**NOVELL'S** ®

# CNA<sup>SM</sup> Study Guide
# for NetWare 5.1

• • • • • • • • • • • • • • •

NOVELL'S®

# CNA<sup>SM</sup> Study Guide
# for NetWare® 5.1

● ● ● ● ● ● ● ● ● ● ● ● ●

DAVID JAMES CLARKE, IV

Novell.
PRESS

Novell Press
Provo, Utah

**Novell's® CNA℠ Study Guide for NetWare® 5.1**

Published by
**Novell Press**
**1800 S. Novell Place**
**Provo, UT 84606**

ISBN: 0-7645-4769-0

Printed in the United States of America

10 9 8 7 6 5 4

1P/SZ/QR/QS/IN

Distributed in the United States by Hungry Minds, Inc.

Distributed by CDG Books Canada Inc. for Canada; by Transworld Publishers Limited in the United Kingdom; by IDG Norge Books for Norway; by IDG Sweden Books for Sweden; by IDG Books Australia Publishing Corporation Pty. Ltd. for Australia and New Zealand; by TransQuest Publishers Pte Ltd. for Singapore, Malaysia, Thailand, Indonesia, and Hong Kong; by Gotop Information Inc. for Taiwan; by ICG Muse, Inc. for Japan; by Intersoft for South Africa; by Eyrolles for France; by International Thomson Publishing for Germany, Austria and Switzerland; by Distribuidora Cuspide for Argentina; by LR International for Brazil; by Galileo Libros for Chile; by Ediciones ZETA S.C.R. Ltda. for Peru; by WS Computer Publishing Corporation, Inc., for the Philippines; by Contemporanea de Ediciones for Venezuela; by Express Computer Distributors for the Caribbean and West Indies; by Micronesia Media Distributor, Inc. for Micronesia; by Chips Computadoras S.A. de C.V. for Mexico; by Editorial Norma de Panama S.A. for Panama; by American Bookshops for Finland.

For general information on Hungry Minds' products and services please contact our Customer Care Department within the U.S. at 800-762-2974, outside the U.S. at 317-572-3993 or fax 317-572-4002.

For sales inquiries and reseller information, including discounts, premium and bulk quantity sales, and foreign-language translations, please contact our Customer Care Department at 800-434-3422, fax 317-572-4002, or write to Hungry Minds, Inc., Attn: Customer Care Department, 10475 Crosspoint Boulevard, Indianapolis, IN 46256.

For information on licensing foreign or domestic rights, please contact our Sub-Rights Customer Care Department at 212-884-5000.

For information on using Hungry Minds' products and services in the classroom or for ordering examination copies, please contact our Educational Sales Department at 800-434-2086 or fax 317-572-4005.

Please contact our Public Relations Department at 212-884-5163 for press review copies or 212-884-5000 for author interviews and other publicity information or fax 212-884-5400.

For information on using Hungry Minds' products and services in the classroom or for ordering examination copies, please contact our Educational Sales Department at 800-434-2086 or fax 317-572-4005.

For press review copies, author interviews, or other publicity information, please contact our Public Relations department at 317-572-3168 or fax 317-572-4168.

For authorization to photocopy items for corporate, personal, or educational use, please contact Copyright Clearance Center, 222 Rosewood Drive, Danvers, MA 01923, or fax 978-750-4470.

**Library of Congress Cataloging-in-Publication Data**

Clarke, David James, 1964-
    Novell's CNA study guide for Netware 5.1 / David James Clarke, IV.
        p.   cm.
    1. NetWare. 2. Operating systems (Computers) I. Title: CNA study guide for Netware 5.1. II. Title.
    QA76.76.O63 C55    2000
    005.7'1369--dc21                                              00-050061

**Hungry Minds™**   is a trademark of Hungry Minds, Inc.

Marcy Shanti, *Publisher, Novell Press, Novell, Inc.*
Novell Press and the Novell Press logo are trademarks of Novell, Inc.

# Welcome to Novell Press

**N**ovell Press, the world's leading provider of networking books, is the premier source for the most timely and useful information in the networking industry. Novell Press books cover fundamental networking issues as they emerge — from today's Novell and third-party products to the concepts and strategies that will guide the industry's future. The result is a broad spectrum of titles for the benefit of those involved in networking at any level: end user, department administrator, developer, systems manager, or network architect.

Novell Press books are written by experts with the full participation of Novell's technical, managerial, and marketing staff. The books are exhaustively reviewed by Novell's own technicians and are published only on the basis of final released software, never on prereleased versions.

Novell Press at Hungry Minds is an exciting partnership between two companies at the forefront of the knowledge and communications revolution. The Press is implementing an ambitious publishing program to develop new networking titles centered on the current versions of NetWare, GroupWise, BorderManager, ManageWise, and networking integration products.

Novell Press books are translated into several languages and sold throughout the world.

**Marcy Shanti**
Publisher
Novell Press, Novell, Inc.

## Novell Press

**Publisher**
Marcy Shanti

## Hungry Minds

**Acquisitions Editors**
John Gravener
Ed Adams

**Project Editor**
Julie M. Smith

**Technical Editor**
Robb Tracy

**Copy Editors**
Lane Barnholtz
Cindy Lai
Julie Campbell Moss

**Proof Editor**
Patsy Owens

**Project Coordinator**
Louigene A. Santos

**Quality Control Technician**
Dina F Quan

**Graphics and Production Specialists**
Robert Bihlmayer
Jude Levinson
Michael Lewis
Ramses Ramirez
Victor Pérez-Varela

**Media Development Specialist**
Travis Silvers

**Media Development Coordinator**
Marisa Pearman

**Illustrators**
Rashell Smith
Gabriele McCann
John Greenough

**Proofreading and Indexing**
York Production Services

# About the Author

**David James Clarke, IV** is the original creator of the CNE Study Guide phenomenon. He is the author of numerous #1 best-selling books for Novell Press, including *Novell's CNE Update to NetWare 5*, *Novell's CNA Study Guide for NetWare 5*, *Novell's CNE Study Guide for NetWare 5*, *Novell's CNE Study Set for NetWare 5*, and the new *Clarke Notes* series.

Clarke is an online Professor for CyberStateU.com (a virtual IT university) and cofounder of the Computer Telephony Institute (home of the CTE certification). He is also the developer of The Clarke Tests v5.0 (an interactive learning system) and producer of the best-selling video series, *"So You Wanna Be a CNE?!"*.

Clarke is a Certified Novell Instructor (CNI), a CNE, and a CNA. He speaks at numerous national conferences and currently serves as the president and CEO of Clarke Industries, Inc. He lives and writes in the heart of Silicon Valley.

*I dedicate this book to all the past, present, and future heroes of ACME.*
*Without their collective imagination and passion*
*the world wouldn't have a chance . . . how about you?!*

# Foreword

The author of this comprehensive, if not voluminous, manuscript asked me to write a few words in the form of a brief foreword. It boggles the mind what I could possibly have to say about technology invented five centuries after my birth, but why not? — *I have done crazier things!* As a matter of fact, the evidence against me is overwhelming. So, here we go. . . .

What you are about to experience can best be described as *life changing*. In simpler terms, "the knowledge presented in this guide will significantly alter your perception of network-based communications in such a way that you will permanently modify your behavior toward technology". There you go — life changing.

NetWare 5.1 provides the means for creating a virtual global community. As such, people anywhere can interact with each other instantaneously. While this concept alone boggles even the largest mind, it slowly gains perspective when you place it in the same company as digital watches, microwave cooking, and daytime television. Now, if you are going to be a successful CNA and help us save the world, you will need to expand your understanding of Novell technology beyond the local LAN and into the global Web. When I say "Web," I mean the pervasive worldwide communications network known as the *Internet*.

In order to help expand your understanding of the Novell Internet, the author of this manuscript presents several exciting new technical advancements — many of which dwarf the significance of daytime television. In this guide, you will learn how to build a global NDS tree and connect to the network with fellow webians — using the new Novell Client. In addition, you will architect a virtual city using the NetWare 5.1 file system, secure the tree with NetWare Administrator, control workstations using ZENworks, and ultimately generate hard-copy output using Novell Distributed Printing Services (NDPS). Stunning!

For the record, I still prefer painting, the sundial, and food cooked over an open flame. However, I am sure that I will eventually adapt to the "virtuosity" of 21st century life. After all, we're all in this together, so we might as well make the best of it.

Yours,

Leonardo Da Vinci

# Preface

**W**elcome to the core of NetWare 5.1 Administration . . . there's no turning back!

Leonardo DaVinci once said that inside every stone is a beautiful statue waiting to be exposed. "The trick", he said, "is chiseling away the pieces that don't belong."

Leonardo DaVinci is my inspiration for the *CNA Study Guide* series of Novell certification companions. Through great effort, I have identified the core of NetWare 5.1 Administration and it *is* very beautiful. The bottom line is—this book is your guide through the jungle of NetWare 5.1 Administration test objectives. It will help you focus your formal education, study guide lessons, and/or hands-on skills. And to aid you during your quest for "life changing" knowledge, I offer two different types of help at key points during the adventure:

**TIP**

**Highlights time-proven management techniques and action-oriented ideas. These tips are great ways of expanding your horizons beyond just CNAship—they're your ticket to true nerddom.**

**REAL WORLD**

Welcome to the real world. I don't want you to be a two-dimensional CNA in a three-dimensional world. These icons represent the other dimension. In an attempt to bring this book to life, I've included various real-world scenarios, case studies, and situational walk-throughs.

Finally, I'm guessing that at some point, you will want to apply all this life-changing knowledge to a physical, practical application—a network, perhaps. One assumes that you will act on this book's technical concepts, philosophies, schematics, lab exercise, puzzles, tips, and examples. In the meantime, I'd like to hear from you as I strive to provide the best certification study materials available. Please feel free to e-mail me at DClarke@iACME.com. Let me know how you liked the book and/or what features you would like added.

So, get prepared for an adventure through Novell's certification jungle. And don't forget your guide . . . there's no limit to where you can go from here!

Enjoy the show and good luck on the exam!

# Acknowledgments

Unless you've lived with a writer, it's hard to understand the divine patience that it takes to accept a writer's crazy hours, strange insights, and constant pitter-patter on the keyboard. Mary, my wife, deserves all the credit in the world for supporting my work and bringing a great deal of happiness into my life. She is my anchor! And, of course, thanks to my two lovely princesses: Leia and Sophie. Somehow they know just when I need to be interrupted—daughter's intuition. Most of all, they both have brought much needed perspective into my otherwise one-dimensional life. For that, I owe my family everything.

Next, I would like to thank the other great architect of this book—my partner Cathryn Ettelson. She has been instrumental in all aspects of this project—research, chiseling away the unneeded stone, testing hands-on clues in the Mad Scientist's laboratory, building exam notes, and the list goes on. In addition, she has helped me understand that "less is more"! I owe a great deal to this brilliant woman, and I truly couldn't have written this book without her.

Behind every great book is an incredible production team. It all started with Kevin Shafer—legendary development boss. His flawless organization, quick wit, and patience were instrumental in bringing this book to life. Kevin did a marvelous job of leading this unique mission from beginning to end. Thanks also to Ed Adams and John Gravener for acquisitions, Cindy Valdez for opening the gateway to Novell, Phil Richardson for guidance, and Julie Smith for always keeping us on our toes. Also, thanks to Lane Barnholtz, Cindy Lai, and Julie Campbell Moss for giving the manuscript a final polish.

Finally, thanks a million to the IDG Books Worldwide's production department, sales staff, marketing wizards, and bookstore buyers for putting this *CNA Study Guide* into your hands. After all, without them I'd be selling books out of the trunk of my car!

I saved the best for last. Thanks to *you* for caring enough about NetWare 5.1, your education, and the world to buy this book. You deserve a great deal of credit for your enthusiasm and dedication. Thanks again, and I hope this education changes your life. Good luck, and enjoy the show!

# Contents at a Glance

# Contents

# CHAPTER 1

# Introduction to NetWare 5.1

**W**elcome to NetWare 5.1 — Novell's solution for *OneNet*. Think of this new operating system as the super glue that connects your intranets, extranets, and the Internet into one supernet. To be a successful CNA (and a OneNet superhero), you will need to expand your understanding of the Novell LAN beyond the server, beyond the NDS tree, to the *collective whole*.

Let me explain . . . .

▶ *What is networking?* — Ever since the beginning of time, people have had an uncontrollable need to communicate. Our nature drives us to exchange ideas, information, and opinions. *Networking* is the ultimate level of communication. It transcends words and pictures to provide a pathway for thoughts, ideas, and dreams. Networking as it exists today is the result of millions of years of evolution and growth — and the fun is only just beginning.

▶ *What does the future of networking hold?* — Network software began with the sharing of files and printers within local area networks (LANs) and evolved into the management of wide area networks (WANs) that enable enterprise-class computing. The future of networking will involve a world in which all types of networks (intranets, the Internet, and extranets; corporate and public; wired and wireless) work together as one Net to simplify the complexities of eBusiness and to provide the power and the flexibility that organizations need to succeed in the Net economy.

▶ *What is NetWare 5.1?* — I'm glad you asked. It's actually more of a solution than a product. NetWare 5.1 extends the Novell LAN to include private intranets and/or the globally shared Internet. The great thing about NetWare 5.1 is that it is fully modular by design. It includes a server-based operating system, Novell Directory Services (NDS), pure IP transport, ZENworks desktop management, and a variety of intranet/Internet products. In addition, NetWare 5.1 is fully compatible with existing NetWare servers, applications, and hardware.

▶ *What's so great about intranets?* — Intranetworks (or *intranets*) enable you to leverage existing Internet technology to create a secure private corporate network. Private intranets rely on a graphical user interface (GUI) based browser to provide access to local and shared information. In addition, paperless communications are encouraged and centrally available. Information can be accessed 24 hours a day. Probably the most exciting feature, however, is the availability of multimedia. That is, data, text, audio, and video are simultaneously available through a single browser to everyone on the WAN. Wow!

▶ *What about the Internet?* — If your company must extend beyond a private intranet, you may want to consider accessing the public Internet. The World Wide Web (WWW) can deliver a variety of information, including product or company data, software updates, press releases, customer support, ordering information, online publications, merchandising, advertising, and/or broadcasting. This is all accomplished using a myriad of Internet services — all available within NetWare 5.1.

NetWare 5.1 is Novell's enterprise solution for building OneNet. It is built on the following foundation:

1. Novell Directory Services

2. NetWare 5.1 Connectivity

3. NetWare 5.1 File System

4. NetWare 5.1 Security

5. NetWare 5.1 Workstation Management

6. NetWare 5.1 Printing

As you can see, NetWare 5.1 is much more than a simple file/print server. It includes numerous intranet/Internet solutions for global connectivity. In this study guide, we're going to explore all six of these NetWare 5.1 topics — which are the focus of Novell Education Course 560, "NetWare 5.1 Administration."

If you plan to go on and obtain a Novell NetWare 5.1 CNE certification as well, you'll need to become an expert in even more facets of global networking. If so, you should study *Novell's CNE Study Guide for NetWare 5.1* to complete your CNE journey and explore the following NetWare 5.1 benefits:

▶ NetWare 5.1 is built on an open standards Web development platform, including support for Microsoft client Web development tools and back-end services.

▶ NetWare 5.1 provides improved Web development support for Java, JavaServer Pages (JSP), Java Database Connectivity (JDBC), Active Server Pages (ASP), and Open Database Connectivity (ODBC) standards. In addition, NetWare 5.1 offers built-in support for third-party authoring tools, with File Transfer Protocol (FTP) services integrated into the Web Server, and support for Microsoft FrontPage 2000 extensions and Office 2000 publishing compatibility.

▶ NetWare 5.1 provides a comprehensive set of open standards and collaborative services for corporate computing, which enables integrators and Information Technology (IT) teams to more easily deploy vertical solutions. This Web integration makes every NetWare server a potential repository of Web server content, enhancing intranet collaboration.

As a NetWare 5.1 network administrator, you will have two key responsibilities: (1) setting up network services; and (2) organizing and configuring network resources. The responsibilities involved in setting up network services include setting up server, workstation, and network hardware and software; establishing personal and shared network data storage; and configuring workstations for automatic connection to the network.

The responsibilities involved in organizing and configuring network resources include managing the network (by maintaining network security and printing systems), protecting the data (by guaranteeing data integrity and establishing system audit procedures), backing up personal and network data, and documenting the network (by creating a printed copy of the NDS tree, tracking user rights, and recording security assumptions).

So, sharpen your mind and enjoy the show.

# NetWare 5.1 CNA Features

Whether you're an aspiring CNA or just want to learn more about NetWare 5.1, you'll need to become intimately familiar with all six features that comprise Novell Course 560, "NetWare 5.1 Administration." Here's a brief peek:

▶ *Novell Directory Services* — We'll start by exploring Novell's highly acclaimed NDS technology, which is a distributed, replicated database that helps you manage network resources as objects in a hierarchical tree. Cool!

▶ *NetWare 5.1 Connectivity* — Once you've mastered the tree, you must learn how to access it. NetWare 5.1 connectivity involves Novell Client software, login scripts, and NDS object management.

▶ *NetWare 5.1 File System* — NetWare 5.1 offers two Directory trees — NDS and the physical file system. The file system mirrors NDS in many ways, but also branches off into more down-to-earth territory including volumes, directories, and files.

▶ *NetWare 5.1 Security* — Of course, with increased resource access and distributed data comes security problems. Fortunately, NetWare 5.1 includes a five-layered security model that restricts access in a number of different ways, including login authentication, login restrictions, NDS security, file system security, and finally, file system attributes.

▶ *NetWare 5.1 Workstation Management* — NetWare 5.1 workstation management is dominated by an NDS-integrated feature called ZENworks. ZEN-works is a desktop-management tool that uses NDS to simplify the process of managing Windows-based workstations. ZENworks is actually an acronym for Zero Effort Networks. So, what does the "Zero Effort" part mean? It refers to the fact that ZENworks reduces the cost and complexity of maintaining network computers by delivering workstation management tasks directly to the user desktop.

▸ *NetWare 5.1 Printing* — Novell Distributed Printing Services (NDPS) replaces the queue-based printing system with improved overall network performance, reduced printing problems, and better administration. That's a pretty tough promise to keep — fortunately, NDPS delivers.

So, that covers the top six CNA solutions offered by NetWare 5.1, and, in a nutshell, identifies the technology covered in this book. It doesn't, however, encompass all of NetWare 5.1. In the next book in this series (*Novell's CNE Study Guide for NetWare 5.1*), we will discover many more advanced features that round out Novell's next-generation information superhighway (which I call the *Infobahn*).

Let's start with a quick look at your life as a NetWare 5.1 CNA, starting with Novell Directory Services.

## Novell Directory Services

Novell Directory Services (NDS) is a fundamental network service that is supplied by all NetWare 5.1 servers. As a matter of fact, it's the most fundamental network service offered by NetWare 5.1, after network communications. As such, NDS management is one of the key responsibilities of a network administrator.

As its name implies, NDS provides access to a database, called the *Directory*, that contains all resources for the entire network. This object-oriented Directory database is organized into a hierarchical structure called the NDS *tree*. (*Directory* is capitalized in this case to differentiate it from the NetWare 5.1 file system directory, which we'll discuss in Chapter 4).

So, what does NDS look like? From the outside, it looks like a big cloud hovering over your network. On the inside, however, it follows a hierarchical tree structure similar to the DOS or Windows file system. As you can see in Figure 1.1, NDS organizes resources into logical groups called *containers*.

So, is NDS worth it? Let's take a quick look at two of the key NDS features we'll cover in this book:

▸ NDS Objects

▸ NDS Naming

▶ · · · · · · · · · · · · · · · · · · · · · · · · · · · · ◀

FIGURE 1.1

*A tree in a cloud — getting to know NDS*

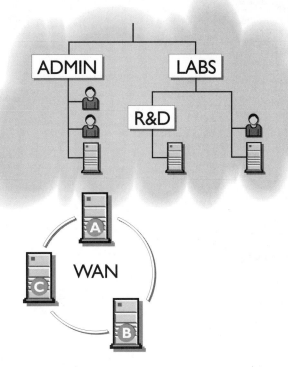

## NDS Objects

As in nature, the NDS tree starts with the [Root] and builds from there. Next, it sprouts container objects, which are branches reaching toward the sky. Finally, leaf objects flutter in the wind and provide network functionality to users, servers, and the file system. As you can see in Figure 1.2, the tree analogy is alive and well.

The logical NDS tree is made up of logical and physical entities that provide organizational or technical function to the network. As you can see in Figure 1.3, they come in three different flavors:

- ▶ [Root]

- ▶ Container objects

- ▶ Leaf objects

▶ · · · · · · · · · · · · · · · · · · · · · · · · · ◀

FIGURE 1.2

*The figurative NDS tree*

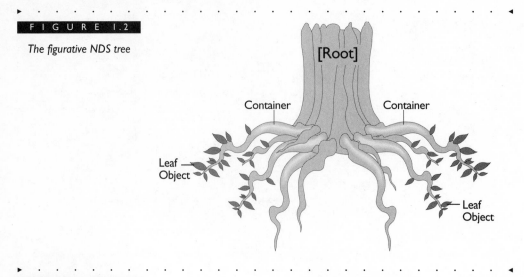

▶ · · · · · · · · · · · · · · · · · · · · · · · · · ◀

FIGURE 1.3

*The real NDS tree*

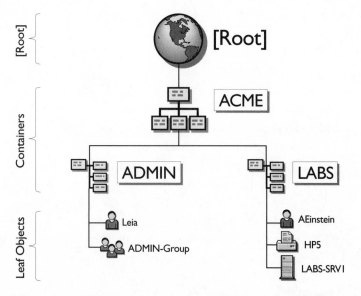

The [Root] is the very top of an NDS tree, and as such, its icon is appropriately a picture of the earth. Container objects define the organizational boundaries of an NDS tree and house other container objects and/or leaf objects. In Figure 1.3, we use container objects to define the ACME organization and two of its divisions—ADMIN and LABS.

Leaf objects are the physical or logical network resources that provide technical services and network functionality. Leaf objects define the lowest level of the NDS structure. In Figure 1.3, leaf objects represent users, a printer, a server, and a group. NDS supports many different leaf object types, enabling you to manage routers, databases, e-mail systems, and so on. Plus, NDS is open, so experienced network administrators can add their own objects using the Schema Manager in ConsoleOne. We'll discuss the main object types in detail in Chapter 2.

The tree can be organized any way you want, as long as it makes sense. AEinstein, for example, is placed near the resources he uses — the HP5 printer and LABS-SRV1 file server. We'll learn more about ACME later in this chapter. But now, it's time to *Save the Net!!*

### NDS Naming

NDS naming defines rules for locating leaf objects. One of the most important aspects of a leaf object is its position in the NDS tree. Proper naming is required when logging in, accessing NDS utilities, printing, and for most other management tasks.

The whole NetWare 5.1 NDS naming scheme is much more complicated than "Hi, I'm Fred." It requires both your name and location. For example, a proper NDS name would be "Hi, I'm Fred in the ADMIN division of ACME." As you can see in Figure 1.4, Fred's NDS name identifies who he is and where he works. This naming scheme relies on a concept called *context*.

**FIGURE 1.4**

*Getting to know the real Fred*

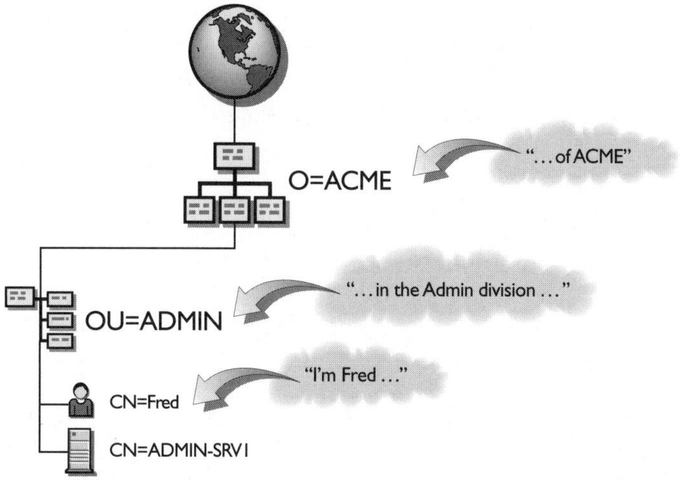

O=ACME — "…of ACME"

OU=ADMIN — "…in the Admin division …"

CN=Fred — "I'm Fred …"

CN=ADMIN-SRV1

Context defines the position of an object within the Directory tree structure. When you request a particular network resource, you must identify the object's context so that NDS can find it. NetWare 5.1 uses specific naming guidelines for creating an object's context — which we'll review in Chapter 2.

Well, that's all there is to it — not really! Remember, every cloud has a silver lining, and this section has yours. Use this information wisely as you expand the horizons of your network. Now, let's continue our discussion of NetWare 5.1 administration features by learning how to *connect* to this mysterious network cloud.

**For more information about Novell Directory Services, refer to Chapter 2.**

TIP

## NetWare 5.1 Connectivity

It is time to get connected!

The OneNet journey must start at the proverbial Point A. The challenge begins today — connecting to the network and building ACME's NDS tree. In NetWare 5.1, connectivity is dominated by the following three topics:

▶ *Connecting to the Network* — First, you must establish network connectivity using special workstation software. In this book, we discuss the NetWare 5.1 Novell Client for Windows 95/98 and the NetWare 5.1 Novell Client for Windows NT/2000.

▶ *Configuring Login Scripts* — Once you log in, these cool batch files take over. Login scripts establish user-specific drive mappings, search mappings, printer connections, and messages each time a user logs into the network.

▶ *Welcome In* — Finally, the world of NDS and NetWare 5.1 is open to your users. At this point, they'll need to learn how to browse the Net using NetWare Administrator, ConsoleOne, and a variety of NDS objects.

Let's get connected . . . now!

**Connecting to the Network**

Throughout this book, we focus on the *network* as a distributed synergistic collection of computers. Throughout the entire NetWare 5.1 CNE program, we'll learn how to design, install, manage, and secure the network. However, we have to start somewhere. *How about the basics of the workstation-to-server connection?* This is the most fundamental principle of local area networking and wide area networking.

At its most fundamental level, a network workstation is made up of three fundamental components:

▶ Network interface card (NIC)

▶ Workstation connectivity software

▶ Local operating system

Once you have connected to the network using the Novell Client, there's only one task left — logging in. As a network administrator, you've already accomplished the hard part — automating the workstation connection. Now it's the user's turn. The good news is that both the Novell Client for Windows 95/98 and the Novell Client for Windows NT/2000 provide a friendly GUI login utility for users (see Figure 1.5).

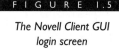

F I G U R E   1 . 5

*The Novell Client GUI
login screen*

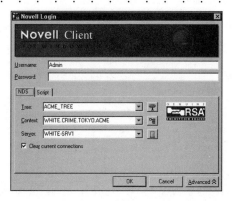

As you can see in Figure 1.5, the GUI login utility provides simple Username and Password input boxes within the native MS Windows environment. In addition, the NDS page enables you to specify an NDS tree, server, and/or login context. Similarly, the Script page enables users to override container and profile scripts with local text files in login script format. We'll discuss the NetWare 5.1 Novell Client for Windows 95/98 and NetWare 5.1 Novell Client for Windows NT/2000 in Chapter 3.

### Configuring Login Scripts

Login scripts are the next phase of NetWare 5.1 connectivity. Once users have been authenticated using a valid username and password, NetWare executes a variety of login script configurations. In short, login scripts are batch files for the network. They provide a simple configuration tool for user customization—drive mappings, text messages, printer connections, and so on.

NetWare 5.1 supports four types of login scripts, which are executed in systematic progression. As you can see in Figure 1.6, there's a flowchart logic to how login scripts are executed. Here's a quick look:

▶ *Container login scripts*—These are properties of Organization and Organizational Unit containers. They enable you to customize settings for all users within a container.

▶ *Profile login scripts*—These are properties of the Profile object. These scripts customize environmental parameters for groups of users. This way, users who are located in different parts of the NDS tree can share a common login script.

▶ *User login scripts*—These are properties of each User object. They are executed after the Container and Profile scripts, and they provide customization at the user level.

▶ *Default login script*—This is executed for any user who does not have an individual User login script. This script contains some basic drive mappings and essential system commands.

All four of these login script types work in concert to provide customization for containers, groups, and users. As you'll quickly learn, login scripts are an integral part of your daily network administrator grind. Login scripts consist of commands and identifiers just like any other program or batch file, and they must follow specific rules and conventions. We'll explore login scripts in more detail in Chapter 3.

FIGURE 1.6

*Understanding NetWare
5.1 login scripts*

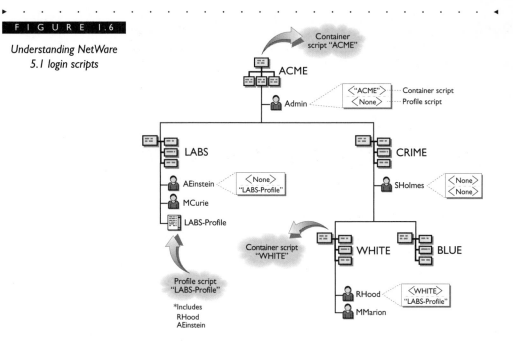

## Welcome In!

Congratulations! You've connected to the network. *Now what?*

The first thing you should do once you gain access to the NDS tree is browse. NetWare Administrator is a Windows-based tool that enables you to graphically manage objects and properties in the NDS tree. NetWare 5.1 also includes a Java-based management tool called ConsoleOne.

In NetWare Administrator, you can view, create, move, delete, and assign rights to any object in the NDS tree. Of course, you can only manage the objects for which you have the appropriate access rights. NetWare Administrator runs as a multiple-document interface application. This means you can display multiple browsing windows at one time. A single browser window is shown in Figure 1.7.

This completes our brief romp through NetWare 5.1 connectivity. As you can see, it is useless without workstations, servers, and network connectivity. Fortunately, NetWare 5.1 offers numerous tools to make these management tasks a breeze. Now, let's expand beyond the NDS tree, into the realm of physical network resources. Let's explore the other NetWare 5.1 directory tree.

▶ · · · · · · · · · · · · · · · · · · · · · · ◀

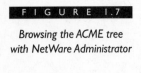

FIGURE 1.7

*Browsing the ACME tree
with NetWare Administrator*

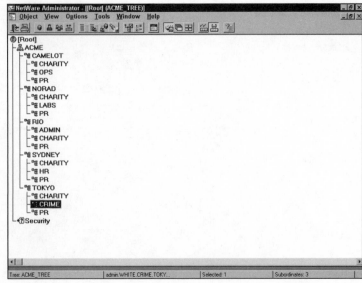

**For more information about NetWare 5.1 Connectivity, refer to
Chapter 3.**

TIP

## NetWare 5.1 File System

The NDS Directory is a database of network resources that is shared by all
servers in an NDS tree. Each NetWare 5.1 server, however, maintains its own separate file system that can be used to store shared applications and data files.

As you can see in Figure 1.8, the Directory tree above the NetWare 5.1 server is
NDS. It organizes network resources into a logical network hierarchy. The directory tree below the server is the file system. It organizes network data files into a
functional file hierarchy.

The NetWare 5.1 file system is similar to the DOS file system. Like the DOS file
system, it is hierarchical in nature and consists of volumes, directories, and files.
*Volumes* exist at the top of the NetWare 5.1 file system. A volume represents both
a physical network device (such as a server hard drive, CD-ROM drive, or optical
disk drive) and a logical NDS object (that is, a Volume leaf object in the NDS tree).
Because of this unique position, a volume acts as a bridge between NDS and the
file system.

FIGURE 1.8

*The two NetWare 5.1 directory trees*

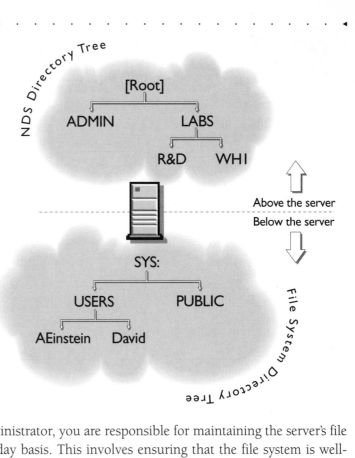

As a network administrator, you are responsible for maintaining the server's file system on a day-to-day basis. This involves ensuring that the file system is well-organized, easily accessible to network users, and contains adequate storage space. These responsibilities include three basic skills:

▶ Managing volume space

▶ Managing directories and subdirectories

▶ Managing files

NetWare 5.1, Windows 95/98, and Windows NT/2000 each ship with utilities that can be used for performing file system management tasks. Because the NetWare file system emulates the Windows file structure, you'll find that you can use many of the same tools and techniques for managing both network and workstation file systems — assuming, of course, that the appropriate Novell Client software is installed on each workstation. For example, you can use Windows Explorer (and, to a limited extent, Windows Network Neighborhood) to access and manage the NetWare file system. You can also use DOS commands, although you may find that they offer limited functionality.

NetWare 5.1 offers a number of file system utilities, including the following file system utilities:

- ▸ NetWare Administrator

- ▸ ConsoleOne

- ▸ FILER

- ▸ NDIR

- ▸ NCOPY

- ▸ FLAG

In addition, NetWare 5.1 includes a *drive mapping* feature which provides backward compatibility for legacy applications. Drive mapping is a built-in file system management scheme that enables you (and users) to assign drive letters to network directories. Typically, physical local devices are referenced using characters at the beginning of the alphabet (such as A: through E:). In NetWare, logical network directories are typically referenced using characters in the remainder of the alphabet (such as F: through Z:).

In general, NetWare 5.1 provides three different strategies for drive mapping:

- ▸ Network Drive Mapping

- ▸ Search Drive Mapping

- ▸ Directory Map Object

This completes our jaunt through NetWare 5.1's second directory structure — the file system. NDS and the file system approach life together with a common purpose — to logically organize user resources, except that this time, the resources are files, not users.

**For more information about the NetWare 5.1 File System, refer to Chapter 4.**

TIP

Now that we agree that all our NetWare 5.1 resources should be organized into two logical trees, it's time to start thinking about security.

## NetWare 5.1 Security

Security in the Information Age poses a very interesting challenge. Computers and communications have made it possible to collect volumes of data about you and me — from our latest purchase at the five-and-dime to our detailed medical records. Privacy has become a commodity to be exchanged on the open market. Information is no longer the fodder of afternoon talk shows. It has become *the* unit of exchange for the 21st century — more valuable than money.

NetWare 5.1 improves on earlier NetWare security models by adding supplemental front-end barriers for filtering unauthorized users. The security features discussed in this study guide can be thought of in terms of the following five-layered model (see Figure 1.9):

- ▸ *Layer 1* — Login/Password Authentication

- ▸ *Layer 2* — Login Restrictions

- ▸ *Layer 3* — NDS Security

- ▸ *Layer 4* — File System Access Rights

- ▸ *Layer 5* — Directory/File Attributes

▶ · · · · · · · · · · · · · · · · · · · · · · · · · · · · ◀

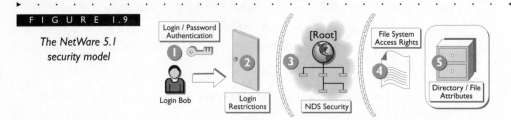

FIGURE 1.9

*The NetWare 5.1
security model*

As you can see, each layer creates an increasingly strong barrier against user access. Each time you pass through a door, you are greeted with another barrier. Let's take a quick look.

### Layer One — Login/Password Authentication

As you can see in Figure 1.9, it all starts with Login/Password authentication. Remember, users don't log into NetWare servers any more, they log into the NDS tree. When a user requests login via a Novell Client login screen, the authentication process begins automatically. If a user supplies the correct parameters during the login process (such as tree name, context, username, and password), the user moves on to Layer 2 of the security model.

### Layer Two — Login Restrictions

After you provide a valid login name and password, you are authenticated. Congratulations! NetWare 5.1 responds with conditional access and NDS rights take over. At this point, I stress the word *conditional* access. Permanent access is made possible by a variety of login restrictions. These login restrictions include the following:

▶ *Account restrictions* — These include anything from "Account Locked" to "Force Periodic Password Changes."

▶ *Password restrictions* — These include restrictions such as "Minimum Password Length" and "Force Unique Passwords."

▶ *Station restrictions* — These can be used to limit users to specific workstation node IDs.

▸ *Time restrictions* — These determine when users can and cannot use the system.

▸ *Intruder detection/lockout* — This is a container-based feature that detects incorrect password attempts.

Each of these restrictions can be configured by network administrators using NetWare Administrator. We'll learn all the details of how and why later in Chapter 5.

### Layer Three — NDS Security

Once you enter the NDS tree, your ability to access leaf and container objects is determined by a sophisticated NDS security structure. At the heart of NDS security is the Access Control List (ACL). Every NDS object includes a property which contains an ACL. It defines who can access the object (trustees) and what each trustee can do (rights). An ACL can contain two types of rights:

▸ *Object rights* — Define an object's trustees and control what the trustees can do with the object.

▸ *Property rights* — Limit the trustees' access to specific properties of the object.

Object and property rights are designed to provide efficient access to NDS objects, without making it an administrative nightmare. You be the judge. Users can acquire object rights in a variety of ways, including trustee assignments, inheritance, and security equivalence. Property rights, on the other hand, are a bit trickier. Global property rights can be inherited, but rights to specific properties must be granted through a trustee assignment or inherited using the [I] Inheritable right.

Regardless of how you acquire object and property rights, the concept of effective rights still applies. This means the actual rights you can exercise over a given object are a combination of explicit trustee assignments, security equivalence, inheritance, and the Inherited Rights Filter (IRF). The mathematical product of this mess is known as *NDS effective rights*. And that effectively ends our discussion of NDS security and moves us on to Layer Four of the NetWare 5.1 security model — file system access rights.

### Layer Four—File System Access Rights

Well, here we are. Before you can access any files on a NetWare 5.1 server, you must have the appropriate file system access rights. Following is a list of the eight rights that control access to NetWare 5.1 files (they almost spell a word):

▸ W—Write: Grants the right to open and change the contents of a file.

▸ (O)—Doesn't exist, but is needed to spell a word.

▸ R—Read: Grants the right to open a file and read its contents (or run an application).

▸ M—Modify: Grants the right to change the attributes or name of a file or directory.

▸ F—File Scan: Grants the right to see files and directories.

▸ A—Access Control: Grants the right to change trustee assignments and IRFs.

▸ C—Create: Grants the right to create new files and subdirectories.

▸ E—Erase: Grants the right to delete a directory, its files, and subdirectories.

▸ S—Supervisor: Grants all rights to a directory and the files and subdirectories below it. This right cannot be blocked by an IRF.

Holy anatomical nematodes, Batman! That spells WoRMFACES. It's not a pretty sight, but certainly a name you will not forget. NetWare 5.1 file system access rights are administered in much the same way as NDS object rights. They are granted with the help of trustee assignments and inheritance. In addition, file system rights are subject to most of the same rules as NDS effective rights. All in all, NDS security and file server security parallel one another—one operating in the clouds (NDS) and one with its feet firmly planted on the ground (file system).

This completes the majority of the five-layered NetWare 5.1 security model. There's only one layer left, and it is seldom used—directory/file attributes. Let's take a closer look.

### Layer Five—Directory/File Attributes

Directory and file attributes provide the final and most sophisticated layer of the NetWare 5.1 security model. These attributes are rarely used, but provide a powerful tool for specific security solutions. If all else fails, you can always turn to attribute security to save the day.

NetWare 5.1 supports three different types of attributes:

▸ *Security attributes*—The main attribute category. Some attributes apply to both directories and files.

▸ *Feature attributes*—Applies to three key features: backup, purging, and the Transactional Tracking System (TTS).

▸ *Disk management attributes*—For file compression, data migration, and block suballocation.

Well, there you have it. That's a brief snapshot of NetWare 5.1's five-layer security model. As a network administrator, it's your job to identify network threats and implement appropriate security countermeasures to eliminate them. This isn't easy. You have many factors working against you—including money, office politics, and user productivity. Fortunately, NetWare 5.1 provides a multilayered security model for creating and maintaining your impenetrable network armor.

 **For more information about NetWare 5.1 Security, refer to Chapter 5.**

**TIP**

Now, let's continue our journey through Novell's OneNet by exploring one of its most fascinating management tools—ZENworks—otherwise known as the *Zen* of NetWare 5.1.

## NetWare 5.1 Workstation Management

NetWare 5.1 workstation management is dominated by an NDS-integrated feature called ZENworks. Unlike the implication of its name, ZENworks has little to do with ancient meditation and wisdom. In actuality, it's a clever acronym for Zero Effort Networks. While it's impossible to achieve actual zero effort networking, ZENworks does greatly improve the manageability of user access to the Net.

ZENworks is a desktop management tool that reduces the hassle of connecting PCs to small, medium, and large networks. ZENworks leverages NDS to help network administrators manage Windows-based desktops by providing policy-enabled workstation management, desktop management, and application control.

ZENworks 2.0 is available in two forms: the ZENworks 2.0 Starter Pack (on the *Novell Client* CD-ROM included with NetWare 5.1) and the ZENworks 2.0 full package (purchased separately). The ZENworks 2.0 Starter Pack, which we study in this course, includes the Application Launcher and Desktop Management components. The full ZENworks 2.0 package includes the functionality found in the Starter Pack, as well as hardware and software inventory management, inventory and distribution reporting, and Help Desk policies.

*So how does it work?* ZENworks extends the NDS schema to include several new objects. These objects allow you to configure and control workstations from within the NDS tree:

▸ Application and Application Folder objects

▸ User and User Group objects

▸ Workstation and Workstation Group objects

▸ Policy Packages

Once ZENworks has been installed, you can take advantage of its three main features: workstation management, desktop management, and application management. Let's take a quick look at these three functional areas and learn what it takes to master the power of NetWare 5.1 ZENworks.

### Workstation Management with ZENworks

The first category of ZENworks features is the largest. Workstation Management encompasses various network administrator tasks associated with daily user productivity. Here's what you have to look forward to when you implement ZEN-works Workstation Management:

▸ *Policies* — ZENworks includes various Policy Packages, which are NDS objects you create to help you maintain Workstation objects in the NDS tree. Each package is a collection of policies that enable you to set up parameters for managing workstations, users, groups, or containers.

▸ *NDS registration* — Workstations must be registered with NDS before they can be imported into the tree and managed as NDS objects. ZEN-works includes a Workstation Registration Agent that registers work-stations via a Workstation Import Policy. Once the policy is in place, you can register workstations by granting NDS rights, choosing a registration method (Application Launcher, Scheduler, or login script), and verifying workstation registration via a local log file. Once a workstation appears in the NDS registration list, it can then be imported into the NDS tree and managed as an NDS object.

As you can see, ZENworks offers many benefits for workstation management in the virtual age. Now, let's cruise over to the user desktop and see what it can do for you.

### Desktop Management with ZENworks

In addition to workstation management, ZENworks offers numerous benefits to the user. This desktop management functionality is employed via two different features:

▸ *Customizing desktop applications* — You can customize user desktops by enabling two specific ZENworks policies: a User System Policy (in a User Policy Package) and a Computer System Policy (in a Workstation Policy Package). A User System Policy allows you to customize the desktop functions available to specific users. For example, hiding applications such as Network Neighborhood, Run, and Find can help reduce access problems and server traffic. Similarly, a Computer System Policy can be used to customize the Windows properties of a specific workstation.

▸ *Standardizing user profiles* — Desktop settings such as Wallpaper, Screen
Saver, and Sounds can be standardized and deployed to every user in the
enterprise. These settings can even be configured so that users cannot
modify them. As a matter of fact, most of the normal user-defined preferences set in the Windows Control Panel can be configured using a Desktop Preference Policy in a User Policy Package.

Now let's complete our brief journey through ZENworks by exploring the final
feature — Application Management.

### Application Management with ZENworks

ZENworks 2.0 includes a special version of the Application Launcher that enables
you to distribute network-based applications to users' workstations and manage
them as objects in the NDS tree. Users then access the applications assigned to them
using the Application Launcher Window or Application Explorer.

Application Launcher consists of four separate programs, including two *administrator* components and two *user* components. The two administrator components are
Application Launcher Snap-In for NetWare Administrator and snAppShot. Application Launcher also provides the following benefits to network administrators:

▸ *Single-point of application administration* — Application Launcher enables
you to create Application objects in the NDS tree and manage a number of
distinct properties.

▸ *Centralized application maintenance and control* — Application Launcher
allows you to control exactly what users see and do at their workstations.

▸ *Push-and-pull software distribution to workstations* — Application Launcher
gives you the option of pulling or pushing software to network workstations. *Pull distribution* places application icons on the user's desktop
and runs remote installation programs when the user requests them.
*Push Distribution* does the same thing — only automatically.

In addition to administrator components, Application Launcher includes the
following two user components: Application Launcher Window and Application
Explorer. Application Launcher also provides the following benefits to users:

▶ *Location-independent access to applications* — Provides users with access to network applications on distributed servers, as well as automated drive mappings and local configurations.

▶ *Application fault tolerance* — Replicates primary applications to backup servers and automatically restores local configurations, if they are deleted. This level of fault tolerance is transparent to users.

▶ *Application load balancing* — Stores applications on multiple servers where they can be distributed to users intelligently and efficiently. Application Launcher sends you an alternate copy of an application when the primary server is overworked.

▶ *Roaming profile support* — Detects your current setup and pushes the components you need to the desktop.

▶ *Rights assignments via applications* — The ZENworks 2.0 Starter Pack includes the ability to assign file system rights to an NDS Application object and, therefore, pass those rights to the user during application association.

This completes our brief romp through ZENworks. As you can see, it is a powerful tool for workstation, desktop, and application management. As a network administrator, you should quickly become a ZENworks master.

 **For more information about NetWare 5.1 Workstation Management with ZENworks, refer to Chapter 6.**

TIP

## NetWare 5.1 Printing

The final stop on our tour down the NetWare 5.1 information superhighway is printing. NetWare 5.1 includes a revolution in network printing — Novell Distributed Print Services (NDPS). NDPS is a next-generation NetWare printing service designed to replace queue-based systems. It is the result of a joint development effort by Novell, Hewlett-Packard, and Xerox. With NDPS, network-based printers are independent of servers, and printer drivers can automatically be made available to every defined printer and user on the network.

So, how does all this fancy printing work? Check out Figure 1.10. As you can see, NDPS consists of three support components surrounding the Printer Agent, which is the heart of printing. Let's take a closer look.

FIGURE 1.10

*NetWare 5.1 NDPS printing architecture*

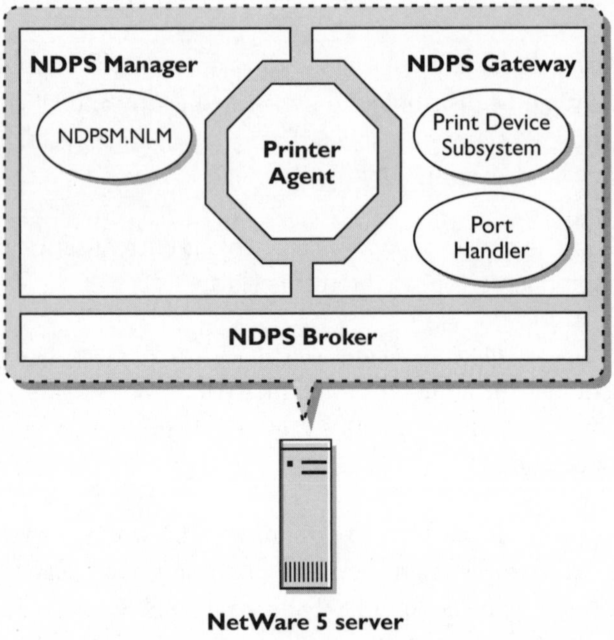

**NetWare 5 server**

▶ *Printer Agent* — A Printer Agent combines the functions previously performed by a queue-based print queue, printer, and print server into one intelligent, integrated entity. Typically, a printer has a one-to-one relationship with a Printer Agent. A Printer Agent can represent either a Public Access printer or a Controlled Access printer (both of which are discussed in Chapter 7). A Printer Agent can exist as software (running on a NetWare 5.1 server) or firmware (embedded within a network-attached printer).

▶ *NDPS Manager* — An NDPS Manager is a logical NDS object that creates and manages Printer Agents. You must create an NDPS Manager object before creating server-based Printer Agents. A good rule of thumb is to create an NDPS Manager object for each server that hosts NDPS printers.

Only one NDPS Manager is allowed per server. The NDPS Manager software runs on a NetWare 5.1 server as NDPSM.NLM. This NLM (NetWare Loadable Module) carries out instructions provided by the NDPS Manager object.

▸ *NDPS Gateway* — NDPS Gateways are a collection of software that run on the NDPS Broker server and ensure backward compatibility for non-NDPS-aware printers. You must select and configure an NDPS gateway whenever you create a Printer Agent. One benefit of NDPS gateways is that they enable you to support unusual printing environments (in other words, printers that are not NDPS-aware). In short, an NDPS gateway acts as a software bridge that directly links Printer Agents to NDPS printers. This is accomplished by translating NDPS instructions into device-specific commands. NDPS currently ships with the following ten gateways: Hewlett-Packard, Xerox, Lexmark, EPSON, Kyocera, Tektronix, IBM, OKIDATA, Canon, and Ricoh. The Novell Gateway is designed to be used with printers that do not have an embedded Printer Agent and do not have a gateway provided by the printer manufacturer.

▸ *NDPS Broker* — An NDPS Broker is a special management component that provides three important services to the NetWare 5.1 printing architecture (explained in more detail in Chapter 7). The Broker is composed of two complementary parts: an NDS leaf object (NDPS Broker) and a server-based NLM (BROKER.NLM). The good news is you don't have to worry about creating your own NDPS Broker. When NDPS is installed, the setup tool ensures that a Broker object is created. An additional Broker is only created automatically if you install NDPS on a server that is more than three hops away from the nearest existing Broker. You don't have to worry about activating an NDPS Broker because it's loaded automatically when NDPS is initialized. To do its job, an NDPS Broker must log into the NDS tree and authenticate itself to the server.

This completes our discussion of NetWare 5.1 NDPS printing services. Printing has always been and continues to be one of your greatest challenges as a network administrator. Fortunately, the revolution is upon us.

**For more information about NetWare 5.1 NDPS, refer to Chapter 7.**

TIP

This concludes our initial tour of Novell's implementation of OneNet via NetWare 5.1. As you can see, it is a powerful operating system for seamlessly connecting intranets, extranets, and the Internet. This section focused on the following six main topics covered by the NetWare 5.1 CNA certification:

▶ Novell Directory Services (see Chapter 2 for more information)

▶ NetWare 5.1 Connectivity (see Chapter 3 for more information)

▶ NetWare 5.1 File System (see Chapter 4 for more information)

▶ NetWare 5.1 Security (see Chapter 5 for more information)

▶ NetWare 5.1 Workstation Management (see Chapter 6 for more information)

▶ NetWare 5.1 Printing (see Chapter 7 for more information)

As you can see from this list, NetWare 5.1 is definitely worthy of ACME and their plight — to save the Net.

*Now it's your turn . . .*

You are the final piece in our globe-trotting puzzle. You will become ACME's management information services (MIS) department and the architect of their communications strategy. As a NetWare 5.1 network administrator, you come highly recommended. Your mission — *should you choose to accept it* — is to build the ACME WAN. You will need courage, design experience, NDS know-how, and this book. If you succeed, you will save the Net and become a CNA! All in a day's work.

Following is a brief synopsis of the ACME case study we use throughout this study guide. For more details, please read the comprehensive mission briefing in Appendix E, "ACME Mission Briefing."

Good luck; and by the way, thanks for saving the Net!

# Getting to Know ACME

ACME has been designed as "A Cure for Mother Earth." It is staffed by some of the greatest heroes from the earth's unspoiled history. These are the founding mothers and fathers of earth's Golden Age—before instant popcorn, talking cars, and daytime television. It's clear that somewhere along the human timeline, progress went amok. We need help from heroes before that time.

To vortex back in history and grab the ACME management, we've used a prototype of the Oscillating Temporal Overthruster (OTO). We've hand-chosen only the brightest and most resourceful characters, then meticulously trained each one of them for special tasks. They're a little disoriented, but more than happy to help.

These historical heroes have been placed in an innovative organizational structure. As you can see in Figure 1.11, ACME is organized around the following five main divisions (read more details in Appendix E):

▸ *Human Rights (Gandhi)*—Taking care of the world's basic needs, including medicine, food, shelter, and peace. These tasks are handled jointly by Albert Schweitzer, Mother Teresa, Florence Nightingale, and Buddha. This division's work has the most positive impact on the World Health Index (WHI).

▸ *Labs (Albert Einstein)*—Putting technology to good use. This division is the technical marvel of ACME. In addition to research and development (R&D) efforts, the Labs division is responsible for the WHI tracking center in NORAD. This division is staffed by the wizardry of Leonardo da Vinci, Sir Isaac Newton, Charles Darwin, Marie Curie, and Charles Babbage.

▸ *Operations (King Arthur)*—Saving the world can be a logistical nightmare. Fortunately, we have King Arthur and the Knights of the Round Table to help us out. In this division, ACME routes money from caring contributors (Charity) to those who need it most (Financial)—there's a little Robin Hood in there somewhere. Also, with the help of Merlin, we will distribute all the Human Rights and Labs material to the four corners of the globe.

▶ *Crime Fighting (Sherlock Holmes and Dr. Watson)* — Making the world a safer place. This division tackles the almost insurmountable task of eradicating world crime. It's a good thing we have the help of Sherlock Holmes and some of our greatest crime-fighting superheroes, including Robin Hood, Maid Marion, Wyatt Earp, and Wild Bill Hickok. These heroes deal with the single most negative factor in WHI calculations — crime. This is very important work.

▶ *Admin (George Washington)* — Keeping the rest of ACME running smoothly. It's just like a well-oiled machine with the help of America's Founding Fathers — George Washington, Thomas Jefferson, Abraham Lincoln, Franklin Delano Roosevelt (FDR), and James Madison. Their main job is public relations under the command of one of our greatest orators, FDR. In addition to getting the word out, Admin tracks ACME activity (auditing) and keeps the facilities operating at their best.

I'd like to begin by thanking you for choosing to accept this mission! ACME has a daunting task ahead of it, so there's no time to waste.

Some NDS schematics are included in Appendix E. They are for your eyes only. Once you have read the inputs, eat them! There's other good news — you don't have to save the world alone. The project team is here to help you. Remember, we're counting on you. Be careful not to let these facts fall into the wrong hands. Believe it or not, the world has forces at work that don't share our love for the human race.

**REAL WORLD**

Throughout this book, we will use ACME as a global case study for key NetWare 5.1 network management tasks. (See Appendix E, "ACME Mission Briefing" for more details.) You will build ACME's enterprise NDS tree, construct a multilayered security model, distribute ZENworks clients, and build a comprehensive NDPS printing system. Pay attention! ACME may just change your life — and help you become a NetWare 5.1 CNA.

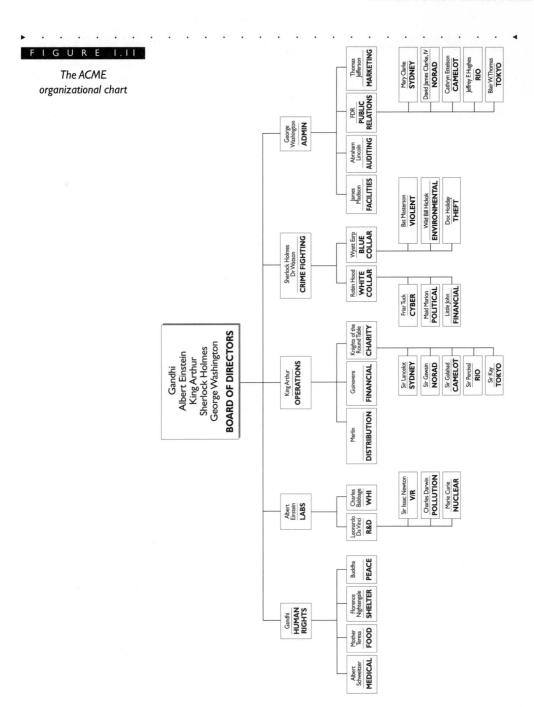

FIGURE 1.11

The ACME
organizational chart

## LAB EXERCISE 1.1: ONENET!

Circle the 15 NetWare 5.1 features hidden in this word search puzzle using the hints provided. No punctuation characters (such as blank spaces, hyphens, and so on) should be included. Numbers should always be spelled out.

```
S  K  Y  I  E  D  Q  Y  M  X  E  R  T
E  N  T  E  R  P  R  I  S  E  Y  S  D
C  O  N  S  O  L  E  O  N  E  L  G  G
U  V  X  I  W  O  R  M  F  A  C  E  S
R  E  W  A  C  M  E  O  N  E  N  E  T
I  L  N  H  C  P  P  P  T  E  E  P  C
T  L  Q  P  O  L  I  C  I  E  S  W  H
Y  C  O  N  N  E  C  T  I  V  I  T  Y
B  L  G  R  A  K  R  F  M  H  H  S  X
C  I  T  X  T  N  T  J  P  Y  X  N  F
B  E  H  T  E  N  A  R  T  X  E  B  C
G  N  I  P  P  A  M  E  V  I  R  D  J
Q  T  C  Y  V  I  E  S  R  H  X  S  H
```

### Hints

1. A property of an NDS object which indicates the trustees for the object (and the rights they have been granted), as well as the IRF for that object.
2. An organization whose mission is to protect Planet Earth from the Alpha Centurions.
3. One of the primary goals of networking.
4. A Java-based server/workstation console utility that provides basic server and NDS management functions.
5. A built-in file system management scheme that enables you to assign drive letters to network directories.
6. The network of a single organization that spans national boundaries.
7. The extension of a company's private intranet to the Internet for use by selected mobile workers, customers, and/or suppliers.

8. A geographically limited network.
9. Network connectivity hardware required for connecting to a network.
10. Network connectivity software required for a workstation to connect to a NetWare 5.1 server.
11. Novell's strategy for connecting intranets, extranets, and the Internet together.
12. ZENworks configuration tools for managing NDS workstations, users, groups, or containers.
13. Protecting your network from unauthorized access.
14. A geographically dispersed network.
15. A memorable pneumonic for file system access rights.
   See Appendix C for answers.

## LAB EXERCISE 1.2: INTRODUCTION TO NETWARE 5.1

### Across

1. Next-generation printing system
6. The ultimate in communication
7. Private network that uses Internet technology
9. Provides access to non-NDPS printers
10. Entry-level Novell certification
11. Zero Effort Networks
15. Identity verification

### Down

2. Pointer to file system directory
3. Foundation of the WWW
4. NDS tree branch
5. The other NetWare 5.1 directory
8. Global object-oriented database
12. NDS location
13. Intermediate Novell certification
14. Bridge between NDS and the file system

See Appendix C for answers.

# CHAPTER 2

# Novell Directory Services

**W**elcome to Novell Directory Services (NDS)!

NDS is an object-oriented database that organizes network resources into a hierarchical tree. The global NDS tree is fully replicated and distributed throughout the network, providing efficient connectivity and network fault tolerance. NDS also features a single login and hidden security system that makes access to any server, volume, or network resource completely transparent to the user. NDS takes care of the complexities of network topology, communications, protocol translation, and authentication in the background, far away from the user.

Simply stated, users no longer belong to servers; they belong to the network as a whole. Users, servers, printers, volumes, and groups are treated equally and given simultaneous access to each other's resources.

**TIP**

**NDS enables you to manage network resources (such as servers, users, and printers) as graphical objects in a logical directory structure. In addition, NDS allows you to control these objects and the file system (directories and files) through two graphical tools: NetWare Administrator (Windows-based) and ConsoleOne ( Java-based).**

As you learned in the first chapter, NDS is a virtual tree structure that helps you organize network resources. It's also referred to as the *Cloud* because it floats above physical resources such as servers, printers, and users. The goal of this chapter is to generate enough neurokinetic energy in your brain to jumpstart your NetWare 5.1 administration lessons. In other words, we're going to make you think until it hurts:

▶ *Getting to Know NDS* — We'll start with a brief introduction to NDS and learn how it differs from the NetWare 3 bindery. Then, we'll explore the composition of the logical NDS tree.

▶ *NDS Objects* — Next, we'll explore the NDS [Root], container, and leaf objects in detail. Objects are the physical foundation of the logical NDS tree.

▶ *Overview of NDS Management* — Finally, we'll begin our CNA/CNE administrative journey with a brief introduction to NDS planning, naming, and current context.

So, without any further ado, let's start at the beginning—with an introduction to the NDS Cloud.

## Getting to Know NDS

Novell Directory Services (NDS) is a fundamental network service that is supplied by all NetWare 5.1 servers. As a matter of fact, it's the most fundamental network service offered by NetWare 5.1 after network communications. As such, NDS management is one of the key responsibilities of a network administrator.

As its name implies, NDS provides access to a database, called the *Directory*, that contains all resources for the entire network. This object-oriented Directory database is organized into a hierarchical structure called the NDS tree. (The word *Directory* is capitalized in this case to differentiate it from the NetWare 5.1 file system *directory*, which we'll discuss in Chapter 4.)

Although all NetWare 5.1 servers on the network use the Directory, you probably don't want to store a complete copy of it on each server. This is particularly true if you have a large network. Fortunately, NetWare 5.1 enables you to break up the Directory into smaller pieces called *partitions* and replicate them on multiple servers. This means that any NetWare 5.1 server can contain a copy of the entire Directory, specific pieces of it (partitions), or none at all. Of course, it's best to keep copies of important partitions closest to the users who need them. This minimizes unnecessary replica synchronization and background network traffic.

Some of the major benefits of NDS are as follows:

- *Central management* of network information, resources, and services

- *Standard method* of managing, viewing, and accessing network information, resources, and services

- *Logical organization* of network resources that are independent of the physical characteristics or layout of the network

- *Dynamic mapping* between an object and the physical resource to which it refers

*So, what does NDS look like?* From the outside, it looks like a big cloud hovering over your network. On the inside, however, it's a hierarchical tree similar to the DOS file system. As you can see in Figure 2.1, NDS organizes resources into logical groups called containers. In Figure 2.1, servers are organized according to function. Then users are placed in the appropriate containers to simplify connectivity. In addition, productivity is enhanced because users are near the resources they use. NDS also creates a global method of interconnectivity for all servers, users, groups, and other resources throughout the network.

▶ · · · · · · · · · · · · · · · · · · · · · · · · · · · · · · ◀

FIGURE 2.1

*The NDS tree structure*

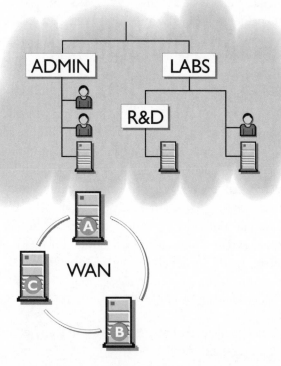

The bottom line is this—users don't access physical resources anymore. Instead, they access logical objects in the NDS tree. This means they don't need to know which NetWare 5.1 server provides a particular resource. All they need to know is where the resource exists in the logical NDS world.

## NDS versus the Bindery

NDS was first introduced in NetWare 4. Prior to that, NetWare operating systems relied on a server-centric model in which each NetWare server had its own flat-file database for tracking network resources, called the *bindery*. The bindery consisted of three files that held object, property, and value information, respectively. With this server-centric model, you had to log into each server that held resources that you wanted (refer to the flat architecture in Figure 2.2). This created considerable overhead, because users had to have a user account on each server they required access to. For example, if you had a network with 15 servers and 150 users, you would have to create 2,250 user accounts, if each user required access to resources on each server.

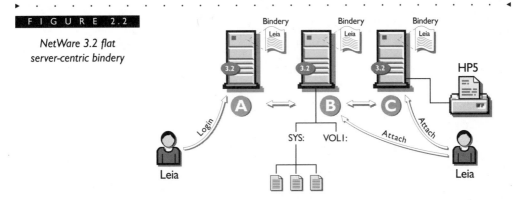

FIGURE 2.2

*NetWare 3.2 flat server-centric bindery*

NetWare 5.1, on the other hand, relies on a network-centric model (see Figure 2.3). In this model, NDS (the directory service) provides access to a global relational database (the Directory), which stores information about all network resources in a hierarchical format (the NDS tree).

In Figure 2.3, each network resource exists only once as a logical object in the Directory. The main benefit of this strategy is that it requires a single login, to the NDS tree, for access to all network-wide resources for which you have trustee rights (permission). This strategy, in turn, provides a single point for accessing and managing most network resources. This is true even if the servers on your network are connected across a wide area network (WAN).

▶ · · · · · · · · · · · · · · · · · · · · · · · · · · · · ◀

FIGURE 2.3

*The NetWare 5.1 hierarchical network-centric NDS tree*

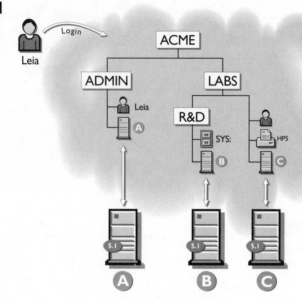

## Composition of the Tree

As in nature, the NDS tree starts with the [Root] and builds from there. Next, it sprouts container objects, which are branches reaching toward the sky. Finally, leaf objects provide network functionality to users, servers, and the file system. As you can see in Figure 2.4, the tree analogy is alive and well.

The real NDS tree is made up of logical network objects. NDS objects define logical or physical entities that provide organizational or technical function to the network. As you can see in Figure 2.5, they come in three different flavors:

- ▶ [Root]

- ▶ Container objects

- ▶ Leaf objects

The [Root] is the very top of the NDS tree. Because it represents the opening porthole to the NDS world, its icon is appropriately a picture of the Earth. Container objects define the organizational boundaries of the NDS tree and house other container objects and/or leaf objects. In Figure 2.5, we use container objects to define the ACME organization and its two divisions: ADMIN and LABS.

FIGURE 2.4

*The figurative NDS tree*

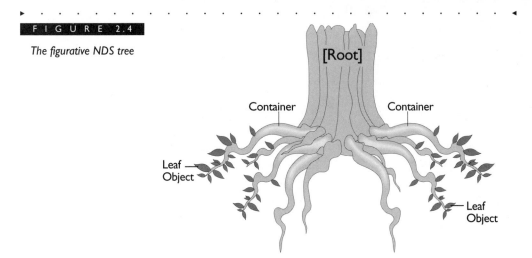

Finally, leaf objects are the physical or logical network resources that provide technical services and network functionality. Leaf objects define the lowest level of the NDS structure. In Figure 2.5, leaf objects represent users, a printer, a server, and a group. We'll discuss the most interesting leaf objects in the next section.

The tree can be organized any way you want, as long as it makes sense. AEinstein, for example, is placed near the resources he uses: the HP5 printer and LABS-SRV1 server.

## NDS Access

When a NetWare client (such as a user, application, or server) requests access to a network resource or service, NDS satisfies the request according to data stored in the network-wide Directory. One of the advantages of this strategy is that client requests are separated from resource physicality—that is, users don't need to know where a physical resource is located. They simply reference its unique Directory name. Because NDS is provided by all NetWare 5.1 servers, any NetWare 5.1 server on the same network can connect you with the resource.

FIGURE 2.5

The real NDS tree

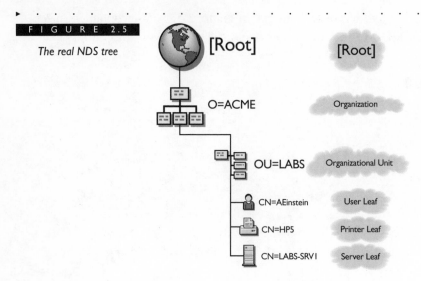

Here's how NDS processes client requests:

**1.** A NetWare 5.1 client requests a resource.

**2.** A NetWare 5.1 server responds.

**3.** NDS locates the object in the Directory.

**4.** The Directory locates the physical location of the resource.

**5.** Client validity and authority are checked.

**6.** The Client is connected to the resource.

Now that you understand the fundamental architecture of NDS, let's take a closer look at its different container and leaf objects. These are the physical foundation of the logical NDS tree.

# NDS Objects

The Directory consists of objects, properties, and values.

An *object* is similar to a record or row of information in a database table. It contains information about a particular network entity. NDS represents each network resource as an object in the Directory. For example, a User object represents a particular user on the network.

An object *property* is similar to a field in a database record. It is a category of information you can store about an object. For example, properties of a User object include such things as Login Name, Password, and Telephone Number. Each type of object has a specific set of properties associated with it; this defines its *class*. Properties are predefined by NDS and determine how a given object can be used. For example, Server properties differ from Printer properties because they are different NDS objects with different functions.

Three important types of NDS properties include the following:

▸ *Required properties* — These properties contain vital object data, and, therefore, must be supplied to create the object. Required properties can't be deleted. For example, when you create a User object, you must indicate values for the Login Name and Last Name properties. As a matter of fact, the name of an object is always a required property. (Otherwise, you would have no way of referring to it.) In contrast, the required properties for a Printer object include Printer Name, Network Address, and Configuration Information.

▸ *Optional properties* — These properties contain nonvital information about an object. As such, you only need to supply values for them if desired. Examples include a User's Title, Telephone Number, and Fax Number.

▸ *Multivalued properties* — These properties support more than one entry. For example, the Telephone Number property associated with a User object can hold multiple phone numbers for that user. Other User-related multivalued properties include Title, Location, and Fax Number. (This type of multivalued property is represented in NetWare Administrator with a "..." button to the right of the property field. If you click this button, you'll be allowed to enter additional entries for the property.)

Finally, a property *value* is similar to a data string in a field of a database record. In other words, it's a data item associated with a property. For example, the value associated with the Password property of a User object would be the actual password for that User object.

Refer to Table 2.1 for an illustration of the relationship between NDS objects, properties, and values.

| T A B L E  2.1<br>*Understanding NDS Objects, Properties, and Values* | OBJECT | PROPERTY | VALUE |
|---|---|---|---|
| | User | Login Name | AEinstein (also known as AEinstein.LABS.NORAD.ACME) |
| | | Title | Super Smart Scientist |
| | | Location | NORAD |
| | | Password | Relativity |
| | Printer (Non NDPS) | Name | WHITE-P1.WHITE.CRIME.TOKYO.ACME |
| | | Default Print Queue | WHITE-PQ1.WHITE.CRIME.TOKYO.ACME |
| | | Print Server | WHITE-PS1.WHITE.CRIME.TOKYO.ACME |
| | NetWare Server | Other Name | LABS-SRV1 |
| | | Version | Novell NetWare 5.00h[DS] |
| | | Operators | Admin |
| | | Status | Up |

## Understanding NDS Objects

As we discussed earlier, the Directory is an object-oriented database that is organized in a hierarchical structure called the NDS tree. It provides a way to view the logical organization of network resources stored in the Directory database. As you can see in Figure 2.6, the tree is similar to the DOS file system. It contains three main classes of objects:

▸ [Root]

▸ Container objects

▸ Leaf objects

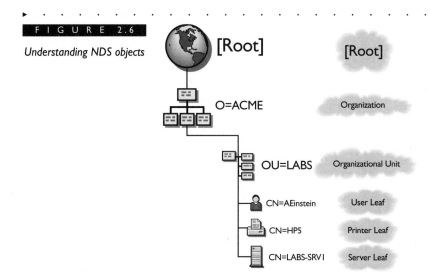

FIGURE 2.6

*Understanding NDS objects*

The top of the tree is called the *[Root]*. *Container objects*, which are analogous to folders, define the organizational boundaries of the Directory and are used to store other container objects and/or leaf objects, depending on which type of container they are. (A container object is called a *parent object* if it contains other objects.) *Leaf objects*, which are analogous to files, are typically stored in container objects. They are the physical or logical network resources that provide technical services and WAN functionality. Leaf objects define the lowest level of the NDS structure and, thus, cannot contain other objects.

The main difference between NDS and DOS architecture is that NDS containers have restrictions on where they can be placed and what can be placed in them. Typically, each NetWare 5.1 network will only have one NDS tree. If a network has more than one tree, each will function as a separate, independent database. In other words, resources cannot be shared between them.

In the Directory, each network resource is defined as a logical object. There are a number of different types of objects. For example, an object can represent a person (such as a user), a physical resource (such as a printer), an NDS resource (such as a group), or an organizational resource (such as an Organizational Unit container).

Now that you've mastered the subtle differences between NDS objects, properties, and values, let's explore some of the most interesting objects in detail, starting with [Root].

## [Root]

The [Root] is a required object that defines the top of the NDS organizational structure. Because it represents the opening porthole to our NDS world, its icon is appropriately a picture of the Earth. Each Directory tree can only have one [Root], which is created during installation of the first server in that tree. The only objects that can be created directly under the [Root] are Country, Organization, and Alias. (In this case, the Alias object can only point to a Country or Organization.) The square brackets ([ ]) are mandatory when referring to this object.

Although some people think of the [Root] as a container object (because it contains all the objects in the Directory), it differs from other container objects in the following ways:

▶ It cannot be created except during installation of the first NetWare 5.1 server on a network.

▶ It is essentially a placeholder; it does not have properties.

▶ It cannot be moved, deleted, or renamed.

▶ The NDS tree name is sometimes confused with the [Root] object. Unlike the [Root] object, however, the tree name can be changed.

Like other objects, the [Root] can be assigned as a trustee of other objects, and other objects can be granted trustee access rights to it. For example, an object can be granted trustee rights to the entire NDS tree by making the object a trustee of the [Root] object. (See Chapter 5 for further information on trustee rights.)

## Container Objects

Container objects are logical objects that organize (store) other container or leaf objects. A container can represent a country, location within a country, company, department, responsibility center, workgroup, or collection of shared resources. Each class of container object has different rules that define what it can contain and where it can be located in the tree. Each class also has different properties.

The following are the most common types of NetWare 5.1 container objects:

▸ *Country* — Designates the country where certain parts of the organization reside.

▸ *Organization* — Represents a company, university, or department. NDS only supports one layer of Organization objects, hence, the term *one-dimensional*. (**Note:** Organizations can hold Organizational Unit containers or leaf objects.)

▸ *Organizational Unit* — Represents a division, business unit, or project team within the Organization. Organizational Units hold other Organizational Units or leaf objects. They are *multidimensional*.

Refer to Figure 2.6 earlier for an illustration of the relationship between the [Root] and container objects. The ACME Organization houses other Organizational Units (including LABS), that in turn house leaf objects (like AEinstein). Let's take a closer look at these three different container objects.

### Country

The *Country* object is an optional container that organizes a Directory tree by country. This type of object can only be defined directly under the [Root] and must be named using a two-character abbreviation. Novell states that you must use a *valid* two-character country abbreviation. Presumably, this is to ensure that your network is in compliance with the two-character abbreviations defined in the ISO X.500 standard.

Interestingly, if you create a Country object using the NetWare Administrator utility, it allows you to use any two-character name. To determine which two-character names are compliant with the ISO X.500 standard, click Help when creating the Country object, and NetWare 5.1 will tell you. The only objects that can exist in a Country container are an Organization or Alias object pointing to an Organization.

**TIP** If you don't have any compelling reasons to use the **Country** object, stay away from it. It only adds an unnecessary level of complexity to your network. As a matter of fact, Novell doesn't even use the Country object in its own multidimensional, worldwide **NDS** tree.

### Organization

If you don't use a Country object, the next layer in the tree is typically an Organization. As you can see in Figure 2.6 earlier, ACME is represented as an *O*. You can use an Organization object to designate a company, a division of a company, a university or college with various departments, and so on. Every Directory tree must contain at least one Organization object. Therefore, it is required. Many small implementations use only the Organization object and place all their resources directly underneath it. Organization objects must be placed directly below the [Root], unless a Country object is used. Finally, Organization objects can contain all objects except [Root], Country, and Organization.

Earlier, we defined the Organization as a one-dimensional object. This means the tree can only support one layer of Organization objects. If you look closer at the icon, you'll see a box with multiple horizontal boxes underneath. Additional vertical hierarchy is defined by Organizational Units; which are multidimensional. We'll describe them in just a moment.

Figure 2.7 illustrates the object dialog box for the ACME Organization using NetWare Administrator. On the right side of the screen are the many page buttons that identify categories of NDS properties for this object. Associated with each page button is an input screen for a specific set of information (on the left side). The Identification page button (shown here) allows you to define a variety of Organization properties including Name, Other Name, Description, Location, Telephone, and Fax Number.

Similar page buttons allow you to configure important Organization parameters, including postal information, print job configurations, trustee assignments, and so on. As far as ACME is concerned, the Organization container defines the top of the functional tree.

### Organizational Unit

The Organizational Unit object is a *natural group*. It allows you to organize users with the leaf objects they use. You can create group login scripts, a user template for security, trustee assignments, security equivalences, and distributed administrators.

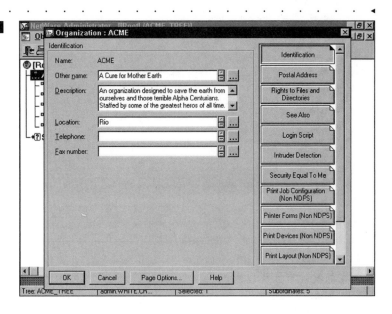

FIGURE 2.7

*Properties of an NDS*
*Organization object*

Organizational Units can represent a division, business unit, project team, or department. In Figure 2.6 earlier, the LABS organizational unit represents a division within the ACME Organization. In this container, AEinstein works with his printers and servers. Organizational Units are multidimensional, in that you can have many hierarchical levels of containers within containers. Remember, Organization objects can only exist at one level in the NDS tree.

Organizational Units are the most flexible containers because they can contain other Organizational Unit objects or leaf objects. As a matter of fact, Organizational Units can contain most of the NDS object types, except the [Root], Country, or Organization containers (or Aliases of any of these).

Now, let's take a look at the real stars of our NDS world — leaf objects.

▶ · · · · · · · · · · · · · · · · · · · · · · · · · · · · · · · · · · ◀

**REAL WORLD**

NDS supports many other special-use container objects. Three that you may frequently run across are Locality, User License Container, and Server License Container.

The "secret" Locality object is similar to the Country object, in that it's optional and not created as part of the default NetWare 5.1 installation. If desired, you can use a Locality object to designate the region where your organization's headquarters resides. Unlike Country objects, Locality objects can reside either under the Country, Organization, or Organizational Unit containers.

In addition, NetWare 5.1 supports two different types of license container objects: a User License container and a Server License container. These objects are added to the NDS tree when NetWare 5.1 is installed. They appear as NDS objects in the container that includes the Server object. License container objects can contain multiple-license Certificate leaf objects. To manage licenses for users, use the "Novell+NetWare 5 Conn SCL+510" license container. This is where the initial user license certificates are placed, by default. This name is a compound fragment made up of the Publisher, Product, and Version attributes. In addition, the number at the end of the license container object's name indicates the version of NetWare that it supports.

## Leaf Objects

Leaf objects represent logical or physical network resources. Because leaf objects reside at the end of the structural NDS tree, they cannot be used to store other objects. In other words, they represent the proverbial "end of the road." As we learned earlier, each class of leaf object has certain properties associated with it. This collection of properties differentiates the various leaf object classes from each other. For example, User objects contain different properties than Printer objects.

The following are some of the key leaf objects covered in this course:

 *Alias* — An Alias object points to another object that exists in a different location in the NDS tree. It enables a user to access an object outside of the user's normal working context (that is, container).

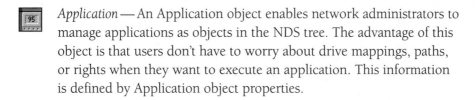

*Application* — An Application object enables network administrators to manage applications as objects in the NDS tree. The advantage of this object is that users don't have to worry about drive mappings, paths, or rights when they want to execute an application. This information is defined by Application object properties.

*Auditing File (AFO)* — An Auditing File object represents an audit trail's log of events associated with a container, workstation, or volume. This object enables you to manage auditing file logs as objects in the NDS tree.

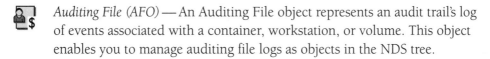

*Directory Map* — A Directory Map object represents a logical pointer to a physical directory in the NetWare 5.1 file system. This object is useful in mapping statements because it enables you to map a drive to a resource without knowing its physical location. If the path to the resource changes, you only need to change the path designated in the Directory Map object, rather than any of the login script mappings statements that refer to it.

*Group* — A Group object defines a list of users for the purpose of assigning access rights or other configuration parameters. The members of a group can be a subset of users in the same container or spread across multiple containers. The difference between containers and groups is that container objects store User objects, whereas Group objects store a list of User objects.

*License Certificate* — A License Certificate object is used by NetWare Licensing Services (NLS) to monitor and control the use of licensed applications on the network.

*NetWare Server* — A NetWare Server object represents a server on your network that is running any version of the NetWare operating system. This object is used by various leaf objects (such as Volume objects) to identify a physical server that provides particular network services. Refer to Figure 2.8 for an illustration of the NetWare Server properties that can be managed using NetWare Administrator.

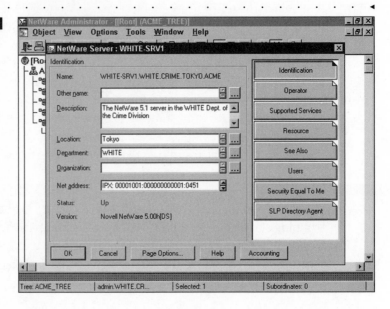

*Organizational Role* — An Organizational Role object defines a position or role within the organization that can be filled by any designated user. The Organizational Role is particularly useful for rotating positions that support multiple employees, where the responsibilities of the job, and the network access required, are static. If a User object is assigned as an occupant of an organizational role, the user "absorbs" all trustee rights assigned to it. Some organizational role examples include PostMaster, Network Administrator, Silicon Valley CEO, or Receptionist.

*Printer (Non NDPS)* — A Printer (Non NDPS) object represents a queue-based physical printing device on the network, such as a printer or plotter. (**Note:** NDPS printing objects are discussed later in Chapter 7.) Refer to Figure 2.9 for an illustration of the Printer (Non NDPS) properties that can be managed using NetWare Administrator.

*Print Queue* — A Print Queue object represents a print queue used to store print jobs sent from client workstations. In NetWare 5.1, each print queue is stored as a subdirectory under the QUEUES directory at the root of a NetWare volume.

*Print Server (Non NDPS)* — A Print Server (Non NDPS) object represents a network print server used for monitoring queue-based print queues and printers.

 *Profile* — A Profile object defines a login script for a subset of users in the same container or spread across multiple containers. (If all of the users in a container need the same login script, you should use a Container login script, instead.)

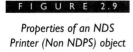

F I G U R E   2 . 9

*Properties of an NDS Printer (Non NDPS) object*

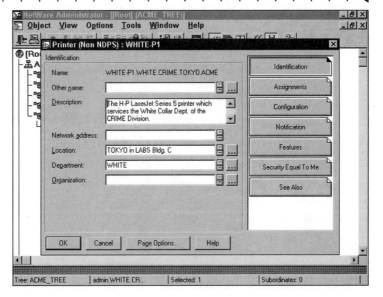

*Template* — A Template object can be used to create User objects with similar properties.

*Unknown* — An Unknown object represents an NDS object that has been corrupted, invalidated, or that cannot be identified as belonging to any of the other leaf classes. For example, an Alias object becomes Unknown when its host is deleted.

*User* — A User object represents a person who uses the network (for example, you, me, or Fred). For security reasons, you should create a separate User object for each user on the network. A User object contains a plethora of interesting properties, including Login Name, Password, Full Name, Login Restrictions, and so on. Refer to Figure 2.10 for an illustration of the User properties that can be managed using NetWare Administrator.

FIGURE 2.10

*Properties of an
NDS User object*

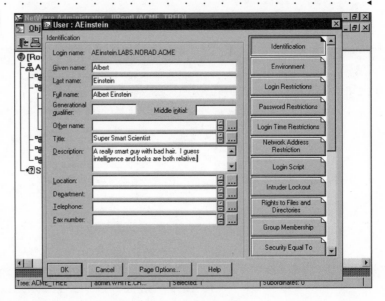

**REAL WORLD**

NDS is a powerful database with much valuable user information. Consider using it as a central company database of employee data. If you can't find what you need in the almost 100 default properties, you can always create your own. The NetWare 5.1 Software Developers Kit (SDK) provides interface tools for modifying and adding NDS properties. This is called *extending* the NDS Schema.

In addition, NetWare 5.1 includes a Schema Manager for viewing and customizing the NDS Schema directly from NetWare Administrator. You can access this GUI (graphical user interface) management tool from the Object menu. Check it out ... it's fun at parties!

*Volume* — A Volume object represents a physical volume on the network. Typically, volumes are created during the server installation process. Remember that a Volume object is a leaf object rather than a container object — even though the NetWare Administrator utility may give you the opposite impression. It stores information about a volume including server name, physical volume mapping, and volume use statistics.

 *Workstation* — A Workstation object enables you to manage network workstations through NDS. This leaf object is automatically created when a workstation is registered and imported into the NDS tree. (We'll explore this process later when we explore ZENworks in Chapter 6.)

 *Workstation Group* — A Workstation Group object lets you manage or maintain a group of Workstation objects. This leaf enables you to apply a change to a Workstation Group object, instead of each individual Workstation object.

Table 2.2 summarizes some important NDS object characteristics.

**T A B L E  2.2**

*NDS Object Characteristics*

| OBJECT | CAN EXIST IN | CAN CONTAIN | EXAMPLES |
|---|---|---|---|
| [Root] | Top of the tree | Country<br>Organization<br>Alias *(of Country or Organization only)* | [Root] |
| Country | [Root] | Organization<br>Alias *(of Organization only)* | US<br>UK |
| Organization | [Root]<br>Country | Organizational Units<br>All leaf objects | Novell<br>MIT |
| Organizational Unit | Organization<br>Organizational Units | Organizational Units<br>All leaf objects | Sales<br>Finance |

*Continued*

| TABLE 2.2 | | | |
|---|---|---|---|
| NDS Object Characteristics (continued) | | | |
| OBJECT | CAN EXIST IN | CAN CONTAIN | EXAMPLES |
| Leaf Objects | [Root] (Alias of Country or Organization only) Country (Alias of Organization only) Organization Organizational Unit | Cannot contain other NDS objects | CRIME-SRV1 DClarkeIV CEttelson |

This completes our discussion of the most interesting NDS objects offered by NetWare 5.1. You'll want to get to know all these leaf objects because future discussions center around how to organize, design, and manage them. Once you understand the relationships between NDS objects, you can start building your tree — that's later in Chapter 3.

**TIP**

**Every leaf object and container object is represented by an icon graphic that depicts its purpose. For example, printers are printers, servers are computers, and users are people. These icons are used throughout this book and in graphical NDS utilities. NetWare Administrator, for example, uses icons to provide a snapshot of an entire NDS tree in a hierarchical structure. This feature makes it easier for administrators and users to locate and use NetWare 5.1 resources. Cool.**

How do you feel? So far, we've explored all the physical and logical objects that make up NetWare 5.1's revolutionary NDS tree. However, this is only the beginning. Your success as a CNA/CNE is defined by your ability to manage NDS objects and their properties.

## LAB EXERCISE 2.1:
## GETTING TO KNOW NDS (MATCHING)

### Part I

Write C for container or L for leaf next to each of the following objects:

1. ___ Volume
2. ___ Country
3. ___ User
4. ___ Group
5. ___ Organizational Unit
6. ___ NetWare Server
7. ___ Print Queue
8. ___ Organizational Role
9. ___ Computer
10. ___ Organization

See Appendix C for answers.

### PART II

Indicate whether you think each item below would be a container or a leaf object. If you think it would be a container object, indicate what type of container (that is, Country, Organization, or Organizational Unit).

1. _____ The Human Resources department
2. _____ David IV
3. _____ A database server
4. _____ The PAYCHECK print queue
5. _____ ACME, Inc.
6. _____ The Administrator Organizational Role
7. _____ UK (that is, United Kingdom)
8. _____ A dot matrix printer
9. _____ The Tokyo office
10. _____ The SYS: volume

See Appendix C for answers.

# NDS Management Overview

Now that you understand what the NDS tree is made of, we need to explore how it works. As you manage the NDS tree, pay particular attention to its structure. A well-designed tree will make resource access and management much easier.

The structure of the NDS tree is both organizational and functional. The location of an object in the tree can affect how users access it and how network administrators manage it. The NDS tree structure impacts the following areas of administrative responsibility:

▶ NDS planning

▶ Resource access

▶ Resource setup

You complete these tasks by implementing NDS planning guidelines, using proper NDS naming structure, and understanding current context. Let's take a closer look.

## Planning Guidelines

An efficient NDS Directory tree provides all the following benefits:

▶ It makes resource access easier for users.

▶ It makes administration easier for network administrators.

▶ It provides fault tolerance for the NDS database.

▶ It decreases network traffic.

The structure of the tree can be based on location, organization, or administration. In many cases, it's a combination of all three. Many factors influence the structure of your NDS tree. Before you design your tree, you might need to study workgroups, resource allocation, and/or learn how data flows throughout your network.

As a CNA, it's your responsibility to navigate and manage the tree, not to design or troubleshoot it — that's what CNEs are for. Novell offers a CNE-level course called Course 575, "NDS Design and Implementation," which explores the network design process. This material is also covered in much greater detail in *Novell's CNE Study Guide for NetWare 5.1*.

## NDS Naming

The name of an NDS object identifies its location in the hierarchical tree. Therefore, each object name must be unique. NDS naming impacts two important NetWare 5.1 tasks:

- ▶ *Login* — Typically, you need to identify the location of your User object in the NDS tree in order for NetWare 5.1 to authenticate you during login.

- ▶ *Resource access* — NDS naming exactly identifies the type and location of NetWare 5.1 resources, including file servers, printers, login scripts, and files.

The whole NetWare 5.1 NDS naming scheme is much more complicated than "Hi, I'm Fred." It requires both your name and location. For example, a proper NDS name would be "Hi, I'm Fred in the ADMIN division of ACME." As you can see in Figure 2.11, Fred's NDS name identifies who he is and where he works.

The NDS tree affects resource access because the organization of objects in the tree dictates how they can be found and used. In fact, the whole NDS naming strategy hinges on the concept of *context*. There are two main types of context: current context and object context. Check it out.

### Context

*Current context* is sometimes referred to as *name context*. It defines *where you are* in the NDS tree at any given time, not *where you live*. This is an important distinction. For example, if you are using a NetWare 5.1 utility, it's important to know what the utility considers as the current context in the NDS tree (that is, the default container to use if one is not specified). This concept is somewhat similar to knowing your current default drive/directory when using a DOS or Windows utility on your workstation.

FIGURE 2.11

Getting to know
the real Fred

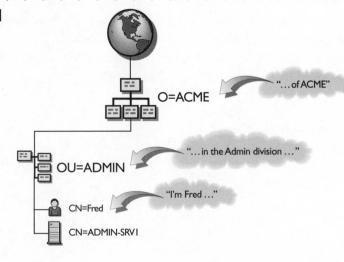

O=ACME — "…of ACME"

OU=ADMIN — "…in the Admin division …"

CN=Fred — "I'm Fred …"

CN=ADMIN-SRV1

## REAL WORLD

Novell recommends that before you implement NDS, you create a document that describes your naming standards. The NDS naming rules we're going to learn here only work if object names are consistent across the network. A naming standards document provides guidelines for naming key container and leaf objects, including users, printers, servers, volumes, print queues, and organizational units. In addition, it identifies standard properties and value formats. Consistency, especially in the naming scheme used for objects, provides several benefits:

▸ A consistent naming scheme provides a guideline for network administrators who will add, modify, or move objects within the Directory tree.

▸ A naming standard eliminates redundant planning and gives network administrators an efficient model to meet their needs, but it leaves implementation of resource objects open and flexible.

▸ Consistent naming schemes help users identify resources quickly, which maximizes user productivity.

▸ Consistent naming enables users to identify themselves easily during login.

In addition, current context affects how much of an object's distinguished name you must provide to find it. (See the section "Distinguished Names" later in this chapter for more information.) Current context also enables you to refer to an object in your current container by its common name because the object's context is the same. Note that current context always points to a container object, rather than a leaf object. Typically, at login, you'll want a workstation's current context set to the container that holds the user's most frequently used resources.

In Figure 2.11, Fred's context is ". . . in the ADMIN division of ACME." This context identifies where Fred lives in the NDS tree structure. It identifies all container objects leading from him to the [Root]. In addition to context, Figure 2.11 identifies Fred's common name (CN). A leaf object's common name specifically identifies it within a given container. In this example, the User object's common name is Fred.

Two objects in the same NDS tree may have the same common name — provided, however, that they have different contexts. This is why naming is so important. As you can see in Figure 2.12, our NDS tree has two Freds, but each has a different context.

▶ · · · · · · · · · · · · · · · · · · · · · · · · · · · · · ◀

*Understanding NDS context*

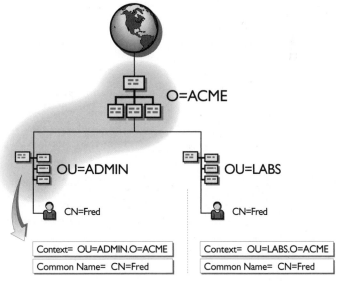

*Object context* (sometimes referred to as *context*) defines where a particular object is located in the NDS tree structure. It is a list of container objects leading from the object to the [Root]. Locating an object through context is similar to locating a file using the directory path. As we learned earlier, object context is used for two important purposes: logging in and accessing resources. Unfortunately, NDS does not have a search path feature (such as NetWare SEARCH drives or the DOS PATH command used in the file system). This means that when you request a particular network resource, you (or your workstation) must provide NDS with enough information to locate the object in the tree.

Each NDS object has a naming type associated with it. This naming type is identified by a one- or two-character abbreviation. Following are examples of naming types:

- ► *C* = Country container

- ► *O* = Organization container

- ► *OU* = Organizational Unit container

- ► *CN* = Common name (specifies a leaf object)

Now that you understand how NDS context works, let's review the naming rules associated with it:

- ► Current context is a pointer to the NDS container that your Novell Client is currently set to.

- ► An object's context defines its location in the NDS tree.

- ► Each object has an identifier abbreviation that defines it for naming purposes, namely the following: C = Country, O = Organization, OU = Organizational Unit, and CN = common name (of leaf object).

- ► Context is defined by listing all containers from the object to the [Root], in that order. Each object is separated by a period.

- ► Context is important for logging in and accessing NDS resources.

So, there you have it. That's how context works. With this in mind, it's time to explore the two main types of NDS names: distinguished names and typeful names.

### Distinguished Names

An object's *distinguished name* is its complete NDS path. It is a combination of common name and object context. Each object in the NDS tree has a distinguished name that uniquely identifies it in the tree. In other words, two objects cannot have the same distinguished name.

In Figure 2.13, AEinstein's context is .OU=R&D.OU=LABS.O=ACME, and his common name is CN=AEinstein. Therefore, Einstein's distinguished name is a simple mathematical addition of the two:

```
.CN=AEinstein.OU=R&D.OU=LABS.O=ACME
```

▶ · · · · · · · · · · · · · · · · · · · · · · · · · · · · ◀

**FIGURE 2.13**

*Building AEinstein's distinguished name*

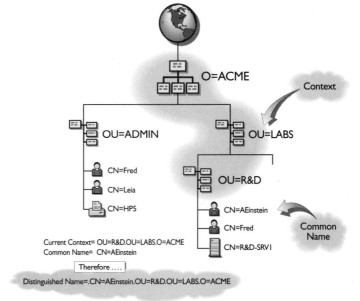

Notice the use of periods. A distinguished name always starts with a leading period. Trailing periods aren't allowed. The leading period identifies the name as distinguished (that is, complete). Otherwise, it is assumed to be incomplete. In other words, a relative distinguished name.

### Relative Distinguished Names

A *relative distinguished name* lists an object's path to the current context, not the [Root]. The relativity part refers to how NDS builds the distinguished name when you supply a *relative* name. By definition, for example, the common name of a leaf object is a relative distinguished name. When you use a relative distinguished name, NDS builds a distinguished name by appending the current context to the end:

Relative distinguished name + current context = distinguished name

For example, if the current context is .OU=LABS.O=ACME and you submit a relative distinguished name of CN=AEinstein.OU=R&D, the distinguished name would be resolved as (refer to Figure 2.14) the following:

```
.CN=AEinstein.OU=R&D.OU=LABS.O=ACME
```

▶ · · · · · · · · · · · · · · · · · · · · · · · · · ◀

FIGURE 2.14

*Building AEinstein's relative distinguished name*

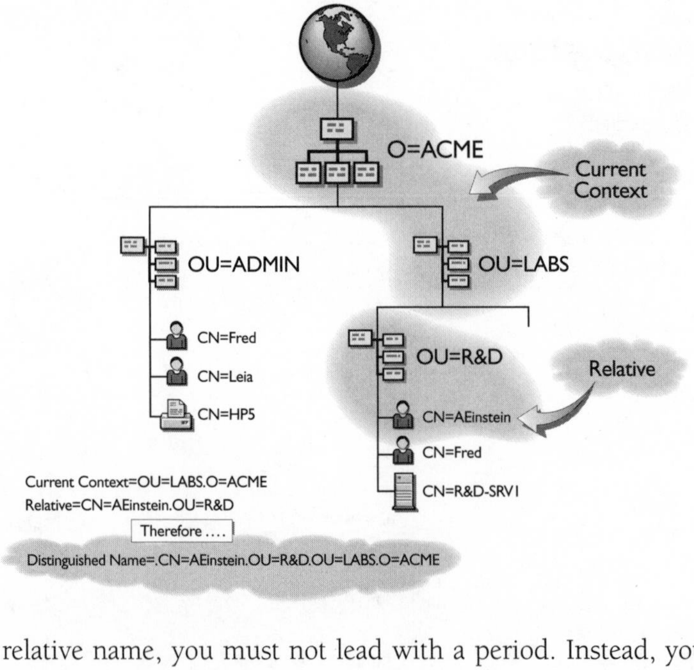

To distinguish a relative name, you must not lead with a period. Instead, you can use trailing periods to change the current context used to resolve the name (as if naming wasn't hard enough already). The bottom line is that each trailing period

tells NDS to remove one object name from the left side of the current context being used. This concept is somewhat similar to the trailing dot feature used in the DOS CD command.

For example, assume that .OU=R&D.OU=LABS.O=ACME is your current context and that CN=LEIA.OU=ADMIN.. is your relative distinguished name. In this case, the distinguished name would resolve as follows (refer to Figure 2.15):

```
.CN=LEIA.OU=ADMIN.O=ACME
```

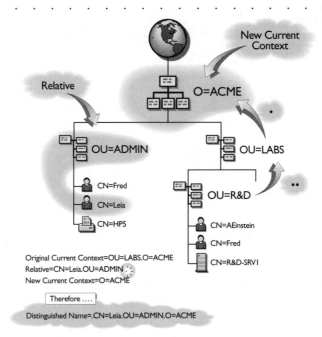

FIGURE 2.15

*Using trailing periods to resolve Leia's distinguished name*

New Current Context

Relative

O=ACME

OU=ADMIN

OU=LABS

CN=Fred

CN=Leia

CN=HP5

OU=R&D

CN=AEinstein

CN=Fred

CN=R&D-SRV1

Original Current Context=OU=LABS.O=ACME
Relative=CN=Leia.OU=ADMIN..
New Current Context=O=ACME

Therefore ....

Distinguished Name=.CN=Leia.OU=ADMIN.O=ACME

As you can see, it's very important where you place your dots! Here's a quick summary:

▸ All objects in an NDS name are separated by dots.

▸ Distinguished names are preceded by a dot. This identifies them as complete.

▸ Relative distinguished names are not preceded by a dot. This identifies them as incomplete.

▸ Trailing dots can only be used in relative distinguished names because they modify the current context to be used. Each dot moves the context up one container as the distinguished name is resolved.

For a complete summary of NDS distinguished naming rules, refer to Table 2.3.

| TABLE 2.3 *Getting to Know Distinguished Naming* | | DISTINGUISHED NAMES | RELATIVE NAMES |
|---|---|---|---|
| | What it is | Complete unique name | Incomplete name based on current context |
| | How it works | Lists the complete path from the object to the [Root] | Lists the relative path from the object to the current context |
| | Abbreviation | DN | RDN |
| | Leading period | Leading periods required | No leading periods allowed |
| | Trailing periods | No trailing periods allowed | Trailing periods optional |

Now, let's step back in reality for a moment and explore the other NDS naming category — typeful names.

### Typeful versus Typeless Names

*Typeful names* use attribute type abbreviations to distinguish between the different container types and leaf objects in NDS names. In all the examples to this point, we've used these abbreviations to help clarify context, distinguished names, and relative distinguished names. Following are the most popular attribute type abbreviations:

▸ C = Country container

▸ O = Organization container

▶ OU = Organizational Unit container

▶ CN = Common name of a leaf object

These attribute types help avoid the confusion that can occur when creating complex distinguished and relative distinguished names. I highly recommend that you use them. Of course, like most things in life — they are optional! You can imagine how crazy NDS naming gets when you choose not to use these attribute abbreviations. This insanity is known as *typeless naming*.

*Typeless names* operate the same as typeful names, but they don't include object attribute types. In such cases, NDS has to guess what object types you're using. Take the following typeless name, for example:

`.Admin.ACME`

Is this the ADMIN Organizational Unit under ACME? Or is this the Admin user under ACME? In both cases, it's a valid distinguished name, except that one identifies an Organizational Unit container, and the other identifies a User leaf object (refer to Figure 2.16).

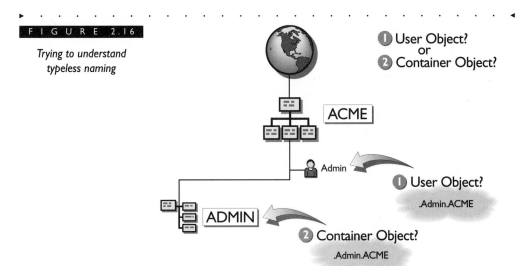

F I G U R E   2.16

*Trying to understand
typeless naming*

Well, here's the bottom line: which one is it? It's up to NDS. If you do not provide a typeful object name, NDS calculates attribute types for each object. Fortunately, NetWare 5.1 has some guidelines for guessing what the object type should be.

**1.** The leftmost object is a common name (leaf object).

**2.** The rightmost object is an Organization (container object).

**3.** All middle objects are Organizational Units (container objects).

Although this works for most cases, it's only a general guideline. Many times, typeless names are more complex. Take our example in Figure 2.16 earlier, for instance. We know now that the rightmost object is an Organization, but what about Admin? Is it a common name or an Organizational Unit? We still don't know. Fortunately, NetWare 5.1 includes a few exceptions to deal with complex typeless scenarios. Here's how it works:

▸ *Exception Rule 1: Container Objects* — Many NetWare 5.1 utilities are intelligent enough to resolve typeless names, depending on what they are trying to accomplish. CX, for example, is used primarily for changing context. If you apply the CX command to a typeless name, it assumes the leftmost object is an Organization or Organizational Unit. This is because you can't change your current context to a leaf object. Other utilities that allow you to change context include NetWare Administrator and ConsoleOne. In summary, here's how our example from Figure 2.16 would look with the CX utility:

```
CX .ADMIN.ACME resolves as ".OU=ADMIN.O=ACME"
```

▸ *Exception Rule 2: Leaf Objects* — Similarly, resource-based utilities recognize the leftmost object of a typeless name as a leaf object. Many of these utilities are expecting to see a common name. The most prevalent are LOGIN, MAP, and CAPTURE. Here's how it works for our example in Figure 2.16:

```
LOGIN .Admin.ACME resolves as ".CN=Admin.O=ACME"
```

▶ *Exception Rule 3: Contextless Login* — If you have Catalog Services and Contextless Login activated, NDS will resolve typeless names by offering the user a list from the NDS Catalog. (**Note:** NetWare 5.1 eDirectory [installed by default] does not support Catalog Services.)

There you have it. This completes our discussion of typeless names and NDS naming in general. As you can see, this is an important topic because it impacts all aspects of NDS design, installation, and management. No matter what you do, you're going to have to use the correct name to log into the tree or access NDS resources. As we've learned, an object's name is a combination of *what it is* (common name) and *where it lives* (context).

Now, let's complete our NDS adventure with a quick lesson in changing your current context.

## Changing Your Current Context

A user's current context can be set in one of the following ways:

▶ Before login, using the Name Context field on the Client tab of the Novell NetWare Client Properties (or Novell Client Configuration) window

▶ During login, using the Context field on the NDS tab of the Novell Login window (which is accessed by clicking the Advanced button)

▶ Using the CONTEXT login script command

▶ Using the CX utility

It's best to set a user's context at login, so the user can have easy access to the network resources he or she uses the most. If a user wants to access resources located in a different context, he or she will need to use correct naming conventions. Let's explore each of these four methods for changing a user's current context before, during, and after login.

### Setting a User's Context Before Login

On Windows 95/98 and Windows NT/2000 workstations, you can set the workstation's current context before login by entering the appropriate context information in the Novell NetWare Client Properties window, as shown in Figure 2.17. The typeless distinguished name in the Name Context field sets the workstation's current context before login. It can be entered with or without a preceding period.

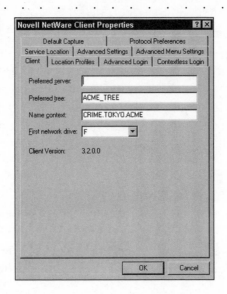

FIGURE 2.17

The Novell NetWare Client
Properties dialog box

To set up a workstation's current context before login, access the Network icon in the Windows 95/98 or Windows NT/2000 Control Panel, select Novell NetWare Client, and then click Properties. When the Novell NetWare Client Properties dialog box appears, enter the current context in the Name Context field on the Client tab. (If you're already logged into the network, a faster way to change this field is to right-click the N icon in the System tray and to select Novell Client Properties from the pop-up menu. When the Novell Client Configuration dialog box appears, enter the current context in the Name Context field on the Client tab.)

### Setting a User's Context during Login

On Windows 95/98 and Windows NT/2000 workstations, you can set a workstation's current context during login by entering the appropriate context information in the Novell Login window. To do so, when the Novell Login window is displayed, click the Advanced button and then enter the current context in the Context field on the NDS tab.

## Using the CONTEXT Login Script Command

Setting a workstation's current context during login sets the current context that will be in effect for the user once the user attaches to the network. This prevents the user from having to use distinguished names to access NDS resources. Remember, NDS attempts to resolve relative distinguished names into distinguished names by appending the current context to the end of the relative name.

The CONTEXT login script command is similar to the NetWare 5.1 CX command-line utility, except that it does not support all the same options (that is, it only sets the current context). To set a workstation's current context during login, add this command to the appropriate Container, Profile, or User login script:

```
CONTEXT distinguished name
```

For example,

```
CONTEXT .LABS.NORAD.ACME
```

Note the use of a preceding period (.) to identify the distinguished name. This method is not workstation-specific; it can be set for an individual or a group.

## Using the CX Command

You can view information about an object's context or change your workstation's current context using the CX command-line utility (which is executed at the DOS prompt on a client workstation). CX is the key NetWare 5.1 utility for dealing with NDS context. It enables you to perform two important tasks: change your workstation's current context and/or view information about a resource's object context.

CX is a relatively straightforward command with a great deal of versatility. As a matter of fact, it's similar to the DOS CD command in its general approach. If you type **CX** by itself, the system displays your workstation's current context. This is marginally interesting, at best. CX really excels when you combine it with one or more command-line switches. Here are some of the more interesting ones:

- ► *CX* — View your workstation's current context.

- ► *CX .* — Move the context up one container for each period (.).

- ► *CX /T* — View the Directory tree structure below your current context.

- ► *CX /A /T* — View all objects in the Directory tree structure below your current context.

▶ *CX /R /A /T* — View all objects in the Directory tree below the [Root].

▶ *CX /CONT* — List containers only, below the current context, in a vertical list, with no directory structure.

▶ *CX /C* — Scroll output continuously.

▶ *CX .OU=ADMIN.O=ACME* — Change your current context to the ADMIN container of ACME.

▶ *CX /?* — View online help, including various CX options.

▶ *CX /VER* — View the version number of the CX utility and the list of files it executes.

Probably the most useful CX option is CX /R /A /T. I'm sure there's a hidden meaning somewhere in the rodent reference. Regardless, the CX /R /A /T option displays the relative location of all objects in the NDS tree.

Congratulations! This completes our lesson on Novell Directory Services.

So far, we've explored the basics of NetWare 5.1 and the intricacies of NDS. Now we're ready for *Prime Time*:

▶ NetWare 5.1 Connectivity (Chapter 3)

▶ NetWare 5.1 File System (Chapter 4)

▶ NetWare 5.1 Security (Chapter 5)

▶ NetWare 5.1 Workstation Management with ZENworks (Chapter 6)

▶ NetWare 5.1 Printing (Chapter 7)

Don't be scared — I'll be with you every step of the way. And we'll explore NDS many times throughout this study guide. This is only the beginning, and pretty soon you'll become a full-fledged superhero . . . .

Speaking of superheroes, remember ACME? It's time to SAVE THE WORLD again!!! Starting with NetWare 5.1 Connectivity.

See ya there!

Answer the following questions using the directory structure shown in Figure 2.18.

FIGURE 2.18

*Understanding NDS naming for Tokyo*

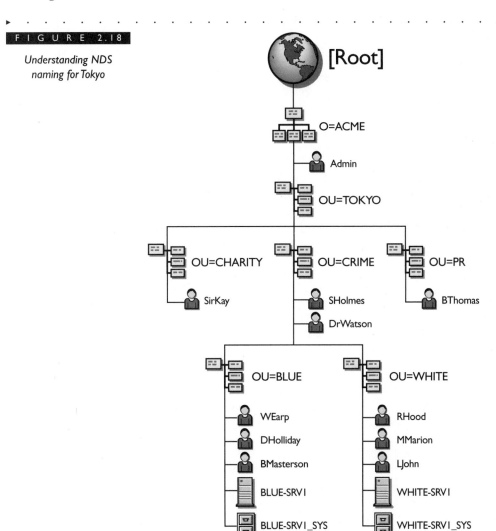

**1.** Indicate a typeless distinguished name for BMasterson.

**2.** Provide a typeful distinguished name for RHood.

**3.** List a typeless relative distinguished name for the CRIME Organizational Unit, assuming that your current context is the [Root].

**4.** Show a typeful relative distinguished name for the BLUE-SRV1 Server object from the default current context.

**5.** If your current context is .CRIME.TOKYO.ACME, what is the shortest name that accurately references the SHolmes User object?

**6.** Assume your current context is .TOKYO.ACME. Indicate a typeless relative distinguished name for the LJohn User object.

**7.** If your current context is .PR.TOKYO.ACME, what would be a typeful relative distinguished name for SirKay?

**8.** Assume your current context is .WHITE.CRIME.TOKYO.ACME. Provide a typeless relative distinguished name for Admin.

**9.** If your current context is .BLUE.CRIME.TOKYO.ACME, what would be a typeful relative distinguished name for BThomas?

**10.** Assume your current context is .WHITE.CRIME.TOKYO.ACME. What is the longest possible typeful relative distinguished name for the SYS: volume on the BLUE-SRV1 server?

**11.** If DHolliday attaches to the BLUE-SRV1 server by default, what is his current context after login? Give two LOGIN commands for DHolliday.

**12.** How would MMarion visit SirKay?

**13.** Provide ten LOGIN commands for SHolmes from .BLUE.CRIME.TOKYO.ACME:

**14.** What is the easiest way to move above ACME from the .PR.TOKYO.ACME context?

See Appendix C for answers.

## LAB EXERCISE 2.3: PLANT A TREE IN A CLOUD

Circle the 15 NDS-related terms hidden in this word search puzzle using the hints provided. No punctuation characters (such as blank spaces, hyphens, and so on) should be included. Numbers should always be spelled out.

```
O R G A N I Z A T I O N Q O E R X V I O
R B I N D E R Y R T N U O C U R R E N T
G L J C H V I K W V J N U G X X N X E W
A J Q E T D O I R E P G N I L I A R T S
N G W H C L I C P W B K O S G Y T Y W Q
I H X Y S T G U H J T Y Y O B S P M A L
Z X L I G Q I Y Q O D A L K Y E E H R N
A B Y D P I Z V G G V N T G F M B D E P
T X G N A T U R A L G R O U P G E W S R
I G R C C I W K O Q O N L X P Y U Y E E
O R G A N I Z A T I O N A L R O L E R L
N T Y P E L E S S N A M E G M Q I V V C
A R C J O J R V M M T H X T O C B V E C
L E A D I N G P E R I O D N E W L M R I
U G Z G B I C C M P Y O X U Z X V L D P
N U Q N J U E R D Y N L Q F Q P X M P L
I H Z R W J T M N Q N O F Y V G Q L G N
T K S C J D F D G X T R W E S B I J U Z
```

### Hints

1. Predecessor to NDS found in pre-NetWare 4 versions of the operating system.
2. Container object that uses predetermined two-character names.
3. The context that would be displayed if you issued the CX command with no options.

4. Command-line utility used to view or change your current context.
5. Identifies a name as a distinguished name.
6. A network process during which each user must provide a valid NDS name context in order to be authenticated.
7. An Organizational Unit is considered to be one of these because its members do not have to be added to a group membership list, but they can't be excluded either.
8. Represents a machine on the network running any version of the NetWare operating system.
9. Item that represents a resource in the NDS database.
10. Container object that can be used to represent a company, university, or association.
11. Object that represents a position or role with an organization.
12. Container object that represents a division, business unit, or project team within the Organization.
13. Changes current context to be used when resolving a relative distinguished name.
14. Name that contains object attribute abbreviations.
15. Name that does not contain object attribute abbreviations.

See Appendix C for answers.

## LAB EXERCISE 2.4: NOVELL DIRECTORY SERVICES

### Across

1. Holds object information
3. NDS database
4. Leaf object name
6. Terminal object
7. Tree-like structure
8. Property data
10. Object location in the Tree
12. The Cloud
13. NDS tree apex

## Down

2. Container ancestor
4. C, O, and OU
5. Multiple entry property
6. User ID
9. Corrupted object becomes one
11. Represents a person

See Appendix C for answers.

# NetWare 5.1 Connectivity

It is time to get connected!

So far, we have learned all about the NDS Cloud, and we have explored the myriad features of NetWare 5.1. Now you get a chance to start the adventure of a lifetime. In the remaining five chapters of this study guide, we will venture through the NetWare 5.1 file system, security, workstation management with ZENworks, and NDPS printing. However, the journey must start at the proverbial Point A. The challenge begins today — connecting to the network and building ACME's NDS tree.

In this chapter, we're going to learn about basic network components, install the Novell Client, and eventually log into the NDS tree. Then we'll discover login scripts, browse our new NDS tree, and eventually add some new users. Here's a sneak peek at what's ahead:

▸ *Connecting to the Network* — Before you can manage NetWare 5.1, you must gain access to the NDS tree. This is accomplished by configuring the NetWare 5.1 Novell Client and logging in using one of its built-in GUI or command-line tools. In addition, we'll learn how user context can help make tree browsing a snap for first-time administrators.

▸ *Configuring Login Scripts* — Next, we'll learn how login scripts can help you customize users' connections and establish important login settings. Think of these as batch files for the network.

▸ *Welcome In!* — Once you gain access to NDS, you can use a variety of Novell and third-party tools to *browse* the tree. Browsing not only acquaints you with the tree, it also aids in NDS navigation — which is required for network administration. However, we're not going to stop there. We'll learn how to create NDS users using a variety of tools and how to manage their access to advanced resources — using Alias, Directory Map, and Group objects.

So, that's how you connect to and browse the NetWare 5.1 NDS tree. Now let's begin with an in-depth lesson in *connectivity*.

# Connecting to the Network

The first rule of NetWare 5.1 administration is "know your network." You must understand the relationship between NDS objects (users, printers, and servers) and the general layout of the NDS tree. As you can see in Figure 3.1, ACME's NDS tree organizes network resources into a hierarchical directory tree.

FIGURE 3.1

*The ACME NDS tree*

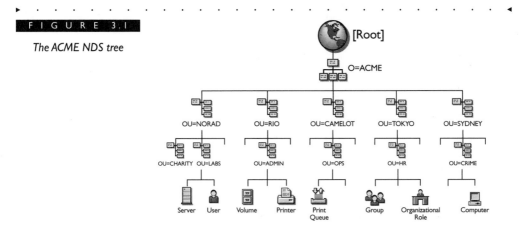

NDS enables these resources to be managed in a single view. This is significant because it dramatically increases administrative flexibility, enabling you to manage the tree and its objects by using various properties and security capabilities. Furthermore, the Directory is network centric; that is, it's distributed and replicated on multiple servers throughout the network. This increases resource availability and fault tolerance.

The NDS tree is only available to authenticated users. Remember, users don't log into NetWare servers any more — they log into the NDS tree. And, to gain access to the Cloud, users must utilize a special set of hardware and software. Now let's learn more about the fundamental components of your network, as well as how to access the NDS tree using a supercharged NetWare 5.1 client.

## Understanding Network Components

By definition, a *network* is a collection of computers that share three important features: the capability to communicate with each other, to share resources (such as hard disks and printers), and to access remote hosts or other networks. NetWare 5.1 administration requires an in-depth familiarity with a variety of network resources and services. A *network resource* is something that you use (such as a network printer or shared volume), whereas a *network service* is the system or method for providing a resource.

NetWare 5.1 is based on a client-server network model. As you can see in Figure 3.2, a client-server network is composed of three main hardware components, each with its own software and/or protocols:

▸ *Server* — The server establishes the communications procedures for network workstations and allocates shared resources. In addition, the server houses the all-important network operating system — in this case, NetWare 5.1.

▸ *Workstations* — Workstations (also known as *clients*) handle 95 percent of the network processing load. Each workstation represents a user's link to the network. Workstations must be as user friendly as they are smart. In a NetWare network, the workstations use the Novell Client for resource access and for connectivity to the server.

▸ *Communications* — The communications media delivers data to the network boards housed inside servers and workstations. This provides the network messages with a highway to travel upon. The communications pathway is made up of a variety of topology components (such as hubs and network interface cards) and cabling. Networks rely on communications media for connectivity, reliability, and speed.

In addition to these key hardware and software components, the network offers a variety of peripherals and remote connectivity. As you can see in Figure 3.2, we included a shared printer as a peripheral resource, as well as access to web pages via the NetWare Enterprise Web Server. NetWare 5.1 includes all these features and more.

FIGURE 3.2

*Understanding network components*

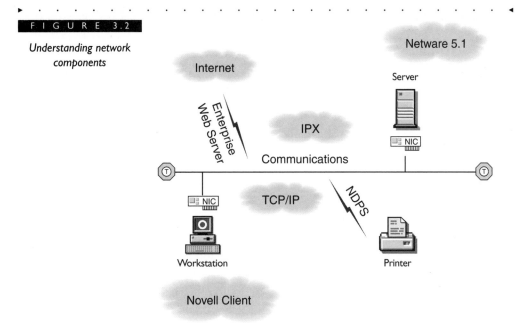

Now, let's take a closer look at each of these main components and learn how they combine to create network synergy. After all, the whole is greater than the sum of its parts when you're talking about NetWare 5.1.

### Server

A *server* is a central computer that runs a network operating system (such as NetWare 5.1). The server's main function is to regulate communication between itself, network workstations, and other shared resources (such as printers and modems). In addition, a server provides workstations and other clients with simultaneous multi-user access to shared resources and services. In a client-server network (such as NetWare 5.1), a server is typically only used as a server (rather than as a combination server/workstation).

In a Novell network, a server runs the NetWare operating system. NetWare 5.1 is a suite of software components designed to connect, manage, and maintain a network and its services. Some components run on the server and others operate on workstations. With NetWare 5.1, most administrative tasks are performed from a workstation, rather than from a server.

Typically, a NetWare 5.1 server runs on an Intel or Intel-compatible Pentium II (or higher) computer and consists of the following:

▸ *Kernel* — The kernel is the core of the NetWare 5.1 operating system. It is loaded into server RAM by executing a file called SERVER.EXE and provides central network functionality — such as processor scheduling, memory management, and input/output (I/O) control. The NetWare kernel performs a similar function to the kernel found in a workstation operating system (such as COMMAND.COM used by DOS).

▸ *Server console* — The server console displays a DOS-like console prompt that enables you to control and to manage the NetWare server. At the server console, you can perform tasks such as shutting down and restarting the server, executing console commands, loading and unloading NetWare Loadable Modules (NLMs), and running Java classes and applets. Other tasks include editing configuration files and other batch files, setting server configuration parameters, adding and removing name spaces on volumes, viewing network traffic, and sending messages.

▸ *NetWare Loadable Modules (NLMs)* — These are software programs that run on the server and provide added functionality. Most of them can be loaded and unloaded while the server is running. There are four main types of NLMs:

  • *Disk drivers (with .CDM and .HAM extensions)* — Control communication between NetWare 5.1 and internal storage devices.

  • *LAN drivers (with a .LAN extension)* — Control communication between NetWare 5.1 and server network interface cards (NICs).

  • *Name space modules (with a .NAM extension)* — Enable files with non-DOS naming conventions to be stored on NetWare 5.1 volumes.

  • *NLM utilities (with a .NLM extension)* — Management utilities or server application modules that enable you to run services that are not part of the kernel.

### Workstation

A *workstation* is a standalone computer (such as an IBM PC or Macintosh) that performs its own local processing and manages its own software and data files. A *network workstation* uses hardware and software that enables it to function as a network client — including a workstation operating system, a network board, communications media, client software (such as the Novell Client), and applications. A *client* is a device such as a personal computer, printer or another server that requests services or resources from a server. As a network client, a workstation can take advantage of the network's distributed resources, centralized management, and enhanced security.

NetWare 5.1 supports the following types of workstations:

- *DOS* — NetWare 5.1 supports Novell DOS 7, MS-DOS (5.*x* or 6.*x*), and PC DOS (5.*x*, 6.*x*, or 7.0) operating systems.

- *Windows* — NetWare 5.1 supports Windows 2000, Windows NT, Windows 95/98, and Windows 3.*x* workstations.

- *Linux* — The Linux client is integrated into many popular Linux distributions (including Caldera OpenLinux and Red Hat Linux). It provides NetWare file, print, and routing services to Linux workstations using native NetWare Internetwork Packet Exchange (IPX) services.

- *Macintosh* — NetWare Client for MacOS is available on the ProSoft Engineering Web site at `www.prosfoteng.com/NetWare.htm`. It provides NetWare file, print, and routing services to Macintosh workstations using native NetWare IPX services.

- *UNIX* — UNIX support is provided by NetWare NFS, which must be purchased separately. NetWare NFS provides support for native UNIX NFS (Network File System) filing and native UNIX Transmission-Control Protocol/Internet Protocol (TCP/IP) communications. You can use NFS services with Linux and Solaris, as well.

Although NetWare 5.1 supports the various types of workstations previously listed, the network can only be administered from DOS and Windows workstations.

Figure 3.3 illustrates the NetWare 5.1 Novell Client architecture. This figure shows how the various workstation hardware and software components interact with each other, and how the flow of data occurs through the workstation. You'll notice that hardware components (such as network boards and cabling) occupy the lower layers, while the software components (such as the Novell Client and workstation operating system) exist at the top of the model.

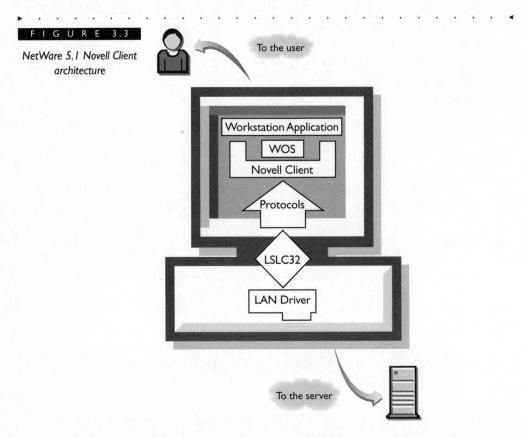

FIGURE 3.3

NetWare 5.1 Novell Client architecture

In Figure 3.3, the workstation hardware enables data to enter and exit the client at the bottom of the model. In general, the workstation hardware is responsible for physically connecting the workstation to the network (via a network interface card and cabling) and for helping to ensure that data sent to and from the workstation is not lost or corrupted.

The workstation network interface card (which is also known as a NIC, network adapter, or network board) facilitates communication between the local workstation operating system (WOS) and the NetWare 5.1 server. The NIC is managed by a series of workstation connectivity files including a LAN driver and

LSLC32.NLM (a Link Support Layer driver that acts as a switchboard to route network protocol packets between the LAN driver and appropriate communications protocols). Protocols determine (through a set of rules) the language used to move data across the network.

The workstation hardware is *not* responsible for the content of the data, how the data is used on the workstation, or guaranteeing network privileges to access any program or resource on the network. All of these are the responsibility of the workstation software.

The remainder of Figure 3.3 is dominated by workstation software. The software has four primary responsibilities:

▶ Create the content sent to and from the network

▶ Format network data so that network devices can understand it

▶ Help ensure that only authorized users access the network

▶ Control the flow of data within the workstation to applications and users

Following is a brief description of the three main software components presented in Figure 3.3:

▶ *Workstation applications* — These applications (such as word processing, spreadsheet, and e-mail programs) produce data that can be sent to and from the workstation. Workstation applications don't communicate directly with the network. Instead, they rely on the workstation hardware, Novell Client, and workstation operating system for access to network programs and services.

▶ *Workstation operating system (WOS)* — This provides a central interface for user access and local and network applications. A workstation operating system offers the following local services: file storage on local or network disks, access to data on the workstation or network, document printing on local or network printers, and data format processing of network data traveling to and from the workstation.

> ▸ *Novell Client* — The Novell Client software makes it possible for the work-station to access the network and to communicate with peripheral devices. The Novell Client handles three primary responsibilities: providing access to NetWare services, enforcing network security, and managing local communications.

### Communications

Communication is the ultimate goal of networking. The communications pathway shown earlier in Figure 3.2 is the road on which all network messages travel. Servers and workstations communicate with each other using the following three technologies:

> ▸ *Topology* — The physical arrangement of network servers, workstations, and peripherals (such as the Ethernet 10Base-T star configuration). Topology components are distributed devices that establish the network protocol and facilitate the movement of messages over cabling throughout the topology.

> ▸ *Protocol* — The set of rules that control the topology (such as TCP/IP and/or IPX).

> ▸ *Communications media* — The physical bound or unbound pathway upon which electronic signals travel (such as twisted pair, fiber optic, coaxial, and wireless).

As a NetWare 5.1 network administrator, it's important that you understand the functional responsibilities of these networking components, as well as understand how these networking components work together to ensure reliable data flow from workstations over communications media to the NetWare 5.1 server.

Now, let's explore Novell Client installation and learn how to build a powerful NetWare-compatible workstation.

## Installing the Novell Client

Both the Novell Client for Windows 95/98 and the Novell Client for Windows NT/2000 were designed to be closely integrated with their respective workstation operating systems. For this reason, you must be intimately familiar with both the Novell Client and the Windows 95/98 and Windows NT/2000 interfaces. Egad!

To perform a local installation of the Novell Client for Windows 95/98 or the Novell Client for Windows NT/2000, you'll need to run the WINSETUP.EXE file from the root directory of the *NetWare 5.1 Novell Client Software* CD-ROM. WIN-SETUP.EXE automatically activates the correct workstation setup file from a platform-specific directory when you insert the CD-ROM (it uses the AutoRun feature of Windows 95/98 and Windows NT/2000).

During the installation process, you'll need to determine whether to do a Typical or Custom installation. If you select the Typical option, the Novell Client is automatically installed and configured using detected (or default) protocols. This option is recommended for most computers.

If you select the Custom option, you will need to establish specific protocol and login configurations. In addition, you will be given the opportunity to select optional workstation installation components — such as the Novell Workstation Manager and Novell Distributed Print Services (NDPS). The Custom option is typically recommended for system administrators and advanced users only.

During a Custom Novell Client installation, you'll need to make the following configuration choices, in order:

- ▸ Protocol preference

- ▸ Login authentication

- ▸ Custom installation components

Let's take a closer look. And feel free to follow along in the "Lab Exercise 3.1: Connecting to the Network with Windows 95/98" section.

### Protocol Preference

Communication protocols are the common language of the network. The Novell Client for Windows 95/98 and the Novell Client for Windows NT/2000 support both TCP/IP and IPX protocols. TCP/IP is the protocol of the Internet, whereas IPX supports previous versions of NetWare. For the most part, IPX support is provided solely by the Novell Client, while Windows itself helps establish TCP/IP communications.

As a network administrator, you must decide which protocol to use on each workstation. Many organizations enable both the TCP/IP and IPX protocols on workstations to ensure network compatibility. This allows each workstation to connect to previous versions of NetWare, the Internet, and/or NetWare 5.1 networks utilizing IP-Only.

As you can see in Figure 3.4, the following four options are available in the Protocol Preference configuration screen: IP only, IP with IPX Compatibility, IP and IPX, and IPX.

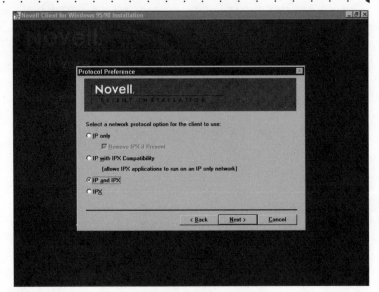

FIGURE 3.4

*Selecting protocol(s) during a Custom Novell Client installation*

### Login Authentication

Authentication is the process of identifying an individual when he or she requests access to the network. This is accomplished when a user enters their username and password in the NetWare 5.1 GUI Login screen.

The Login Authenticator configuration screen shown in Figure 3.5 provides two authentication options: NDS (NetWare 4.x or later) and Bindery (NetWare 3.x).

### Custom Installation Components

Near the end of the Custom Novell Client installation procedure, the Optional Components screen provides a myriad of optional client components. The specific components available depend on which NetWare 5.1 client is being installed. For example, Figure 3.6 illustrates the optional components that are supported by the Novell Client for Windows 95/98.

FIGURE 3.5

*Specifying an NDS connection during a Custom Novell Client installation*

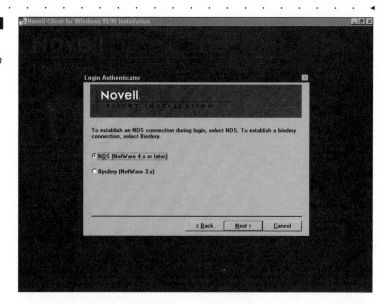

FIGURE 3.6

*Selecting optional components during a Custom Novell Client installation*

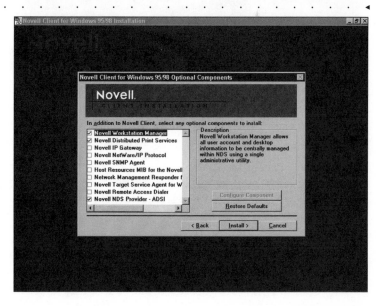

Once you've installed the Novell Client, there's only one task left — logging in. Let's get connected!

## Logging In

As a network administrator, you've already accomplished the hard part — automating the workstation connection. Now it's the user's turn. The good news is that both the Novell Client for Windows 95/98 and the Novell Client for Windows NT/2000 provide a friendly GUI login utility for users. As you can see in Figure 3.7, the Novell Login window provides simple Username and Password input boxes within the native MS Windows environment. The good news is that NetWare 5.1 supports a single login for access to all authorized network resources. In other words, once the user logs in, he or she is granted automatic access to all authorized resources in the NDS tree.

▶ · · · · · · · · · · · · · · · · · · · · · · · · · · · · · · · · · · · ◀

| FIGURE 3.7 |  |
|---|---|
| *Novell Login window* | |

To log into a NetWare 5.1 tree, the user must have a workstation with the current Novell Client software installed. The user must also have a "live" connection to the network, including a functioning NIC and a correctly configured protocol stack. Finally, the user must have a valid username and password. The username (also known as a *login ID*) is the same as the user's User object name. NDS also requires a valid NDS context so that it can differentiate between users with similar names.

So how do you get access to the NetWare 5.1 GUI Novell Login window on a Windows 95/98 or Windows NT/2000 workstation? Good question. NetWare 5.1 offers numerous choices:

▶ On a Windows 95/98 workstation, the Novell Login window appears when the workstation boots up. On a Windows NT/2000 workstation, you'll need to press Ctrl+Alt+Delete simultaneously to activate login.

▸ You can click Start ➪ Programs ➪ Novell ➪ NetWare Login. Typically, the NetWare 5.1 login utility is placed in the Novell folder.

▸ You can right-click the *N* icon in the Windows System tray and select NetWare Login.

▸ You can run the LOGINW95.EXE or LOGINW32.EXE file from the C:\NOVELL\CLIENT32 subdirectory on a Windows 95/98 workstation.

▸ You can run the LOGINWNT.EXE file from the C:\WINNT\SYSTEM32 subdirectory on a Windows NT/2000 workstation.

▸ At the DOS prompt, you can type the following (where *<distinguished name>* is the full distinguished name of the User object, preceded by a period):

```
F:\LOGIN> LOGIN <distinguished name>
```

Here are a few important things to remember about the NetWare login process: login is mandatory, login is primarily a security issue, and NDS provides a single point of login to all authorized network services in an NDS tree (that is, once a user is authenticated, he or she should not have to enter a login name or password again).

Here are other things to remember:

▸ A user's login ID is the same as his or her User object name.

▸ Passwords are initially established by network administrators and may (or may not) be modified by users (depending on how User object properties have been configured).

▸ Passwords should be unique.

▸ Passwords may need to be changed periodically for security reasons.

As you can see in Figure 3.7, the Novell Login window contains an Advanced button for login script and NDS configuration. This allows you to configure three different types of login information:

▶ *NDS* — The NDS tab shown in Figure 3.8 (which is displayed by default when you click on the Advanced button on the Novell Login window) enables you to configure critical Directory information during login. This includes the tree name, server, and most importantly, user context. The Context field defines where the user's User object lives in the NDS tree and, thus, changes the workstation's current context to match it during login. If this field is configured correctly, the user can simply type his or her User object name in the Username field above. Another nice feature of this tab is that it enables you to specify whether or not any connections the user currently has to the network should be cleared upon login. (In most cases, you'll want to mark this check box.)

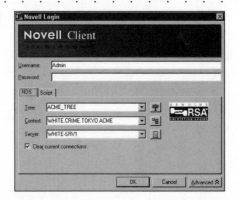

*NDS tab on expanded Novell Login window*

▶ *Script* — The Script tab shown in Figure 3.9 enables you to establish specific login script settings. With this tab, you can suspend the running of login scripts, run alternate login scripts, and/or define specific login script identifier variables. (Login scripts are described in the "Configuring Login Scripts" section later in this chapter.) You can also indicate whether to display a Results window upon login and, if so, whether to close it automatically or to require user intervention. There are some important rules to be aware of with respect to the Script page. If a Container or User login script is specified in the Login Script field, only that login script will be executed at login. If a Profile object is specified in the Profile Script field, that script will run in addition to the other login scripts with which the user is associated. You can avoid running login scripts altogether by unmarking the Run Scripts check box.

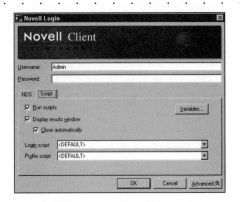

FIGURE 3.9

*Script tab on expanded Novell Login window*

▶ *Variables* — The Variables window appears when you click the Variables button on the Script page. This window enables you to define four login script variables: %2, %3, %4, and/or %5. For example, the following command will MAP ROOT the H: drive to the path defined as %2 in the Variables window:

```
MAP ROOT H:=WHITE-SRV1_SALES:%2
```

Congratulations . . . you're in! Now that you've learned the basics of network hardware and software and gained access to the NetWare 5.1 NDS tree, it's time to browse network resources. In order to automate resource connectivity, you should spend some time customizing login script settings. Login scripts are batch files for the network that provide a variety of user configurations — including drive mappings, printer redirection, and environmental variables.

Let's learn more about how network administrators can use these scripts to achieve greater network synergy.

## LAB EXERCISE 3.1: CONNECTING TO THE NETWORK WITH WINDOWS 95/98

In this book, we will explore many of the NetWare 5.1 tools you need to master NetWare 5.1 administration — including the Novell Client, NetWare Administrator, ConsoleOne, the NetWare 5.1 file system, NDS security, ZENworks, and NDPS. Periodically along the way, you'll want to practice the various technologies discussed by performing lab exercises.

Let's start with Novell Client installation, Windows 95/98 connectivity, and logging in.

**Warning: All exercises in this book should be performed in an isolated, nonproduction environment!**

TIP

To perform this exercise, you will need the following:

▶ A NetWare 5.1 server called WHITE-SRV1.WHITE.CRIME.TOKYO.ACME (which can be installed using the directions found in Appendix D)

▶ A Windows 95/98 workstation that meets the minimum requirements for running the NetWare 5.1 Novell Client for Windows 95/98

▶ A *NetWare 5.1 Novell Client Software* CD-ROM

**Although this exercise is designed for Windows 95/98 workstations, you'll find that the steps are similar for Windows NT/2000 workstations.**

TIP

In the next section, we'll explore the detailed steps for performing a Custom installation of the Novell Client for Windows 95/98.

### Part I: NetWare 5.1 Novell Client for Windows 95/98 Installation

Complete the following steps to perform a local installation of the NetWare 5.1 Novell Client for Windows 95/98 on a workstation:

**1.** Exit any applications that you are running.

**2.** Install the NetWare 5.1 Novell Client for Windows 95/98 on your workstation:

**a.** Insert the *NetWare 5.1 Novell Client Software* CD-ROM in your workstation's CD-ROM drive.

**b.** When the WinSetup — Novell Clients window appears, click Windows 95/98 Client.

**c.** When the Novell Client for Windows 95/98 License Agreement window appears, do the following:

- Read the agreement.

- Click Yes to accept its terms and conditions.

**d.** When the Welcome to Novell Client for Windows 95/98 Install window appears follow these steps:

- Click Custom to indicate that you'd like to perform a Custom installation.

- Click Next.

**e.** Follow these steps when the Protocol Preference window appears:

- Ensure the "IP and IPX" radio button is marked to indicate that you'd like the Novell Client to use the IP and IPX protocols.

- Click Next.

**f.** Follow these steps when the Login Authenticator window appears:

- Verify that the "NDS (NetWare 4.x or Later)" radio button is selected.

- Click Next.

**g.** When the Novell Client for Windows 95/98 Optional Components window appears, do as follows:

- Make sure that the following check boxes are marked:

  ```
  Novell Workstation Manager
  ```

```
Novell Distributed Print Services

Novell NDS Provider—ADSI
```

- Click Install.

**h.** Wait while the NetWare 5.1 Novell Client for Windows 95/98 software is installed.

**i.** When the Novell Client for Windows 95/98 Installation window appears, click Reboot to reboot the computer.

**j.** When the Novell Login dialog box appears, log into your tree as the Admin user as follows:

- Make sure the following is listed in the Username field:

  ```
  admin
  ```

- Type the following in the Password field:

  ```
  ACME
  ```

  (You'll notice that asterisks, rather than the actual password, are displayed for security reasons.)

- Click OK.

**Part II: Novell Client Connectivity for Windows 95/98**

Now, let's walk through some important Client 32 workstation connectivity steps — namely connection and login. In this section, we will use an alternate method for logging into the network. Follow carefully and try this at home — if you dare!

**1.** Follow these steps on a Windows 95/98 workstation:

**a.** Right-click the red *N* icon in the System Tray. (The System Tray is located, by default, on the right end of the Windows taskbar.)

**b.** Select NetWare Login from the pop-up menu that appears.

**2.** When the initial Novell Login window appears, do the following:

  **a.** Verify that the following username is listed in the Username field:

  `admin`

  **b.** Type the following in the Password field:

  `ACME`

  **c.** Click Advanced.

**3.** When the expanded Novell Login window appears, the NDS tab should be selected, by default.

  **a.** Ensure the following is listed in the Tree field:

  `ACME_TREE`

  **b.** Ensure the following is listed in the Context field:

  `WHITE.CRIME.TOKYO.ACME`

  **c.** Ensure following is listed in the Server field:

  `WHITE-SRV1`

  **d.** Ensure the Clear Current Connections check box is marked. This will clear any current connections to the network if you are already logged in.

**4.** Click the Script tab.

  **a.** This tab allows you to control the processing of login scripts. It enables you to override existing User and Profile login scripts assigned to this user, as well as to bypass all login scripts. For example, if you want to override your existing User login script (if any), you could indicate the alternate login script name in the Login Script field. If you wanted to override your existing Profile login script (if any), you could indicate the alternate login script name in the Profile Script field.

**b.** You'll notice three check boxes on this page: Run Scripts, Display Results Window, and Close Automatically.

- Ensure that the Run Scripts check box is marked. This will cause any login scripts that have been set up for you to be executed during the login process, including any listed on this dialog box.

- Ensure that the Display Results Window check box is marked. This will cause a Results dialog box to be displayed upon login.

- Close Automatically check box is unmarked. This will force you to click the Close button to close the Results window upon login. (**Note:** It is often helpful to have this check box unmarked when debugging login scripts.)

**5.** Click Variables:

**a.** A Variables dialog box will appear. (If you wanted to pass on any variables to the login script processor, you would indicate them here.)

**b.** Click Cancel. (**Note:** Make absolutely sure you click Cancel on the Variables window, rather than on the Script page. Otherwise, you may run into a variety of problems.)

**6.** Click OK to initiate the login process.

**7.** A Results window should appear onscreen:

**a.** You will notice that the Results window lists information such as your current context, your User object's context, your current tree, the server to which you are currently attached, and any drives that are mapped.

**b.** Review the contents of the window and then click Close.

Congratulations! You have successfully logged into the network.

# Configuring Login Scripts

Once your users have been authenticated with a valid username and password, NetWare 5.1 greets the user with one or more login scripts. A *login script* is a set of instructions used by NetWare to establish environmental configurations during login. These instructions establish user-specific drive mappings, search mappings, printer connections, and messages each time a user logs into the network. Login scripts can also be used to execute applications and/or menus during login. In summary, they provide a simple configuration tool for automated user customization upon login.

Login scripts are one of your most important configuration responsibilities. From one central location, they enable you to customize all users or specific groups of users. Many of the configurations we've talked about are session specific and disappear when users log out. Login scripts give you the ability to reestablish these settings every time your users log in. This is amazing stuff.

NDS supports four types of login scripts, which are executed in systematic progression. As you can see in Figure 3.10, there's a flowchart logic to how login scripts are executed. Here's a quick look:

- ▶ *Container login script* — A Container login script is a property of an Organization or Organizational Unit container. It enables you to customize settings for all users within the container.

- ▶ *Profile login script* — A Profile login script is a property of a Profile object. It is used to customize environmental parameters for a group of users. This way, users who are not in the same container in the NDS tree can share a common login script.

- ▶ *User login script* — A User login script is a property of a User object. It is executed after the Container and Profile script and provides customization at the user level.

- ▶ *Default login script* — The Default login script is executed for any user who does not have an individual User script. This script contains only essential commands, such as a drive mapping to the SYS:PUBLIC directory.

▶ · · · · · · · · · · · · · · · · · · · · · · · · · · · ◀

FIGURE 3.10

*The flow of NetWare 5.1
login script execution*

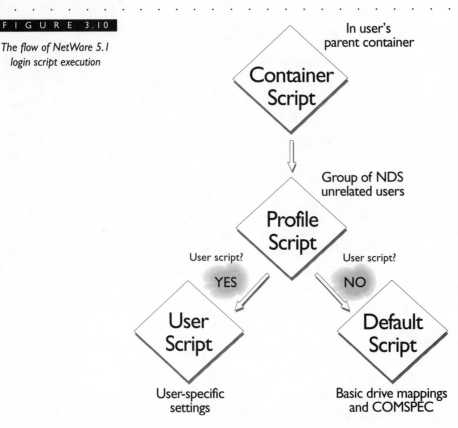

Login scripts consist of commands and identifier variables, just like any other program or batch file. In addition, login script syntax must follow specific rules and conventions. Let's start our discussion with a more detailed look at the four login script types and then explore the commands that make them productive.

### Login Script Types

We just saw that there are four types of login scripts available — Container, Profile, User, and Default. All four work in concert to provide network customization for containers, groups, and users. As you'll quickly learn, login scripts are an integral part of your daily grind. Let's start with a description of the four different login script types.

### Container Login Script

A Container login script is a property of an Organization or Organizational Unit container. It is used to set general environments and/or provide login actions for all users in an Organization or Organizational Unit.

In NetWare 3.*x*, there was a single System login script, per server, that was executed for all users on that server. In NetWare 5.1, however, it is possible for every container to have its own login script. As you could see earlier in Figure 3.10, the Container login script is the first login script executed — Profile and User scripts follow.

There is one important difference between a Container login script and the System login script found in early versions of NetWare. A Container script is only executed for users within a given container. As you can see in Figure 3.11, the Admin user executes the ACME Container login script. SHolmes, on the other hand, doesn't execute any Container login script because the CRIME Organizational Unit doesn't have a login script. Similarly, RHood executes the WHITE Container login script, whereas AEinstein executes none.

▶ · · · · · · · · · · · · · · · · · · · · · · · · · · · · · · · · · · · · ◀

**F I G U R E   3.11**

*Understanding NetWare
5.1 login script types*

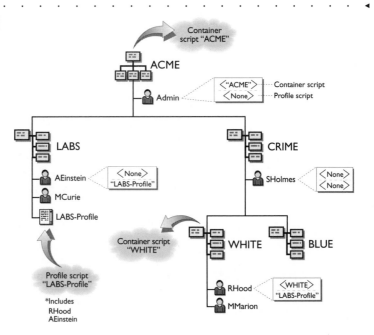

This is an important point because many network administrators assume that Container login scripts can be inherited by lower containers. This is not the case. Only the Container login script of the User object's home container is executed at login. If it does not have a Container login script, no Container login script is executed. If you wish to have one login script that is shared by all users, you have three options: (1) you can create a Profile login script and have all users execute it; (2) you can use the copy-and-paste feature within NetWare Administrator to copy one script to all containers; or (3) you can use an INCLUDE statement in each Container login script, which executes a text file containing these commands. Regardless, the moral of the story is that NDS does not provide a single login script for all users.

As you plan login scripts for your network, keep in mind that at some point you'll need to maintain them. Use Container login scripts to provide access to network resources, Profile scripts for a specific group's needs, and User login scripts only in special circumstances. Following are the types of things you might do within a Container login script:

- Send messages to all users within a given container

- Establish a search drive mapping to the SYS:PUBLIC directory

- Create other search drive mappings for application directories

- Establish a network drive mapping (such as U:) to each user's home directory

- Use IF . . . THEN (conditional) statements for access to specific resources based on times, group memberships, and other variables

- Activate menus or applications used by all the members of a given container

**Drive mappings are logical pointers to local and network file system directories. We'll learn all about them in Chapter 4, "NetWare 5.1 File System."**

TIP

CHAPTER 3

NETWARE 5.1 CONNECTIVITY

### Profile Login Script

A Profile login script is a property of a Profile object. This script customizes environmental parameters and login actions for a group of users, regardless of where they are defined in the NDS tree. This way, users who are not directly related in the NDS tree can share a common login script.

Each User object can be assigned to only one Profile login script. For example, earlier in this chapter Figure 3.11 shows how the AEinstein and RHood objects share the LABS-Profile login script, even though they live in different parts of the tree. Also, note that a Profile login script executes after the Container script, but before a User login script or the Default login script. In Mr. Einstein's case, the Profile login script is the only script that executes.

Figure 3.12 shows an example of how a Profile login script is created in NetWare Administrator. Once the script has been defined, two more tasks remain: (1) ensure that each user has the Browse right to the Profile object and the Read property right to the Profile object's Login Script property (assuming the user and Profile are defined in different containers); and (2) ensure the complete name of the Profile object is defined in each user's Profile property.

FIGURE 3.12

*Creating the LABS-Profile login script in NetWare Administrator*

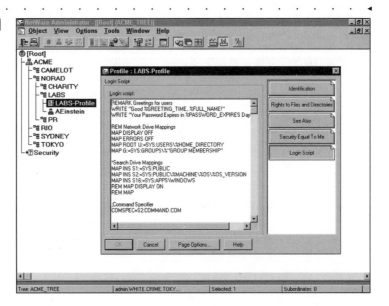

105

**TIP**

**To execute a Profile login script, a User object must be made a Trustee of the Profile object and assigned Read property rights to the Profile object's Login Script property. Please see Chapter 5, "NetWare 5.1 Security," for more information on NDS trustee rights.**

### User Login Script

A User login script is executed after Container and Profile login scripts and provides customization all the way down to the user level. Although User login scripts are a nice feature, they can quickly become a maintenance nightmare. Just imagine hundreds and hundreds of User login scripts constantly needing to be updated and maintained. A better strategy is to use Container and Profile login scripts as much as possible, while attempting to eliminate User login scripts altogether.

The primary purpose of a User login script is user-specific customization. This level of customization can be accomplished in Container and Profile login scripts by using IF . . . THEN login script commands. If it's absolutely necessary for you to create a user-specific login script, it's nice to know that it's there. Typically, however, a User login script is not used.

User login scripts should only be created in special circumstances. Remember, you have to maintain any login scripts you create. A User login script is defined within the Login Script property of a User object. Following are some instances when a User login script might be justified:

▸ Establish network drive mappings to specific user directories, provided that these directories do not correspond with drive mappings included in the Container login script. This enables a user to move more efficiently to network directories located on different servers in the NDS tree.

▸ Connect to commonly used printers, in addition to the ones selected in Container and Profile login scripts.

▸ Activate special user-specific menus and/or applications that a user requires each time he or she logs in.

### Default Login Script

A Default login script is executed for any user (including Admin) who does not have an individual User login script. (It has an either/or relationship with User login scripts.) After you create a User login script, the default script is blocked for the corresponding User object. This poses an interesting dilemma. Earlier, we said it's a good idea not to have a User login script—which means the Default script will automatically execute. This is a problem because the Default login script could override already established drive mappings.

Fortunately, Novell has recognized this problem and provides you with the means to prevent the Default login script from executing—simply insert the following command in a Container or Profile login script:

```
NO_DEFAULT
```

 **TIP** **The Default login script cannot be edited because it is embedded in the LOGIN.EXE file in SYS:LOGIN and SYS:PUBLIC. It can, however, be disabled by including the NO_DEFAULT command in a Container or Profile login script.**

This completes our discussion of the different login script types. In leaving this discussion, consider the factors that determine how you use login scripts and which types you'll need. These factors include the needs of users, their knowledge level, the size of your network, the complexity of your network, ease of administration, the types of groups, and access requirements for different containers.

Remember, login script design can go a long way toward increasing your quality of life and decreasing your daily workload.

## Login Script Commands

Login script commands help customize each user's environment. Login scripts consist of commands and identifier variables just like any other program or batch file. Login script syntax must follow specific rules and conventions. The syntax for login script programming is quite simple, but you must be sure to organize identifier variables and commands using appropriate grammar. For example, consider the following line:

```
MAP U:=SYS:USERS\%LOGIN_NAME
```

This statement uses proper login script syntax. It starts with the MAP login script command and uses appropriate identifier variable grammar — %LOGIN_NAME. The cool thing about this line is that it changes for each user. For example, when Dr. Watson logs in, the system creates a U: drive for him, and it points to SYS:USERS\DRWATSON. On the other hand, when SHolmes logs in, his U: drive points to SYS:USERS\SHOLMES. Cool!

Another good example of login script syntax is the WRITE command. Consider the following statement:

```
WRITE "Good %GREETING_TIME, %LOGIN_NAME!"
```

Depending on the time of day and user who logs in, this single statement will provide a custom message. For example, Leia gets the following message when she turns on her machine in the morning:

```
"Good Morning, Leia!"
```

This can go a long way in making users feel warm and fuzzy about the network. As a matter of fact, some users get the perception that NetWare 5.1 actually cares about them and is personally wishing them a nice day. Regardless of the network's motivation, the point is that users feel good about using the network!

### Identifier Variables

Identifier variables enable you to enter a variable (such as LAST_NAME) rather than a specific name (Watson). When the login script executes, it substitutes real values for the identifier variables. This means that you can make your login scripts more efficient and more flexible. In addition, it makes the concept of a single Container login script more feasible.

As we saw in earlier examples, identifier variables are preceded by a percent sign (%) and written in all uppercase. This is the ideal syntax for identifier variables because it allows you to use them anywhere in the script, including inside quotation marks (" "). Table 3.1 lists some of the most interesting identifier variables available in NetWare 5.1. Learn them. These cute little guys can go a long way in customizing Container and Profile login scripts.

TABLE 3.1

*Login Script Identifier
Variables for NetWare 5.1*

| CATEGORY | IDENTIFIER VARIABLE | DESCRIPTION |
|---|---|---|
| Date | DAY | Day number 01 through 31. |
| | DAY_OF_WEEK | Day of week (Monday, Tuesday, and so on). |
| | MONTH | Month number (01 through 12). |
| | MONTH_NAME | Month name (January, February, and so on). |
| | NDAY_OF_WEEK | Weekday number (1 through 7, where 1 equals Sunday). |
| | SHORT_YEAR | Last two digits of year. |
| | YEAR | All four digits of year. |
| Time | AM_PM | a.m. or p.m. |
| | GREETING_TIME | Time of day (morning, afternoon, or evening). |
| | HOUR | Hour of day on a 12-hour scale. |
| | HOUR24 | Hour of day on a 24-hour scale. |
| | MINUTE | Minutes (00 through 59). |
| | SECOND | Seconds (00 through 59). |
| User | CN | User's full login name as it exists in NDS. |
| | LOGIN_ALIAS_CONTEXT | Y if REQUESTER_CONTEXT is an Alias. |
| | FULL_NAME | User's unique full name as it appears in both NDS and the bindery. |
| | LAST_NAME | User's surname in NDS or full login name in bindery-based NetWare. |
| | HOME_DIRECTORY | Determines home directory location for User object. Can be used to provide automated drive mapping to user's home directory. |
| | LOGIN_CONTEXT | Context where user exists. |
| | LOGIN_NAME | User's unique login name, truncated to eight characters. |

*Continued*

TABLE 3.1

Login Script Identifier
Variables for NetWare 5.1
(continued)

| CATEGORY | IDENTIFIER VARIABLE | DESCRIPTION |
|---|---|---|
| User | MEMBER OF "GROUP" | Group that object user is assigned to. |
| | NOT MEMBER OF "GROUP" | Group that object user is not assigned to. |
| | PASSWORD_EXPIRES | Number of days before password expires. |
| | REQUESTER_CONTEXT | Context when login started. |
| | USER_ID | Unique hexadecimal ID assigned to each user. |
| Workstation | MACHINE | Type of computer (either IBM_PC or other name specified during configuration). |
| | NETWARE_REQUESTER | Version of Requester being used (NetWare Requester for OS/2 or VLM users). |
| | OS | Type of operating system on workstation (MSDOS, OS/2, and so on). |
| | OS_VERSION | Operating system version loaded on workstation. |
| | P_STATION | Workstation's 12-digit hexadecimal node ID. |
| | SHELL_TYPE | Version of workstation's DOS shell for NetWare 2 or NetWare 3 user, and NetWare 4 Requester for DOS. |
| | S_MACHINE | Short machine name (IBM, and so on). |
| | STATION | Workstation's connection number. |
| Miscellaneous | FILE_SERVER | NetWare 5.1 server name that workstation first attaches to. |
| | NETWORK_ADDRESS | IPX external network number for cabling system (8-digit hexadecimal number). |
| | ACCESS_SERVER | Shows whether access server is functional (true or false). |
| | ERROR_LEVEL | An error number (0 equals no errors). |
| | %n | Replaced by parameters entered after LOGIN command (starting with %0). See NetWare 5.1 documentation for more details. |

In addition to these identifier variables, you can use any NDS property name within a NetWare 5.1 login script. Just be sure to use the same syntax — that is, uppercase and preceded by a percent sign (%). In addition, the property name must be written inside its own set of quotation marks, if it contains a space.

The identifier variables shown in Table 3.1 must be used with valid login script commands. As you can see in Figure 3.13, NetWare 5.1 includes a plethora of commands that can be used in various configurations. In the remainder of this section, we'll present the commands as part of a sample NetWare 5.1 Container login script (see Figure 3.13). In each case, refer to Figure 3.13 for appropriate syntax. Also, use the reference letter ("A," for example) as a pointer to the correct section in the sample script.

**FIGURE 3.13**

*A typical NetWare 5.1 login script*

```
A   REMARK Greetings for users
    WRITE "Good %GREETING_TIME, %FULL_NAME!"
    WRITE "Your Password Expires in %PASSWORD_EXPIRES Days"

B   REM Network Drive Mappings
    MAP DISPLAY OFF
    MAP ERRORS OFF
    "MAP ROOT U:=%HOME_DIRECTORY"
    "MAP G:=SYS:GROUPS\%"GROUP MEMBERSHIP"

C   *Search Drive Mappings
    MAP INS S1:=SYS: PUBLIC
    MAP INS S2:=SYS: PUBLIC \%MACHINE\%OS\%OS_VERSION
    MAP INS S16:=SYS:APPS\WINDOWS
    MAP DISPLAY ON
    MAP

D   ; Command Specifier
    COMSPEC= S2:COMMAND.COM

E   SET PROMPT= "$P$G"
    SET TEMP= "U:\USERS\%LOGIN_NAME\TEMP"

F   IF DAY_OF_WEEK= "Friday" THEN BEGIN
        MAP R:=.REPORTS.LABS.NORAD.ACME
        DISPLAY R:FRIDAY.TXT
        PAUSE
    END

G   IF MEMBER OF "OPS-Group" THEN #CAPTURE P=HP4S1-P1 NT TI=10
    IF MEMBER OF "ADMIN-Group" THEN #CAPTURE P=HP5-P1 NFF NT
    IF MEMBER OF "LABS-Group" THEN #CAPTURE P=CANONBJ-P1 NB

H   NO_DEFAULT

I   PCCOMPATIBLE
    DRIVE U:
    EXIT "Start"
```

### A: WRITE and REMARK

Login scripts should always start with documentation. This is accomplished using the REMARK command. Any line beginning with REMARK is ignored by NDS when the LOGIN utility executes the login script. It does, however, provide a useful tool for documenting the different sections of your Container, Profile, and User login scripts.

Besides the word REMARK, NetWare 5.1 supports three other variations — REM, an asterisk (*), and a semicolon (;). As you can see in Figure 3.13, all possibilities have been used. Another use of documentation is edit tracking. When multiple supervisors are maintaining the same container login script, it's a good idea to document who does what, when. For example, another network administrator looking at the script might not know what an INCLUDE subroutine will accomplish without logging in to execute it. A REM could be used to indicate the purpose of the included file. Finally, a REMARK can also be used to troubleshoot problems in a login script. Placing REM at the beginning of the line causing the problems will allow you to make sure that the rest of the script executes properly.

One of the most popular login script commands is WRITE. With it, you can display a variety of friendly messages during login script execution. WRITE displays the information presented inside quotation marks. In a WRITE statement, variables must be displayed in all uppercase letters and preceded by a percent sign (%). One of the friendliest was shown earlier in Figure 3.13. Here are other identifier variables you can use with the WRITE command:

```
Your password expires in %PASSWORD_EXPIRES days.

Today is %MONTH_NAME %DAY.

At the tone, the time is %HOUR:%MINUTE %AM_PM.

You're connected as workstation %STATION.

You're attached to %FILE_SERVER.
```

Don't underestimate the power of communication. Goodwill flourishes with a quick note to your users now and again.

**REAL WORLD**

Here's a list of things to think about when creating login scripts. It's always a good idea to have a few guidelines in mind before you begin exploring all the possibilities:

▸ *Minimum* — One (with a maximum of three). Even though all four login scripts are optional, the Default login script will run if the User has no User login script. To avoid this, you can include a NO DEFAULT command in a Container or Profile login script.

▸ *Case* — Login scripts are not case sensitive, except for identifier variables in quotation marks (where they must be typed in uppercase and preceded by a percent sign (%). See the WRITE example later in this chapter.

▸ *Characters per line* — 512 maximum, although 78 is recommended for readability.

▸ *Commands per line* — One. Press Enter to mark the end of each line. Lines that automatically wrap are considered one command and do not require another REM character in front of subsequent wrapped lines. However, if a RETURN is issued at the end of the first line, the first statement on the next line must be preceded by REMARK, REM, an asterisk(*), or a semicolon (;).

▸ *Blank lines* — Have no effect. Use them to visually separate groups of commands.

▸ *Documentation* — Use any variation of the REMARK command to thoroughly document what's going on.

### B: Network Drive Mappings

The next section in Figure 3.13 establishes user-specific and group-specific drive mappings. Drive mapping is the single most important command within login scripts. Mappings are essential to NetWare 5.1 navigation and provide a facility for representing large directory paths as single drive letters. The problem with mapping is that it's both session-specific (meaning drive pointers disappear when users log out) and user-specific (meaning they're unique for each user). The temporary nature of drive mappings makes them particularly annoying — because MAP commands must be entered each time a user logs in. Fortunately, this process can be automated using NetWare 5.1 login scripts.

**TIP**

**In addition to standard MAP statements, NetWare 5.1 login scripts support MAP NEXT and MAP *n commands. MAP NEXT automatically chooses the next available drive letter, while MAP *n maps the *network drive number* indicated to the directory or volume specified. For example, if the first network drive on a workstation is F:, then MAP *2 will map the G: drive.**

The display of drive mappings can be turned off using the MAP DISPLAY OFF command and turned on using the MAP DISPLAY ON command. The display of drive mapping errors can be turned off using the MAP ERRORS OFF command and turned on using the MAP ERRORS ON command.

The MAP command is most useful when combined with identifier variables, thereby enabling you to accomplish user-specific or group-specific mappings with only one command. In the first network drive mapping in Figure 3.13, we are using the %HOME_DIRECTORY variable to map root the U: drive to each user's own home directory. In the second example, we are using a value stored in the Group Membership property of the User objects to define a network drive mapping.

### C: Search Drive Mappings

Once network drive mappings have been established, it's time to shift your attention to search drive mappings. By default, the first search drive should always be SYS:PUBLIC. On legacy DOS workstations, you may want to map the second search drive to the DOS directory structure on the server if DOS is being run from the network (as in the case of a diskless workstation). Notice our creative use of identifier variables in search mapping 2. This single statement intelligently maps every workstation to the appropriate version of DOS. Of course, these statements must be combined with the exact DOS structure outlined in Chapter 4, "NetWare 5.1 File System."

Next, you may want to create a search drive mapping for network-based applications. In these cases, you can use MAP INS S16 to systematically create mappings in order. In each case, S16 will use the next available search number.

### D: COMSPEC

COMSPEC stands for COMmand SPECifier. It indicates where a DOS-based or Windows-based workstation should look for COMMAND.COM if something goes wrong. Normally, this parameter is set by your workstation operating system. (For instance, on a Windows 95/98 workstation, it would typically be set to C:\ WINDOWS\COMMAND.COM.)

However, if you have workstations running DOS off the network (such as in the case of legacy diskless workstations), you will need to use the COMSPEC login script command to ensure that this parameter points to the correct location of COMMAND.COM for each workstation. This can be accomplished using the S2: drive mapping that we created earlier.

### E: SET

The SET command enables you to configure DOS environment variables within a login script. You can use the SET command exactly the same as you would in DOS, except that you'll need to surround the values with quotation marks. (**Note:** Most SET variables are configured in the user's AUTOEXEC.BAT file.)

In Figure 3.13, we've included two important SET variables:

```
SET PROMPT="$P$G"
```

This variable configures the local and network prompt to display the current directory path. We want users to feel like they're at home.

```
SET TEMP="U:\USERS\%LOGIN_NAME\TEMP"
```

This variable points the Windows TEMP directory to a NetWare 5.1 drive within the user's home directory structure. Whatever you do, don't use the SET PATH command in a Container login script; it overwrites local and network search drives.

### F: IF ... THEN ... ELSE

IF . . . THEN commands enable you to use script programming logic. They check a given condition and execute your command(s) only if the condition is met. You can also add the ELSE statement to selectively execute another command only when the condition is not met. For example, you can have the system display a fancy message and fire phasers on the user's birthday (using MONTH and DAY identifier variables). You can also display a message pointing out that it's not his/her birthday the other 364 days of the year.

IF . . . THEN commands are versatile login script tools. They effectively enable you to execute any command based on condition, including login name, context, day of the week, or group membership. As you saw earlier in Figure 3.13, we are executing these three commands only on Friday:

- ▸ *MAP* — This statement maps the R: drive to a Directory Map object.

- ▸ *DISPLAY* — This statement displays a text file that is stored on the R: drive.

- ▸ *PAUSE* — This statement temporarily stops execution of the login script to allow the user time to read the display. Just as with the DOS PAUSE command, execution resumes when the user presses any key.

Also, notice the use of BEGIN and END statements. If you plan on including multiple commands within a nested IF . . . THEN statement, you must use BEGIN to mark the start and END to mark the bottom of the nest. (**Note:** IF . . . THEN statements can be nested up to ten levels.)

Before you resign yourself to creating Profile and User login scripts, explore the use of IF . . . THEN statements in Container login scripts.

### G:# (External Program)

The DOS executable (#) command has been included by Novell to support external programs, such as those that end with .EXE, .COM, or .BAT. Because NetWare 5.1 has a limited number of login script commands, you may run across a case where you need to run a nonlogin script program. External programs should be included in Container and Profile scripts, and preceded by one of the following characters:

*[handwritten: Immediate Call]*

- ▸ # — Initiates external execution of an .EXE., .COM, or .BAT file. If an executable filename is preceded by a pound sign (#), login script execution continues *after* the program is exited. For example, to launch the Application Launcher from a login script, you would type: #NAL.

*[handwritten: Call after login]*

- ▸ @ — Initiates external execution of an .EXE, .COM., or .BAT file. Using this symbol enables the remainder of the login script to execute *before* the external executable loads.

The difference between the # symbol and the @ symbol is the point at which the login script is executed in relation to the external program: # (after) and @ (before).

In Figure 3.13 earlier, we combined the #CAPTURE program with IF . . . THEN statements to customize group-specific printing captures within a single Container login script. Once again, the goal is to satisfy all of your users' needs from within a single, centrally managed login script.

### H: NO_DEFAULT

As you remember from our earlier discussion, the Default login script is contained in LOGIN.EXE and cannot be edited. In addition, it may conflict with drive mappings in Container and Profile login scripts. Finally, the Default login script executes only if there is no User login script for a particular user, which conflicts with our goal of having one centrally managed Container login script.

Fortunately, by using the NetWare 5.1 NO_DEFAULT statement, you can skip the Default login script even without a User script. Simply place it toward the end of a Container or Profile script, and everything will be fine.

### I: EXIT

EXIT is a legacy login script command that is typically used on DOS workstations. It terminates the execution of a login script and executes the specified program at a DOS prompt. The program can be an .EXE, .COM, or .BAT file and must reside in the default directory. When combined with the DRIVE command (as shown earlier in Figure 3.13), EXIT can facilitate a smooth transition from a login script to a menu system. In our example, we're exiting to a START batch file residing in either SYS:PUBLIC or the user's home directory.

In Figure 3.13, the DRIVE command dumps Leia into her own home directory, where the menu system resides. In addition, the PCCOMPATIBLE line ensures that her clone workstation returns a %MACHINE value of IBM_PC.

It's important to note that the EXIT command skips all other login scripts. For this reason, you'll want to be careful where you place it. Only use EXIT in a Container login script if you're convinced there are no Profile or User scripts for the affected users, or if you'd rather not execute those scripts because they've been created by nonauthorized personnel. For example, on a DOS workstation, you can use this command for skipping unnecessary login scripts and making a smooth transition to a menu system.

### Other Login Script Commands

In addition to the commands shown in Figure 3.13, NetWare 5.1 includes a potpourri of other login script commands. Here's a few of the more interesting system configuration tools:

▸ *BREAK* — If BREAK ON is included in a login script, the user can press Ctrl+C or Ctrl+Break to abort the normal execution of a login script. The default is BREAK OFF.

▸ *CLS* — Use CLS to clear the user's screen during login script execution.

▸ *CONTEXT* — This command changes the workstation's current NDS context during login script execution.

▸ *FDISPLAY* — Works the same as DISPLAY, except that it filters out formatting codes, printer codes, and other garbage before showing the file onscreen. In other words, it can be used to display the text of an ASCII file without showing ASCII formatting codes.

▸ *FIRE PHASERS* — "Beam me up, Scotty." FIRE PHASERS can be combined with identifier variables to indicate the number of times the phaser sound should be sounded. For example, FIRE PHASERS %NDAY_OF_WEEK will fire five phasers on Thursday. This noise-making login script command is an excellent tool for drawing attention to an onscreen message or a breach of network security.

▸ *GOTO* — This command enables you to execute a portion of the login script out of regular sequence. GOTO jumps to login script labels — text followed by a colon (TOP:, for example). (**Note:** Do not use GOTO to enter or exit a nested IF . . . THEN statement.)

▸ *INCLUDE* — The INCLUDE command branches to a subscript from anywhere in a login script. A subscript can be a DOS text file containing valid login script syntax or an entire login script that belongs to a different object in the NDS tree (use distinguished naming to call other login scripts). After the commands in the subscript have been executed, the system continues to the next line in the original script. Consider using INCLUDE subscripts with IF . . . THEN statements to ultimately customize Container login scripts.

This completes our discussion of login scripts. I hope you've gained an appreciation for how these powerful tools can help you customize user and group connections. Once Container and Profile scripts have been executed, NetWare 5.1 opens the door to a whole new world — the expansive NDS tree.

## LAB EXERCISE 3.2: CONFIGURING ACME'S LOGIN SCRIPTS

Just when you think you're finally going to have a moment to get to some items on your to-do list, SHolmes comes cruising into your office. He said that he'd like to be able to have the members of a special gang-prevention interdepartmental task force share some applications, reports, and other data — and asks if you have any ideas. Of course you have ideas; after all, you are a network administrator!

To perform this exercise, you will need the following:

▸ A NetWare 5.1 server called WHITE-SRV1.WHITE.CRIME.TOKYO.ACME (which can be installed using the directions found in Appendix D).

▸ A workstation running the NetWare 5.1 Novell Client for Windows 95/98 or NetWare 5.1 Novell Client for Windows NT/2000 (which can be installed using the directions found in Lab Exercise 3.1). This workstation must also meet the minimum hardware requirements for running the ConsoleOne utility (namely, a Pentium Pro 200 or better with a minimum of 64MB of RAM).

### Part I: Design a Profile Login Script

**1.** Construct a login script from the following notes you made for yourself:

**a.** Insert a comment at the top of the login script indicating the purpose of the login script, the author (you), and the date the file was created.

**b.** Allow users to access utilities in the SYS:PUBLIC directory.

**c.** Allow users to access executable files in the SYS:APPS\WHITE\TF-GP directory. (Comment out this line for the moment.)

**d.** Map the S: drive to the SYS:SHARED\WHITE\TF-GP directory. (Comment out this line for the moment.)

**e.** Map root the U: drive to each user's home directory under SYS:USERS\WHITE\TF-GP. (Comment out this line for the moment.)

**f.** Display a greeting that is displayed each time a user logs in, including the user's full name, day, date, time, and station number.

**g.** Display a file called SYS:SHARED\WHITE\TF-GP\MESSAGE.TXT containing the important news of the day. (Comment out this line for the moment.)

**h.** On Wednesdays, fire phasers twice and display a reminder to members of the task force that the weekly meeting is at 9:00 a.m. in Conference Room 3-D.

**i.** If the user is a member of the TF-GPMGR group, run the DrWatson login script. Assume that his User object is located in the WHITE container. (Comment out this line for the moment.)

**j.** Here are some general notes:

- Whenever appropriate, don't forget to insert a PAUSE statement so that messages don't scroll off the screen before the user has a chance to read them.

- Insert appropriate remarks through the login script so that someone else who looks at it can easily understand what you have done.

- **Note:** In real life, you would probably want to create the directories and files required by this login script next. However, because we don't discuss the NetWare 5.1 file system until Chapter 4 (or Security until Chapter 5), we'll just leave the affected lines commented out for now.

**Part II: Install the ConsoleOne Utility**

**1.** Log into the network as Admin, if you haven't already done so.

**2.** Before you can use ConsoleOne for the first time, you must install it on your workstation. Follow these simple instructions to install ConsoleOne:

**a.** Exit any other applications that are currently running on your workstation.

**b.** Map a drive to the SYS: volume.

- If you originally installed the WHITE-SRV1 server using the directions in Appendix D, skip this step (because you should already have a search drive mapped to the SYS: volume).

- Otherwise, consult Chapter 4 for directions on how to map a search drive to the SYS: volume using the Network Neighborhood utility.

**c.** Click Start ➪ Run. When the Run dialog box appears, browse to SYS:PUBLIC\MGMT\CONSOLEONE\1.2\INSTALL\SETUP.EXE and then click OK.

**d.** Follow the prompts.

**e.** Wait until the installation process is complete and the workstation reboots.

**f.** Log into the network as Admin.

### Part III: Create the DrWatson User Object

**1.** Launch the ConsoleOne utility by double-clicking the new ConsoleOne icon on your workstation desktop. You'll notice that the ConsoleOne browser window is relatively similar to the browser window found in other Windows-based utilities.

**2.** Display the WHITE container in the right pane.

**a.** Browse the ACME_TREE to the CRIME container (which is the parent of the WHITE container) and then display its contents:

- In the left pane, double-click The Network.

- In the left pane, double-click ACME_TREE.

- In the left pane, double-click ACME.

- In the left pane, double-click TOKYO.

- In the left pane, double-click CRIME.

**b.** You'll notice that the contents of the CRIME container appear in the right pane, including the WHITE container.

**3.** Create the DrWatson User object.

  **a.** Use *one* of the following methods for selecting the parent object for the DrWatson User object:

  - In the right pane, click the parent (that is, WHITE in this case) and then select File ⇨ New ⇨ User, *or*

  - In the right pane, click the parent (that is, WHITE in this case) and press Insert, *or*

  - In the right pane, right-click the parent (that is, WHITE in this case) and then select New ⇨ User.

  **b.** Follow these steps if the New Object dialog box appears:

  - Select User in the Class list box.

  - Click OK.

  **c.** When the New User dialog box appears, do as follows:

  - In the Name field, enter the following:

    ```
    DrWatson
    ```

  - In the Surname field, enter the following:

    ```
    Watson
    ```

  - In the Unique ID field, verify that DrWatson appears.

  - Mark the Define Additional Properties check box.

  - Click OK.

  **d.** When the Create Authentication Secrets dialog box appears, do as follows:

  - In the Tree field, verify that ACME_TREE is listed.

  - In the Context field, verify that WHITE.CRIME.TOKYO.ACME is listed.

- In the Username field, verify that DrWatson is listed.
- In the New Password field, enter the following:

  ACME

- In the Confirm New Password field, enter the following:

  ACME

- Click OK.

**d.** When the Properties of DrWatson dialog box appears, click the General tab.

**e.** Follow these steps when the General page appears:

- In the Full Name field, enter the following:

  Dr. Watson

- Click the Login Scripts tab.

**f.** When the Login Scripts page appears, do as follows:

- In the Login Script field, enter the following. (Make sure it is all on one line):

  Write "The DrWatson User login script is being executed."

- Click OK to save your changes to the DrWatson User object.

**Part IV: Create the TF-GP Profile Object**

**1.** Create the TF-GP Profile object.

**a.** Use *one* of the following methods for selecting the parent object for the TF-GP Profile object:

- In the right pane, click the parent (that is, WHITE in this case) and then select File ➪ New ➪ Object, *or*

- In the right pane, click the parent (that is, WHITE in this case) and press Insert, *or*

- In the right pane, right-click the parent (that is, WHITE in this case) and then select New ⇨ Object from the pop-up menu that appears.

**b.** When the New Object dialog box appears, follow these steps:

- In the Class list box, select Profile.

- Click OK.

**c.** When the New Profile dialog box appears, do the following:

- In the Name field, enter the following:

  `TF-GP`

- Mark the Define Additional Properties check box

- Click OK.

**d.** When the Properties of TF-GP dialog box appears, do the following:

- The General tab will be displayed by default.

- In the Description field, enter the following:

  `Gang Prevention Task Force`

- Click the Login Script tab.

**e.** Follow these steps when the Login Script page appears:

- In the Login Script field, key in the Profile login script you created in Part II of this exercise.

- Click the NDS Rights tab and then select "Trustees of This Object" from the drop-down menu that appears.

**f.** When the NDS Rights page appears, click Add Trustee.

**g.** When the Select Objects dialog box appears, follow these steps:

- Select DrWatson.

- Click OK.

**h.** When the Rights Assigned to Selected Objects dialog box appears, do the following:

- In the Property field, verify that [Entry Rights] is selected.

- In the Rights section, verify that the Browse check box is marked.

- In the Property field, click [All Attributes Rights].

- In the Rights section, verify that the Compare and Read check boxes are marked.

- Click OK to return to the previous page.

- Click OK to save your changes to this Profile object.

**2.** Assign the TF-GP Profile to the DrWatson User object.

**a.** In the right pane, double-click WHITE to display its contents.

**b.** In the right pane, double-click the DrWatson User object to display its properties.

**c.** When the Properties of the DrWatson dialog box appears, click the Login Script tab.

**d.** When the Login Script page appears, click the Browse button to the right of the Profile field.

**e.** When the Select Object dialog box appears, follow these steps:

- Select TF-GP.

- Click OK.

**f.** If a message appears indicating that the user does not have the Read rights to the Profile's login script property, click Yes to indicate that you'd like the Profile assignment to be created anyway.

- Click OK to save your change to the DrWatson object.

- Exit the ConsoleOne utility.

**3.** Test the new Profile login script.

    **a.** Log into the network as the DrWatson user to check things out:

       • Don't forget that the password for the DrWatson User object is "ACME".

       • When logging in, make sure that the Close Automatically check box is unmarked. (See Part II of Lab Exercise 3.1 for details.)

    **b.** Watch the screen carefully as the Profile login script is executed and determine the following:

       • Was a search drive mapped to SYS:PUBLIC?

       • Was a greeting displayed that includes Dr. Watson's full name, the day of the week, and the date?

       • Was your station number displayed?

       • If today is Wednesday, was a notice about the staff meeting displayed and two phasers fired?

       • If at any point, you are instructed to "press any key," do so.

       • Was a message displayed indicating that Dr. Watson's User login script is being executed?

    **c.** Click Close to close the Results window.

**4.** Log in as Admin.

    **a.** If you encountered any errors, log into the network as Admin, fix the problems, and then log into the network as DrWatson to see if the problems have been fixed.

    **b.** **Note:** If during login, the Results screen flashed too fast for you to read it, it probably means you forgot to unmark the Close Automatically check box. (See Part II of Lab Exercise 3.1 for details.)

# Welcome In!

Welcome to the NetWare 5.1 NDS tree!

As a NetWare 5.1 network administrator, you must appreciate the delicate balance of life on the network. To be a CNA/CNE means that you appreciate your users and their resources. It means that you like the smell of laser printer toner, the feel of NDS objects between your toes, and the sound of disgruntled users breathing down the back of your neck.

Once you've found your way into the NetWare 5.1 tree, it's time to learn a little bit about management. So, what is tree management all about? It involves a combination of tools, knowledge, and experience. In this section, we will learn how to browse the NetWare 5.1 tree, create NDS users, and help these users gain access to valuable resources. In summary, we'll explore the following three areas:

- *Just Browsing* — We'll learn how to browse NDS resources using a variety of tools — including NetWare Administrator, ConsoleOne, Windows 95/98 or Windows NT/2000 Explorer, and Netscape Navigator.

- *Creating NDS Users* — You'll finally get an opportunity to build the ACME tree with help from NetWare Administrator, ConsoleOne, and BULKLOAD.

- *Managing Resource Access* — Finally, we'll learn how to support nomadic users with Alias, Directory Map, and Group objects.

Are you ready for a tour of the NetWare 5.1 tree? Tour guide optional.

## Just Browsing

*Browsing* is a technical term that means "to walk around the NDS tree looking at stuff." Browsing not only acquaints you with the tree, it also aids in NDS navigation. NDS navigation is required for a myriad of management tasks (such as creating users, adding security, configuring volumes, and partitioning).

In the world of NetWare, Novell and their friends (Microsoft and Netscape) offer a variety of tools for NDS browsing. In this section, we'll explore the four most powerful tools:

▸ *NetWare Administrator* — A Windows-based tool that enables you to graphically manage various objects and properties in the NDS tree.

▸ *ConsoleOne* — A network-compatible Java tool that enables you to administer network resources from a central browser.

▸ *Windows 95/98 and Windows NT/2000* — A native Windows-based workstation environment that provides resource browsing using Network Neighborhood.

▸ *Netscape Navigator* — A network-compatible browser tool that enables you to view web pages and execute GUI applications (such as the NetWare 5.1 documentation viewer).

Now, let's begin our tour of the NDS tree with a quick look at NetWare Administrator.

### Browsing with NetWare Administrator

NetWare Administrator is a Windows-based tool that enables you to graphically manage objects and properties in the NDS tree. You can also browse the tree by double-clicking specific container objects and expanding their contents. Then, detailed resource information is just a double-click away. With this utility, you can view, create, move, delete, and assign rights to any object in the NDS tree (provided that you have the appropriate NDS access rights).

Once you access the NDS tree using the Novell Client, you can perform a variety of management tasks with NetWare Administrator:

▸ Create and delete objects (such as users and groups)

▸ Assign rights to the NDS tree and file system

▸ Set up Novell Distributed Print Services (NDPS)

▸ Set up and manage NDS partitions and replicas

▸ Browse object and property information throughout the tree

▶ Move and rename NDS objects

▶ Set up and manage licensing services

**TIP**

**You may restrict access to NetWare Administrator by moving it from SYS:PUBLIC into another, more restricted subdirectory (such as SYS:SYSTEM). Everyday users don't need this powerful tree-browsing utility.**

NetWare Administrator runs as a multiple-document interface application. This means you can display multiple browsing windows at one time. The primary browser window is shown in Figure 3.14.

▶ · · · · · · · · · · · · · · · · · · · · · · · ◀

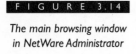

F I G U R E   3.14

*The main browsing window in NetWare Administrator*

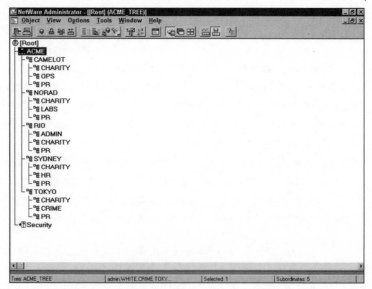

In order to view multiple windows in NetWare Administrator, select the Tile option from the Windows menu. Figure 3.15 shows three browser windows tiled for [Root], CRIME, and WHITE. Once again, notice how easy it is to view multiple ACME resources — regardless of their location. You'll notice that the title for each of the browser windows displays its context. This helps you track where all of your resources are in the logical NDS world.

**REAL WORLD**

NetWare 5.1 includes two versions of NetWare Administrator: (1) Windows 3.1 (SYS:PUBLIC\NWADMN3X) and (2) Windows 95/98 and Windows NT/2000 (SYS:PUBLIC\WIN32\ NWADMN32.EXE). In this study guide, we'll focus on the 32-bit Windows 95/98 and Windows NT/2000 version.

FIGURE 3.15

*Three tiled NetWare Administrator browsing windows*

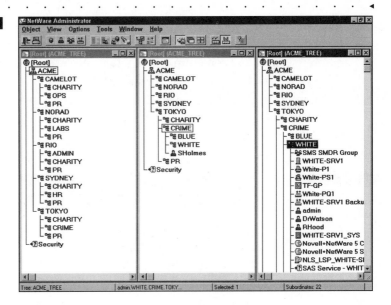

You can also browse the NDS tree by moving through container objects. Of the several ways to expand the contents of a container, here are just a few:

- ▶ *Double-click the container object* — When you double-click a container, it expands its contents — which shows all subordinate container and leaf objects. If a container is expanded, you can collapse it by double-clicking it again.

▶ *Select a container object in the tree and choose the Expand option from the View menu* — This will expand the contents of the container. You can collapse the container by using the Collapse option from the same menu.

▶ *Select a container object and press plus (+) on the numeric keypad of your keyboard* — The container object will expand and show its contents (sounds embarrassing). You can collapse the container by pressing minus (–) on the numeric keypad. (**Note:** The plus [+] above the equals sign [=] doesn't work. You must use the numeric keypad.)

▶ *Select a container object and press the right mouse button* — Select the Browse option from the pull-down menu that appears. This launches a new browser window containing the contents of the selected container object. Figure 3.16 shows the short menu that appears when the right mouse button is pressed. By the way, this is a great shortcut feature. In this case, *right* is right.

F I G U R E   3.16

*Right mouse button shortcut in NetWare Administrator*

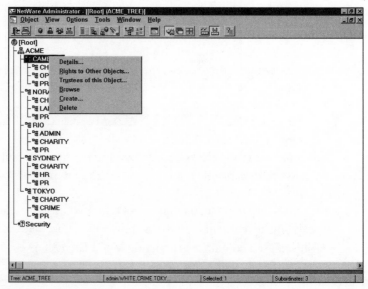

The object dialog box is organized into pages that you can access using the page buttons along the right side. As you can see in Figure 3.17, the Identification page always appears first, by default. You can browse specific NDS properties by selecting the corresponding page button. Each object type has a different set of page buttons because each object type has a different set of properties. Figure 3.17 shows the page buttons for the O=ACME container object.

▶ · · · · · · · · · · · · · · · · · · · · · · · · · · · · · · · · · ◀

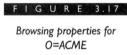

FIGURE 3.17

*Browsing properties for O=ACME*

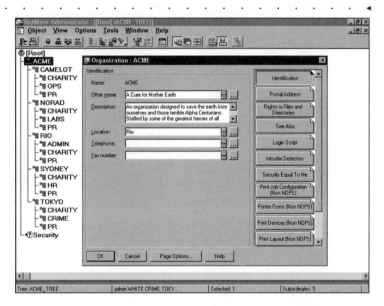

**TIP**

**The property pages in an object dialog box are all part of the same dialog. In other words, when you select a different page, you are still in the same dialog. If you press OK or Cancel on any page, you are affecting the entire dialog box, not just the individual page. For example, OK will save modifications to all of the pages and Cancel will exit the dialog box without saving changes to any page. You can move between pages of the dialog box by selecting the desired page button in each case.**

You can also locate object and property information in the NDS tree by using the Search feature. Fortunately, you can perform this function without having to expand each of the container objects. It's much easier, trust me. The search operation will browse the entire tree, unless you narrow the search criteria.

For example, in Figure 3.18, the search criteria is configured to find all the Users in the ACME tree who have a Department property equal to Charity. You can further narrow the search by starting at a subcontainer instead of the [Root]. Or you can expand the search criteria to include all objects in the Charity container, not just Users. As you can see, the NetWare Administrator search engine is very sophisticated. Maybe you'll find what you're looking for.

**FIGURE 3.18**

*Searching the ACME tree for CHARITY users*

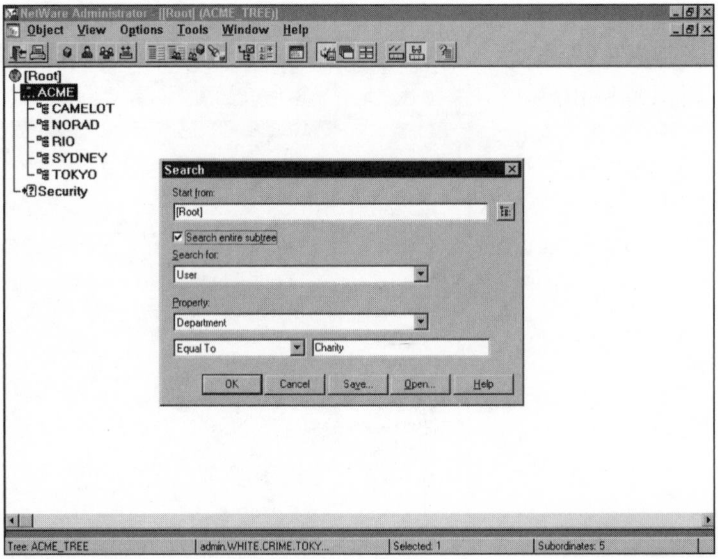

This completes our brief tour through NetWare Administrator. Now, let's explore its Java-based cousin — ConsoleOne.

### Browsing with ConsoleOne

In addition to NetWare Administrator, NetWare 5.1 includes a Java-based administration browser called ConsoleOne. ConsoleOne is designed like a file manager utility with a left pane (where you browse containers) and right pane (where you manage network resources and NDS objects).

As a Java-based GUI tool, ConsoleOne supports cross-platform compatibility from both the Novell Client workstation and NetWare 5.1 server. Both platforms require Java support. On the server, this is provided by the Java Virtual Machine, which is loaded by default when the server boots. On the workstation, the Java platform is installed as a custom option during Novell Client setup.

ConsoleOne provides the following NetWare administration capabilities:

▸ Manage NDS and the file system from within a single application

▸ Browse large trees, and administer large numbers of objects

▸ Expand your leaf object set

▸ Administer NDS objects at the NetWare 5.1 server console

Prior to configuring ConsoleOne, make sure that your workstation meets the following minimum system requirements: Pentium Pro processor with at least 64MB of RAM and Novell Client v3.1 (or later) installed. You can access the ConsoleOne setup utility as the file SETUP.EXE in the SYS:PUBLIC\MGMT\ CONSOLEONE\1.2\INSTALL directory. (**Note:** You can download the latest version of ConsoleOne at `http://www.novell.com/download/`.) Once the installation process is complete, you can start ConsoleOne by double-clicking the ConsoleOne icon on your Windows desktop.

Once ConsoleOne has been activated, you will be presented with a GUI browser screen similar to Figure 3.19. As you can see, ConsoleOne resembles a typical workstation-based GUI *Explorer* tool. The left window pane enables you to browse objects, while the right side displays the contents of the highlighted icon.

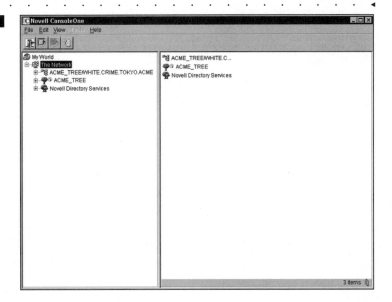

FIGURE 3.19

*ConsoleOne GUI browser tool*

The ConsoleOne browser relies on a variety of different object types:

▶ *My World* — The highest-level container object. By default, My World includes the following second-level links: My Server, Shortcuts, and The Network. As you can see in Figure 3.19, clicking The Network in the left-hand pane brings NDS trees and containers into view in the right pane.

▶ *Container objects* — These second-level objects contain other icons that pertain to the NetWare 5.1 server, the GUI interface, the file system, or NDS. For example, when you browse the file system, volumes and subdirectories appear as configurable objects. When browsing NDS, Organization and Organizational Unit objects appear.

▶ *Leaf objects* — These represent the physical or logical resources associated with second-level containers. Leaf objects include servers, volumes, configuration files, tools, and a variety of typical NDS leaves.

ConsoleOne enables you to manage your server's file system using the Volumes object. From ConsoleOne you can perform the following file system functions: navigate the file system, rename a file, delete a file, copy a file, and edit text files.

### Browsing with Windows 95/98 and Windows NT/2000

In addition to NetWare Administrator and ConsoleOne, NetWare 5.1 also supports GUI browsing by using the Windows 95/98 and Windows NT/2000 Network Neighborhood and Explorer utilities. This capability is only available when Windows is integrated with the Novell Client. This integration provides the following additional capabilities to Windows 95/98 and Windows NT/2000 workstations:

▶ *Support for long filenames* — Long filenames are files with names that are longer than 8 or 11 characters.

▶ *Full integration with Windows Explorer, Network Neighborhood, and other Windows programs* — This allows you to access NetWare resources from native Windows applications.

▸ *Use of the System tray* — The Novell Client places an *N* icon in the
Windows System tray that allows you to access many frequently used
Novell Client features. To do so, simply right-click the icon.

The initial Network Neighborhood screen lists all NDS trees and servers available on the network. You can browse a particular tree by double-clicking the tree
icon and navigating its subsequent container objects (see Figure 3.20). In addition, you can view properties about servers and volumes by double-clicking their
respective icons within the Network Neighborhood Explorer.

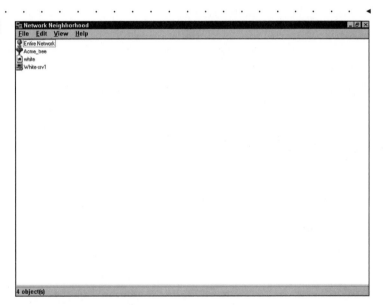

**FIGURE 3.20**

*Browsing the NDS tree with
Windows 95/98 Network
Neighborhood*

### Browsing with Netscape Navigator

Browsers are specialized workstation programs that provide TCP/IP connectivity to Internet/intranet Web servers and other Java applications. Browsers (such as
Netscape Navigator) augment the functionality of the Novell Client by offering the
following networking features in addition to Web browsing:

▸ Allowing you to display network resources (provided that Lightweight
Directory Access Protocol (LDAP) is running).

▸ Providing a GUI login window for access to networks and network services, including printing and file storage resources. (**Note:** This feature requires either LDAP or the Novell Portal Server.)

▸ Enabling you to call and execute local and network applications.

▸ Providing a user interface and user utilities to access and use network resources (provided that the Portal Server is running).

Unlike the Novell Client (which can be configured to support both IPX and TCP/IP), browsers rely exclusively on the TCP/IP protocol for network communications. In addition, browsers rely on the host WOS (such as Windows 95/98 or Windows NT/2000) as an application platform. Some of the newer browsers (such as Microsoft Internet Explorer) are fully integrated with the WOS and can extend its capabilities by providing important new services.

Workstation browsers (such as Netscape Navigator) are the primary GUI platform for Java applications. Java is a programming language that enables computer programmers to create a program that can run on virtually any computer platform—from Windows to MacOS to mainframes. This ability is particularly important on computer networks. Because networks already connect many different kinds of platforms, Java enables those platforms to support a single application without costly translation. The use of Java-based programs is likely to increase in the future. Therefore, any browser you choose should support Java.

Installing Netscape Navigator is similar to installing the Novell Client. The WINSETUP.EXE installation program used to install the Novell Client can also be used to install Netscape Navigator. Once the browser has been installed, an icon appears on your workstation desktop that enables you to launch the browser. To begin the installation process, simply run the setup program from the *Novell Client* CD-ROM or download it for free from Netscape's Web site (www.netscape.com).

This completes our browsing tour of the NetWare 5.1 NDS tree. Now that you're familiar with all administrative aspects of the tree, it's time to get down to business. To succeed in the NDS tree, you must be down to earth (literally) and focus on the NDS objects themselves. Now it's time to create some NDS Users.

## Creating NDS Users

Now that you understand the fundamentals of NDS browsing, it's time to put your knowledge to the test. Today is your big day. We finally get to build ACME's tree. In Chapter 1, we learned all about ACME and their mission to save the world. Then, in Chapter 2, we learned about NDS objects and the layout of the ACME tree. Finally, in this chapter, we get to build the ACME tree, starting with NDS users.

The User object is the most fundamental NDS leaf object because it represents the distributed humans who access your network. Each person on the network should be represented by a unique User object because that's where NDS stores property information, defines the user environment, and regulates access to network resources. For example, you should have a unique User object to log into the NDS tree, access distributed Application objects (through Novell Application Launcher, also known as NAL), and use network-attached printers (through NDPS).

By default, Admin is the only NDS User object created automatically. It is defined when NDS is installed on the first server in your network. Initially, the Admin object has complete authority to manage all aspects of the network and is the primary User object used for initial network setup. You are not limited to one object with supervisory authority. You can create additional User objects with the same rights as the Admin object (see Chapter 5 to learn how). Interestingly, because Admin is a User object, it can be deleted, modified, or have its security access revoked, just like any other User object.

Fortunately, NetWare 5.1 provides us with three powerful tools for creating NDS users:

- *NetWare Administrator* — Enables you to create and manage NDS objects quickly and easily from a Windows-based workstation.

- *ConsoleOne* — Is a Java-based tool that enables you to create and manage NDS objects from either a workstation or a NetWare 5.1 server.

- *BULKLOAD* — Is a command-line NLM that enables you to import users from a database application into the NDS tree.

Now, let's build ACME's NDS tree starting with NetWare Administrator.

### Creating NDS Users with NetWare Administrator

NetWare Administrator is a Windows-based utility that enables you to create, delete, modify, rename, move, and view detailed information about an NDS object — assuming, of course, that you have the appropriate access rights.

Following are the detailed steps for creating a user account in NetWare Administrator:

**1.** Log into the network.

**2.** Launch the NetWare Administrator utility. Follow these steps to do so:

    **a.** Click Start ➪ Run.

    **b.** When the Run dialog box appears, in the Open field, browse to the following file on the SYS: volume of the WHITE-SRV1 server and click OK:

```
\PUBLIC\WIN32\NWADMN32.EXE
```

**3.** Browse the tree and locate the User object's target parent container.

**4.** Use *one* of the following methods to create the User object:

    **a.** Highlight the container and select Object ➪ Create, *or*

    **b.** Highlight the container and press Insert, *or*

    **c.** Highlight the container and click the Create a New Object button in the toolbar (it looks like a 3D box.), *or*

    **d.** Right-click the container and select Create from the pop-up menu that appears.

**5.** When the New Object dialog box appears, select User and click OK.

**6.** Do the following when the Create User dialog box appears (as shown in Figure 3.21):

    • (Required) In the Login Name field, indicate the username for this user.

    • (Required) In the Last Name field, indicate the last name of this user.

**REAL WORLD**

Make sure that ConsoleOne is closed before you open NetWare Administrator on the same workstation. Both utilities draw on the same NDS resources and, therefore, can lock up your machine if they are both open at the same time on the same machine.

F I G U R E   3.21

*Creating new users in WHITE*

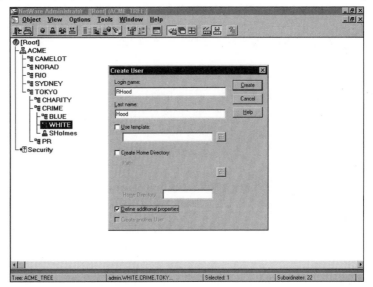

- (Optional) Mark the Use Template check box if you want to use a template to create this user. Then, browse to locate the Template object. You can use the Template object to create multiple users with similar characteristics — such as phone numbers, addresses, and account restrictions. Multiple Template objects can exist in the Directory. In fact, multiple Template objects can exist within a container.

- (Optional, but recommended) Mark the Create Home Directory check box if you want to create a home directory for this user. Next, browse to locate the path for the home directory. Finally, in the Home Directory field, modify the directory name listed if the user's home directory name is different from his or her username. A home directory serves as a user's personal storage space in the NetWare 5.1 file system (and usually matches his or her login name). Typically, all user home directories are grouped under a common parent directory, such as SYS:USERS.

- (Optional) Mark the Define Additional Properties check box if you want to configure additional properties for this user.

- (Optional) Mark the Create Another User check box if you want to create an additional user.

- Click Create to create the new user.

**7.** Collapse the container and expand it again to view the User object you just created.

The Template is a special user-oriented leaf object that enables you to create and manage a series of user accounts with similar property values. You can automatically copy the properties of a Template object to a User object when creating it (via the Use Template check box). This feature allows global changes (such as a company address or fax number) to be made in one place and passed on to all User objects created using the Template. In addition, the Template object maintains a live link with all of its subordinate users. When a change is made to one or more Template object properties using the "Details on Multiple Users" option, the change is copied to all the associated User objects.

---

### REAL WORLD

Practice creating users (with and without home directories) using NetWare Administrator. You should know how to add/modify properties of a User object both at the time of creation (Define Additional Properties) or after the fact (by double-clicking the leaf object). When viewing or modifying properties for a User object, try clicking the page buttons on the right side of the User object dialog box to familiarize yourself with the properties available in each page. Then, practice creating multiple users at one time by marking the Create Another User check box. Finally, practice deleting a User object by highlighting it and pressing Delete.

---

Follow these steps to create a Template object using NetWare Administrator:

**1.** Log into the network.

**2.** Launch the NetWare Administrator utility.

**3.** Browse the tree and locate the Template object's target parent container.

**4.** Highlight the container and press Insert.

**5.** When the New Object dialog box appears, select Template and click OK.

**6.** Follow these steps when the Create Template dialog box appears:

- (Required) In the Name field, indicate the name for this template.

- (Optional) Mark the Use Template or User check box if you want to use another template or user to create this template. Then, browse to locate the Template or User object.

- (Optional) Mark the Define Additional Properties check box if you want to configure additional properties for this template.

- (Optional) Mark the Create Another Template check box if you want to create an additional template after this one is created.

- Click Create to create the new template.

**7.** Collapse the container and expand it again to view the Template object you just created.

Once you have created one or more user accounts, you can use NetWare Administrator to modify them individually or as a group:

▶ *Individually* — Each User object can be modified separately by highlighting it and selecting Object ⇨ Details. Some properties (such as username, last name, and password) can only be changed on an individual basis.

▶ · · · · · · · · · · · · · · · · · · · · · · · ◀

**REAL WORLD**

Practice using NetWare Administrator to change the property values of multiple users with the Object ⇨ "Details on Multiple Users" option. In addition, you should practice selecting the users to be modified by using each of the following four methods: selecting individual users (using Shift-click or Ctrl-click), selecting one or more Group objects, selecting one or more containers, and selecting a Template object that has already been used to create User objects.

▶ *As a group using the "Details on Multiple Users" option* — This option enables you to make sweeping changes to multiple user accounts from a central location. To change properties common to multiple users (such as an address or fax number), highlight the appropriate object(s) and select Object ⇨ "Details on Multiple Users." You can either select multiple User objects or one or more Organization, Organizational Unit, Template, or Group objects. To select contiguous objects, click the first object and shift-click the last. To select discontiguous objects, control-click the objects.

NetWare Administrator is your friend. However, it's not the only tool provided by NetWare 5.1 for NDS user creation. Now, let's take a look at a cool new Java-based tool called ConsoleOne. This is undoubtedly the future of NetWare user management.

### Creating NDS Users with ConsoleOne

ConsoleOne is a GUI Java-based utility that runs on a NetWare 5.1 server or Novell Client workstation. It is included in NetWare 5.1 as a glimpse of the future direction of administrative utilities. And because ConsoleOne is written in Java, it can run on a variety of platforms — including Windows, Macintosh, and UNIX clients, as well as NetWare 5.1 servers.

Currently, only a limited number of objects can be created using ConsoleOne, including Users, Groups, Organizations, and Organizational Units. Although you can establish most properties for these objects, any advanced NDS management tasks must be made using NetWare Administrator.

As you can see in Figure 3.22, the ConsoleOne interface resembles Windows with a number of administrative enhancements—such as a graphical toolbar, Explorer-like navigation, and context-sensitive menu system.

F I G U R E   3.22

*The ConsoleOne administrative browser*

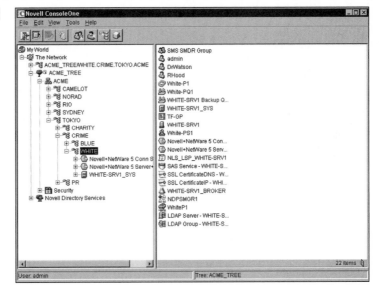

Follow these steps to create a user account using ConsoleOne:

**1.** You must install ConsoleOne on your workstation before you can use it. To do so, execute the SYS:\PUBLIC\MGMT\CONSOLEONE\1.2\INSTALL\SETUP.EXE file and follow the prompts. When the process is complete, a ConsoleOne shortcut will appear on your desktop. (If ConsoleOne is already installed on your workstation, skip this step.)

**2.** Log into the network as Admin. (**Note:** You need to log in *before* launching ConsoleOne so that the utility will display the NDS tree and the containers that you connected to during login.)

**3.** Launch the ConsoleOne utility on your workstation by double-clicking the ConsoleOne shortcut on your desktop.

**4.** When the ConsoleOne screen appears, do as follows:

   **a.** In the left pane, browse the tree and locate the User object's target parent container.

   **b.** Select File ➪ New ➪ User.

**5.** When the New User dialog box appears, follow these steps:

- (Required) In the Login Name field, enter the username for the new user.

- (Required) In the Last Name field, enter the last name for the new user.

- (Optional) Mark the Define Additional Properties check box if you want to configure additional properties for this user.

- (Optional) Mark the Create Another User check box if you want to create an additional user.

- Click Create to create the new user.

**6.** When the Create Authentication Secrets dialog box appears, in the New Password field, enter a password for the new user, and then click OK.

**7.** The User object you created appears in the right pane.

ConsoleOne also enables you to manage existing NDS objects from the administrative browser. To do so, simply browse to the object's home container in the left window pane. Then, right-click the object you want to administer in the right side of the display.

At this point, ConsoleOne returns a pop-up menu. Click Properties and the details of the NDS object display—as shown in Figure 3.23. In this example, we're managing the Identification property tab of the Admin User object. Remember, once you've made your modifications, click Apply to save the changes.

Now, let's explore the final NDS user creation tool—BULKLOAD. This is actually more of a database import tool than a GUI NDS manager. Check it out.

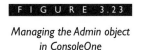

F I G U R E   3.23

*Managing the Admin object in ConsoleOne*

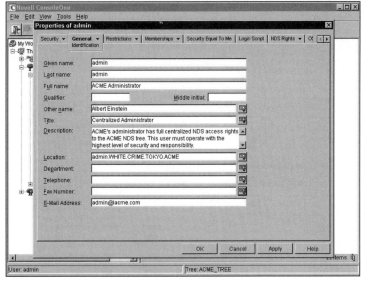

## Creating NDS Users with BULKLOAD

BULKLOAD.NLM is a command-line server utility that enables you to import user-related database information from a delimited ASCII file into the NDS database. This utility can be used to create, delete, and modify User objects and their properties in a batch process.

BULKLOAD uses LDAP Data Interchange Format (LDIF) files for batch processing. LDIF files can be generated from most e-mail programs.

Congratulations! You've taken a big step today toward saving the world. ACME's tree is in place. I bet you didn't think NetWare 5.1 administration could be so much fun.

Now, let's finish off this chapter with a quick look at managing resource access. After all, the NDS tree is a big place, and many times users need help getting in touch with their "resources".

## Managing Resource Access

NetWare 5.1 and NDS present special management challenges to network administrators if users need to access distributed multicontext resources. Following are some important planning guidelines for multiple resource access:

▶ *File System and File System Security* — When planning file system access rights, consider global objects (containers, Group objects with global membership, [Root], and [Public]). To grant an object (User, Group, container, and so on) rights to a volume in another context, make the object a trustee and grant the rights. When you map drives (network or search), use the distinguished name of the Volume object, create a Directory Map object in the current container, or create an Alias object in the current context.

▶ *Network Printing* — Rely on a single Print Manager for managing printers in multiple contexts. Also, make sure to grant public access, rather than controlled access, to printers needed by everyone.

▶ *NDS and NDS Security* — Use default rights assignments (when appropriate). Delegate responsibility by creating additional network administrators. Consider whether to grant distributed administrators the Supervisor object right or something less risky (such as Create, Delete, and Rename rights).

NetWare 5.1 provides three different strategies for maintaining NDS accessibility:

▶ Use an Alias object to refer to an object in another container.

▶ Use an Application object or Directory Map object to refer to file system resources in another container.

▶ Use a Group object to refer to group members from anywhere in the NDS tree.

Let's gain access.

### Creating Alias Objects

The *Alias* object is an NDS leaf that refers to (or points to) an NDS object elsewhere in the tree. This is a great strategy for making a resource available to users in a different container. However, users still need rights to the original object. For instance, if users in the MARKETING container need access to a Volume object in the SALES container, you can create an Alias object in the MARKETING container. This way, the users in MARKETING will be able to map a drive to the volume using only the Alias object's common name — because the Alias object is in their current context.

In Figure 3.24, an Alias object in the ADMIN container points to the AEinstein User object in the LABS container. This means that AEinstein can log in from either the ADMIN or LABS context — giving him easier access to his user identity.

▶ · · · · · · · · · · · · · · · · · · · · · · · · · · · · · ◀

F I G U R E   3.24

*Creating an Alias object
in NDS*

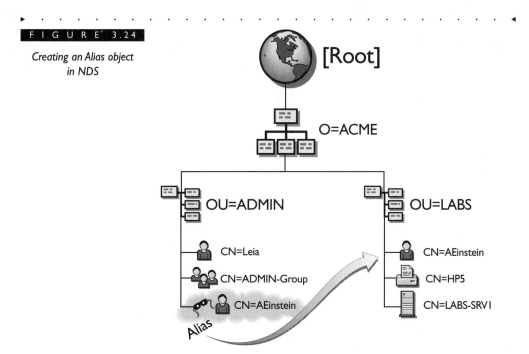

Follow these simple steps to create an Alias object using NetWare Administrator:

**1.** Log into the network.

**2.** Launch the NetWare Administrator utility.

**3.** Browse the tree and locate the Alias object's target parent container.

**4.** Click the container and select Object ⇨ Create.

**5.** When the New Object dialog box appears, select Alias and click OK.

**6.** Follow these steps when the Create Alias dialog box appears:

- (Required) In the Alias Name field, indicate the name for this Alias object.

- (Required) In the Aliased Object field, browse to or enter the distinguished name of the host object.

- (Optional) Mark the Define Additional Properties check box if you want to configure additional properties for this Alias object.

- (Optional) Mark the Create Another User check box if you want to create an additional Alias Object after this one.

- Click Create to create the new Alias object.

**7.** Collapse the container and expand it again to view the Alias object you just created.

### Creating Application and Directory Map Objects

NetWare 5.1 and NDS offer two leaf objects for accessing files and directories in multiple containers: the *Application* and *Directory Map* objects. Pointing an Application object to an application file on a volume in another container is helpful when you can't install the application on multiple servers. Similarly, pointing a Directory Map object to a directory on a volume in another container is helpful when a directory is needed in more than one container, but must be kept on a single volume.

For example, if the users in the MARKETING container need access to an application or volume in the SALES container, you can use either of these two strategies:

▸ You can create an Application object in the MARKETING container and use Application Launcher to launch the application.

▶ You can create a Directory Map object in the MARKETING container and map network drives to the SALES volume.

Application and Directory Map objects operate in a similar way to the Alias object. However, whereas Application and Directory Map objects point to locations on file system volumes, Aliases point to NDS objects.

### Creating Group Objects with Global Membership

The *Group* object can contain members from anywhere in the NDS tree and can be used to grant trustee rights to any NDS object. If User objects are members of a Group object, rights granted to the Group pass to the members (this is known as *security equivalence*). The Group object's location in the NDS tree is not important. The critical factors are *who* are the members of the Group and *what* NDS rights they have.

Using a Group object in this way provides a single point of management. Group Members can use resources (such as applications, directories, or data files) on all volumes that the Group objects has rights to. Keep in mind that a Group can be assigned as a trustee of any NDS object, as well as any volume (or directory or file) in any container.

Congratulations — you made it! Together we have survived our safari through NetWare 5.1's expansive NDS tree. As we learned at the beginning of this chapter, tree management requires an excellent balance of watering, love, sunshine, and weeding. In the remaining chapters of this book, we will apply our connectivity lessons to four realms of the NetWare 5.1 administration kingdom:

▶ File system

▶ Security

▶ ZENworks

▶ NDPS Printing

So, brace yourself for more fun. Only superheroes need apply!

## LAB EXERCISE 3.3: JUST BROWSING THE NDS TREE

In this exercise, we will explore the NDS tree structure using two different utilities: NetWare Administrator and ConsoleOne.

To perform this exercise, you will need the following:

▶ A NetWare 5.1 server called WHITE-SRV1.WHITE.CRIME.TOKYO.ACME (which can be installed using the directions found in Appendix D).

▶ A workstation running the NetWare 5.1 Novell Client for Windows 95/98 or NetWare 5.1 Novell Client for Windows NT/2000 (which can be installed using the directions found in Lab Exercise 3.1).

**Part I: NetWare Administrator**

The NetWare Administrator utility is undoubtedly the most versatile utility available in NetWare 5.1.

**1.** Log into the tree as Admin, if you haven't already done so.

**2.** Create a shortcut to the NetWare Administrator utility on your desktop.

    **a.** Execute the Windows Explorer utility.

    **b.** Browse to SYS:\PUBLIC\WIN32.

    **c.** Drag NWADMN32.EXE to your desktop.

    **d.** Exit the Windows Explorer utility.

**3.** Execute the NetWare Administrator utility.

    **a.** Execute the NetWare Administrator utility by double-clicking the NWADMN32.EXE shortcut you just created on your desktop.

    **b.** If a Welcome to NetWare Administrator dialog box appears, read the "tip" that is listed and then click Close.

**4.** Set the context for the NetWare Administrator browser screen to the WHITE container.

**a.** Determine the context that is currently set for this browser window. To do so, look to see what container is listed in the top-left corner. For example, if [Root] is at the top, it means that the context is currently set to the [Root].

**b.** Select View ⇨ Set Context.

**c.** Follow these steps when the Set Context dialog box appears:

- In the Tree field, verify that the following container is listed:

  ACME_TREE

- Click the Browse button to the right of the Context field.

**d.** Follow these steps when the Select Object dialog box appears:

- To navigate the tree, double-click a container in the right pane to move down one level in the tree or double-click the up arrow in the right pane to move up one level in the tree. The contents of each container that you select in the right pane will display in the left pane. Practice walking up and down the tree until you feel comfortable with the procedure.

- Next, navigate the tree until the WHITE container is shown in the left pane, and then click it and click OK.

- When the Set Context dialog box reappears, WHITE.CRIME.TOKYO.ACME should be listed in the Context field. (If you had wanted to, you could have manually typed in this context, rather than browsing the tree to find it.)

- Click OK to return to the browser screen.

- When the browser screen reappears, the WHITE container should be displayed in the top-left corner.

**5.** Set the context for the NetWare Administrator browser screen to the [Root].

**a.** A quick way to move up one level in the tree is to use the Backspace key on your keyboard. Press Backspace four times to change the context from the WHITE container to the [Root].

**b.** The [Root] should now be displayed in the top-left corner of the browser.

**6.** Expand or collapse a container object.

    **a.** Follow these steps to expand a container:

- Double-click the container object, *or*

- Click the container object and then select View ⇨ Expand, *or*

- Click the container object and then press the plus sign (+) on the numeric keypad portion of your keyboard.

    **b.** To collapse a container, do as follows:

- Double-click the container object, *or*

- Click the container object and then select View ⇨ Collapse, *or*

- Click the container object and then press the minus sign (-) on the numeric keypad portion of the keyboard.

    **c.** Practice using each of the three methods listed above for expanding containers. Try to determine the type of containers that are contained in each container (if any), as well as the type of leaf objects. Also, practice using each of the three methods previously listed for collapsing containers.

**7.** View the object dialog (for example, details) of a container object.

    **a.** The object enables you to display and edit information relating to an object's properties. When you display the object dialog for a container, you'll notice there is a column of page buttons along the right side of the screen. You can click each button, one at a time, to view the category of information available on that page. Two methods are available for viewing the information relating to a container object:

- Click the container object and then select Object ⇨ Details.

- Right-click the container object and then select Details from the pop-up menu that appears.

**b.** Practice using both of these methods to view the property information that is available for various types of container objects, including the [Root], the ACME Organization object, and the WHITE Organizational Unit object.

**8.** View the object dialog (for example, details) of a leaf object.

　　**a.** Three methods are available for viewing the information relating to a leaf object:

　　　　• Double-click the leaf object, *or*

　　　　• Click the leaf object and then select Object ⇨ Details, *or*

　　　　• Right-click the leaf object and then select Details from the pop-up menu that appears.

　　**b.** Practice using all three of these methods to view the property information that is available for various types of leaf objects in the WHITE container.

**9.** Exit the NetWare Administrator utility.

**Part II: ConsoleOne**

The ConsoleOne utility is a Java utility that can be used to manage NDS objects and their properties. This utility has both a server and a client component. We will use the Client component in this exercise.

**I.** Launch ConsoleOne.

**2.** Set the context for the ConsoleOne browser screen.

　　**a.** Determine the context that is currently set for this ConsoleOne browser window. To do so, look to see what container is listed in the top-left corner of the browser window. For example, if ACME is at the top, it means that the context is set to ACME.

**b.** If the container that you would like to become the new context is currently available in the left pane, right-click the container and then select Set as Root from the pop-up menu that appears.

**c.** If the container that you would like to become the new context is higher in the tree than the current context, double-click the left arrow in the top-left corner of the browser screen, until the desired container appears. (Each time you double-click the arrow, it moves the context up one level in the tree.)

**d.** If you'd like to reset the context to My World, right-click the left-arrow in the top-left corner of the browser screen and then select Show My World from the drop-down menu that appears.

**e.** Practice setting the context to various containers until you are comfortable with the procedure. When you're done, set the context to My World.

**3.** Practice navigating the ConsoleOne browser window.

**a.** If you click a container in the left pane, its contents will appear in the right pane.

**b.** To expand a container in the left pane, you can either double-click the container or click the plus sign (+) to the left of its icon. To collapse an expanded container, double-click the container or click the minus sign (-) to the left of its icon.

**c.** To display the contents of a container that is currently displayed in the right pane, you can either double-click the container in the left pane or in the right pane.

**d.** Practice expanding and collapsing containers in the left pane and displaying the contents of a container selected in the left pane in the right pane until you are comfortable with the procedures.

**4.** View the properties of a container object.

   **a.** When you display the Properties dialog box for a container, you'll notice there is a row of tabs along the top of the screen. You can click each tab, one at a time, to view the category of information available on a particular page. In some cases, if you click a tab, a drop-down menu will appear listing further choices. If so, simply select the desired menu option. Two methods are available for viewing the information relating to a container object:

     • Click the container object and then select File ⇨ Properties.

     • Right-click the container and then select Properties from the pop-up menu that appears.

   **b.** Practice using both of these methods to view the property information that is available for various types of container objects, including the ACME Organization object and the WHITE Organizational Unit object.

**5.** View the properties of a leaf object.

   **a.** Three methods are available for viewing property information for a leaf object:

     • Double-click the leaf object, *or*

     • Click the leaf object and then select File ⇨ Properties, *or*

     • Right-click the leaf object and then select Properties from the pop-up menu that appears.

   **b.** Practice using all three of these methods to view the property information that is available for various types of leaf objects in the WHITE container.

**6.** Exit the ConsoleOne utility.

## LAB EXERCISE 3.4: BUILDING ACME'S NDS TREE

In this exercise, you will begin building the ACME tree structure. Some sections of the tree will be built using NetWare Administrator, while others will be built using ConsoleOne.

To perform this exercise, you will need the following:

▶ A NetWare 5.1 server called WHITE-SRV1.WHITE.CRIME.TOKYO.ACME (which can be installed by using the directions found in Appendix D).

▶ A workstation running the NetWare 5.1 Novell Client for Windows 95/98 or NetWare 5.1 Novell Client for Windows NT/2000 (which can be installed by using the directions found in Lab Exercise 3.1).

In this exercise, you will create Organizational Unit, Template, and User objects for CAMELOT and RIO using the following information:

▶ The Location property for each container or leaf object should always contain the city or location (such as Camelot or Rio). The Department should always be the full name of the container (such as Administration, Financial, Marketing, and so on).

▶ The address, phone, and fax information for the CAMELOT Organizational Unit and its subcontainers is as follows:

London Road
Bracknell, Berkshire RG12 2UY
United Kingdom
Phone: (44 344) 724000
Fax: (44 344) 724001

▶ The address, phone, and fax information for the RIO Organizational Unit and its subcontainers is as follows:

Alameda Ribeirao Preto 130-12 Andar
Sao Paulo 01331-000
Brazil

Phone: (55 11) 253 4866
Fax: (55 11) 285 4847

▶ Each Organizational Unit will have the following Intruder Detection/Lockout limits:

- Incorrect Login Attempts — 5

- Intruder Attempt Reset Interval — 10 days

- Intruder Lockout Reset Interval — 20 minutes

▶ Template objects (and User objects) should contain the following account restrictions, unless otherwise specified:

- Each user will be limited to three concurrent logins.

- Each user will be required to have a unique password consisting of eight characters or more, and will be required to change their password every 60 days. Each user will be allowed six grace logins.

- Each user will be restricted from logging in each day between 3:00 a.m. and 4:00 a.m. (when backups and system maintenance are finished).

Now that you know the plan, let's go ahead and implement it!

**Part I: NetWare Administrator**

**1.** Log into the network as Admin, if you haven't already done so.

**2.** Launch the NetWare Administrator utility.

**3.** Create the CAMELOT Organizational Unit under the ACME Organization.

    **a.** To create the Camelot Organizational Unit, use *one* of the following methods:

- Click ACME and then press Insert, *or*

- Click ACME and then select Object ⇨ Create, *or*

- Right-click ACME and then choose Create from the pop-up menu that appears.

**b.** When the New Object dialog box appears, do as follows:

- Click Organizational Unit.

- Click OK.

**c.** When the Create Organizational Unit dialog box appears, do as follows:

- In the Organizational Unit Name field, enter the following:

  CAMELOT

- Mark the Define Additional Properties check box.

- Click Create.

**d.** Because you marked the Define Additional Properties check box in Step 4c, the Organizational Unit: CAMELOT dialog box appears.

- You'll notice that the Printer Forms (Non NDPS) page button is selected by default.

- Click the Identification page button.

**e.** Follow these steps when the Identification page appears:

- In the Other Name field, enter the following:

  CAMELOT

- In the Location field, enter the following:

  CAMELOT

- In the Telephone field, enter the following:

  44 344 724000

- In the Fax Number field, enter the following:

  44 344 724001

- Click the Postal Address page button.

**f.** When the Postal Address page appears, follow these steps:

- In the Street field, enter the following:

  London Road

- In the City field, enter the following:

  Bracknell

- In the State or Province field, enter the following:

  Berkshire, United Kingdom

- In the Postal (Zip) Code field, enter the following:

  RG12 2UY

- Click the Intruder Detection/Lockout page button

**g.** When the Intruder Detection page appears, follow these steps:

- Mark the Detect Intruders check box.

- In the Incorrect Login Attempts field, replace the default value with the following default value:

  5

- In the Days field in the Intruder Attempt Reset Interval field, replace the default value with the following default value:

  10

- In the Hours field in the Intruder Attempt Reset Interval field, verify that the following value is listed:

  0

- In the Minutes field in the Intruder Attempt Reset Interval field, replace the default value with the following default value:

  0

- Mark the Lock Account after Detection check box.

- In the Days field in the Intruder Lockout Reset Interval field, verify that the following value is listed:

  0

- In the Hours field in the Intruder Lockout Reset Interval field, verify that the following value is listed:

  0

- In the Minutes field in the Intruder Lockout Reset Interval field, replace the default value with the following default value:

  20

- Click OK to save your changes.

4. Create a Template object in the CAMELOT container.

  a. To create a Template object in the CAMELOT Organizational Unit container, use *one* of the following methods:

  - Click CAMELOT and then press Insert, *or*
  - Click CAMELOT and then select Object ⇨ Create, *or*
  - Right-click CAMELOT and then choose Create from the pop-up menu that appears.

  b. When the New Object dialog box appears, follow these steps:

  - Click Template.
  - Click OK.

  c. When the Create Template dialog box appears, follow these steps:

  - In the Template Name field, enter the following:

    CAM-UT

  - Mark the Define Additional Properties check box.
  - Click Create to create the new Template called CAM-UT.

**d.** When the Template: CAM-UT dialog box appears, follow these steps:

- You'll notice that the Identification page button is selected, by default.

- Fill in the same location, telephone, fax, and address information as you did for the CAMELOT Organizational Unit in Step 4d.

- You won't be able to set any Intruder Detection parameters for this User Template, as Intruder Detection parameters are set per container, not per leaf object.

- Click the Login Restrictions page button.

**e.** When the Login Restrictions page appears, follow these steps:

- Mark the Limit Concurrent Connections check box.

- In the Maximum Connections field, replace the default value with the following default value:

  3

- Click the Password Restrictions page button.

**f.** When the Password Restrictions page appears, follow these steps:

- Verify that the Allow User to Change Password check box is marked.

- Mark the Require a Password check box.

- In the Minimum Password Length field, replace the default value with the following default value:

  8

- Mark the Force Periodic Password Changes check box.

- In the Days Between Forced Changes field, replace the default value with the following default value:

  60

- Mark the Require Unique Passwords check box.

- Mark the Limit Grace Logins check box.

- In the Grace Logins Allowed field, verify that the following value is listed:

  6

- Click Set Password After Create.

- Click Login Time Restrictions page button.

**g.** When the Login Time Restrictions page appears, follow these steps:

- A grid will be displayed showing days of the week along the left edge and time of day across the top. Each cell in the grid represents a half-hour period during the week. You'll notice that when you place the mouse cursor in a cell, the day and time represented by that cell is displayed. White (blank) cells represent times during which the user is allowed to log in. Gray cells indicate times that the user is prevented from logging in.

- Click the 3:00 and 3:30 cells for each day of the week. (Alternately, you can drag the cursor to select multiple cells.)

- When you finish updating the Time Restrictions, click OK to save your changes.

**5.** Create the CHARITY Organizational Unit under the CAMELOT container.

  **a.** Use the same methods described in Step 4 to create a CHARITY Organizational Unit under the CAMELOT Organizational Unit.

  **b.** In the appropriate fields enter the department, location, phone, fax, address, and Intruder Detection information listed at the beginning of this exercise.

  **c.** Click OK to save your changes.

**6.** Create a Template object for the CHARITY Organizational Unit. Use the same method described in Step 4 to create a Template for the CHARITY Organizational Unit called CHR-UT. This time, however, we'll save time by copying the properties from the Template you created in the CHARITY Organizational Unit earlier, rather than having to key them in again. Make the following modifications to the directions in Step 4:

   **a.** On the Create Template dialog box, mark the Use Template or User check box instead of the Define Additional Properties check box when you create the Template.

   **b.** Click the Browse button to the right of the Use Template or User field.

   **c.** When the Select Objects screen appears, in the left pane, double-click the CHR-UT User Template object and then click Create.

**7.** Create the SirGalahad User object.

   **a.** To Create the Sir Galahad User object, use *one* of the following methods:

   • Click CHARITY and then press Insert, *or*

   • Click CHARITY and then select the Object ➪ Create, *or*

   • Right-click CHARITY and then choose Create from the pop-up menu that appears.

   **b.** When the New Object dialog box appears, follow these steps:

   • Click User.

   • Click OK.

   **c.** When the Create User dialog box appears, follow these steps:

   • In the Login Name field, enter the following:

   `SirGalahad`

   (**Note:** Login Name is a required property for a User object.)

- In the Last Name field, type the following:

  Galahad

  (Last Name is also a required property for a User object.)

- Mark the Use Template check box.

- Click the Browse button to the right of the Use Template field.

**d.** When the Select Object dialog box appears, follow these steps:

- The CAM-UT Template object appears in the Available Objects pane on the left side of the screen. Double-click this object to select it.

- Normally, you would also create a home directory for this user, but you can't at this time because the CAM-CHR-SRV1 server has not yet been installed.

- Click Create to create this user using the defaults in the CHR-UT template.

**8.** Create the .OPS.CAMELOT.ACME Organizational Unit and then create the following objects under it: the OPS-UT Template object and the KingArthur User Object.

**9.** Create the .PR.CAMELOT.ACME Organizational Unit and then create the following objects under it: the CAM-PR-UT Template object and the CEttelson User object.

**10.** Create the .FIN.OPS.CAMELOT.ACME Organizational Unit and then create the following objects under it: the FIN-UT Template object and the Guinevere User object.

**11.** Create the .DIST.OPS.CAMELOT.ACME Organizational Unit and then create the following objects under it: the DST-UT Template object and the Merlin User object.

**12.** Exit the NetWare Administrator utility.

**Part II: ConsoleOne**

**1.** Execute the ConsoleOne utility.

**2.** Create the RIO Organizational Unit under the ACME Organization.

**a.** In the left pane, browse to the ACME Organization object. When you do so, you'll notice that it appears in the right pane, as well.

**b.** To create the RIO Organizational Unit, use *one* of the following methods:

- In the right pane, click ACME and then select File ⇨ New ⇨ Organizational Unit, *or*

- In the right pane, click ACME and then press Insert, *or*

- In the right pane, right-click ACME and then select New ⇨ Organizational Unit from the pop-up menu that appears.

**c.** If the New Object dialog box appears, follow these steps:

- Select Organizational Unit in the Class list box.

- Click OK.

**d.** When the Organizational Unit dialog box appears, follow these steps:

- In the Organizational Unit Name field, enter the following:

  RIO

- Mark the Define Additional Properties check box.

- Click Create.

**e.** When the Properties of RIO dialog box appears, follow these steps:

- Enter the appropriate department, location, phone, fax, address, and Intruder Detection information indicated at the beginning of this exercise.

- Click OK to save your changes to this Organizational Unit object.

**3.** Create the ADMIN, CHARITY, and PR Organizational Units under the RIO Organizational Unit and then create the AUDIT, FAC, and MRKT Organizational Units under the ADMIN Organizational Unit.

**4.** Create Template objects. Using ConsoleOne, create a Template object for the RIO Organizational Unit. Then, create a separate Template object for the ADMIN, CHARITY, and PR Organizational Units under the RIO Organizational Unit and the AUDIT, FAC, and MRKT Organizational Units under the ADMIN Organizational Unit.

**5.** Create the GWashington User object under the ADMIN.RIO.ACME Organizational Unit object using the Template object in that container.

**6.** Create the SirPercival User object under the CHARITY.RIO.ACME Organizational Unit object using the Template object in that container.

**7.** Create the JHughes User object under the PR.RIO.ACME Organizational Unit object using the Template object in that container.

**8.** Create the ALincoln User object under the AUDIT.ADMIN.RIO.ACME Organizational Unit object using the Template object in that container.

**9.** Create the JMadison User object under the FAC.ADMIN.RIO.ACME Organizational Unit object using the Template object in that container.

**10.** Create the TJefferson User object under the MRKT.ADMIN.RIO.ACME Organizational Unit object using the Template object in that container.

**11.** Modify an NDS User object using ConsoleOne.

    **a.** Navigate to the SirPercival.CHARITY.RIO.ACME object and then right-click it.

    **b.** Select Properties from the pop-up menu that appears.

    **c.** When the Properties of SirPercival window appears, click the triangle on the Restrictions tab and then select Login Restrictions from the drop-down list.

**d.** When the Login Restrictions window appears, follow these steps:

- Mark the Account Has Expiration Date check box.

- Click the Date/Time icon to the right of the Expiration Date and Time field.

**e.** When the Date and Time window appears, change the expiration date to 12:01 a.m. of today's date one year from now. (In other words, if today is December 1, 1999, you would change the expiration date to December 1, 2000, at 12:01 a.m.):

- Select the appropriate year using the up arrow or down arrow to the right of the Year field.

- Use the single arrows and double arrows to the left and right of the Time field to change the time to 12:01 a.m. (Double arrows change the hour; single arrows change the minutes.)

- Click OK to exit the Select Date and Time window.

**f.** When the Properties of SirPercival dialog box reappears, follow these steps:

- Click Apply.

- Click Close.

**12.** If you want to change properties values for multiple users, you can either make the changes manually (which is too much work) or use the Details on Multiple Users feature. In our case, we want to experiment with limiting the users in the RIO branch of the tree to one concurrent connection.

**a.** To select the User objects to be modified, we need to choose *one* of the following methods:

- Shift-click or Ctrl-click multiple objects of the same type, *or*

- Click a Template object to modify its members, *or*

- Click a Group object to modify its members.

**b.** In this case, we'll want to select the RIO Organizational Unit:

- Click the RIO Organizational Unit.
- Select File ⇨ Properties of Multiple Objects.

**c.** When the Properties of Multiple Objects dialog box appears, follow these steps:

- Click User.
- Click OK.

**d.** When the Properties of Multiple Objects dialog box appears, follow these steps:

- The Objects to Modify page will be displayed, by default. Review the User objects listed in the "Changes Will Be Applied to the Following Objects" list box to ensure that they correspond to the users that you created in the previous Steps 5 through 10.
- Select Restrictions ⇨ Login Restrictions.

**e.** When the Login Restrictions page appears, follow these steps:

- Mark the Limit Concurrent Connections check box.
- In the Maximum Connections field, replace the default value with the following:

  1

- Click OK to save your changes.

**13.** Exit the ConsoleOne utility.

## Part III: SPECIAL CASES

Now that you've had an opportunity to build certain sections of the ACME tree, let's explore some of their special conditions. Following is a list of some of ACME's more challenging NDS management requirements. Please help them out.

**1.** ACME needs a site administrator in each location. This will be a revolving position among each of the division heads. For example, the NORAD

administrator (named NORAD-Admin) will have administrative access to
all divisions of NORAD, and the position will alternate among AEinstein,
DClarke, and SirGawain.

2. In addition, all of the site administrators will share a common login script.
It will be a mechanism for global security, drive mappings, and special
messaging.

3. The Human Rights Tracking application is constantly being updated. Can
you think of an easier way to manage its search drive mappings?

4. Also, each of the Human Rights department administrators needs access to
the Human Rights Tracking program. Security could be a problem.

5. All the employees in the Auditing department need easy access to all the
resources in the Financial container for auditing purposes. Also, the
auditors don't want to have to navigate the tree to see them.

6. In addition, the Auditing application is constantly being updated.
Searching drive mapping is becoming a problem.

7. As a matter of fact, the Financial database is due for some major changes,
as well. I see a pattern forming here. Please help us out.

8. The following traveling users need a simpler context for accessing ACME
from distributed locations: AEinstein, DHoliday, and MCurie.

9. Everyone in the Crime Fighting division needs to share a common login
script.

10. Finally, Leonardo daVinci believes in empowering his scientists. After all,
he's a "lab rat," not a bureaucrat. To distribute the administrative load
evenly, he and his scientists take turns managing the R&D department —
each scientist takes the helm for three months out of the year.

## LAB EXERCISE 3.5: CONNECTING TO THE NETWARE 5.1 NETWORK

Circle the 15 connectivity-related terms hidden in this word search puzzle using the hints provided. No punctuation characters (such as blank spaces, hyphens, and so on) should be included. Numbers should always be spelled out.

```
B  U  L  K  L  O  A  D  C  E  L  P  T  M
R  W  O  H  U  C  E  K  L  Q  Y  I  T  M
E  O  G  T  P  I  B  G  R  P  C  N  K  A
A  O  I  F  D  I  S  P  L  A  Y  F  K  P
K  J  N  Z  Z  E  B  K  P  V  M  N  N  D
S  V  S  U  W  D  M  X  Q  L  N  E  E  I
T  H  C  F  I  R  E  P  H  A  S  E  R  S
A  G  R  E  E  T  I  N  G  T  I  M  E  P
T  U  I  S  T  E  N  T  B  Q  X  C  H  L
I  F  P  Q  X  T  C  Y  E  I  M  R  Q  A
O  Z  T  M  A  P  L  O  I  F  D  V  O  Y
N  O  D  E  F  A  U  L  T  M  N  B  A  F
K  P  H  D  U  U  D  I  M  M  G  U  Y  S
Q  J  J  O  J  S  E  W  V  X  S  P  S  R
N  B  A  F  B  E  N  Q  H  C  Q  Q  M  L
```

### Hints

1. Login script command that can be set to allow or to disallow users from pressing Ctrl+C or Ctrl+Break to abort the normal execution of a login script.
2. Utility that enables you to import users from a database application into the NDS tree.
3. Login script command that is similar to the DISPLAY command, except that it filters out formatting codes.
4. Login script command that uses a noisemaker to draw attention to something on the screen or a breach of security.

5. Login script identifier variable that returns a value of "morning," "afternoon," or "evening."
6. Login script command that executes a DOS file written in login script format.
7. Property that may contain search mappings, drive mappings, printer connections, messages, and other commands.
8. Login script command that is used to assign drive pointers.
9. Login script command that can be used to turn on or turn off the displays of drives being mapped.
10. Login script identifier variable that prevents the execution of the Default login script.
11. Login script command that suspends operation of the login script until a key is pressed.
12. Login script command that can be used to add a comment to a login script.
13. Login script identifier variable that displays the workstation connection number.
14. Number of levels deep a login script IF . . . THEN statement can be nested.
15. Login script command that allows you to display information listed in quotation marks.

See Appendix C for answers.

**LAB EXERCISE 3.6: LET ME IN!**

## Across

1. Runs the Novell Client
5. Netscape Navigator, for example
7. Second login script executed
8. Main topic of chapter
10. Java-based NDS manager
11. Physical pathway of network signals
12. Executed if no User login script

## Down

1. Controls the workstation (abbreviation)
2. Operating system core
3. NetWare server program

4. Last login script executed
6. Also known as network board
7. Set of rules
8. First login script executed
9. Physical layout of network

See Appendix C for answers.

# CHAPTER 4

# NetWare 5.1 File System

**A**s we discussed in Chapter 2, the NDS Directory is a database of network resources that is shared by all servers in an NDS tree. Each NetWare 5.1 server, however, maintains its own separate file system that can be used to store shared applications and data files.

As you can see in Figure 4.1, the Directory tree above the NetWare 5.1 server is NDS. It organizes network resources into a logical network hierarchy. The Directory tree below the server is the file system. It organizes network data files into a functional application hierarchy.

▶ · · · · · · · · · · · · · · · · · · · · · · · ◀

FIGURE 4.1

The two NetWare 5.1
Directory trees

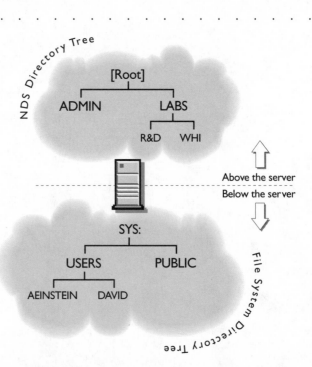

Every NetWare 5.1 file server contains a hierarchical directory structure for storing shared data files and applications called the *file system*. The file system organizes internal disks into one or more volumes. Volumes are then divided into directories that contain subdirectories or files. On the surface it looks a lot like an electronic filing cabinet (see Figure 4.2).

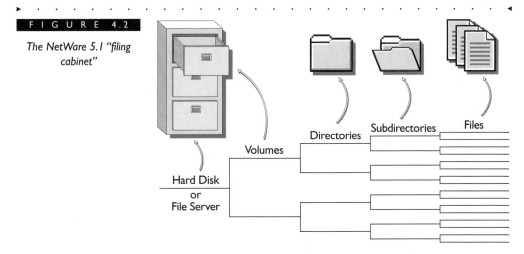

FIGURE 4.2

*The NetWare 5.1 "filing cabinet"*

**TIP**

**In earlier versions of NetWare, the *file system* was referred to as the *directory structure*. In NetWare 5.1, it is referred to as the *file system* to distinguish it from the NDS Directory structure.**

Network administrators are responsible for maintaining the network file system. This involves keeping the file system well organized with adequate storage space and accessible to appropriate network users.

With the above analogy in mind, we're going to explore the three key components of NetWare 5.1's file system: volumes, directories, and files. In the first section, we'll learn a little about the file system architecture and then discover some time-proven strategies for extending beyond the default directory structure. Then, we'll discover a slew of NetWare 5.1 file system utilities and learn how to use them to manage network volumes, directories, and files. Finally, we will study drive mapping—a built-in file system management scheme that enables you (and users) to assign drive letters to network volumes and directories.

Let's begin the adventure with file system design.

# Designing the NetWare 5.1 File System

Each NetWare 5.1 file server contains a hierarchical directory structure for storing shared data files and applications—called the *file system*. The file system organizes server disks into one or more volumes. Volumes are then divided into directories that contain subdirectories and/or files.

In general, you should plan your file system based on the following three goals:

▸ Ease of use

▸ Ease of administration

▸ Ease of file system security enforcement

In this lesson, we will explore guidelines for creating volumes and learn how to build an effective directory structure on top of the system-created file system.

## Understanding Volumes

A volume can be a subdivision of a disk, an entire disk, or can span multiple disks. It is a physical amount of server storage space that is fixed in size. A volume represents the highest level in the NetWare 5.1 file system and is the root of the server directory structure. Each volume also has an associated Volume object in the NDS tree.

The first volume on each NetWare 5.1 server is named SYS:. It is created automatically during NetWare 5.1 installation. You can define up to 63 additional volumes (for a total of 64). Up to eight volumes are allowed per NetWare partition. Because each volume can span up to 32 hard disks, it means a NetWare 5.1 server can support up to 2,048 hard disks. In addition, a volume can support user files up to 2GB long, up to 32TB of total disk space, and as many as 16 million directory entries (if using only the DOS name space).

Because volumes are at the top of the file system tree, they should be planned first. Here are a few guidelines to consider when creating NetWare volumes:

▸ Reserve the SYS: volume for files needed by the NetWare 5.1 operating system. Additional volumes can be created for applications, data files, and print queues.

▸ Create a separate volume for each client operating system that allows long filenames. For example, if you have OS/2, Windows 95/98, or Macintosh users in addition to DOS users, you might want to create separate volumes for OS/2 (which allows filenames up to 255 characters long), Windows 95/98 (which allows filenames up to 255 characters long), and Macintosh files (which allows filenames up to 32 characters long). This is particularly important because it enhances administration, backup procedures, and disk space usage. (**Note:** Name space modules add performance (and table entry) overhead on a volume, so only required ones should be loaded on a particular volume.)

▸ If fault tolerance is more important than performance, create one volume per disk. If performance is more important than fault tolerance, span one NetWare 5.1 volume over multiple hard disks (with one segment of the volume on each hard disk). If fault tolerance and performance are equally important, you can still spread volumes across multiple hard disks, but you should ensure that they are duplexed. (*Duplexing* is a system fault tolerance strategy where all of the data on one hard disk is duplicated on another hard disk on a different channel. If the original hard disk or channel fails, the duplicate takes over automatically.)

▸ Consider using descriptive volume names. For example, application volumes can be named APPS, while data volumes can be called DATA.

NetWare 5.1 volumes are further organized into directories and files. *Directories* are logical volume subdivisions that provide an administrative hierarchy to network applications and data files. *Files* represent the bottom level of the file-server food chain. They can contain valuable system or user data or network applications.

The ultimate goal of the NetWare 5.1 file system is to organize directories and files according to function and security needs. In this lesson, we will start with the system-created directory structure and then expand to include user, configuration, application, and shared data directories.

To accomplish this goal, you must follow specific file syntax and naming rules. As with NDS object naming, filenames define the data's name and location:

```
Server\Volume:Directory\(Subdirectory)\Filename
```

Standard directory names and filenames support eight characters and an optional three-character extension. Special non-DOS filenames can extend as far as 32 characters (Macintosh) or even 255 characters (OS/2 and Windows 95/98).

These non-DOS files require an additional volume feature called *name space*. Also, be sure to support the path conventions of standard or special filenames. NetWare 5.1 allows 255 characters in a directory path (counting the drive letter and delimiters), whereas DOS only allows a maximum of 127 characters.

Refer to Table 4.1 for more NetWare 5.1 file-system naming rules.

| TABLE 4.1 | PATH COMPONENT | RULES |
|---|---|---|
| *NetWare 5.1 Standard File-System Naming Rules* | File Server | Name is limited from 2 to 47 characters. |
| | | First character in name cannot be a period. |
| | | Name cannot contain spaces or special characters such as * + , \ /, : ; = < > [ ]. |
| | Volume | Name length is limited from 2 to 15 characters. |
| | | Physical name must end with a colon (:), which is added automatically. |
| | | First volume on server must be SYS:. |
| | | Two physical volumes on the same server cannot have the same name. |
| | | Name cannot contain spaces or special characters such as * + , \ /, : ; = < > [ ]. |
| | Directory | Name length is limited to a maximum of 11 characters (a directory name consisting of 1 to 8 characters, plus an optional directory name extension of up to 3 characters). |
| | | A period (.) is used to separate the directory name from the (optional) extension. |
| | | Directories should be limited to functional groups. |
| | | Name cannot contain spaces or special characters such as * + , \ /, : ; = < > [ ]. |

| T A B L E   4.1 | PATH COMPONENT | RULES |
|---|---|---|
| *NetWare 5.1 Standard File-System Naming Rules (continued)* | Subdirectory | Name length is limited to a maximum of 11 characters (a directory name consisting of 1 to 8 characters, plus an optional directory name extension of up to 3 characters). |
| | | A period (.) is used to separate the directory name from the (optional) extension. |
| | | Subdirectories share common functionality. |
| | | The size of subdirectories is limited by disk size. |
| | | Name cannot contain spaces or special characters such as * + , \ /, : ; = < > [ ]. |
| | Files | Name length is limited to a maximum of 11 characters (a filename consisting of 1 to 8 characters, plus an optional filename extension of up to 3 characters). |
| | | A period (.) is used to separate the directory name from the (optional) extension. |
| | | Name cannot contain spaces or special characters such as * + , \ /, : ; = < > [ ]. |

Once the volumes are in place, it's time to shift your focus to directories. This is when it gets interesting. Fortunately, NetWare 5.1 gives you a big head start with system-created directories and files.

Let's check them out.

## System-Created Directories

During NetWare 5.1 server installation, a number of system-created directories and files are automatically placed on the SYS: volume. This default directory structure is designed to maintain normal server operations. Therefore, these directories should not be deleted, moved, or renamed.

Following is a brief discussion of some common NetWare 5.1 system-created directories (refer to Figure 4.3). You may find that some of these directories do not exist on your server because they are reserved for special circumstances:

▸ *CDROM$$.ROM* — Contains the index for a mounted CD-ROM.

▸ *DELETED.SAV* — Contains deleted files from removed directories — until the files are salvaged or purged. This directory is only created when needed.

▸ *ETC* — Contains sample files to aid network administrators in configuring the server for TCP/IP protocols.

▸ *JAVA* — Contains Java programming support files.

▸ *JAVASAVE* — Contains configuration files used for Java programming.

▸ *LIB* — Contains a Structured Query Language (SQL) Connector Manager INI file

▸ *LICENSE* — Contains license-related files.

▸ *LOGIN* — Contains utilities such as LOGIN.EXE, CX.EXE, and MAP.EXE. (**Note:** LOGIN is the only directory available to users prior to login.)

▸ *MAIL* — May (or may not) contain subdirectories or files. If you upgrade your server from a previous version of NetWare, this directory may contain user-specific system configuration files — such as bindery login scripts (LOGIN) and queue-based print job configurations (PRINTCON.DAT). In NetWare 5.1, such items are stored as properties of each User object, rather than as separate files.

▸ *NDPS* — Contains administration and support files for Novell Distributed Print Services (NDPS).

▸ *NETBASIC* — Contains NetBasic programming support files and sample templates.

- *NI* — Contains NetWare installation files.

- *NOVONYX* — Contains various web server installation and execution files.

- *NSN* — Contains Novell Script for NetWare files.

- *ODBC* — Contains ODBC.INI files and a driver.

- *PERL* — Contains PERL script-related support files and sample templates.

- *PUBLIC* — Contains general user commands and utilities. By default, all users in a server's home container have access to PUBLIC — but only after they've logged in.

- *PVSW* — Contains client and license files.

- *QUEUES* — Contains one B9830000.QDR directory, by default. This directory provides backward-compatibility for QMS support in NDPS.

- *README* — Contains simple documentation in the form of various README files.

- *SENLM* — Contains NetWare-specific Application Program Interfaces (APIs) and NLM files.

- *SYSTEM* — Contains special administrative tools and utilities, including operating system files, NetWare Loadable Modules (NLMs), and NDS maintenance programs. For this reason, access to the SYSTEM directory should be limited to centralized and distributed administrators only.

- *TMP* — May not (or may) appear as a temporary directory. Created, as needed, by the system.

- *UCS* — Contains various NLMs for UCS support. UCS stands for Universal Component System. It provides developers with networking programming tools.

▶ · · · · · · · · · · · · · · · · · · · · · · · ◀

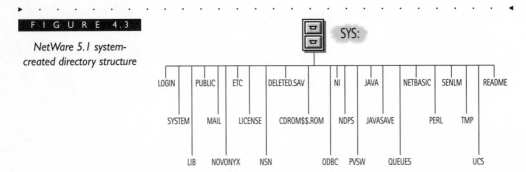

F I G U R E   4.3

*NetWare 5.1 system-created directory structure*

This completes our brief pilgrimage through the NetWare 5.1 system-created directory structure. Be sure that you do not accidentally delete, move, or rename any of these system-created directories—especially LOGIN, SYSTEM, PUBLIC, and MAIL. Next, let's expand our horizons beyond the default directory structure and explore the land of additional directories. You'll be amazed at what you can find there.

## Expanding Beyond the Default Directory Structure

The system-created directory structure provides an excellent foundation for your file system tree. The next step is to add custom user, configuration, application, and data directories (refer to Figure 4.4):

▶ *Home directories* — Each user should be given a private, secure home directory under a parent directory, such as DATA:USERS. Home directories serve two functions: security and organization. From a security viewpoint, they provide a secure place for private user files, where a user can create, delete, modify, move, and copy their own documents. From an organizational viewpoint, home directories become the parent of a complex user-specific directory structure. Each user's home directory name should exactly match their login name.

▶ *Configuration directories* — A server's NetWare file system should support two types of configuration files: application and user. Application-specific configuration files (such as style sheets) should be placed in a CONFIG directory under the application directory. User-specific configurations (such as ZENworks Profiles and interface files) should be placed in user home directories.

▶ *Application directories* — A subdirectory structure should be created under a directory such as DATA:APPS for each network application. For security's sake, restrict this structure to application program files only (that is, those with a .EXE, .BAT, or .COM extension). Users can store their data in home directories, group areas, or a directory such as DATA:SHARED.

▶ *Shared data directories* — The proper organization of network data (or lack thereof) strongly impacts user productivity. Your file system should support three types of data: personal data should be stored in user home directories; group-specific data should be stored in group directories under a directory such as DATA:SHARED; and globally shared data should be stored in a shared parent directory such as DATA:SHARED.

▶ · · · · · · · · · · · · · · · · · · · · · · · · · · · ◀

**FIGURE 4.4**

*Beyond the default directory structure*

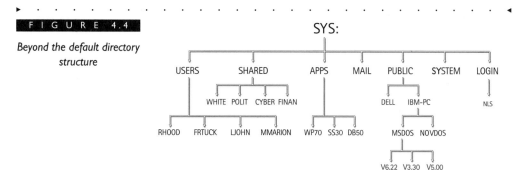

That's the NetWare 5.1 file system. So, the only question that remains is, *"What should it look like?"* You have two choices: flat or deep. Check them out.

## Directory Structure Design Scenarios

The design of a server's directory structure will vary, depending on individual and organizational needs. You can either create a flat tree with many directories stored off the root of the volume, or you can have a deep directory structure with many levels of subdirectories. As you can see in Figure 4.5, there are two primary directory structure design scenarios:

▶ Flat directory structure

▶ Deep directory structure

Let's compare and contrast them.

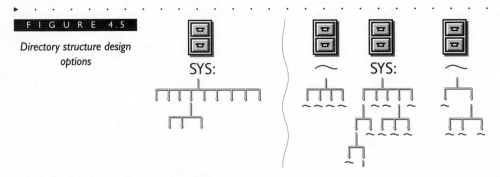

**FIGURE 4.5**

*Directory structure design options*

### Flat Directory Structure

The flat directory structure in Figure 4.6 uses a single volume and is appropriate for a small company with few users.

On the upside, this design limits file storage to a single volume, with short path names. Application programs are separated from data files. File storage has no limitations, except for the physical size of the hard disk.

On the downside, the SYS: volume shares its space with all application and data directories. Home directories are located in the root of the volume with no shared data area. This means there is no mechanism to prevent the server from crashing, if, for example, user data files exceed the hard disk size.

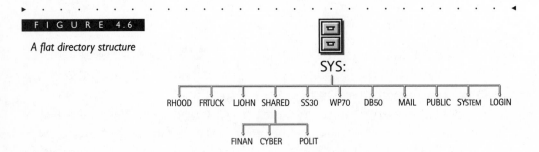

**FIGURE 4.6**

*A flat directory structure*

### Deep Directory Structure

A deep directory structure relies on multiple volumes. In this scenario (refer to Figure 4.7), the system-created directories and applications share SYS:, with other components having their own volumes.

On the upside, the SYS: volume is more stable because files are not added or deleted very often. You can also use a different file system administrator for each volume, if desired.

On the downside, it is harder to manage file system rights when users, applications, and shared files are on different volumes. Also, you may run out of room on a given volume, even though you have sufficient total disk space on the server.

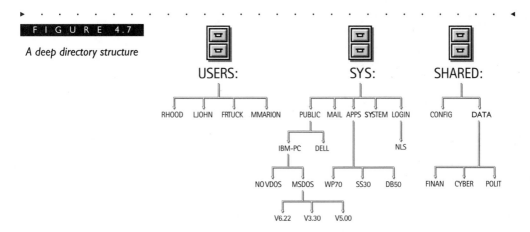

**F I G U R E   4.7**

*A deep directory structure*

This completes our jaunt through NetWare 5.1 file system design. Now we will continue this chapter with a detailed lesson in NetWare 5.1 file management tools. In the next section, we will explore all the file system utilities that apply to NetWare 5.1 and provide some examples of how they can be used to simplify your life.

So, without further ado, let's build a NetWare 5.1 file system tool belt.

## LAB EXERCISE 4.1: DESIGNING A DIRECTORY STRUCTURE FOR ACME

You're ready to create the initial file-system directory structure for the WHITE-SRV1 server. Using the scenario listed here, design the directory structure on paper first and then use ConsoleOne to create the directory structure for your ACME system.

To perform this exercise, you will need the following:

▸ A NetWare 5.1 server called WHITE-SRV1.WHITE.CRIME.TOKYO.ACME (which can be installed using the directions found in Appendix D).

▸ A workstation running either the NetWare 5.1 Novell Client for Windows 95/98 or NetWare 5.1 Novell Client for Windows NT/2000 (which can be installed using the directions found in Lab Exercise 3.1).

Initially, the Crime Fighting division, the White-Collar Crime department, and the three White-Collar Crime units (Cyber Crime, Financial Crime, and Political Crime) will all share the same server (WHITE-SRV1.WHITE.CRIME.TOKYO. ACME). Although there will be some sharing of programs and data, each group will essentially function as an independent workgroup with a separate network administrator.

Because the WHITE-SRV1 server has already been installed, the system-created LOGIN, SYSTEM, PUBLIC, MAIL, and ETC directories already exist.

The USERS directory should be created in the root of the volume. Under this directory, each workgroup will have a parent directory for its home directories (called CRIME, WHITE, CYBER, FIN, and POL, respectively). The home directories themselves will be created when you actually create the users at a later time.

Each of the workgroups will have access to the SHARED directory, which will be located in the root of the volume. This directory will be used for the sharing of files between workgroups. In addition, each workgroup will have exclusive access to its own group directory under the SHARED directory (called CRIME, WHITE, CYBER, FIN, and POL, respectively).

The first three applications that will be installed on the server include the following:

- ▸ A word processing application (in the WP70 directory)

- ▸ A spreadsheet application (in the SS30 directory)

- ▸ A database application (in the DB50 directory)

Each of these subdirectories will be stored under the APPS directory, which will be located in the root of the volume.

Now, let's implement your new structure:

**1.** Log in as Admin, if you haven't already done so.

**2.** Launch the ConsoleOne utility.

**3.** Create the APPS, SHARED, and USERS directories.

    **a.** In the left pane, browse to and click the WHITE-SRV1_SYS volume.

    **b.** Press Insert or select File ➪ New ➪ Object.

    **c.** When the New object dialog box appears, ensure that Directory is selected, and then click OK.

    **d.** Follow these steps when the New Directory dialog box appears:

        • In the Name field, type the following:

        APPS

        • Mark the Create Another Directory check box

        • Click OK.

    **e.** Follow these steps when the New Directory dialog box appears:

        • In the Name field, type the following:

        SHARED

- Verify that the Create Another Directory check box is marked.

- Click OK.

  **f.** Follow these steps when the New Directory dialog box appears:

  - In the Name field, type the following:

    USERS

  - Unmark the Create Another Directory check box.

  - Click OK.

**4.** Create the subdirectories under the APPS directory.

  **a.** Using the method of your choice, create the DB50, SS30, and WP70 subdirectories under the APPS directory.

**5.** Create the subdirectories under the SHARED directory.

  **a.** Using the method of your choice, create the CRIME, WHITE, CYBER, FIN, and POL subdirectories under the SHARED directory.

**6.** Create the subdirectories under the USERS directory.

  **a.** Using the method of your choice, create the CRIME, WHITE, CYBER, FIN, and POL subdirectories under the USERS directory.

**7.** Exit ConsoleOne.

# File System Utilities

As a network administrator, you are responsible for maintaining the server's file system on a day-to-day basis. This involves ensuring that the file system is well-organized, easily accessible to network users, and contains adequate storage space. These responsibilities include three basic skills:

- Managing volume space

- Managing directories and subdirectories

- Managing files

NetWare 5.1, Windows 95/98, and Windows NT/2000 each ship with utilities that can be used for performing file system management tasks. Because the NetWare file system emulates the Windows file structure, you'll find that you can use many of the same tools and techniques for managing both network and workstation file systems—assuming, of course, that the Novell Client software is installed on each workstation. For example, you can use Windows Explorer (and, to a limited extent, Windows Network Neighborhood) to access and manage the NetWare file system. You can also use DOS commands, although you may find that they offer limited functionality.

NetWare 5.1 offers a number of file system utilities, including the following:

- NetWare Administrator

- ConsoleOne

- FILER

- NDIR

- NCOPY

- FLAG

- RENDIR

Of the file system tools listed, you'll find that NetWare Administrator, ConsoleOne, and FILER allow you to perform the broadest range of file management tasks.

**Although the courseware mentions the RENDIR command found in earlier versions of NetWare, you'll probably find that it is not available on your server.**

**TIP**

## NetWare Administrator

NetWare Administrator is the most versatile of the NetWare 5.1 file management utilities. It runs under Windows 95/98 and Windows NT/2000 and enables you to create, delete, rename, copy, and/or move directories and files. In addition, NetWare Administrator can be used to grant trustee rights, modify Inherited Rights Filters (IRFs), determine effective rights, and assign directory/file attributes. NetWare Administrator also allows you to view and/or manage a variety of volume statistics, as well as salvage and purge deleted files.

Following is a summary of the file system management capabilities provided by NetWare Administrator:

▶ Create, move, delete, and rename directories

▶ Copy, move, and delete entire subdirectory structures

▶ View or change directory information, such as owner, attributes, trustees, Inherited Rights Filter, or space limitations

▶ Set up search and view filters (include and exclude options)

▶ Mark multiple files for copying, moving, and deleting

▶ Manage file compression and data migration

▶ Salvage and purge files

Now, let's take a closer look at how you can use NetWare Administrator to manage NetWare 5.1 volumes, directories, and files.

**Managing Volumes with NetWare Administrator**

The NetWare Administrator utility treats file system volumes as NDS objects. As you can see in Figure 4.8, NetWare Administrator includes the following configuration pages (on the right side of the screen) for Volume objects:

▸ Identification

▸ Statistics

▸ Dates and Times

▸ User Space Limits

▸ Trustees of the Root Directory

▸ Attributes

▸ See Also

▸ Security Equal to Me

To display volume information using NetWare Administrator, walk the tree until you find your desired volume — in our case it's .CN=WHITE-SRV1_SYS.OU= WHITE.OU=CRIME.OU=TOKYO.O=ACME. When you view Details about a volume, the Identification page is displayed by default. As you can see in Figure 4.8, the Identification page includes information such as volume name, host server, NetWare 5.1 version, host volume, and location.

The Statistics page is the really interesting NetWare Administrator volume page (see Figure 4.9). It displays statistical information including the volume type (non-removable), available disk space, deleted files, compressed files, block size, installed name spaces, and installed volume optimization features (such as block suballocation, file compression, and data migration). Colorful pie charts are also displayed, showing the percentage of disk space and directory entries used.

Identification page for
volumes in NetWare
Administrator

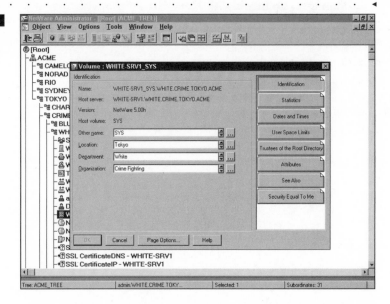

Statistics page for volumes
in NetWare Administrator

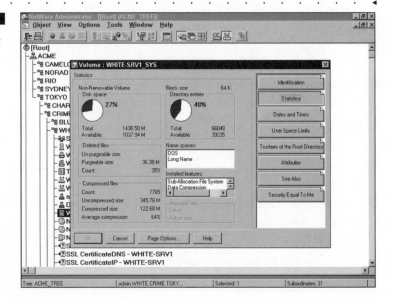

As you can see in Figure 4.10, NetWare 5.1 enables you to restrict the amount of disk space each user can use on a volume via the User Space Limits page. You can also use this same screen to track the amount of space any particular user has available.

FIGURE 4.10

Setting User Space Limits in
NetWare Administrator

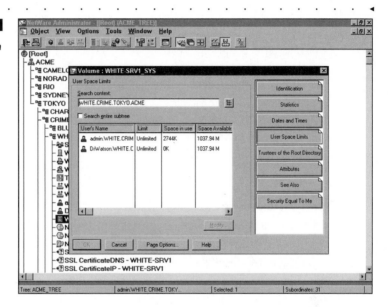

**TIP**

**Volume space usage is tracked by file *ownership*. This means that users are charged for disk space whenever they copy or create a file on the host volume. If users are continually running out of space, they may be getting charged for ownership of files they don't actually "own." To solve this problem, consider using NetWare Administrator to change the Ownership property of certain files to Admin or some other unrestricted user.**

In addition to Identification, Statistics, and User Space Limits, NetWare Administrator provides a few other volume-related page buttons:

▶ *Dates and Times* — Displays values for the volume creation date and time, owner, last modified date and time, last archived date and time, and "user last archived by." The latter options offer valuable information for managing data backup.

▸ *Trustees of the Root Directory* — Displays security information concerning the trustees of the root directory, their effective rights, and the directory's Inheritance Filter. You should be careful about who gets access rights to the root directory of any volume — especially SYS:. We'll learn more about this in Chapter 5.

▸ *Attributes* — Displays directory attributes for the root directory of the given volume. This is another security option that will be discussed in Chapter 5.

▸ *See Also* — Displays who and what is related to this Volume object. It is basically a manual information record for tracking special volume details.

▸ *Security Equal to Me* — Lists the users who are security equivalent to this object.

### Managing Directories with NetWare Administrator

In order to manage NetWare 5.1 directories with NetWare Administrator, you must first click the desired directory and then click the Object menu. If you look at the options in the Object menu, you'll notice that you can perform the following file management tasks: create, delete, rename, copy, and/or move a directory.

You can also select the Details option to view information about the directory. If you then select the Facts page button, as shown in Figure 4.11, another screen appears with more detailed directory information, including the owner, the directory creation date/time, the last modified date/time, the last archived date/time, and the archiver. It also lists the volume space available to this directory and the disk space restrictions — if any.

### Managing Files with NetWare Administrator

NetWare Administrator also enables you to perform a variety of useful file management tasks. First of all, walk the tree until the desired file is in view. Click the file and then click the Object menu. If you look at the options in the Object menu, you'll notice file management options that enable you to delete the file, rename it, copy it, or move it. The same options can be accessed from the Details menu by highlighting the file and right-clicking the mouse.

FIGURE 4.11

*Facts page for directories in NetWare Administrator*

If you select the Facts page button, a screen appears with the size, file creation date/time, file's owner, last modified date/time, modifier, last accessed date, last archived date, and archiver (see Figure 4.12). If you have the appropriate rights, you can modify all of these parameters, except for the size and creation date.

FIGURE 4.12

*Facts page for files in NetWare Administrator*

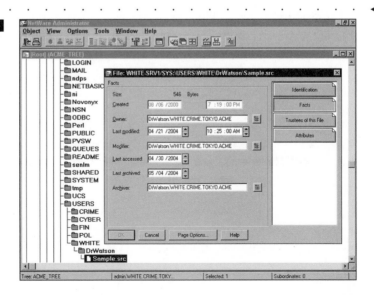

That's enough of NetWare Administrator for now. We'll explore some more advanced file-system management tasks in the next section. Now, for something completely different. Let's explore the Java-based workstation and server tool—ConsoleOne.

### REAL WORLD

Using NetWare Administrator, practice browsing the Directory tree to locate individual volumes, directories, and files—and to view their properties. Next, in NetWare Administrator, practice searching for Volume objects using the Object ⇨ Search feature and for volumes, directories, and files using the little-known GOTO feature. (To see how the GOTO feature works, be sure the item you want to select is currently displayed onscreen, and then simply start typing the name of the volume, directory, or file, and see what happens.) Finally, as you read through each section in this study session, try to perform the tasks described.

## ConsoleOne

The Java-based ConsoleOne tool enables you to manage the NetWare 5.1 file system using The Network object under the My World link (refer to Figure 4.13). This tool supports both traditional NetWare volumes, as well as new Novell Storage Services (NSS) volumes. ConsoleOne enables you to create, delete, rename, copy, and/or move directories and files. You can also grant trustee rights, modify Inherited Rights Filters (IRFs), determine effective rights, and view volume usage statistics.

**ConsoleOne does not currently allow you to salvage or purge deleted files. These tasks are reserved for NetWare Administrator and selected text-based utilities. See Table 4.3 later for more information.**

**TIP**

Now, let's take a closer look at how you can use ConsoleOne to manage NetWare 5.1 volumes, directories, and files.

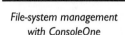

FIGURE 4.13

*File-system management with ConsoleOne*

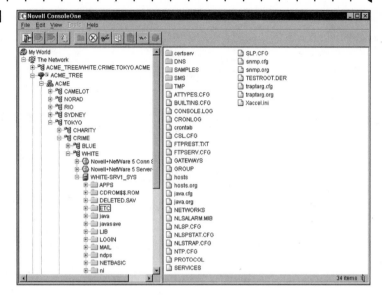

## Managing Volumes with ConsoleOne

ConsoleOne allows you to view volume statistics through the Volume object properties screen. As you can see in Figure 4.14, the Statistics page includes volume information such as the following

- ▸ Volume name (WHITE_SRV1_SYS in Figure 4.14)

- ▸ Total volume size

- ▸ Name space status (installed)

- ▸ Compression statistics

- ▸ Deleted file information

- ▸ Block size

FIGURE 4.14

*Volume Statistics page in ConsoleOne*

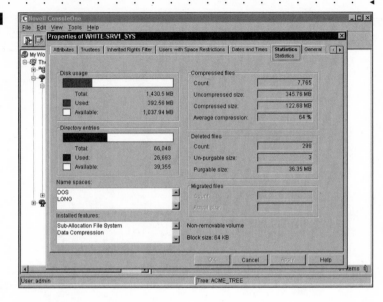

## Managing Directories with ConsoleOne

You can also use ConsoleOne to view the contents of a directory, or information regarding the directory. As you can see in Figure 4.15, the directory Facts page includes the following directory-specific information:

- ► Directory name and extension

- ► Date/time created and Owner name

- ► Modified and archived information

- ► Folder size restriction information

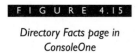

*Directory Facts page in ConsoleOne*

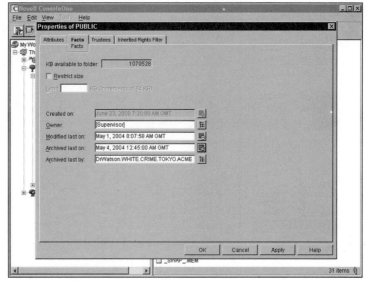

### Managing Files with ConsoleOne

Finally, ConsoleOne allows you to view creation and ownership information regarding NetWare 5.1 data and program files. As you can see in Figure 4.16, the file Facts page displays information such as the following:

- ▶ Filename, including extension

- ▶ File size and Owner name

- ▶ File date and time information, including date/time created, data/time last modified, and date/time last accessed.

- ▶ Archiver

This completes our brief lesson in file system management with ConsoleOne. We'll explore some more advanced file system management tasks in the next section. Now, let's leave the graphical world and explore some text-based utilities. Yes, they still exist!

▶ · · · · · · · · · · · · · · · · · · · · · · · · · ◀

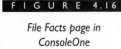

F I G U R E   4.16

*File Facts page in
ConsoleOne*

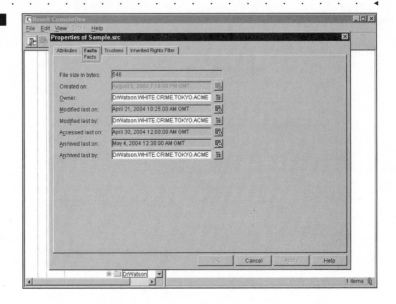

## FILER

FILER is a text-based (menu) utility that runs at the DOS prompt. It can be used to perform many of the same file management tasks as NetWare Administrator and ConsoleOne. As you can see in Figure 4.17, FILER includes menu choices for managing files and directories, and viewing volume information. In addition, it provides salvaging, purging, and searching options.

▶ · · · · · · · · · · · · · · · · · · · · · · · · · ◀

F I G U R E   4.17

*Available Options menu
in FILER*

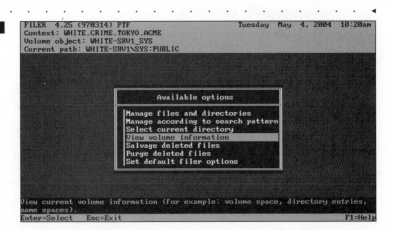

## NDIR

NDIR is a command-line utility that runs at the DOS prompt. It can be used to display volume information such as volume space usage, maximum directory entries, available directory entries, compression statistics, and name spaces loaded. It can also be used to view a variety of directory and/or file information such as owner, creation date, archive information, IRF, effective rights, and attributes.

Table 4.2 lists some of the most common NDIR commands. Know them well.

| T A B L E  4.2 | COMMAND | RESULT |
|---|---|---|
| *Common NDIR Commands* | NDIR | Displays subdirectories and files in the current directory |
| | NDIR *.BAT /FO | Displays files only in the current directory with an extension of .BAT |
| | NDIR \MAP.EXE /SUB /FO | Displays all occurrences of the MAP.EXE file, starting the search at the root of the volume |
| | NDIR /VOL <br> NDIR /VOLUME | Displays volume information |
| | NDIR /DO /SUB <br> NDIR /DO /S | Displays directories and subdirectories in the current directory and below |
| | NDIR *.* /FO /C | Displays the files in the current directory — scrolling continuously while displaying the list |
| | NDIR *.* /ACCESS BEF 01-01-00 <br> NDIR *.* /AC BEF 01-01-00 | Displays all files in the current directory that were last accessed before the new millennium |
| | NDIR /FO /SORT UP | Displays files only in the current directory — sorted by last modified date |
| | NDIR /FO /SORT OW | Displays files only in the current directory — sorted by owner |

*Continued*

| TABLE 4.2 | COMMAND | RESULT |
|---|---|---|
| Common NDIR Commands (continued) | NDIR *.* /FO /REV SORT SIZE | Displays files in the current directory, sorted in reverse order by size (from largest to smallest) |
| | NDIR *.* /OWNER EQ DClarke | Displays subdirectories and files in the current directory owned by DClarke |
| | NDIR R*.* /SIZE GR 1000000 | Displays files and subdirectories in the current directory whose filenames begin with R and that exceed 1MB in size |
| | NDIR /SPA | Displays space limitations for the current directory |
| | NDIR /? | Displays help information for the NDIR command |

## NCOPY

NCOPY is a command-line utility that offers similar functionality to the DOS XCOPY command. NCOPY enables you to copy network directories and files from one location to another. For example, the following command copies the 2000 directory on the G: drive (as well as its subdirectories and their files—including empty subdirectories) to an ARCHIVE directory under the current directory's parent directory:

```
NCOPY G:2000 ..\ARCHIVE /S /E
```

## FLAG

FLAG is a command-line utility that enables you to view or modify directory and file attributes. In addition, it enables you to modify the ownership of a directory or file and to view or modify the search mode of executable files.

For example, the following command sets the Immediate Compress (IC) attribute for all files in the current directory:

```
FLAG *.* +IC
```

### Windows 95/98

As we discussed earlier, if the Novell Client software is installed on your workstation, you can use Windows utilities to perform file management tasks in the NetWare 5.1 file system. Windows Explorer (and, to a more limited extent, Windows Network Neighborhood) can be used to perform many of the same file management tasks as NetWare Administrator and ConsoleOne.

For example, the Network Neighborhood NetWare Info screen (shown in Figure 4.18) allows you to view typical network file system information such as owner, space restriction (if any), creation date/time, modification date/time, archive date/time, and attributes. To do so, simply right-click a volume, directory, or file and click Properties.

▶ · · · · · · · · · · · · · · · · · · · · · · · · · ◀

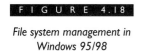

F I G U R E   4 . 1 8

*File system management in Windows 95/98*

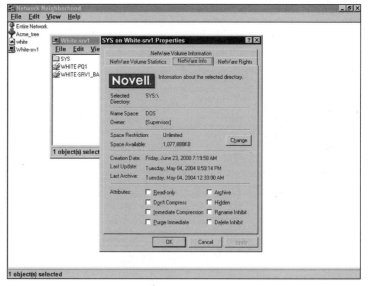

### Using the Correct Utility

As a network administrator, you are responsible for setting up and managing the network directory structure on each volume. Table 4.3 lists a variety of important directory management tasks and the NetWare 5.1 utilities you can use to perform them.

TABLE 4.3

*NetWare 5.1 File
Management Utilities
Summary*

| MANAGEMENT OBJECT | MANAGEMENT TASK | MANAGEMENT UTILITY |
|---|---|---|
| Managing Volumes | Display volume space usage | NetWare Administrator<br>ConsoleOne<br>FILER<br>NDIR |
| | Display the name spaces loaded on a NetWare 5.1 volume | NetWare Administrator<br>ConsoleOne<br>FILER<br>NDIR |
| | Manage file compression | NetWare Administrator<br>ConsoleOne (View Only)<br>FILER<br>NDIR (View Only) |
| | Manage data-migration attributes | NetWare Administrator<br>ConsoleOne<br>FLAG |
| Managing Directories | View directory information such as creation date, last access date, owner, and security attributes | NetWare Administrator<br>ConsoleOne<br>FILER<br>NDIR |
| | Modify directory information such as creation date, last access date, owner, and security attributes | NetWare Administrator<br>ConsoleOne<br>FILER |
| | Create, rename, and move a directory | NetWare Administrator<br>ConsoleOne<br>FILER |
| | Remove a directory and its contents, including subdirectories | NetWare Administrator<br>ConsoleOne<br>FILER |
| | Remove multiple directories simultaneously | NetWare Administrator<br>ConsoleOne<br>FILER |

**TABLE 4.3**

*NetWare 5.1 File
Management Utilities
Summary (continued)*

| MANAGEMENT OBJECT | MANAGEMENT TASK | MANAGEMENT UTILITY |
|---|---|---|
| Managing Directories (continued) | Copy a directory structure (while maintaining all NetWare 5.1 information) | NetWare Administrator ConsoleOne FILER NCOPY |
| | Move an entire directory structure (while maintaining allNetWare 5.1 information) | NetWare Administrator ConsoleOne FILER |
| Managing Files | View file information such as creation date, last access date, owner, and security attributes | NetWare Administrator ConsoleOne FILER NDIR |
| | Modify file information such as creation date, last access date, owner, and security attributes | NetWare Administrator ConsoleOne FILER |
| | Copy files (and preserve NetWare 5.1 attributes) | NetWare Administrator ConsoleOne FILER NCOPY |
| | Salvage deleted files | NetWare Administrator FILER |
| | Purge deleted files | NetWare Administrator FILER PURGE.EXE |
| | Set a file or directory to "Purge Upon Deletion" | NetWare Administrator FILER FLAG |

Well, there you have it — the wonderful collection of NetWare 5.1 file system utilities. In this section, we focused on the three main components of the NetWare 5.1 file system — volumes, directories, and files. We discovered a variety of tools and learned how they help us manage each of these components. See Table 4.3 for a summary.

The important thing is to focus on the file system, not the tool — a unique, but effective approach. Speaking of which, let's explore some common file-system management tasks. And remember to bring your tool belt with you!

# File System Management

Now that you understand the capabilities of each NetWare 5.1 file-system management tool, it's time to put that knowledge to the test. Most NetWare 5.1 file-system management tasks focus on volume space usage and security. Specifically, NetWare 5.1 network administrators must be able to do the following:

- View volume space usage information — including locating files by their access date, ownership, and/or size

- Restrict volume space

- Change file and/or directory ownership

- Copy, salvage, and/or purge files

- Optimize volume space — including setting file compression, block suballocation, and/or file migration attributes

Let's take a closer look.

## Viewing Volume Space Usage Information

Ensuring sufficient available volume space is critical in maintaining an efficient NetWare 5.1 file system. Therefore, you'll want to track volume space utilization using NetWare Administrator, ConsoleOne, FILER, and/or NDIR.

In ConsoleOne, volume space usage information is tracked as a property of the Volume object. You can view information such as available disk space, directory entries, installed name spaces, installed features, compressed files, and deleted files (see Figure 4.19).

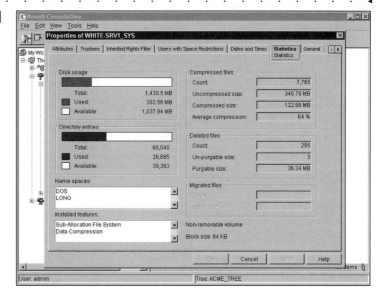

FIGURE 4.19

*Volume space usage information in ConsoleOne*

## Restricting Volume Space

If disk space becomes a scarce commodity, consider removing files that have not been used in a while. You may also want to consider tracking files by size and ownership. Obviously, large files owned by deleted users are often attractive candidates for archiving or deletion.

A common method of managing volume space is to restrict volume space usage. NetWare 5.1 enables you to restrict volume space according to two criteria:

▶ *By user* — User space restrictions must be set independently for each volume. To do so using ConsoleOne, right-click the volume on the browser screen and then select Properties from the pop-up menu that appears. When the Properties dialog box appears, click the Users with Space Restrictions page tab. When the Users with Space Restrictions page appears, click Add. When the Select Object dialog box appears, browse to and select the context containing the user, select the user, and then click OK. When the User Space Restriction dialog box appears, make sure the User Space Limit check box is marked, enter the correct size in the Space Limit (in KB) field, and then click OK. Finally, click OK or Apply in order to save the space restriction.

▶ *By directory* — Any space limitation set for a directory also affects the space available for files in the directory and its subdirectories. To limit the total size of a directory, modify the Restrict Size property of the directory using either ConsoleOne (see Figure 4.20), NetWare Administrator, or FILER. To do so using ConsoleOne, click the directory on the browser screen to highlight it and select File ⇨ Properties. When the Properties dialog box appears, click the Facts page tab. When the Facts page appears, mark the Restrict size check box and then enter the correct size in the Limit KB (increments of 64KB) field. Finally, click OK or Apply in order to save the space restriction.

**F I G U R E   4.20**

*Volume space usage information in ConsoleOne*

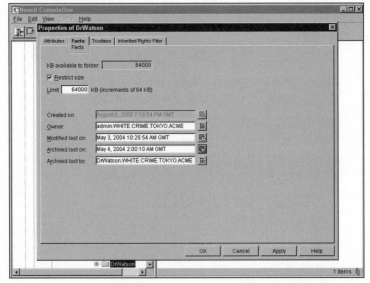

**Keep in mind that user volume space restrictions override directory restrictions.**

TIP

## Changing File and/or Directory Ownership

Volume space usage is tracked by file *ownership*. A user is designated as the owner of a file when he or she creates it. If users are continuously running out of space, you may find that they are being charged for files that they are listed as the owner of, but are not responsible for. If this is the case, you can use NetWare Administrator, ConsoleOne, or FILER to change the Owner property of each file to the appropriate user. In NetWare Administrator, double-click the file in the browser window, click the Facts page tab, and then change the object listed in the Owner field.

## Copying, Salvaging, and/or Purging Files

You can use any utility, such as Windows Explorer or the DOS COPY command, to copy directories and files from one location to another. However, copying files with NetWare Administrator, ConsoleOne, FILER, or NCOPY enables you to do the following:

▶ Copy an entire directory structure

▶ Copy NetWare 5.1's extended file information

▶ Verify that the copy procedure was executed accurately

▶ Copy files using either a logical Volume object name or a physical volume name

Once files have been deleted, they can be salvaged using NetWare Administrator, FILER, or Windows Explorer (assuming, of course, that they have not yet been purged). To salvage a file, you must have the Read and File Scan rights to the file and the Create right to the directory. The good news is that the salvaged file will retain all of its original trustee rights and extended attributes.

The NetWare Administrator Salvage menu (shown in Figure 4.21) provides three choices:

▶ Include pattern using wildcards or filenames

▶ Sort options (deletion date, deletor, filename, file size, or file type)

▶ Source (current directory or deleted directories)

When all the options are set correctly, click the List button to list the files indicated. As with any Windows 95/98-based utility, you have a variety of options for selecting a desired object. First, you can select a single file by clicking it. Or you can select sequentially listed files by clicking the first file, holding down Shift, and then clicking the last file in the range. And finally, you can select nonsequentially listed files by holding down Ctrl while selecting files.

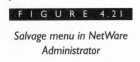

F I G U R E   4.21

Salvage menu in NetWare Administrator

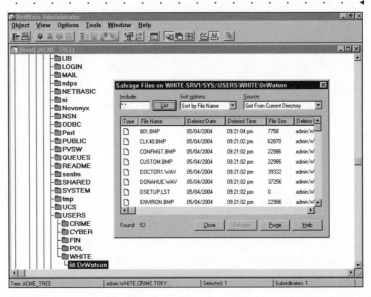

When you have selected all the desired files, you can click either the Salvage or Purge button at the bottom of the screen to salvage or purge the selected file(s). If salvaged, the NetWare 5.1 files will be restored with their original trustee rights and extended attributes intact. If you choose to purge the files, they will not be available for salvaging at a later date. However, if you leave the files alone, NetWare will purge them by itself when the volume gets low on space — on a first-in, first-out basis.

Salvageable files are normally saved in their parent directory (that is, the directory from which they were deleted). If the parent directory is deleted, then salvageable files are stored in the DELETED.SAV directory located in the volume's root directory.

As we discussed earlier, deleted files are available for salvaging until they are *purged*. Files can be purged manually or automatically. One of the ways files can be purged automatically is by using server SET parameters. Typically, NetWare will purge old files when a volume gets low on disk space — on a first-in, first-out basis. A file is also deleted automatically if the file (or its parent directory) is assigned the Purge Immediate (P) attribute using NetWare Administrator, ConsoleOne, FILER, or FLAG. If so, the file is purged upon deletion. This strategy is useful for confidential files, print queues, or to free large, contiguous blocks of space.

Deleted files can also be purged manually using NetWare Administrator, FILER, PURGE.EXE, or Windows Explorer. If you don't have the Supervisor file system right, however, you can only purge files that you own.

## Optimizing Volume Space

One of NetWare 5.1's key benefits is enhanced filing security and control through centralized disk storage. Along these lines, NetWare 5.1 offers three useful volume optimization strategies aimed at solving disk space shortage problems:

▸ *Block suballocation* — This increases available disk space by storing portions of multiple files in a single disk allocation block.

▸ *File compression* — This increases available disk space by compressing inactive files.

▸ *Data migration* — This increases available disk space by moving inactive files to near-line storage.

Let's take a closer look at how you can optimize NetWare 5.1 volume space.

### Block Suballocation

Technically speaking, a *block* is a discrete allocation unit of disk space. Each NetWare 5.1 volume has a predefined block size, ranging from 4K to 64K, based on the size of the volume. A file is stored in one or more blocks. A disk storage inefficiency problem can arise when using medium or large block sizes to store numerous small files.

As you can see in Figure 4.22, a 64K block is fully occupied by a 5K or 63K file — it can't tell the difference. The problem is that the 5K file results in 59K of unusable wasted disk space. A couple thousand 5K files later, and you've wasted more than 100MB of server disk space — not a good thing.

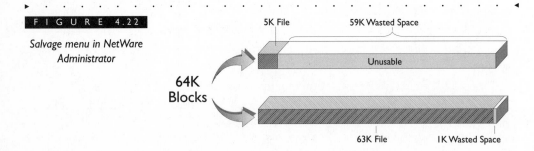

FIGURE 4.22

Salvage menu in NetWare
Administrator

5K File          59K Wasted Space

64K
Blocks

Unusable

63K File          1K Wasted Space

Block suballocation solves this problem of wasted disk space by dividing partially used disk blocks into 512-byte suballocation blocks. These suballocation blocks can be used by multiple files.

In Figure 4.23 (with block suballocation enabled), a 5K file would still take the first 5K of a 64K block. But the remaining 59K would be available for leftovers from other full blocks. A 100K file, for example, would take up another 64K block and send the remaining 36K over to the first block (as shown in Figure 4.23). Without block suballocation, the remaining 36K would occupy another entire 64K block — thereby, wasting another 28K of space in addition to the 59K already wasted from the 5K file.

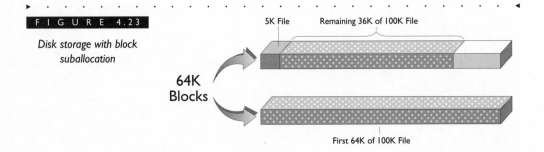

FIGURE 4.23

Disk storage with block
suballocation

5K File          Remaining 36K of 100K File

64K
Blocks

First 64K of 100K File

Here's the bottom line:

▶ *Without block suballocation* — The two files totaling 105K would occupy three 64K blocks and waste 87K of volume space.

▶ *With block suballocation* — The two files totaling 105K would occupy two suballocated blocks, leaving 23K of volume space to be used by portions of one or more other files.

Block suballocation is used when the size of a file exceeds the block size. It's important to remember that a file always starts at the beginning of a new block. In other words, you can't start a new file in the middle of a partially used block. You can, however, store the remainder of a large file within the suballocation area of a partially used block.

Block suballocation is turned on by default and operates at the volume level. You can use NetWare Administrator, ConsoleOne, or FILER to determine if this feature is installed on a volume. To do so using NetWare Administrator, highlight the volume, click the "View or Modify Object Properties" icon in the toolbar, click the Statistics page tab, and then see if "Sub-Allocation File System" is listed in the Installed Features list box. To do so using ConsoleOne, highlight the volume, click File ⇨ Properties, click the Statistics page tab, and then see if "Sub-Allocation File System" is listed in the Installed Features box.

### File Compression

The second volume optimization feature included with NetWare 5.1 is file compression. File compression enables NetWare 5.1 volumes to hold more data by automatically compressing inactive files. Users can save up to 63 percent of the server's disk space when file compression is activated — that's 1GB of files in 370MB of space. (**Note:** This feature is not yet available on NSS volumes.)

File compression is managed internally by the core NetWare operating system. Normally, once file compression is turned on, a number of server SET parameters determine exactly when files will be *compressed*. A file is automatically *uncompressed* when it is accessed.

You can override compression SET parameters by assigning the Immediate Compress (IC) attribute for a file, which means it is automatically compressed after use. Alternately, you can assign the Don't Compress (DC) attribute for a file, which means the file will never be compressed. The DC attribute is particularly useful for large, heavily used database files. If you assign the IC or DC attribute to a directory, it affects all files within the directory. These attributes can be viewed or set using the ConsoleOne, NetWare Administrator, FILER, or FLAG utilities. They can also be displayed (but not modified) using the NDIR utility.

### REAL WORLD

Practice changing file compression attributes (such as DC and IC) using the Windows-based graphical NetWare Administrator utility. To do so, double-click the directory or file, select the Attributes page tab, and then mark the appropriate attribute check box.

You can enable file compression during or after NetWare 5.1 installation. Once compression is enabled, however, you cannot disable it without re-creating the host volume. ConsoleOne, NetWare Administrator, FILER, and FLAG enable you to view or modify file compression attributes. NDIR allows you to view, but not modify, such attributes.

### Data Migration

Data migration provides near-line storage by automatically transferring inactive files from a NetWare volume to a tape drive or optical disk (that is, *jukebox*). One advantage of this strategy is that it is transparent to the user. When a user attempts to access a migrated file, the file still appears to be stored on the original volume. This means that the user can easily access the file without having to worry about where it is actually stored.

Data migration is part of NetWare 5.1's High-Capacity Storage System (HCSS), which extends the storage capacity of a NetWare server by integrating an optical disk library or jukebox. HCSS uses rewriteable optical disks to move files between faster, low-capacity storage devices (such as a server hard disk) and slower, high-capacity storage devices (such as a jukebox). HCSS requires specialized hardware and is fully integrated into NetWare 5.1. It can be activated at the server using special post-installation drivers.

Several SET parameters can be used for managing data migration. You can also prevent a file from being migrated by assigning the Don't Migrate (DM) attribute to a directory or file by using the ConsoleOne, NetWare Administrator, or FLAG utilities. Because migration is activated at the volume level, you can use any of the volume management utilities discussed previously for viewing migration statistics — including ConsoleOne, NetWare Administrator, FILER, or NDIR.

Be forewarned, however, there are performance sacrifices for installing HCSS. You should only consider data migration if you need real-time access to archived files. Typical implementations include law libraries, financial information, and medical records.

I guess we're done then, huh? Wrong! We haven't journeyed into the mysterious land of drive mapping yet. I'm sure you'd rather not go there, but buck up, soldier, you're a CNA — you can handle it.

*But can your users?*

**REAL WORLD**

Once HCSS has been activated, migration is performed on a file-by-file basis, according to two criteria:

- ▶ Capacity threshold — The percentage of the server's hard disk that can be used before HCSS starts migrating files from the hard disk to the jukebox.

- ▶ Least Recently Used (LRU) — A series of guidelines that determines which files are moved from the server's hard disk to the jukebox. These guidelines move the least-active files first.

Near-line data migration is still much slower than on-line disks, so the system must have a way of informing users that the file is on its way. Many near-line tape manufacturers provide terminate-and-stay-resident programs (TSRs) that display a message while NetWare is searching for the near-line file — something like, "Hold your horses, we're working over here!"

## LAB EXERCISE 4.2: NETWARE 5.1 FILE SYSTEM MANAGEMENT WITH NETWARE ADMINISTRATOR AND CONSOLEONE

In this exercise, we will use NetWare Administrator and ConsoleOne to manage NetWare 5.1 directories and files.

To perform this exercise, you will need the following:

▸ A NetWare 5.1 server called WHITE-SRV1.WHITE.CRIME.TOKYO.ACME (which can be installed using the directions found in Appendix D).

▸ A workstation running either the NetWare 5.1 Novell Client for Windows 95/98 or NetWare 5.1 Novell Client for Windows NT/2000 (which can be installed using the directions found in Lab Exercise 3.1).

### Part I: File System Management with NetWare Administrator

**1.** Log in as Admin, if you haven't already done so.

**2.** Launch NetWare Administrator.

**3.** Make sure the current context for this browser window is set to the [Root].

**4.** Open an independent browser window for the WHITE container.

   **a.** Navigate to and click the WHITE container.

   **b.** Select Tools ➪ NDS Browser.

   **c.** Follow these steps when the Set Context dialog box appears:

   • In the Tree field, verify that the following is listed:

   ACME_TREE

   • In the Context field, confirm that the following is listed:

   WHITE.CRIME.TOKYO.ACME

   • Click OK.

- Two browser windows will now be visible, with the new browser window being the *active* one. The current context for the active window will be set to the WHITE container.

- Click the Maximize button in the upper-right corner of the new browser window to make it take up the full screen.

**5.** Create a RESEARCH subdirectory under the SHARED\POL directory.

  **a.** Navigate to the SHARED\POL directory under the SYS: volume (that is, under the WHITE-SRV1_SYS object).

  **b.** To create the RESEARCH subdirectory under the POL directory, use *one* of the following methods:

  - Click POL, then press Insert, *or*

  - Click POL, then select Object ⇨ Create, *or*

  - Right-click POL, then choose Create from the pop-up menu that appears.

  **c.** When the Create Directory dialog box appears, follow these steps:

  - In the Directory Name field, enter the following:

    RESEARCH

  - Click Create to create the directory.

  - Double-click the POL directory to expand it and display its contents.

**6.** Create the following subdirectories under the RESEARCH directory: PROJECT1, PROJECT2, and PROJECT3.

  **a.** Click the RESEARCH directory.

  **b.** Press Insert.

  **c.** When the Create Directory dialog box appears, follow these steps:

  - In the Directory Name field, enter the following:

    PROJECT1

- Mark the Create Another Directory check box.

- Click Create to create the directory.

**d.** Follow these steps when the Create Directory dialog box reappears:

- In the Directory Name field, enter the following:

PROJECT2

- Click Create to create the directory.

**e.** Follow these steps when the Create Directory dialog box reappears:

- In the Directory Name field, enter the following:

PROJECT3

- Unmark the Create Another Directory check box.

- Click Create to create the directory.

- Double-click the RESEARCH directory to expand it and display its contents.

**7.** Open an independent browser window for the SYS: volume.

**a.** Navigate to and click the SYS: volume.

**b.** Select Tools ⇨ NDS Browser.

**c.** Follow these steps when the Set Context dialog box appears:

- In the Tree field, verify that the following is listed:

ACME_TREE

- In the Context field, confirm that the following is listed:

WHITE-SRV1_SYS:WHITE.CRIME.TOKYO.ACME

- Click OK.

- Three browser windows will now be visible, with the newest one being the *active* one. The current context for the active window will be set to the SYS: volume.

**d.** Select Windows ⇨ Tile to reshape the browser windows and view the contents of all three windows at the same time.

- Locate the NDS browser window where the current context is set to the SYS: volume (that is, where WHITE-SRV1_SYS is the object that appears in the top-left corner of the window). We'll refer to this window as the *source* window in this section.

- Locate the NDS browser window where the current context is set to the WHITE container (that is, where WHITE is the object that appears in the top left corner of the window). We'll refer to this window as the *destination* window in this section.

- In the source window, navigate to and expand the SYS:ETC directory to display its contents.

- In the destination window, navigate to and expand the SYS:\ SHARED\POL\RESEARCH directory to display its contents.

**8.** Copy each of the following files to the directory indicated, using the procedures found in Steps 8a and 8b. (**Note:** You can use these same procedures for copying a directory, as well as its subdirectories and files.)

- Copy the SYS:\ETC\ATTYPES.CFG file to the SYS:SHARED\POL\ RESEARCH\PROJECT1 directory

- Copy the SYS:\ETC\BUILTINS.CFG to the SYS:SHARED\POL\ RESEARCH\PROJECT2 directory

- Copy the SYS:\ETC\CONSOLE.LOG to the SYS:SHARED\POL\ RESEARCH\PROJECT3 directory

**a.** To select a file, use *one* of the following methods:

- Click the source file in the source window and select Object ⇨ Copy, *or*

- Drag the source file in the source window to the destination directory in the destination window.

**b.** Follow these steps when the Move/Copy dialog box appears:

- You'll notice that the Copy button is selected by default.

- Verify that the correct source and destination paths are listed in the From and Destination fields. (If the Destination field is empty, use the Browse button to the right of it to select the appropriate destination directory.)

- If desired, mark the Copy Trustee Assignments to copy trustee assignments.

- Click OK to copy the file.

**c.** When you are done copying the three files, confirm that the files were copied. In the destination browser window, double-click each destination directory to confirm that the files were successfully copied.

**d.** Close the source browser window. (**Note:** The remainder of the steps in Part I of this exercise will be performed in the destination window.)

**9.** Move the BUILTINS.CFG file (in the PROJECT2 subdirectory) and CONSOLE.LOG file (in the PROJECT3 subdirectory) to the PROJECT1 directory. (**Note:** You can use these same procedures for moving a directory, as well as its subdirectories and files):

**a.** To select the files, follow these steps:

- Click the BUILTINS.CFG file.

- Hold down Ctrl and click the CONSOLE.LOG file.

**b.** To indicate that the files should be moved, use *one* of the following methods:

- Drag the selected files on top of the PROJECT1 directory, *or*.

- Select Object ⇨ Move.

**c.** Follow these steps when the Move/Copy dialog box appears:

- Depending on which method you are using, either the Move or Copy radio button will be selected by default. Mark the Move radio button, if it isn't selected.

- Ensure that the correct source and destination paths are listed in the From and Destination fields. (If the Destination field is empty, use the Browse button to the left of it to select the appropriate destination directory.)

- Click OK to move the designated files to the PROJECT1 directory.

10. Rename the PROJECT1 directory to PROJECT4.

   **a.** Click the PROJECT1 directory.

   **b.** Click Object ⇨ Rename.

   **c.** Follow these steps when the Rename dialog box appears:

   - In the New Name field, replace the existing value with the following:

     PROJECT4

   - Click OK to rename the directory.

   - You'll notice that the PROJECT1 directory has been renamed to PROJECT4.

11. Set the Purge attribute for the CONSOLE.LOG file.

   **a.** Double-click the CONSOLE.LOG file (in the PROJECT4 directory).

   **b.** When the Identification page for this object appears, click the Attributes page button.

   **c.** Follow these steps when the Attributes page appears:

   - Click the Purge Immediate check box.

   - Click OK to save your changes.

12. Delete the three files in the PROJECT4 directory.

   **a.** To select the files in the PROJECT4 directory, do as follows:

   - Click the first filename listed in the PROJECT4 directory.

- While holding down Shift, click the last filename listed in the PROJECT4 directory.

- Press Delete.

**b.** When the Delete dialog box appears, select Yes to confirm the deletion.

**13.** Salvage the files you deleted in Step 12.

**a.** Click the PROJECT4 directory.

**b.** Select Tools ⇨ Salvage.

**c.** Follow these steps when the Salvage dialog box appears:

- Click the List button near the top left of the window. You'll notice that the CONSOLE.LOG file is not listed because you set the "immediate purge" attribute before deleting it.

- Click the first filename listed.

- While holding down Shift, click the second name.

- Click the Salvage button.

- Click the Close button to close the Salvage window.

**d.** Confirm the salvage process. Double-click the PROJECT4 directory to confirm that the two files have been salvaged.

**14.** Limit the DrWatson user to 5,120K of disk storage space on the SYS: volume.

**a.** To select the SYS: volume, use *one* of the following methods:

- Click the WHITE-SRV1_SYS volume and select Object ⇨ Details, *or*

- Right-click the WHITE-SRV1_SYS volume and select Details from the pop-up menu that appears.

**b.** When the volume dialog box appears, click the User Space Limits page button.

**c.** When the Users Space Limits page appears, click the Browse button to the right of the Search Context field.

**d.** When the Select Object dialog box appears, follow these steps:

- In the left pane, click the WHITE container.

- Click OK.

**e.** When the User Space Limits page reappears, follow these steps:

- Click the DrWatson User object.

- Click Modify.

**f.** Follow these steps when the Volume Space Restriction dialog box appears:

- Mark the Limited Volume Space check box.

- Type the following in the "Volume Space Limit (KB)" field:

  5120

- Click OK to save your changes and return to the User Space Limits page.

- Click OK to return to the main NetWare Administrator screen.

**15.** Limit the maximum size of the PROJECT3 directory to 2560K.

**a.** Follow these steps on the main NetWare Administrator screen:

- Right-click the PROJECT3 directory you created earlier in this exercise.

- Select Details from the pop-up menu that appears.

**b.** When the directory dialog box appears, click the Facts page tab.

**c.** Follow these steps when the Facts page appears:

- Mark the Restrict Size check box.

- In the Limit field, enter the following:

  2560

- Click OK to save your changes and return to the main NetWare Administrator screen.

**16.** Delete the RESEARCH directory and its contents.

**a.** Using the method of your choice, delete the RESEARCH directory and its contents.

**b.** Close the destination browser screen (that is, the one whose context is set to the WHITE container).

**c.** Maximize the remaining browser screen (that is, the one whose context is set to the [Root].

**17.** Exit NetWare Administrator.

**Part II: File System Management with ConsoleOne**

Now, let's try to perform some of the same file management tasks using the ConsoleOne utility.

**1.** Execute ConsoleOne.

**2.** Using the method of your choice (see Lab Exercise 4.1), create the following directories:

**a.** SYS:SHARED\POL\RESEARCH

**b.** SYS:SHARED\POL\RESEARCH\PROJECT1

**c.** SYS:SHARED\POL\RESEARCH\PROJECT2

**3.** Copy each of the two files in the following list to the directory indicated, using *one* of the procedures found in Steps 8a and 8b. (**Note:** You can use these same procedures for copying a directory, as well as its subdirectories and files.)

- Copy the SYS:\ETC\ATTYPES.CFG file to the SYS:SHARED\POL\ RESEARCH\PROJECT1 directory

- Copy the SYS:\ETC\BUILTINS.CFG to the SYS:SHARED\POL\ RESEARCH\PROJECT2 directory

**a.** To select a file to be copied, use *one* of the following methods:

- Click the source file and select Edit ⇨ Copy, *or*

- Right-click the source file and select Copy.

**b.** To copy the file to the destination directory, use *one* of the following methods:

- Click the destination directory and select Edit ⇨ Paste, *or*

- Right-click the destination directory and select Paste, *or*

- When the Copy Trustees dialog box appears, click Yes if you want to copy trustees. Otherwise, click No.

**c.** When you finish copying the files, click each destination directory in the left pane to confirm that the files were copied successfully. (When you click a directory in the left pane, its contents will appear in the right pane.)

**4.** Move the BUILTINS.CFG file (in the PROJECT2 subdirectory) to the PROJECT1 directory. (**Note:** You can use these same procedures for moving a directory, as well as its subdirectories and files):

**a.** To select a file to be moved, use *one* of the following methods:

- Click the source file and select Edit ⇨ Cut, *or*

- Right-click the source file and select Cut.

**b.** To move the file to the destination directory, use *one* of the following methods:

- Click the destination directory and select Edit ⇨ Paste, *or*

- Right-click the destination directory and select Paste.

**5.** Rename the PROJECT1 directory to PROJECT3.

**a.** To select a directory to be renamed, use *one* of the following methods:

- Click the directory and select File ⇨ Rename, *or*

- Right-click the directory and select Rename.

**b.** Follow these steps when the Rename dialog box appears:

- In the New Name field, replace the existing value with the following:

  PROJECT3

- Click OK to rename the directory.

- You'll notice that the PROJECT1 directory has been renamed to PROJECT3.

**6.** Set the Purge attribute for the BUILTINS.CFG file.

**a.** Double-click the BUILTINS.CFG file (in the PROJECT3 directory).

**b.** When the Properties of BUILTINS.CFG dialog box appears, the Attributes page should be displayed by default.

- Click the Purge Immediate check box.

- Click OK to save your changes.

**7.** Limit the DrWatson user to 9,600K of disk storage space on the SYS: volume.

**a.** To select the SYS: volume, use *one* of the following methods:

- Click the WHITE-SRV1_SYS volume and select File ⇨ Properties, *or*

- Right-click the WHITE-SRV1_SYS volume and select Properties from the pop-up menu that appears.

**b.** When the Properties of WHITE-SRV1_SYS dialog box appears, click the Users with Space Restrictions page button.

**c.** When the Users with Space Restrictions page appears, you'll notice that a space restriction already exists for the DrWatson user.

- Verify that the DrWatson object is highlighted.

- Click Modify.

**d.** Follow these steps when the User Space Restriction page reappears:

- Verify that the Limit User Space check box is marked.

- In the Space Limit (in KB) field, replace the existing value with the following:

  9600

- Click OK to save your changes and return to the User Space Restrictions page.

- Click OK to return to the main ConsoleOne screen.

**8.** Limit the maximum size of the PROJECT2 directory to 2,560K.

  **a.** To select the PROJECT2 directory use *one* of the following methods:

  - Click the PROJECT2 directory and select File ➪ Properties, *or*

  - Right-click the PROJECT2 directory and select Properties from the pop-up menu that appears.

  **b.** When the Properties of PROJECT2 dialog box appears, click the Facts page tab.

  **c.** Follow these steps when the Facts page appears:

  - Mark the Restrict Size check box.

  - In the Limit KB (Increments of 64KB) field, enter the following:

    2560

  - Click OK to save your changes and return to the main ConsoleOne screen.

**9.** Delete the RESEARCH directory and its contents using the method of your choice.

**10.** Exit ConsoleOne.

# Drive Mapping

Many non-network-aware legacy applications (such as DOS applications) don't recognize NetWare volume names. Instead, they rely on DOS-like drive letters. In an attempt to provide backward compatibility for these applications, NetWare 5.1 supports a drive pointer system called *drive mapping*.

In Figure 4.24, for example, the A: and B: letters point to floppy drives, C: and D: point to hard drives, and E: points to a CD- ROM drive. Pretty simple, huh? Well, it works fine on workstations because they typically use multiple storage devices.

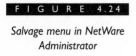

**FIGURE 4.24**

*Salvage menu in NetWare Administrator*

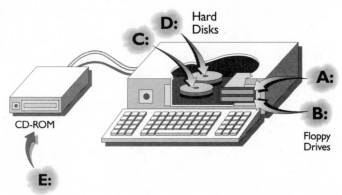

So, how does this theory apply to NetWare 5.1 drives? If we extrapolate from the local theory, we would use 21 different drive letters (F–Z) to point to 21 physical devices — not very likely. So, Novell returned to the proverbial drawing board and came up with a slightly different approach:

*NetWare 5.1 drive letters point to* **logical** *directories instead of* **physical** *drives.*

Drive mapping is a built-in file system management scheme that enables you (and users) to assign drive letters to network directories. Typically, physical local devices are referenced using characters at the beginning of the alphabet (such as A: through E:). In NetWare, logical network directories are typically referenced using characters in the remainder of the alphabet (such as F: through Z:). See Figure 4.25.

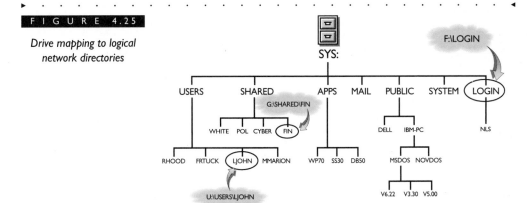

*Drive mapping to logical
network directories*

In general, NetWare 5.1 provides three different approaches to drive mapping:

▸ Network drive mapping

▸ Search drive mapping

▸ Directory Map object

A *network drive* uses a single letter to point to a logical directory path. The previous example uses network drives. A *search drive*, on the other hand, provides additional functionality by building a search list for network applications. Finally, a *Directory Map object* is a centralized NDS resource that points to a logical directory path. It helps ease the transition from one application version to another. Let's take a closer look.

**REAL WORLD**

NetWare 5.1 does not track information on local drive assignments. Even though a map will show that drives A: through E: are assigned to local drives, that does not necessarily mean they point to real devices. Remember that unless otherwise specified, drive mappings pointing to Drives A: through E: are reserved for physical devices on the workstation (not the server).

## Network Drive Mapping

When you map a network drive, you assign a drive letter (that is, *drive pointer*) followed by a colon (:) to a particular network directory. By default, NetWare 5.1 supports five local drive letters (A: through E:) that can point to physical devices on the workstation and 21 network drives (F: through Z:) that can be assigned to network directories.

A network workstation may use more than five drive letters for pointing to physical devices (for example, if it has multiple hard drives, a CD-ROM drive, a ZIP drive, and so on). In this case, the remaining drive letters would be available for assignment as network drives. Interestingly, you can actually remap a drive letter that normally points to a physical device on the workstation—so it instead points to a network directory. Your users may not see the humor in this, however. You can also map multiple drive letters to the same directory.

Once a drive letter has been mapped to a NetWare 5.1 directory, you can navigate the file system using NetWare utilities, Windows utilities, or DOS commands. Simply use the same procedures you would use for accessing local drives via a drive letter. To change your default drive at the DOS prompt, type the drive letter followed by a colon (:) and press Enter.

Network drive mappings are user-specific, temporary environment variables. Each user can have a different set of drive mappings stored in workstation RAM. When a user logs out or turns off the workstation, these mappings are lost. For this reason, you'll want to consider automating the creation of drive mappings using the MAP command in Container and/or Profile login scripts. (See the "Mapping with the MAP Command" section later in this Chapter.)

Alternately, you can use a Windows utility such as Explorer or Network Neighborhood to make the drive mappings permanent on a workstation by storing them in the Windows 95/98 or Windows NT/2000 Registry. (See the "Mapping with Windows 95/98" section later in this study session.) Using either method, the drive mappings will then be available whenever the user accesses the network from this workstation.

Consider creating any or all of the following drive mappings for your users:

▸ *U:*—Each user's home directory (for example, SYS:USERS\LJOHN)

▸ *F:*—SYS:LOGIN (typically created by default unless occupied by local devices)

▸ *G:* — Group-specific data directories (for example, SYS:SHARED\FINAN)

▸ *H:* — A global shared directory (for example, SYS:SHARED)

Now, let's expand our understanding of NetWare 5.1 drive mapping with search drives. They help us build an internal search list for network applications.

**TIP**

**Remember that drive mappings are stored in workstation RAM and, thus, are lost when the user logs off the network and/or powers off the workstation. To solve this problem, you should automate the creation of drive mappings by placing them in a login script or by using a Window utility such as Explorer or Network Neighborhood to make them permanent by storing them in the Windows 95/98 or Windows NT/2000 Registry.**

## Search Drive Mapping

Search drive mappings extend one step beyond network mappings by helping users search for network programs, commands, or batch files (that is, those that have an .EXE, .COM, or .BAT extension), as well as other files (such as .DLL or .MSG files).

Whereas mapping network drives is somewhat comparable to using the DOS SUBST command — mapping search drives is similar to using the DOS PATH command. In fact, because assigning search drives in NetWare 5.1 actually updates the DOS path, you may unintentionally overwrite items in the DOS path if you're not careful! One way this problem can be avoided is by using the MAP INSERT or MAP S16 command. (See the "Mapping with the MAP Command" section later in this chapter for further details.)

When a user specifies an application, batch file, or command without specifying the full path, NetWare 5.1 searches the following locations, in order:

1. Workstation RAM

2. The current directory

3. The directories in the DOS path, in the order listed

If the program is still not found, an error is displayed.

**TIP**

**Most DOS applications cannot access NetWare 5.1 volumes by their volume name. Instead, they typically rely on network drive mappings and search drive mappings.**

The beauty of the NetWare 5.1 search list is that it enables you to prioritize application directories. NetWare 5.1 searches for programs in the order in which they are listed. The list can be a combination of local and network directories. For example, the following search list would find Windows on the local drive first; otherwise, it would use the network version in SYS:APPS\WINDOWS:

```
S1:=SYS:PUBLIC

S2:=SYS:PUBLIC\IBM_PC\MSDOS\V6.22

S3:=C:\WINDOWS

S4:=SYS:APPS\WINDOWS

S5:=SYS:APPS\SS30
```

Because search drive mappings are primarily used to build search lists, you should be more concerned with the order of the list than with the letter assigned to each directory. As you can see from this list, NetWare 5.1 assigns search drive mappings in search order—and each is preceded by the letter *S*. As a matter of convenience, NetWare 5.1 also automatically assigns a drive letter to each search directory—in reverse order (to avoid using network drive letters).

For example, the first search drive (S1:) inherits the letter Z:, the second mapping (S2:) gets the letter Y:, and so on (see Figure 4.26). This enables you to navigate through search directories if necessary, although I don't recommend it. You are limited to a total of 16 search drives that inherit network drive letters. That is, you can have more than 16 search drives, but the extra ones will have to point to local drive letters—such as C:.

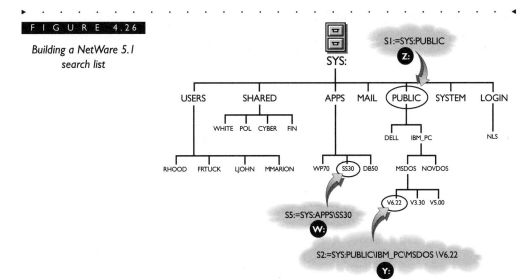

*Building a NetWare 5.1
search list*

Because the NetWare 5.1 search list and DOS PATH statements accomplish the same thing, there can be a definite conflict of interest. As a matter of fact, the NetWare 5.1 search list systematically eliminates directories in the DOS path. To avoid this problem, consider merging your DOS path and NetWare 5.1 search list. This is accomplished using the MAP INSERT command (see the "Mapping with the MAP Command" section later in this chapter).

**TIP**

**When a search drive is being created, both a search drive number and a network drive letter are assigned. The network drive letter assigned is the next available drive letter, in reverse alphabetical order. If the drive letter that would normally be assigned is already in use, the search mapping skips the letter and grabs the next one. For this reason, you should always assign network drive mappings first, to avoid network and search drive mapping conflicts.**

This completes our discussion of network and search drive mappings. Refer to Table 4.4 for a summary of how they work.

| TABLE 4.4                                       | FUNCTION                     | NETWORK DRIVE MAPPING | SEARCH DRIVE MAPPING |
| ----------------------------------------------- | ---------------------------- | --------------------- | -------------------- |
| *Comparing Network and Search Drive Mappings*   | Purpose                      | File System Access    | Searching            |
|                                                 | Assignment method            | As the letter         | In search order      |
|                                                 | Letter assignment            | By you                | By NetWare 5.1       |
|                                                 | First letter (if available)  | F:                    | Z:                   |
|                                                 | Suggested Directory Contents | Data                  | Applications         |

Now, let's take a moment to explore Directory Map objects before we dive into the MAP command.

## Directory Map Objects

In earlier chapters, we learned about a special NDS leaf object that helped you deal with drive mapping in the NetWare 5.1 file system—the Directory Map object. This special-purpose object enables you to map to a central logical resource instead of to the physical directory itself. The advantage of this strategy is obvious—physical directories change, while logical objects don't have to.

This level of independence is very useful. Let's say, for example, that you have a central application server in the TOKYO container that everybody points to. On the server is an older copy of WordPerfect (WP5). You have two options for adding this application to your internal search lists:

1. *Search drive mapping*—Use a traditional search drive mapping in each container's login script (this is, five of them). This mapping would point to the physical directory itself—TOKYO-SRV1\SYS:APPS\WP5.

2. *Directory Map object*—Create a Directory Map object in the TOKYO container called WPAPP and then configure it to point to the physical directory (TOKYO-SRV1\SYS:APPS\WP5). Each of the five search drive MAP commands would then be configured to point to the logical (Directory Map) object, instead of the physical directory (TOKYO-SRV1\SYS:APPS\WP5).

Both of these scenarios accomplish the same thing: They create a search drive mapping to WordPerfect 5 for all users in the Tokyo location. But once you upgrade WordPerfect, you'll find the second option is much more attractive. In the first scenario, you'll need to monitor five different search drive statements in five login scripts (potentially). This is a lot of work!

In the second scenario, however, you'll only need to change the one Directory Map object reference, and all the other MAP statements will automatically point to the right place. Amazing! In the next section, we'll explore the MAP command and learn how it can be used to reference Directory Map objects.

To map a search drive to the Directory Map object WPAPP (without overwriting an existing search drive in the DOS path), you would enter the following command:

```
MAP INS S16:=path:WPAPP
```

**REAL WORLD**

When using the MAP command to map a drive to a Directory Map object, do not place a colon (:) at the end of the Directory Map object.

## Mapping with the MAP Command

So, now that you know everything there is to know about network and search drive mappings, the next logical question is, "How?" One option is to use the MAP command — either at the DOS prompt or in a login script. The MAP command can be used to map network or search drives to volumes, directories, or a Directory Map object. (Although there are a couple of exceptions, most MAP commands can be used either at the DOS prompt or in a login script.)

The NetWare 5.1 MAP command enables you to do the following:

▸ View drive mappings

▸ Create or modify network or search drive mappings

▸ Point to Directory Map objects

- Map drives to a fake root — to fool users or install special applications

- Change mappings from one type to another

- Integrate the network and local search lists

- All sorts of other stuff

**TIP**    **The DOS CD command will change the MAP assignment in the DOS window, but not in current Windows applications. Also, using a mapped driver is faster than manually changing to the correct directory using the CD command because it uses drive letters. Finally, the NetWare 5.1 MAP command is most like the DOS SUBST command.**

Following is the syntax for the MAP command:

```
MAP [[option] drive: = [drive path]]
```

where *option* is a MAP option, *drive* is a letter from A to Z, followed by a colon (:), and *drive path* is any acceptable NetWare volume or directory name. A volume can be specified using a physical or Volume object name. Unlike DOS, both backslashes (\) and forward slashes (/) are acceptable in a drive path.

The MAP command can be used to assign network drive letters to home and shared directories that users need to access on a regular basis. Network drive mappings typically point to directories where user-generated data files (such as word processing documents) are stored.

The MAP ROOT command can be used to create a false root. This is useful for two purposes. First, when you want to prevent a user from using the DOS CD command to move higher up the file system directory tree. It is also useful for legacy applications that must be installed in the root directory. For both security and administrative reasons, you should never install an application in the actual root directory of a volume — so this is a great alternative.

The MAP command can also be used to map search drives that point to network directories containing applications, commands, or batch files (that is, that that have an .EXE, .COM, or .BAT extension) as well as other files (such as .DLL or .MSG files). As we discussed earlier, mapping a search drive updates the DOS path. If you're not careful, you may unintentionally overwrite necessary items in the DOS path. For example, MAP S1:=SYS:\PUBLIC would map the first search drive to the SYS:PUBLIC directory — and overwrite the directory in the first position of the DOS path (if one existed).

The MAP INSERT command enables you to insert a new search drive into the DOS path, at the position specified, without overwriting an existing drive mapping in that position (if one exists). All existing search drives above the new pointer are then bumped up one level in the list and renumbered accordingly.

The MAP S16 command adds a new directory at the end of the DOS path, assuming of course, that the existing DOS path has less than 16 items. (If not, it would replace the directory in the 16th position.) The reason this works is that you cannot have any holes (empty positions) in the DOS path. For example, if you had only three items in the DOS path and attempted to assign an S7: search drive, the new search drive would be inserted in the fourth (rather than seventh) position in the DOS path.

**TIP**

**Search drive mappings share the same environment space as the DOS path. As a result, if you assign a NetWare 5.1 search drive number using the MAP SEARCH command, it will overwrite the corresponding pointer in the DOS path. (For example, if you use the MAP S1: command, it will overwrite the first pointer in the DOS path.) The only way to retain existing pointers in the DOS path is to use the MAP INS or MAP S16: commands, which insert new search drives into the DOS path, rather than replacing existing ones.**

Figure 4.27 displays a sample Login Results window with Network, Search, and Root drive mappings.

Refer to Table 4.5 for an explanation of some of the more common MAP commands in NetWare 5.1.

T A B L E   4.5

*Getting to Know MAP
Commands*

| COMMAND | RESULT |
| --- | --- |
| MAP | Displays a list of current NetWare 5.1 network drive and search drive mappings. |
| MAP G:=WHITE-SRV1\ SYS:SHARED\FINAN | Maps the G: drive as a network drive that points to the SHARED\FINAN directory on the SYS: volume of the WHITE-SRV1 server (using the physical volume name). |
| MAP H:=.WHITE-SRV1_SYS. WHITE:SHARED\FINAN | Maps the H: drive as a network drive that points to the SHARED\FINAN directory on the SYS: volume of the WHITE-SRV1 server (using the Volume object name). |
| MAP I:=.WHITE-SRV1_VOL1.WHITE. CRIME.TOKYO.ACME: | Maps the I: drive as a network drive that points to the root of the VOL1: volume of the WHITE-SRV1 server in the WHITE.CRIME.TOKYO.ACME container (using the distinguished Volume object name). |

TABLE 4.5

Getting to Know MAP
Commands (continued)

| COMMAND | RESULT |
|---|---|
| MAP ROOT J:=SYS:ACCT\REPORTS | Maps the J: drive as a false root pointing to the ACCT\REPORTS directory on the SYS: volume. Because this is a false root, the user cannot access the SYS:ACCT directory, for example, using this drive letter. |
| MAP NEXT SYS:DATA<br>MAP N SYS:DATA | Maps the next available network drive letter to the SYS:DATA directory. (This mapping command is not available for use in a login script.) |
| MAP C M:<br>MAP C S3: | The first command changes the M: network drive to the next available search drive number. The second command changes the S3: search drive to a network drive. |
| MAP INS S1:=SYS:PUBLIC | Maps a new S1: search drive pointing to SYS:PUBLIC, inserts it at the beginning of the DOS path, and then renumbers all existing search drives accordingly. Also, assigns the next available drive letter, in reverse alphabetical order, as a network drive associated with this search drive. |
| MAP S3:=SYS:APPS\WP70 | Maps the S3: search drive pointing to SYS:APPS\ WP70 and inserts it in the third position of the DOS path (overwriting the existing directory, if one exists). Also, assigns the next available drive letter, in reverse alphabetical order, as a network drive. |
| MAP S5:=WPAPP | Maps the S5: search drive pointing to the WPAPP Directory Map object in the *current context* and inserts it in the fifth position of the DOS path (overwriting the existing directory, if one exists). (You'd have to supply the path if WPAPP wasn't in the current context.) Also, assigns the next available drive letter, in reverse alphabetical order, as a network drive. |

*Continued*

T A B L E   4 . 5

*Getting to Know MAP*
*Commands (continued)*

| COMMAND | RESULT |
|---|---|
| MAP S16:=SYS:APPS\WP70 | Inserts a search drive to the SYS:APPS\WP70 directory at the end of the DOS path (assuming, of course, that the DOS path currently contains less than 16 items. If the DOS path contains 16 or more items, it would overwrite the directory in the 16th position). Also assigns the next available drive letter, in reverse alphabetical order, as a network drive. |
| MAP DEL G:<br>MAP REM G: | Deletes the G: drive. |
| MAP /VER | Displays version information about the MAP utility, including the files it needs for execution. |
| MAP /? | Displays online help information for the MAP command. |

## Mapping with Windows 95/98

If you open the My Computer window in Windows 95/98, you'll notice that drive pointers that have been assigned to local and network drives are displayed in parentheses. Lower drive letters are typically assigned to physical workstation drives (such as floppy drives, hard disks, CD-ROM drives, ZIP disks, and so on) while higher drive letters, when assigned, identify network volume or directory locations.

Newer Windows-based programs do not require drive mappings. Instead, they can locate workstation and network resources using a UNC path (which follows the new *Universal Naming Convention* file system standard). As we discussed earlier, if the Novell Client software is installed on a workstation, Windows utilities can be used to view or access network drives. If the Novell Client software is installed on a workstation, any time a network drive is mapped using a Windows utility (such as Explorer or Network Neighborhood), the drive is accessible and visible everywhere else in Windows. When a drive letter is reassigned to a different directory, however, the directory change affects only that specific instance of the drive mapping.

Following are the general steps required to create a network drive mapping using Windows 95/98 Network Neighborhood:

1. In Network Neighborhood, browse to and click the volume or directory you want to map to.

2. Select File ⇨ Novell Map Network Drive.

3. When the Map Drive window appears (see Figure 4.28), follow these steps:

   • In the "Choose the Drive Letter to Map" drop-down box, select the drive letter to be mapped. (You can choose any drive letter listed. If you choose a drive letter already mapped, your new path will be mapped to the drive letter.)

   • In the "Enter the Network Path to the Resource" field, ensure that the correct path is selected.

   • If you want to make this drive a search drive, mark the "Map Search Drive" check box. (If you do so, two radio buttons will appear. Mark either "Put Search Drive at Beginning of Path" or "Put Search Drive at End of Path.")

   • Mark the "Check to Always Map This Drive Letter When You Start Windows" check box if you want this drive to be available each time you log into the network (that is, to create a permanent drive mapping).

   • Click Map to create the drive mapping.

In the beginning . . . there was the NDS Directory tree. We discovered the [Root], leaf objects, and proper naming. We learned how to name the NDS Directory tree, browse it, manage it, and groom it. Just when we thought we understood the true meaning of NetWare 5.1 life, another tree appeared — the non-NDS Directory tree.

This strange new tree is very different. Instead of a [Root], it has a *root*; and instead of leaf objects, it has *files*. But once you get past its rough exterior, you'll see that the non-NDS tree shares the same look and feel as the NDS one. And they approach life together with a similar purpose — to logically organize user resources, except this time the resources are files, not printers.

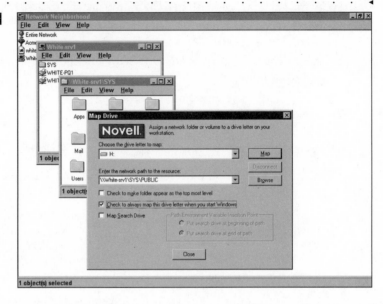

*Mapping drives with
Windows 95/98*

In this chapter, we explored file system design and discovered a slew of NetWare 5.1 file system utilities. Then, we learned how to build drive pointers for quick-and-easy access to server-based volumes, directories, and files.

So, what does the future hold? Well, now that we've learned everything about NDS and non-NDS trees, we can expand our minds to the rest of NetWare 5.1 management. We will combine our new skills and forge ahead into the great network administrator forest:

▶ NetWare 5.1 Security — Chapter 5

▶ NetWare 5.1 Workstation Management — Chapter 6

▶ NetWare 5.1 Printing — Chapter 7

During your journey through the rest of this study guide, look back to the fun times you had in previous chapters. Count on your NDS and non-NDS skills — because you will need them.

Good luck, and by the way . . . thanks for saving the world.

## LAB EXERCISE 4.3: MAPPING DRIVES WITH MAP

Follow the steps in this lab exercise to design sample drive mappings for the directory structure that was created in Lab Exercise 4.1, "Designing a Directory Structure for ACME."

Indicate which MAP command you would use to perform each of the following tasks:

**1.** Display online help information for the MAP command.

**2.** Display your current drive mappings.

**3.** Map drive U: to each user's home directory under the SYS:USERS\WHITE directory.

**4.** Map drive G: to the POL subdirectory under the SHARED directory, using the physical name of the volume.

**5.** Map the J: drive to the same directory as the F: drive.

**6.** Map drive S: to the SHARED directory, using the Volume object name.

**7.** Map the S1: search drive to the SYS:PUBLIC directory without overwriting the existing pointers in the DOS path.

**8.** Map the S2: search drive to the V6.22 directory without overwriting the existing pointers in the DOS path.

**9.** Map the S3: search drive to the SS30 subdirectory.

**10.** Map the S4: search drive as a false root to the DB50 subdirectory.

**11.** If you typed **MAP** at the DOS prompt, how would a mapped root be indicated? How would a mapped root be indicated in the Results window when logging into the network from a Windows 95/98 or Windows NT/2000 workstation?

**12.** Map the S5: search drive to the WP70 subdirectory, specifying that W: be assigned as the associated network drive.

**13.** Assume the Z: drive is associated with a search drive that is mapped to SYS:PUBLIC. If you switched to a DOS prompt, switched to the Z: drive, and then typed **CD ..** to move to the root directory of the volume, what would happen? What could you do to fix the problem?

**14.** Delete the J: drive.

**15.** Delete the S3: search drive using a different command than you did in Step 14. What would happen to your other search drive mappings? What would happen to the network drive associated with those search drives?

**16.** Change the S4: drive from a search drive to a network drive. What would happen to the search drive itself? What would happen to the network drive associated with it?

See Appendix C for answers.

## LAB EXERCISE 4.4: MAPPING DRIVES WITH WINDOWS

In addition to the MAP command, NetWare 5.1 also enables you to create network and search drive mappings using Network Neighborhood on Windows 95/98 and Windows NT/2000 workstations.

To perform this exercise, you will need the following:

▶ A NetWare 5.1 server called WHITE-SRV1.WHITE.CRIME.TOKYO.ACME (which can be installed using the directions found in Appendix D).

▶ A workstation running either the NetWare 5.1 Novell Client for Windows 95/98 or NetWare 5.1 Novell Client for Windows NT/2000 (which can be installed using the directions found in Lab Exercise 3.1).

Complete the following steps on your client workstation:

**1.** Launch Network Neighborhood. To do so, double-click the Network Neighborhood icon on your Windows 95/98 or Windows NT/2000 desktop.

**2.** Select the directory to be mapped.

  **a.** When the main Network Neighborhood screen appears, double-click WHITE-SRV1.

  **b.** When the WHITE-SRV1 window appears, double-click SYS:.

  **c.** When the \\WHITE-SRV1\SYS dialog box appears, click the PUBLIC folder.

**3.** Map the drive.

  **a.** Select File ⇨ Novell Map Network Drive.

  **b.** Follow these steps when the Map Drive dialog box appears:

  • In the "Choose the Drive Letter to Map" field, the next available drive letter will be listed, by default. Using the drop-down box, select a different drive letter, if desired.

- In the "Enter the Network Path to the Resource" field, the path to the directory you have selected will be listed, by default. Using the drop-down box, select a different path, if desired.

- If you want this drive to be available the next time you log in, mark the "Check to Always Map This Drive Letter When You Start Windows" check box.

- If you want this drive to be a search drive, mark the "Map Search Drive" check box. If you do so, in the "Path Environment Variable Insertion Point" section, mark either the "Put Search Drive at Beginning of Path" or "Put Search Drive at End of Path" radio button. (The latter is the default.)

- Click MAP to map the drive.

4. Exit the Network Neighborhood utility.

## LAB EXERCISE 4.5: FILE CABINET OF LIFE

Circle the 15 file-system-related terms hidden in this word search puzzle using the hints provided. No punctuation characters (such as blank spaces, hyphens, and so on) should be included. Numbers should always be spelled out.

```
Y  D  I  R  E  C  T  O  R  Y  J  M  O  U  P
P  U  R  G  E  E  J  F  P  X  B  L  K  K  J
O  O  D  A  T  A  M  I  G  R  A  T  I  O  N
C  T  T  B  K  T  D  N  G  O  E  C  P  Q  N
N  E  T  W  O  R  K  D  R  I  V  E  H  K  M
S  S  E  A  R  C  H  D  R  I  V  E  M  G  O
U  X  K  W  R  U  N  D  I  R  H  S  I  M  J
F  I  L  E  C  O  M  P  R  E  S  S  I  O  N
I  I  A  J  B  T  K  M  C  S  E  T  I  G  L
L  T  L  U  F  E  H  T  F  U  G  O  F  Y  Q
E  G  H  E  U  J  R  P  B  D  A  F  V  D  Q
R  M  N  V  S  Q  J  R  G  A  V  U  Z  T  O
F  U  N  U  W  C  R  F  A  W  L  D  R  M  Z
L  H  I  W  Z  F  A  Z  T  R  A  C  Q  F  Q
Y  H  W  C  I  J  E  N  Q  P  S  T  K  U  T
```

### Hints

1. Directory right required for salvaging files you own.
2. Transfer of inactive or infrequently used data to near-term storage.
3. File system component on which you can impose a disk space limitation.
4. File storage method used to save disk space.
5. File right required for salvaging files you own.
6. NetWare 5.1 menu utility used for salvaging and purging files.
7. NetWare 5.1 command-line utility used for copying files.
8. NetWare 5.1 command-line utility used for viewing file information.
9. Drive mapping to server directory.
10. Process used to prevent deleted files from being recovered.

11. Another file right required for salvaging files you own.
12. Process used to recover deleted files.
13. Type of drive mapping that modifies the DOS path.
14. Console command that can be used to configure file compression parameters.
15. Object whose disk space usage can be limited.

See Appendix C for answers.

## LAB EXERCISE 4.6: NETWARE 5.1 FILE SYSTEM

### Across

3. Letter assigned to device
5. Highest level in the file system
7. DOS directory deletion utility
9. Purpose of MAP command
12. Required NetWare volume
13. Don't migrate attribute
14. Unit of disk space

### Down

1. Analogous to folder contents
2. Analogous to file cabinet
3. Home of deleted files
4. Analogous to folder contents

6. Mapping command-line utility

8. Analogous to a file folder

10. DOS directory creation utility

11. Immediate compression attribute

See Appendix C for answers.

# CHAPTER 5

# NetWare 5.1 Security

**S**ecurity is interesting. Everyone wants it, but how much are you willing to pay for it? Security in the Information Age poses an interesting challenge. Computers and communications have made it possible to collect volumes of data about you and me — from our last purchase at the five-and-dime to our detailed medical records.

And, unsurpringly, Fortune 500 companies are very concerned about network security. For this reason, network security is one of your primary responsibilities as a network administrator. To be truly effective, you must control physical access to network devices (such as keeping servers in secured rooms), as well as protecting programs and data.

Fortunately, NetWare 5.1 provides a variety of security options to help you protect your network and its resources, including login security, NDS security, file system security, operating system licensing (covered in Appendix D), printing security (covered in Chapter 7), and server security (covered in *Novell's CNE Study Guide for NetWare 5.1*). As you can see, NetWare 5.1 security does not consist of a single system. Rather, it is controlled by a combination of different security features working together and independently to protect various aspects of the network.

Three security systems work together to control access to the network and to its file system resources: login, NDS, and file system. They are implemented as five increasingly secure layers of protection (see Figure 5.1).

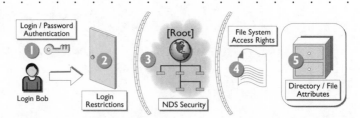

FIGURE 5.1

*The NetWare 5.1 security model*

- ▶ *Layer 1: Login/Password Authentication* — It all starts with Login/Password Authentication. Remember, users don't log into NetWare servers any more — they log into the NDS tree. When a user requests login via a Novell Client login screen, the authentication process begins automatically. If a user supplies the correct parameters during the login process (such as tree name, context, username, and password) — the user moves on to Layer 2 of the security model.

▶ *Layer 2: Login Restrictions* — At Layer 2, the user is presented with a number of account restrictions that must be met, including login restrictions, password restrictions, station restrictions, time restrictions, and Intruder Detection/Lockout restrictions. If a user successfully meets all of these restrictions, he or she is allowed to continue on to Layer 3.

▶ *Layer 3: NDS Security* — Once you enter the NDS tree, a sophisticated NDS security structure determines your ability to access leaf and container objects. At the heart of NDS security is the Access Control List (ACL). The ACL is a property of every NDS object. It defines who can access the object (trustees) and what each trustee can do (rights). The ACL is divided into two types of rights: object rights and property rights.

▶ *Layer 4: File System Access Rights* — Before you can access any files on the NetWare 5.1 server, you must have the appropriate file system access rights. Following is a list of the eight rights that control access to NetWare 5.1 files: Supervisor, Read, Write, Create, Erase, Modify, File Scan, and Access Control.

▶ *Layer 5: Directory/File Attributes* — Directory and file attributes provide the final layer of the NetWare 5.1 security model. These attributes are rarely used, but they provide a powerful tool for specific security solutions. NetWare 5.1 supports three different types of attributes: Security attributes, Feature attributes, and Disk Management attributes.

Well, there you have it. That's a brief snapshot of NetWare 5.1's five-layered security model. Now we'll take a much closer look at each of these layers and learn how they can be used to create your own impenetrable network armor.

## Layer One — Login/Password Authentication

The first two layers of the NetWare 5.1 security model are concerned with login security. Login security controls who can access the network, as well when the network can be accessed and from where it can be accessed. Login security also provides continuing verification of a user's identity.

In this section, we begin with an overview of the login process flowchart. Then, we explore the first layer of login security — Login/Password Authentication.

## Login Security Overview

Login security is activated when a user attempts to log into the network. As you can see in Figure 5.2, this process involves a number of important security features, including the following:

▶ *Authentication* — This is an automatic process that verifies the origin and identity of a request from a client (such as a user).

▶ *Account restrictions* — This includes account balance, login, password, time, and workstation restrictions.

▶ *Intruder detection* — This can be used to track invalid access attempts, as well as to prevent unauthorized users from making unlimited attempts to guess a password and from breaking into the system.

When you login to the network you need to provide, at a minimum, your distinguished (complete) username, including NDS context, as well as your password. If you click the Advanced button on the login screen, you also are allowed to specify the preferred tree, context, preferred server, and so on. NDS then goes to the nearest writeable (that is, Master or Read/Write) replica of your parent partition and attempts to match the information you supplied against specific user properties in the NDS database. In other words, to verify that your User object exists. If your username does not exist in the context specified, you are denied access.

If you provide a valid username and context, the system continues to decision two — account restrictions. Using the information provided by the writeable (Master or Read/Write) replica, NDS checks all your major account restrictions, including login restrictions, time restrictions, station restrictions, network address restrictions, accounting balance, and account lockout. If you try to log in from an unauthorized workstation or during the wrong time of day, for example, access will be denied.

FIGURE 5.2

*Login process flowchart*

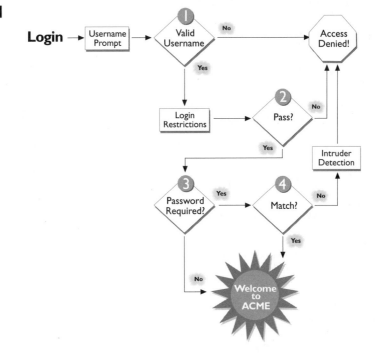

If you pass login restrictions, NDS moves on to the final two decisions—passwords. First, it uses your NDS information to determine whether a password is required. If a password is not required, you are authenticated automatically and granted access. Bad idea. If a password is required, you are prompted for it. Good idea. That brings us to the final login decision: Does the password you provided match the one in the NDS database? If not, access is denied and Intruder Detection parameters are updated.

If you provide the correct password, NetWare 5.1 uses it to decrypt the private authentication key. This completes login authentication and grants access.

In summary, the NetWare 5.1 login process consists of four decisions:

**1.** Are you using a valid username (including context)?

**2.** Do you pass login restrictions?

**3.** Is a password required?

**4.** Does your password match?

If all of these conditions are met, access is granted. As you can see in Figure 5.2, access can be denied in three ways: you type an invalid username, you don't pass login restrictions, or you provide the incorrect password. Now you should have a new appreciation for all the work that's involved when you log into the tree.

Now, let's take a closer look at the first layer of login security — Login/Password Authentication.

### Login/Password Authentication

Authentication is an automatic process that occurs in the background and is transparent to the user. It is used to verify a request from a client (such as a user). For example, when a user submits a login request, the network replies with a unique code. This code is combined with login information (such as password, workstation address, and time) to create a unique identification key. This key is then used to authenticate the user's network requests during the session.

NetWare 5.1 authentication is based on the Rivest, Shamir, and Adleman (RSA) scheme. This is a public key encryption algorithm that is extremely difficult to break. In addition to RSA, authentication uses an independent private key algorithm as well. As you can see in Figure 5.3, Login/Password Authentication consists of four sophisticated steps:

▶ *Step One: Client Requests Authentication* — NetWare 5.1 authentication requires the Novell Client to run. It uses a special workstation module to control the encryption and decryption of public and private keys — RSA.NLM. In Step One, Admin logs in by providing his or her full NDS context. The client requests authentication from the NetWare 5.1 server. The request is then handled by a special program within the core OS (Authentication Services).

▶ *Step Two: Server Returns Encrypted Key* — Once the authentication request has been accepted, NetWare 5.1 matches the user information with an encrypted private key. This private key can only be decrypted by the user password. That's Step Three.

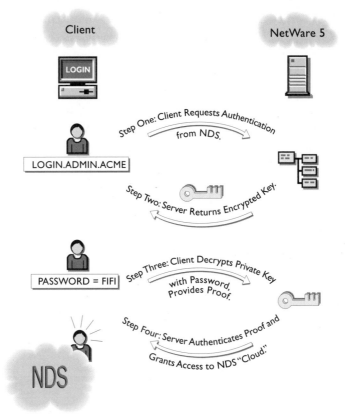

FIGURE 5.3

*NetWare 5.1
login/password
authentication*

▸ *Step Three: Client Decrypts Private Key* — In Step Three, the user provides
a valid password to decrypt the private key. With the private key, the client
creates an authenticator. This credential contains information identifying
the user's complete name, the workstation's address, and a validity period
(the duration of time the authenticator is valid). The client then creates
an encryption called a signature using the authenticator and private key.
Finally, the client requests authentication using a proof. The proof is
constructed from the signature, the request for authentication, and a
random-generated number.

> ► *Step Four: The User Is Authenticated* — During the final step, Authentication Services validates the proof as an authentic construct of the authenticator, the private key, and the message (request for authentication). Once the proof has been validated, the user is granted conditional access to the NDS tree.

The authentication process is designed to enable a user to access all network resources (for which the user has been granted rights) by using a single login. It is an ongoing process that can be used at any time (for example, by a server or client to request authentication from a workstation, or by a user to request authentication from a client or workstation).

The NetWare 5.1 authentication process is designed to guarantee the following:

► Only the purported sender built the message.

► The message came from the workstation where the authentication data was created.

► The message pertains to the current session.

► The message contains no information counterfeited from another session.

► The message has not been tampered with or corrupted.

Once you have been authenticated, you only have conditional access to the network. To become a permanent resident of the NDS tree, you must successfully pass through the second layer of the NetWare 5.1 security model — Login Restrictions. Login restrictions offer much more administrative flexibility because you can limit users according to a large number of criteria including time of day, workstation, intruder detection, and so on.

► · · · · · · · · · · · · · · · · · · · · · · · · · · · · ◄

# Layer Two — Login Restrictions

The first layer of NetWare 5.1 security (Login/Password Authentication) restricts invalid users. Login restrictions, on the other hand, restrict valid users.

Login restrictions are stored as properties of a User object. They perform two key security functions: designating account restrictions and providing intruder detection status. They control such issues as which workstation(s) a particular user can utilize to access the network, the number of concurrent connections the user is allowed, the day(s) and time(s) the user is allowed access, the expiration date for the user account, and so on.

The NetWare Administrator utility has five account restriction page tabs on the right side of a User object's Information property page, four of which are shown in Figure 5.4. These user-specific pages enable you to govern network access according to five key property categories: login restrictions, password restrictions, login time restrictions, network address restrictions, and account balance restrictions. In addition, the container-level Intruder Detection/Lockout feature enables network administrators to track unauthorized login attempts.

▶ · · · · · · · · · · · · · · · · · · · · · · · · · · · · · ◀

FIGURE 5.4

*Account restrictions for
Maid Marion*

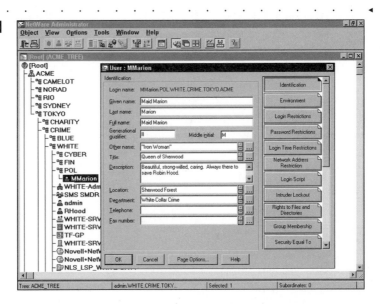

In summary, NetWare 5.1 account restrictions fall into six different categories:

▶ *Login restrictions* — Login Restrictions are set for each user. Maid Marion, for example, can have her account disabled by the network administrator, her account access automatically expire at a predetermined date/time, or have a limit placed on the number of concurrent connections she is allowed to have.

▶ *Password restrictions*— Password Restrictions impact login authentication. On this screen, we can define a variety of Maid Marion's password settings, including requiring her to have a password, requiring a minimum password length, enabling her to change her password, forcing periodic password changes, requiring a unique password, and limiting grace logins. Remember, the password is used by the client to decrypt the authentication private key.

▶ *Login time restrictions*— Time Restrictions determine when a user can be connected to the NDS tree. Time restrictions are not login restrictions per se — but rather, connection restrictions. This means users cannot login or be connected to the tree during prohibited time periods.

▶ *Network address restrictions*— Network Address Restrictions do not allow users to log in or attach from unauthorized workstations. NetWare Administrator calls these network address restrictions, because they enable you to limit user access to a specific protocol, LAN address, or node ID.

▶ *Account balance restrictions*— NetWare 5.1 includes an Accounting feature that enables you to manage Account Balance restrictions for user access to network resources. Users can be charged for a variety of NetWare 5.1 activities, including connection time, processor utilization, and disk space usage.

▶ *Intruder detection/lockout*— Finally, Intruder Detection/Lockout is a global feature that is activated at the container level. Options that can be set include whether to track unsuccessful login attempts, the maximum number of unsuccessful login attempts allowed, the time span during which unsuccessful login attempts can occur, and the amount of time an account remains locked due to intruder detection.

Now let's take a much closer look at each of these six types of NDS login restrictions, starting with login restrictions.

## Login Restrictions Page

NDS login restrictions provide a method for controlling and restricting user access to the NDS tree. They can be found on the Login Restrictions page in NetWare Administrator (see Figure 5.5). As you can see, four main options exist:

▶ *Account Disabled* — Disables and enables the user account. A network administrator can manually disable a user account by marking the "Account Disabled" box and then reenable it by unmarking the check box.

▶ *Account Has Expiration Date* — Sets a date to automatically disable the account and prevent login. To reenable an account that has been disabled by this feature, simply change the Expiration Date and Time fields to represent a future date and time.

▶ *Limit Concurrent Connections* — Limits the number of workstations a user can be simultaneously logged in from.

▶ *Last Login* — An information-only parameter that enables you to track activity on a given account by identifying the last login date and time.

FIGURE 5.5

*Login restrictions in NetWare Administrator*

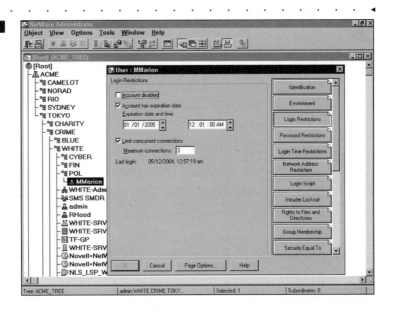

▶ · · · · · · · · · · · · · · · · · · · · · · · · · · · · ◀

## REAL WORLD

Disabling an account causes any connections in use by that account to be terminated (within a grace period tolerance) and prevents future tree logins from that account. However, it does not prevent anyone who is already logged in from authenticating to another server. Therefore, the only way to force a user off the network immediately is to delete the User object for that user. Once this change has propagated throughout the tree, the user is blocked from authenticating to any server!

## Password Restrictions Page

Password restrictions directly impact login authentication. As we saw in Figure 5.2 earlier, NetWare 5.1 access can be granted in one of two ways—by providing the correct password (if one is needed) *or* automatically (if no password is required). Although NDS does not require each User object to have a password, you should make it mandatory within your organization. Otherwise, authentication is crippled. Once you require a password, the question remains, "Who manages it?"—you or the user.

The Password Restrictions property page provides the following six security parameters for managing user account passwords (follow along in Figure 5.6):

- ▶ *Allow User to Change Password*—Allows a user to change his or her own password.

- ▶ *Require a Password*—Requires a password for the user account. You should always mark this check box to prevent unauthorized access. Marking this check box enables you to optionally set the next two password restrictions in this list.

- ▶ *Minimum Password Length*—Sets a minimum password length. The default is 5 characters, although NDS supports up to 128 characters.

- ▶ *Force Periodic Password Changes*—Specifies how often the password must be changed. The default is every 40 days. Alternately, you can indicate a specific date/time for the password to expire.

Marking this check box allows you to optionally set the two remaining password restrictions in this list.

▶ *Require Unique Password* — Prevents the user from reusing a previous password. NDS retains the eight most recent passwords for this user.

▶ *Limit Grace Logins* — Specifies how many times the user can decline to change his or her password once it has expired, without locking the account. If a user account has been disabled by this feature, simply change the value in the "Remaining Grace Logins" field from "0" to a higher number (typically the same value as in the "Grace Logins Allowed" field) to reenable the account.

▶ . . . . . . . . . . . . . . . . . . . . . . . . . . . ◀

**FIGURE 5.6**

*Password restrictions in NetWare Administrator*

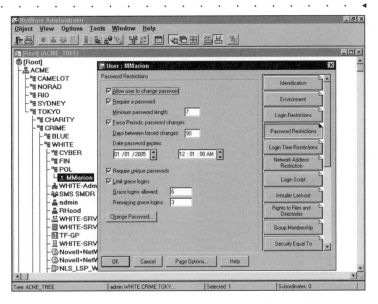

That completes our discussion of password restrictions. Aren't they fun? As you can see, there's much more to NetWare 5.1 passwords than meets the eye. Remember, this is the foundation of our login authentication strategy. Don't underestimate the importance of passwords. Use them — or suffer the consequences.

**REAL WORLD**

Many times password expiration and grace logins cause unneeded friction between network administrators and users, especially when users abuse the privilege and network administrators ultimately have to change the passwords anyway. Consider making password expiration a *big event*. In container login scripts, use the PASSWORD_EXPIRES login script identifier variable to count down the number of days until password expiration (see Chapter 3 earlier). Then when the day arrives, throw a party, bring in balloons and cake, and have everyone change their passwords at once. Turning this event into a party makes password transition every 90 days fun and unobtrusive. It's also a great excuse to have four parties a year.

## Login Time Restrictions Page

The Login Time Restrictions property page provides a weeklong grid for indicating *when* a user is allowed to log into the network. As you can see in Figure 5.7, the grid is organized into 30-minute intervals on a 7-day, 24-hour schedule. A white cell indicates that login is allowed; a gray cell indicates that login is restricted.

FIGURE 5.7

*Login time restrictions in NetWare Administrator*

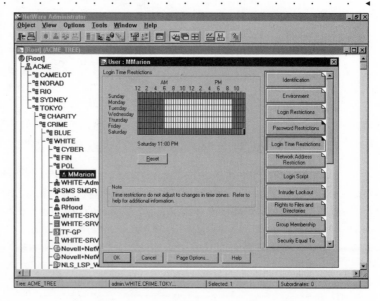

For example, a user can be assigned a login window of 6:00 a.m. to 9:00 p.m. on Monday through Friday by ensuring that the corresponding cells are white on the schedule grid — and the rest are gray. This feature can be configured for an individual user or for multiple users using the Details on Multiples Users feature.

Each square in Figure 5.7 represents a 30-minute interval. The shaded area represents inactive time periods. The white area shows that users can log in any time between 6:00 a.m. and 9:00 p.m. Time restrictions go beyond login restrictions and become connection restrictions. Not only can they not log in — they can't even be connected. If a user fails to heed a time restriction warning, the user connection is cleared without saving any open files. This is a very serious problem. Clearing Maid Marion's connection could result in data corruption or data loss. Make sure users understand that when they receive such a message, they need to immediately save their work and log out.

Don't go crazy with time restrictions. Intelligent time restrictions increase network security, but careless time restrictions can significantly hinder user productivity. (It also causes angry users to call you in the middle of the night when they're trying to meet a contract deadline.) In other words, you want to give users time to work, but not leave the network susceptible to after-hours hacking.

### Network Address Restrictions Page

The Network Address Restrictions property page (shown in Figure 5.8) enables you to limit users to specific protocols, network segments, or physical machines. This page includes two main security parameters:

- *Network Address Restrictions* — Indicates the network addresses (workstations) from which the user can log in. The format of each network address depends on the protocol.

- *Network Protocol* — Allows you to restrict a user to a specific protocol on a multiprotocol network.

▶ · · · · · · · · · · · · · · · · · · · · · · · · · · · · ◀

F I G U R E   5.8

*Network address restrictions in NetWare Administrator*

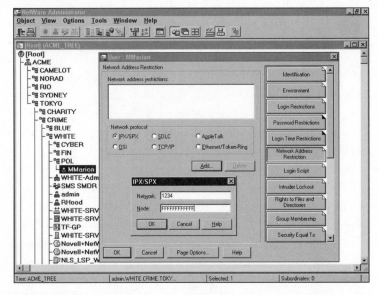

**TIP**

**Unfortunately, NetWare Administrator doesn't dynamically interrogate the network to determine network addresses for you. You must use other NetWare 5.1 or third-party utilities to gain network and node ID information.**

Like other login restrictions, network address restrictions can significantly impede user productivity if they are misconfigured. What happens, for example, when Maid Marion travels to another location? Or, what if we restrict her to one workstation and the machine goes down? These are all important considerations. Although station restrictions are a useful security tool, they can also be detrimental to user relationships.

## Account Balance Restrictions Page

The NetWare 5.1 *Accounting* feature enables you to "charge" a user for the use of certain network resources and services. If this feature has been activated on a particular server, the Account Balance Restrictions property page of a User object can be used to set a current account balance for the user, as well as to indicate either a low balance limit or to allow unlimited credit. The user's account balance is then charged (that is, decreased) each time the user utilizes a resource or service that is being tracked (such as connecting to the network, launching an application, or utilizing network storage space).

Ultimately, the user account is disabled once the account balance is exhausted — assuming, of course, that the "Allow Unlimited Credit" check box has not been marked. This is a way to track the cost of shared network resources by user. This feature can be configured for an individual user or for multiple users using the "Details on Multiples Users" feature.

### REAL WORLD

In NetWare Administrator, practice setting the various types of Login Restrictions available. Know the property page used to set each parameter, and understand the purpose of each restriction. For example, know the correct method for unlocking a user account — whether it is locked because the Account Disabled check box is marked, the Expiration Date and Time has expired, the Grace Logins Remaining parameter has been exceeded, or the Intruder Detection/Lockout feature has been triggered.

## Intruder Detection/Lockout

Welcome to *Whoville*. Intruder Detection/Lockout tracks invalid login attempts by monitoring users who try to log in without correct passwords. As you recall from Figure 5.2 earlier, this feature increments every time a valid user provides an incorrect password. Once Intruder Detection has reached a threshold number of attempts, the account is locked completely.

There's one very important concept you need to know about this final login restriction — it's a container-based configuration. All the previous restrictions have been user-based. As you can see in Figure 5.9, intruder detection is activated at the Organization or Organizational Unit level. Once an account has been locked, it must be reactivated at the user level. Two main configuration elements exist:

  ▸ Intruder detection limits

  ▸ Lock account after detection

▶ · · · · · · · · · · · · · · · · · · · · · · · · · · · · · · · · · · · · · · ◀

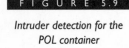

FIGURE 5.9

*Intruder detection for the POL container*

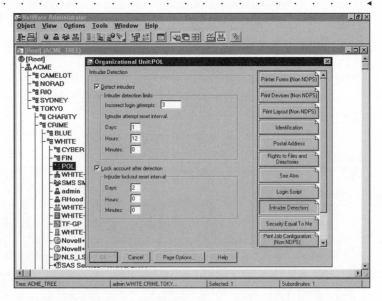

Once Intruder Detection/Lockout has been activated at the container level, all users in that container are tracked. Let's take a closer look.

### Intruder Detection Limits

Intruder Detection is turned off by default. To activate it, you simply click the Detect Intruders check box. Once you activate Intruder Detection, it begins tracking incorrect login attempts. This parameter is set to seven by default. As soon as the incrementing number exceeds the threshold, account lockout occurs (if this feature has been specified). Finally, the Intruder Attempt Reset Interval is a window of opportunity, so to speak. The system uses it to increment the incorrect login attempts. It is set to 30 minutes by default.

Here's how it works. Assume the Incorrect Login Attempts parameter is set to 3 and Intruder Attempt Reset Interval is set to 1 day, 12 hours (see Figure 5.9 earlier). The system tracks all incorrect login activity and locks the user account if the number of incorrect login attempts exceeds 3 in the 36-hour window. Pretty simple, huh? Now let's take a look at what happens once Intruder Detection is activated.

### Lock Account After Detection

This is the second half of Intruder Detection/Lockout. After all, the feature wouldn't be much good if you didn't punish the intruder for entering the wrong password. When you activate the Lock Account After Detection parameter, NDS asks for an Intruder Lockout Reset Interval. By default, this value is set to 15 minutes. Doesn't make much sense, does it? This invites the hacker to come back 15 minutes later and try all over again. Typically, a value equal to or exceeding the Intruder Attempt Reset Interval is adequate. As you saw in Figure 5.9 earlier, we're locking the account for two days, giving you enough time to track down the intruder.

So, what happens to the user when the account is locked? As you can see in Figure 5.10, NetWare 5.1 tracks account lockout at the user level. The Intruder Lockout screen provides three important pieces of information:

▶ *Incorrect Login Count* — A dynamic parameter that tells the user how many incorrect login attempts have been detected during this reset interval. If the account is locked, the incorrect login count should equal the lockout threshold.

▶ *Account Reset Time* — Informs the user how much time is remaining before the account is unlocked automatically.

▶ *Last Intruder Address* — Shows the network and node address of the workstation that attempted the last incorrect login. This parameter provides you with valuable information, regardless of whether the account is locked. This is pretty undeniable evidence that someone tried to hack this account from a specific workstation. You don't have to worry about disputed evidence or planted gloves.

So, who's going to unlock Maid Marion's account? You! Only Admin or distributed administrators can unlock accounts that have been locked by the Intruder Detection feature (in other words, someone with the Supervisor right to the User object). But what about Admin? After all, Admin is the most commonly hacked account — with good reason. If you don't have an Admin-like user to unlock the Admin account, consider using the ENABLE LOGIN command at the file server console. It's always nice to have a back door.

**FIGURE 5.10**

*Intruder lockout for MMarion*

In summary, the Intruder Detection/Lockout feature enhances NetWare 5.1 login security by providing the following security tracking features:

▶ Controls how many times a user can provide an incorrect password within a specified time period.

▶ Prevents intruders from guessing account passwords.

▶ Records the network address of an intruder.

▶ Locks targeted user accounts (if this feature has been set).

Congratulations, you are in! You've successfully navigated the first two layers of the NetWare 5.1 security model—Login/Password Authentication and Login Restrictions. As you learned, the first two layers allow you in, but what you can do once you are inside the tree relies on NDS and file system security.

**For some great hands-on experience with NetWare 5.1 Login Restrictions, check out Lab Exercise 5.4 at the end of the chapter.**

**TIP**

# Layer Three — NDS Security

Welcome to the NDS tree!

Access to the tree is one thing; being able to do *anything* in the tree is another. Until you've been granted sufficient NDS access rights, most network objects are unavailable to you. NDS security controls access to NDS objects and their properties in the Directory. It determines who can access the information and what can be done with it. NDS security is the main method of controlling network resources because it manages access to the Directory (where all resource information is stored).

At the heart of NDS security is the Access Control List (ACL) — which is stored in the Object Trustees property of every NDS object. It defines who can access the object (trustees) and what they can do with it (access rights). In this section, we discuss the six NDS object rights and the six NDS property rights, as well as explore three steps for assigning and restricting trustees. In addition, we examine NDS security guidelines and investigate troubleshooting suggestions.

Although NDS security and file system security are separate, you find that many similarities exist between the two. We discuss many of these similarities and differences when we discuss file system security later in this chapter.

## Understanding NDS Access Rights

Access to NDS objects is controlled by 12 different access rights, which are arranged in two categories:

▸ *Object rights* — These are rights granted to a trustee of an NDS object. They control what a trustee can do with an object, such as browsing (viewing), creating, renaming, or deleting it. These rights don't apply to the object's properties (except for the Supervisor right).

▸ *Property rights* — These are rights granted to a trustee of an NDS object. They control what a trustee can do with the object's properties, such as reading (viewing), comparing, or modifying them. Interestingly, NDS security allows you to assign access rights for all properties within an object or just selected ones.

Let's use the famous "box analogy" to understand the difference between these two different sets of NDS access rights. Think of an NDS object as a box. Like any other three-dimensional rectangloid, the box has external characteristics. You can look at the box and describe its color, size, and shape. By describing the outside of the box, you have a good idea of the type of box it is. But you don't know anything else about it, especially what's inside the box. With object rights, you can look at the box, destroy the box, relabel the box, or create a new one. But you can't get specific information about what's inside the box — that requires property rights.

The contents of the box are similar to what's inside an NDS object — in other words, properties. In most cases, the contents of different boxes vary. One box may contain caviar, while another contains video games. To see what's inside the box, you need permission to open it and look inside. With the proper rights, you can compare properties in this box with properties in other boxes, you can read the packing list, or you can change the contents of the box altogether. It all depends on which property rights you have.

### Object Rights

Object rights control what trustees can do with an NDS object. As you can see in Figure 5.11, the object rights spell a company name — BCDRSI (that is, B.C. Doctors, Inc.). So, what do NDS object rights have to do with dinosaurs? Absolutely nothing, but it's an easy way to remember these rights. Just visualize Jurassic Park and all the sick dinosaurs.

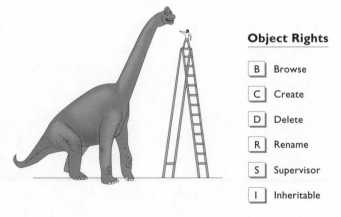

**FIGURE 5.11**

*A Jurassic set of object rights*

**Object Rights**

| B | Browse |
| C | Create |
| D | Delete |
| R | Rename |
| S | Supervisor |
| I | Inheritable |

Following are the six object rights supported by NDS and their functions:

▸ *Supervisor (S)* — Grants an object trustee all access privileges to the object. It also provides the object trustee with the Supervisor right to All Properties of the object.

▸ *Browse (B)* — Enables an object trustee to see the object while browsing the NDS tree.

▸ *Create (C)* — Enables an object trustee to create objects below the designated object in the NDS tree. This right is only available for container objects (because a leaf object cannot contain other objects).

▸ *Delete (D)* — Enables an object trustee to delete the object from the NDS tree.

▸ *Rename (R)* — Enables an object trustee to change the name of the object.

▸ *Inheritable (I)* — Enables an object trustee of a container to inherit the assigned object rights to subcontainer and leaf objects within the container. This right is granted by default to facilitate inheritance. If this right is revoked, an object trustee is limited to the rights assigned for the container only and does not inherit any rights to the objects it contains. This right is only available for container objects.

Except for a few minor exceptions, object rights have no impact on properties. Remember, we're dealing with the outside of the box at this point. If you want to have control over the contents of the box, you need to be granted Property rights.

**TIP**

**Because an NDS object is an entry in the NDS database, it can also be referred to as an *entry object*. As a result, object rights can also be known as *Entry Rights*. Furthermore, property rights can be known as *Attribute Rights* because they grant access to the attributes of a property. However, for the purpose of clarity, we use the terms *Object Right* and *Property Right* from this point forward.**

### Property Rights

Property rights control access to the information stored within an NDS object. They enable users to see, search for, and change the contents of the box. At a minimum, you must be a trustee of an object in order to be granted rights to its properties. As you can see in Figure 5.12, the property rights almost spell a word — SCRAW(L)I(NG). To cure the dinosaur, you have to write a pretty big prescription. This involves that unique medical skill known as SCRAWlIng. (Wait 'til you see my signature at the end of Chapter 7.)

▶ · · · · · · · · · · · · · · · · · · · · · · · · · · · · ◀

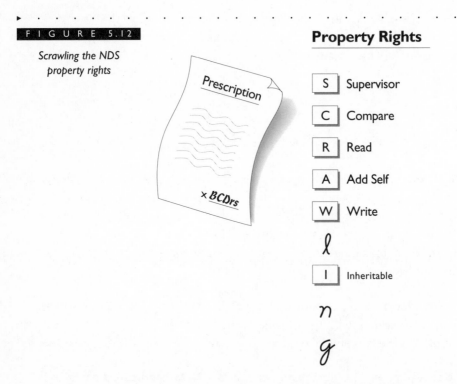

FIGURE 5.12

Scrawling the NDS property rights

**Property Rights**

| S | Supervisor |
| C | Compare |
| R | Read |
| A | Add Self |
| W | Write |
| ℓ |  |
| I | Inheritable |
| n |  |
| g |  |

Following are the six property rights supported by NetWare 5.1 and their functions:

▶ *Supervisor (S)* — Grants an object trustee all access privileges to an object's properties.

▶ *Compare (C)* — Enables an object trustee to compare a specified value to the value(s) stored within the property. With the Compare right, an operation can return True or False, but does not indicate the value(s) of the property. The Compare right is automatically granted when a user is assigned the Read property right.

▶ *Read (R)* — Grants an object trustee the right to see the value(s) of the property. This is better than Compare because it actually enables you to view the property values rather than having to guess what they are.

▶ *Write (W)* — Enables an object trustee to modify, add, change, and/or delete property values. Granting the Write right automatically grants the Add/Remove Self right.

▶ *Add/Remove Self (A)* — Enables an object trustee to add or remove itself as a value of the object property.

▶ *Inheritable (I)* — Enables an object trustee of a container to inherit the assigned property rights to subcontainer and leaf objects within the container. This right is granted by default when the All Properties option is selected and removed by default when the Selected Properties option is chosen. If this right is revoked, an object trustee is limited to the rights assigned for the container's properties only and does not inherit any rights to the properties of the objects it contains. This right is only available for container objects. Finally, the Inheritable rights is only available on NetWare 5.*x* servers.

**One of the most notable object/property exceptions involves the Supervisor [S] object right. Be careful. It gives the user Supervisor [S] property rights to All Properties.**

TIP

In NetWare Administrator, property rights can be granted using two different options: All Properties or Selected Properties (see Figure 5.13).

FIGURE 5.13

*Assigning selected property rights in NetWare Administrator*

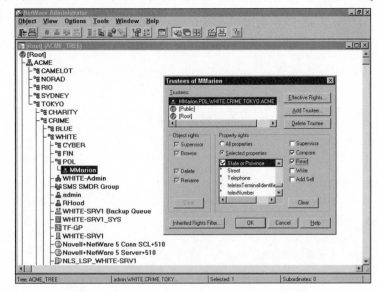

The *All Properties* option assigns the rights you indicate for all properties of the object. A list of these properties is displayed in the Selected Properties window. As you can see in Figure 5.13, the All Properties radio button sits above the Selected Properties button. If it was marked, then MMarion would be able to read and compare all properties, not just the selected ones. Interestingly, ConsoleOne refers to the All Properties option as All Attributes.

The *Selected Properties* option, on the other hand, enables you to fine-tune NDS security for specific properties. In Figure 5.13, the Selected Properties radio button is marked, and the State or Province property is highlighted. Also, we have marked the check box corresponding to each property right that we want to assign (which is Read and Compare in this example). It's important to note that the list of properties available is different for each type of object. For example, notice that a Group object has fewer properties than a User object. Finally, granting trustee rights to Selected Properties overwrites any rights granted through the All Properties option. This is very powerful because it enables you to grant additional rights to certain properties, even though a general assignment already exists.

For example, suppose that an administrative assistant must maintain the phone numbers and fax numbers for specific users. First, assign the administrative assistant as a trustee of all the User objects he or she will be managing. Then, grant him or her selected rights [RW] to the Fax Number and Telephone properties of each User object. This enables the administrative assistant to manage only the telephone numbers and fax numbers of the target users.

**TIP**

**Trustees of an NDS container can be granted the Inheritable property right. By default, the Inheritable property right is granted to an object trustee when container rights are assigned through the All Properties option. However, the Inheritable right must be manually assigned to an object trustee when container property rights are assigned through the Selected Properties option. If you then need to block the inheritance of selected property rights lower in the tree, you can create a new trustee assignment which revokes the Inheritable right.**

Now that you understand the function of Object and Property access rights, let's learn how they work. NDS security supports a three-step model for granting and restricting object/property rights:

▸ *Step One: Assigning Trustee Rights* — First, grant NDS object and property rights using trustee assignments, inheritance, and security equivalence.

▸ *Step Two: Blocking Inherited Rights* — Next, you can block inherited rights by granting a trustee a new trustee assignment lower in the tree (which affects only the trustee) or by using one or more Inherited Rights Filters (which affects everyone).

▸ *Step Three: Calculating Effective Rights* — Finally, a trustee's effective rights are calculated as the combination of trustee assignments, inheritance (minus any rights blocked by an Inherited Rights Filter [IRF] or a trustee assignment lower in the tree), and security equivalence.

Let's get started.

## Step One: Assigning Trustee Rights

The NDS security model is as easy as 1-2-3. So far, we've talked about object and property rights. Understanding these rights is a prerequisite to building an NDS security model. But it's certainly not enough. Now you have to learn how to implement these rights in the ACME NDS tree.

Step One deals with assigning NDS access rights using one of two methods:

▸ Trustee Assignments

▸ Inheritance

*Trustee Assignments* involve work — this is bad, of course, because our goal is to minimize the amount of work we do. But you have to start somewhere. Trustee assignments are granted using NetWare Administrator, ConsoleOne, and/or FILER.

*Inheritance*, on the other hand, doesn't involve work — this is good. Inheritance normally happens automatically when you assign trustee rights at the container level and include the Inheritable (*I*) right. Just like water flowing down a mountain, trustee rights flow down the NDS tree — from top to bottom. The beauty of this feature is that you can assign sweeping rights for large groups of users with a single trustee assignment.

### Trustee Assignments

A *trustee* is any NDS object with rights to another object. Trustees are tracked through a target object's Access Control List (ACL), which is stored in the target object's Object Trustees (ACL) property. Every object has an Object Trustees (ACL) property listing the trustees of the object and the rights each trustee has been assigned. NetWare 5.1 supports the following types of trustees:

*User object* — This is a leaf object that represents a single user. Assign trustee rights to a User object if the rights are unique to that user. A User object can also receive NDS and file system rights by being granted security equivalence to another object in the NDS tree. Security equivalence gives one User object the same rights as another object, typically another User object. This method of trustee assignment is accomplished using the Security Equivalence property.

*Group object* — This is a leaf object that represents a group of users. Any rights that are granted to a Group object are automatically passed on to all members of the group. Assign trustee rights to a Group object if they are needed by a variety of people in a subset of a container or in different containers.

*Organizational Role* — This is a leaf object, similar to a Group object, except that users are identified as occupants rather than members. This object is used to specify a particular role in the organization, rather than just a group of users. Any rights granted to an Organizational Role object are automatically passed on to all occupants of the organizational role. You should grant rights to an Organizational Role object when the rights pertain to a specific job position rather than a person. For example, over the course of a year, one role or job might be staffed by five or six different people. Without an Organizational Role object, these changes would require frequent network administration.

 *Container object* — This is considered a *natural group*. If you make a container object a trustee of any other object, all users and subcontainers of the container inherit those same rights (provided, however, that the *I* right is assigned).

 *[Root]* — When NetWare 5.1 is installed on the first server in your tree, the [Root] object is automatically created at the highest level in the tree. All users who successfully log into the tree are made security equivalent to the [Root]. As such, assigning the [Root] as a trustee of another object gives all NDS users the same rights as those granted to the [Root]. Unlike the [Public] trustee, users must be authenticated to receive rights that have been granted to the [Root]. To protect NDS resources and services, avoid using the [Root] trustee for granting access to objects in the NDS tree. The [Root] object is found inside "The Network" container in ConsoleOne.

 *[Public]* — This is a special system-owned trustee. When NetWare 5.1 is installed on the first server in your tree, [Public] is automatically made a trustee of the [Root] object and is assigned the Browse right. All NDS objects are security equivalent to [Public]. In fact, anyone who is connected to the tree (whether or not they are logged in) has the same rights as [Public]. This means, for example, that anyone who is connected to the tree (whether or not they are logged in) can view every object in the tree. To protect NDS resources and services, avoid using the [Public] trustee for granting access to objects in the NDS tree.

Once you identify *who* is going to get the rights, you have to determine *what* rights you're going to give them and *where* the rights will be assigned: *which* of the twelve object and property rights, and *where* can the object be in the NDS tree. Take Figure 5.14, for example. As you can see, Sherlock Holmes is granted all object rights to the .OU=TOKYO.O=ACME container. In the figure, we have satisfied all three of the trustee assignment elements — who, what, and where.

F I G U R E   5.14

*Understanding NetWare*
*5.1 trustee assignments*

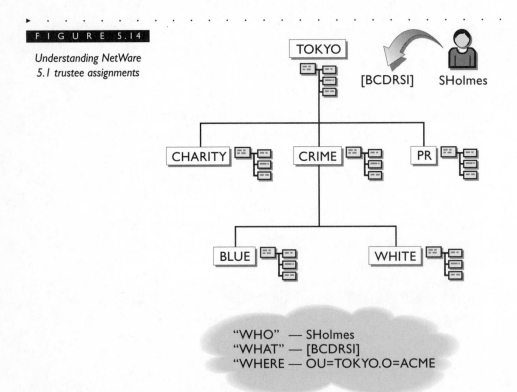

So, how is this accomplished in NetWare Administrator? It depends on your point of view. You have two choices:

▸ *Rights to Other Objects* — This is from Sherlock Holmes' point of view.

▸ *Trustees of This Object* — This is from OU=TOKYO's point of view.

It really doesn't matter which option you choose. You can either assign rights from the user's point of view or the object's point of view. In the first example, we assign security from Sherlock Holmes' point of view. In NetWare Administrator, highlight the SHolmes object and click the right mouse button. An abbreviated dialog box appears. As you can see in Figure 5.15, two security options exist. In this case, we're interested in "Rights to Other Objects."

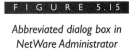

F I G U R E   5.15

*Abbreviated dialog box in NetWare Administrator*

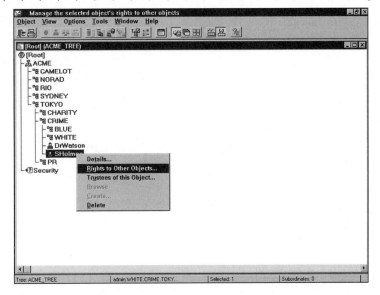

**TIP**

**You can also make an object a trustee of another object in NetWare Administrator by dragging the object over another object. Naturally, any trustee rights indicated are not actually assigned until you click the OK button on the dialog box that appears.**

The "Rights to Other Objects" dialog box is shown in Figure 5.16. This displays the NDS security window from Sherlock Holmes' point of view. As you can see, he has been granted all object rights to the TOKYO Organizational Unit. Specifically, the Supervisor object right implies the Supervisor property rights to All Properties. This was accomplished using the Add Assignment button.

FIGURE 5.16

*Assigning NDS rights from the user's point of view*

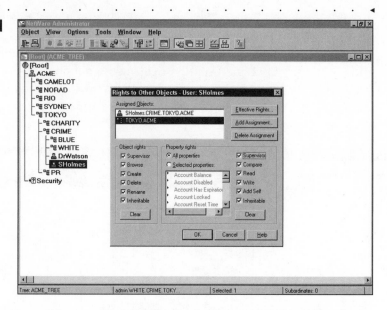

The second option enables you to assign NDS rights from TOKYO's point of view. In this case, you would select OU=TOKYO.O=ACME from the Browse window and click using the right mouse button. The same abbreviated menu appears (as shown earlier in Figure 5.15). This time, though, choose Trustees of This Object. Figure 5.17 shows the NDS security window from TOKYO's point of view. Notice the default trustee. In addition, SHolmes has been added with all object and property rights. This was accomplished using the Add Trustee button.

It is important to note that check marks and object rights appearing in gray are not assigned rights. Assigned rights appear in boldface with a boldface check mark. In addition, some trustees may unexpectedly appear in the Trustee list of a target object as the result of default object or property rights assigned automatically by NetWare. These default rights can be overwritten by an explicit rights assignment.

There you have it. As you can see, it doesn't matter how you assign trustee rights. Both methods get the same result—Sherlock Holmes (who) is granted [BCDRSI] object rights (what) to .OU=TOKYO.O=ACME (where). Now, let's explore a simpler method of assigning NDS access rights—inheritance.

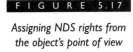

FIGURE 5.17

*Assigning NDS rights from the object's point of view*

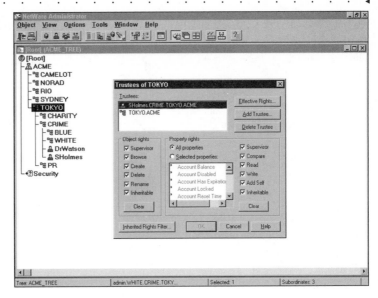

## Inheritance

NDS rights can also be obtained through inheritance. Inheritance minimizes the individual rights assignments needed to administer the network because object/property rights can automatically flow down the tree from containers to subcontainers to leaf objects. The Create right does not flow down to leaf objects, however, because the Create right only pertains to container objects. Both object rights and property rights can be inherited. However, in the case of property rights, the Inheritable right must be explicitly granted to a selected property.

NDS inheritance is an automatic side effect of trustee assignments. As you can see in Figure 5.18, Sherlock Holmes ends up with a lot more than he bargained for. When you assign him the [BCDRSI] object rights to .OU=TOKYO.O=ACME, he actually inherits these rights for all containers and objects underneath TOKYO as well. Now he has all object rights to all containers and all objects in that portion of the tree — this might not be good. We'll figure out how to resolve this problem in the next section.

FIGURE 5.18

*NDS inheritance for
Sherlock Holmes*

TOKYO

[BCDRSI]

Trustee
Assignment

SHolmes

CHARITY
[BCDRSI]

CRIME
[BCDRSI]

PR
[BCDRSI]

Inheritance

BLUE
[BCDRSI]

WHITE
[BCDRSI]

Both object and property rights can be inherited. However, in the case of property rights, only the All Properties option allows automatic inheritance. With the Selected Properties option, you must manually assign the *I* (Inheritable) right to each specific property, if desired. This is because the Inheritable selected property right is not marked by default when the Selected Properties option is used. The Inheritable right is, however, marked by default for object and All Properties rights assignments.

### REAL WORLD

In previous versions of NetWare, rights granted to selected properties could not be inherited. With the version of NDS that comes with NetWare 5.1, however, selected property rights can be inherited if the Inheritable (*I*) right is explicitly granted. (By default, the Inheritable right is not granted when the Selected Properties option is selected.) In addition, if you attempt to use NetWare Administrator to assign rights to specific properties, you notice that the utility automatically assigns default object and All Properties rights at the same time. Make sure you modify the default assignments to reflect the appropriate rights.

There you have it, rights have been assigned. In Step One, we learned two different ways exist for assigning rights to NDS trustees: trustee assignments and inheritance. We also learned that a variety of different trustee types exist, including [Root] and [Public]. The good news is, most of your work stops here. Only in special cases do you need to go on to Steps Two and Three.

Let's explore the remaining two steps, anyway.

## Step Two: Blocking Inherited Rights

Inheritance provides an excellent method for assigning sweeping sets of rights to large numbers of users. However, it can get out of hand very quickly, as shown earlier in Figure 5.18. As you recall from our ACME overview in Chapter 1, Sherlock Holmes heads up the Crime Fighting division. He probably shouldn't have Supervisor object rights to Charity and PR. Fortunately, we can rectify the situation. NetWare 5.1 provides two methods for blocking the inheritance of rights:

- ▸ Granting a new trustee assignment

- ▸ Blocking inherited rights with an Inherited Rights Filter (IRF)

Let's take a closer look.

### Granting a New Trustee Assignment

Inherited object and property rights can be overwritten by granting new assignments lower in the NDS tree. This strategy is particularly useful when you want to overwrite specific property rights that have been granted using the All Properties option. Remember, the Inheritable property right is granted by default when rights are assigned using the All Properties option. So, you can block specific property rights from being inherited by granting a new Selected Properties trustee assignment lower in the tree.

For example, if we assign SHolmes [B] rights to the CHARITY and PR in Figure 5.18 earlier, then he would lose his inheritance for these containers. The new trustee assignment would become his effective right. Creating a new trustee assignment is particularly useful for overwriting Property rights granted with the All Properties option.

### Blocking Inherited Rights with an Inherited Rights Filter (IRF)

As it turns out, there's a problem with Sherlock Holmes' inheritance. Because he's been assigned [BCDRSI] object rights to .OU=TOKYO.O=ACME, he becomes the distributed administrator of that entire section of the tree — this is bad. Sherlock

Holmes is responsible for the Crime Fighting division. He has no authority over CHARITY or PR. However, his inheritance model shows [BCDRSI] object rights to both OU=CHARITY and OU=PR (see Figure 5.18 earlier). We're obviously going to have to do act on this right away.

An object's IRF can be used to block the inheritance of either object and/or property rights. Here's a summary of the rules governing IRFs:

▶ The IRF is an inclusive filter, which means the rights that are in the filter are the ones that are allowed to pass through.

▶ An IRF can only block rights that have been *inherited* from trustee assignments higher in the tree. Remember, inheritance requires the Inheritable (*I*) object and/or property right. Therefore, IRFs only work on rights inherited in conjunction with (*I*).

▶ An object's IRF does not apply to trustee assignments themselves. In other words, if your User object is assigned rights to the object via a trustee assignment, that assignment would not be affected by the object's IRF.

▶ An object's IRF blocks the inheritance of everyone in the tree. Once you've modified an object's IRF, everyone is affected, including Admin — assuming, of course, that they don't have an explicit trustee assignment to the object. To block rights inheritance for specific users only, grant the users a new trustee assignment at the level where the new rights should take effect, rather than using an IRF.

▶ The NDS Supervisor object right can be blocked by an IRF in the NDS tree. It cannot be blocked, however, by an IRF in the file system.

▶ If you attempt to block the Supervisor [S] right with an IRF, NetWare Administrator first requires that you make an explicit Supervisor [S] trustee assignment to someone (assuming, of course, that one does not already exist). This is so that access to that portion of the tree is not permanently blocked.

▸ An object's IRF can be used to block the inheritance of either object and/or property rights. If used to block inherited property rights, it can block property rights originally granted through either the All Properties option, or the Selected Properties option (assuming, of course, that the Inheritable [I] right was granted at the time).

Figure 5.19 shows how the IRF can be used to solve our Sherlock Holmes problem. We create an inclusive IRF of [B] to block everything under CHARITY and PR except the Browse right. His inheritance in OU=CRIME, however, remains unaffected.

FIGURE 5.19

*Blocking NDS rights with the IRF*

So, *how do we assign an IRF?* Once again, NetWare Administrator is our friend. Earlier we learned that trustee assignments can be assigned in one of two ways — "Rights to Other Objects" and "Trustees of This Object." IRFs are accomplished using only one of these two choices. Can you figure out which one? Correct — it's "Trustees of This Object." Remember, IRFs are host-object specific. They work from the host's point of view and apply to every object in the NDS tree.

Figure 5.20 shows the IRF dialog box for .CHARITY.TOKYO.ACME. Notice the downward arrows that appear next to each check box. These differentiate IRF rights from trustee assignments. Also notice that the IRF window doesn't include the Inheritable (I) right. This is logical because the Inheritable right *allows* inheritance, rather than blocking it. As you can see in the figure, IRFs are created from the target object's point of view. This is because IRFs affect all objects in the NDS tree, not just individual users.

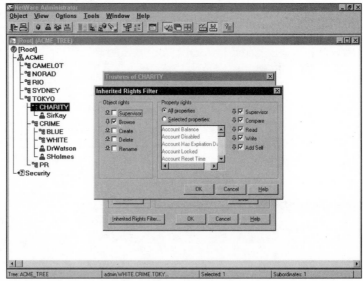

If the IRF applies to all objects in the tree, who is going to administer the OU=CHARITY and OU=PR containers? As you can see in Figure 5.19 earlier, no one can have the [CDRS] object rights. Fortunately, trustee assignments override the IRF. Remember, the *I* in IRF stands for *Inherited*. It only works on inherited rights.

Figure 5.21 introduces two new players—SirKay (the distributed administrator of OU=CHARITY) and BThomas (the distributed administrator of OU=PR). We simply assign BThomas the [BCDRSI] object rights to OU=PR. Now he is the container administrator for this section of the tree and everyone else, including Sherlock Holmes and Admin, has been locked out. The same holds true for SirKay and OU=CHARITY.

So, let me ask you—which activity occurs first? The IRF or the new trustee assignment? Correct . . . the new trustee assignment. Remember, NetWare Administrator does not allow us to set an IRF for OU=PR until someone else has explicitly been granted Supervisor privileges. So, first we assign BThomas [BCDRSI] privileges and then we set the IRF to [B].

Good work.

So, what's the bottom line? What can Sherlock Holmes really do in the TOKYO portion of the tree? The answer can be found in "Step Three: Calculating Effective Rights."

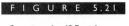

Covering the IRF with new
trustee assignments

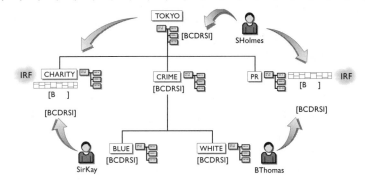

## Step Three: Calculating Effective Rights

The final step in the NDS security model is to determine an object's *effective rights*. NDS effective rights are the actual privileges one object can exercise over another. This is the resulting combination of the following:

- ► Explicit trustee assignments made to an object

- ► Inheritance minus rights blocked by an IRF (or another trustee assignment) lower in the tree

- ► Rights granted to the [Root]

- ► Rights granted to the special [Public] trustee

- ► Security equivalences to parent containers, groups, organizational roles, and so on.

**TIP**

**Remember that NDS effective rights are the actual privileges one object can exercise over another. As such, any object's effective rights are the combination of NDS privileges received through explicit trustee assignments made to an object, inheritance minus rights blocked by an IRF lower in the tree, rights granted to the [Root], rights granted to the special [Public] trustee, and security equivalences to parent containers, groups, organizational roles, and so on.**

NetWare 5.1 includes four utilities that automatically calculate effective rights for you: NetWare Administrator, ConsoleOne, NDIR, and FILER. In NetWare Administrator, for example, you can right-click a trustee object and choose Rights to Other Objects or right-click a target object and choose Trustees of this object (this second option requires less navigation).

ConsoleOne, on the other hand, has one window where you can determine the effective rights of any object in the tree. You can access the window in two ways:

▸ Right-click the object you want to receive effective rights for and then select Properties ➪ NDS Rights ➪ Effective Rights.

▸ Right-click a User object and then select Trustees of this Object.

Sometimes, however, you may need to calculate NDS effective rights manually. Follow along with Figure 5.22 as you review the following ACME example.

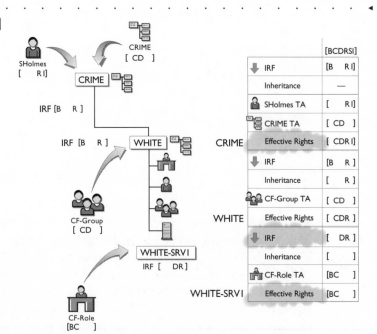

**FIGURE 5.22**

*Calculating simple NDS effective rights*

This effective rights calculation begins with a gentleman named Sherlock Holmes who lives in the CRIME container, is a member of CF-Group, and occupies the CF-Role. The SHolmes user object is given an explicit trustee assignment in which he is granted the [RI] rights to the CRIME container. The CRIME container is also granted an explicit trustee assignment of [CD] rights to itself. Because the SHolmes User object is located in the CRIME container, it is security equivalent to the CRIME container and, thus, gets the same rights. Combining the rights from both sources gives SHolmes effective rights of [CDRI] for the CRIME container. At this point, the CRIME object's IRF is ignored because explicit trustee assignments granted for a target object override the IRF of the target object.

The [CD] rights granted to the CRIME container do not flow down to the next level because the [I] right was not granted. The [RI] rights granted to SHolmes do flow down, but the [I] right is blocked by the WHITE container's IRF of [BR] — leaving just the [R] right as an inherited right. CF-Group is granted a trustee assignment of [CD] to the WHITE container. Because the SHolmes User object is a member of the CF-Group, he is security equivalent to the CF-Group, and gets the same rights. Combining the rights from the two sources gives SHolmes effective rights of [CDR] for the WHITE container.

SHolmes inherited right of [R] does not flow down to the next level because no [I] right exists there. The CF-Group rights of [CD] also do not flow down for the same reason. CF-Role is granted an explicit trustee assignment of [BC] for WHITE-SRV1. Because SHolmes is an occupant of that role, he is security equivalent to CF-Role, and gets the same rights. Therefore, SHolmes has effective rights of [BC] for WHITE-SRV1.

**TIP**

**One of the trickiest aspects of NDS effective rights is deciding when trustee assignment (TA) rights override inherited rights (IR), and when they are combined. It's simple: If the trustee is the same, then TA overrides IR; if trustees are different, then TA combines with IR. In summary**

**Same = override; Different = combine!**

You see . . . that wasn't so hard. In this simple example, we had a limited number of different elements — one user trustee assignment, one group trustee assignment, and one IRF. Of course, the world is not always this simple. Now let's take a look at a more complex example. In this example (see Figure 5.23), there's one user assignment, one group trustee, an Organizational Role equivalent, and three IRFs.

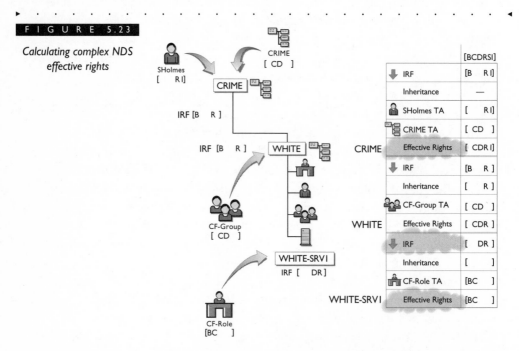

**FIGURE 5.23**

*Calculating complex NDS effective rights*

Once again, we're going to use the effective rights calculation worksheet in Figure 5.23. As before, it begins with Sherlock Holmes at the OU=CRIME container — trustee assignment of [RI]. In addition, the container is granted [CD] rights to itself. Because Sherlock Holmes lives in this context, he gains an ancestral inheritance of [CD]. This, combined with his user assignment, gives the effective rights [CDRI]. In this case, the IRF is useless — simple window dressing. Remember, trustee assignments override the IRF in the same container.

Sherlock Holmes' effective rights in OU=CRIME flow down to become his inherited rights in the OU=WHITE subcontainer. The IRF, however, blocks [CDSI] so his inheritance becomes [R]. This combines with a CF-Group trustee assignment of [CD] to give the effective rights [CDR].

Now, here's the tricky part. The OU=WHITE effective rights would normally flow down to the WHITE-SRV1 object. However, we restricted the Inheritable right at the OU=WHITE container. Therefore, the [CDR] effective rights stay in OU=WHITE and no inheritance is at the WHITE-SRV1 level.

*So what's the bottom line?* Let me tell you — the effective rights for WHITE-SRV1 are equivalent to any trustee assignments (TA) to the object. So, WHITE-SRV1 gets [BC] from the CF-Role Organizational Role and that's the effective rights. No sweat!

As you can see, effective rights get very complicated, very quickly. This is probably because there're so many forces at work. Remember, effective rights are the combination of trustee assignments, inheritance, [Public], and security equivalence. The default NDS rights are looking better and better all the time.

There you have it, the simple three-step NDS security model:

▸ *Step One: Assigning NDS Rights* — Through trustee assignments, inheritance, and/or security equivalence.

▸ *Step Two: Filtering IRF Rights* — The inclusive filter enables you to block inherited rights. Remember to avoid isolating sections of the tree by using new trustee assignments with IRFs.

▸ *Step Three: Calculating Effective Rights* — The actual rights that users can exercise in a given container.

Now, I bet you're glad you made it through Layer 3: NDS Security. Fortunately, there's a sophisticated foundation of NDS default rights to work from. As a matter of fact, that's just the tip of the iceberg.

Let's explore some more advanced NDS Security topics.

## LAB EXERCISE 5.1: CALCULATING NDS EFFECTIVE

OK, now that you're a pro with NetWare 5.1 NDS security, let's experiment with "modern math." In this section, we explored NetWare's version of calculus — calculating effective rights. We learned that effective rights are calculated according to the following formula:

Effective Rights = trustee assignments + inheritance – IRF
(Inherited Rights Filter)

In this exercise, we'll begin Calculus 101 with NDS access rights. Then, in Lab Exercise 5.3 (later in the chapter), you get an opportunity to explore file system effective rights. Also, we've included some beautiful graphic worksheets to help you follow along. You can create your own at home with a pencil, some paper, and a ruler.

So, without any further ado, let's get on with Case #1.

### Case #1

In this case, we are helping Sherlock Holmes gain administrative rights to the Crime Fighting division of ACME. Refer to Figure 5.24. It all starts at .CRIME. TOKYO.ACME, where he is granted [CDI] NDS privileges. No IRF (meaning all rights are allowed to flow) and no inheritance in CRIME exist.

In the next container, WHITE, SHolmes gets [SI] from his CF-Group. Also, there's an IRF of [DI]. Finally, these privileges flow down to the WHITE-SRV1 Server object and become inherited rights. But the server's IRF is set to [BR], so some of them are blocked. Also, SHolmes has an explicit trustee assignment of [D] to the WHITE-SRV1 server. Finally, Sherlock's home container, OU=WHITE, is granted [C] privileges to the Server object.

### Case #2

After careful consideration, you decide that these rights are inadequate for Sherlock and his administrative needs. So, let's try it one more time. But, in this case, we're going to use the "CF-Role" Organizational Role instead of the CF-Group. This gives us more administrative flexibility and narrows the scope of rights assignments. For this case, refer to Figure 5.25.

*Calculating NDS effective rights — Case #1*

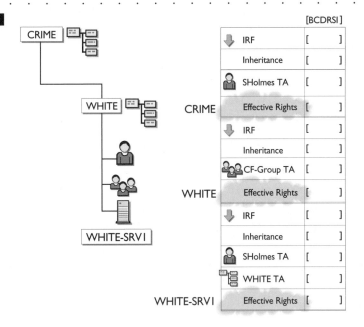

*Calculating NDS effective rights — Case #2*

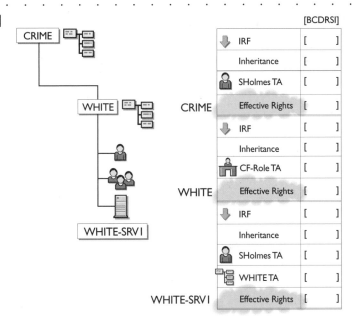

As before, it starts in the .CRIME.TOKYO.ACME container. Sherlock Holmes is granted the [BRI] rights to the container. Also, no inheritance exists in CRIME, but the IRF has been set to [CD] anyway.

In the next container, WHITE, SHolmes gets [BCD] through his CF-Role Organizational Role. Also, there's an IRF of [CDRS]. Finally, the WHITE-SRV1 Server's IRF is set to [BR]. In addition, SHolmes has an explicit trustee assignment of [CD] to the WHITE-SRV1 server. Finally, Sherlock's home container, WHITE, is granted [C] privileges to the Server object. Now, let's see what he ends up with.

**Case #3**

In this final case, let's bounce over to the .BLUE.CRIME.TOKYO.ACME container and help out Wyatt Earp — their administrator. Refer to Figure 5.26. As with most NDS trees, it actually starts much higher up — above TOKYO. Wyatt Earp inherits [BCDRI] to .TOKYO.ACME through his User object. The IRF is wide open, so all rights are allowed to flow through. In addition, he's granted Rename privileges as a user and Browse privileges through his home container — BLUE.

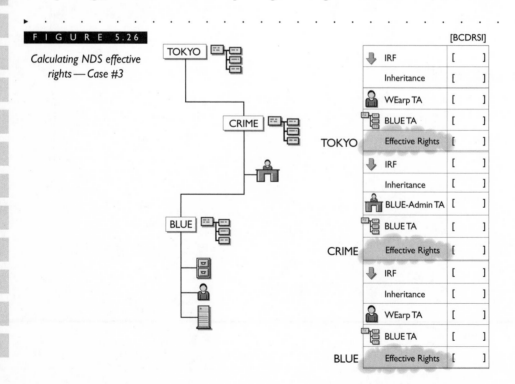

In the next container, CRIME, WEarp gets all object rights through his BLUE-Admin Organization Role. This overshadows the Browse privileges he ancestrally inherits from BLUE. Also, don't forget the CRIME IRF of [BCDI]. Finally, all rights flow down to the BLUE container and become inherited. But the Organizational Unit's IRF is set to [DR], so most of them are blocked. In addition, WEarp has an explicit trustee assignment of [C] to BLUE. This assignment is enhanced by the Browse privilege he inherits from BLUE. Good luck.

See Appendix C for the answers.

# Advanced NDS Security

So far we have focused on the comprehensive NetWare 5.1 security model that enables you to restrict network access according to a variety of criteria such as login authentication, NDS object and property rights, and file system privileges.

Now, we will expand our knowledge of NDS security into the realm of advanced NDS management. In this lesson, we study the following advanced NDS security topics:

▶ *Default NDS Rights* — first, we learn how to use NetWare's built-in NDS security model for limiting potential security loopholes. Specifically, we discover NetWare 5.1's built-in security foundation for the following activities: initial NDS installation, file server installation, user creation, and container creation.

▶ *NDS Administration* — Then, we discuss NDS administration and explore the roles of the Admin User object, distributed managers, and exclusive container administrators.

▶ *NDS Security Management* — Finally, we complete this advanced NDS security lesson with some important administrative guidelines and troubleshooting tips. Once you have established a secure foundation of NDS access rights, you should shift your focus toward distributed resource access and troubleshooting.

Let's get secure.

## Default NDS Rights

NetWare 5.1 assigns certain default NDS rights when NDS is installed on the first server in a network (also known as "initial NDS installation"). The system also grants specific NDS object and property rights each time a file server, user, or container is created. The following default security structure should be used to form the foundation of your advanced NDS management strategy. Additional security assignments can then be made, as needed.

### Initial NDS Installation

During initial NDS installation, two key objects are created: [Root] and Admin. The [Public] trustee (which is not considered an object or object class) is also created at the same time. The *[Root]* object represents the very top of the NDS tree (its icon looks like the Earth). *[Public]* is a special system-owned trustee that is somewhat (but not entirely) analogous to the EVERYONE group in NetWare 3.12. Every object in the NDS tree automatically inherits the rights of [Public]. *Admin* is the first User object in the tree. Because of this, it is granted Supervisor control over the entire network. (These privileges, however, can be modified after the fact, if desired.)

(**Note:** By default, the Admin User object is stored in the same container as the first Server object in the tree. However, with NetWare 5.1, you can customize the location of the Admin User object during server installation.)

The following default rights are assigned during initial NDS installation:

▶ *Admin* — By default, the Admin User object is granted the Supervisor and Inheritable [SI] object rights to the [Root]. This enables Admin (that is, the first User object) to administer the entire NDS tree. Distributed administrators can then be created, if needed, with appropriate rights.

▶ *[Public]* — By default, the [Public] trustee is granted the Browse and Inheritable [BI] object rights to the [Root]. This enables users in the NDS tree to see both the tree and the objects in it.

### File Server Installation

When a new file server is installed in the NDS tree, default rights are granted to the creator of the Server object, the server itself, and [Public]. Remember, to create a Server object, you must have the Supervisor [S] object right to the container that houses the Server object. The default rights assigned during server installation include the following:

▶ *Creator* — By default, the user that installs the server is granted the Supervisor [S] object right to the Server object — which enables the user to manage it. This assignment also gives this user the Supervisor [S] file system right to the root directory of all volumes on the server. Typically, the creator of a server is either Admin or a container administrator.

▶ *Server* — The Server object is granted the Supervisor [S] object right to itself. This enables the server to modify the parameters of its own object.

▶ *[Public]* — The [Public] trustee is granted the Read [R] property right to a specific server property — Messaging Server. This enables any network client to identify the messaging server assigned to this file server, which is a requirement of NetWare's Message Handling Services (MHS). [Public] is also granted the Read [R] property right to the Network Address property. This enables any network client to identify the server.

### User Creation

When you create a new User object in NDS, certain necessary rights are granted automatically. These rights are granted to provide the user with some degree of access to WAN resources. Remember, default NDS rights provide a very good beginning. In many cases, these rights are enough for users to be productive. In general, the User object receives enough rights to modify its own login script and print job configurations. Let's take a closer look:

▶ *User* — The User object is assigned three sets of property rights to its own properties. First, it is granted the Read [R] right to All Properties. This enables the user to view information about his/her own User object. Next, the User object is granted the Read and Write [RW] property rights to two selected properties — Login Script and Print Job Configuration (Non-NDPS). This enables the user to execute and change his/her own User login script and print job configurations. Notice that an obvious object right appears to be missing — the Browse [B] right to the User object.

While this right is not explicitly granted at user creation, it is available to the user through the [Public] trustee, by default. As we discussed earlier, during initial NDS installation, [Public] is granted the Browse [B] right to the [Root] — which enables a user to see all objects in the tree, including his/her own User object.

▸ *[Root]* — The [Root] is granted the Read [R] property right to two specific User object properties — Network Address and Group Membership. This enables any user in the tree to identify the user's network address, location, and group memberships.

▸ *[Public]* — The [Public] trustee is granted the Read [R] property right to a selected User property — Default Server. This enables any user in the tree to determine the default server for this user.

(**Note:** The difference between assigning rights to [Public] versus assigning them to the [Root] is that rights assigned to [Public] are automatically available to a user upon attachment to the network, whereas rights assigned to the [Root] require a valid login authentication.)

### Container Creation

Any NDS container you create receives default rights to itself. This is to ensure that all objects in the container receive the rights they need to access the resources within the container.

▸ *Container* — First, each new container gets the Read [R] property right to its own Login Script property. This enables users in the container to execute the Container login script. Next, the container receives the Read [R] property right to its own Print Job Configuration (Non-NDPS) property. This enables users in the container to read the container's print job configurations.

This completes our discussion of the default NDS rights. Refer to Table 5.1 for a summary. Hopefully, you've gained an appreciation for the sophistication of NDS default security. As you can see, users and servers are well taken care of. The only additional security you need to add is for special container administrators, traveling users, or groups — aka, NDS administration.

| | NDS EVENT | TRUSTEE | DEFAULT RIGHTS |
|---|---|---|---|
| **TABLE 5.1**<br><br>*Default NDS Security Summary* | Initial NDS installation | Admin | [SI] — Supervisor and Inheritable object rights to [Root] |
| | | [Public] | [BI] — Browse and Inheritable object rights to [Root] |
| | File server installation | Creator | [S] — Supervisor object rights to server |
| | | Server | [S] — Supervisor object rights to self |
| | | [Public] | [R] — Read right to selected server property (Messaging Server) |
| | User creation | User | [R] — Read right to All Properties<br>[RW] — Read and Write rights to selected user property (Login Script)<br>[RW] — Read and Write rights to selected user property (Print Job Configuration) |
| | | [Root] | [R] — Read right to two selected user properties (Network Address and Group Membership) |
| | | [Public] | [R] — Read right to a selected user property (Default Server) |
| | Container creation | Container | [RW] — Read and Write rights to Login Script property<br>[RW] — Read and Write rights to Print Job Configuration property |

## NDS Administration

The default rights assignments described previously are adequate for most NDS users. You only need to assign additional rights to users who manage NDS objects on a regular basis. When doing so, try to avoid using the All Properties option because you may inadvertently assign the [W] right to the Object Trustees (ACL) property of an object.

(**Note:** Having the [W] right to the Object Trustees (ACL) property of an object effectively gives the trustee the ability to grant anyone (including themselves) all rights, including the Supervisor [S] right.)

NDS enables you to use either a central or distributed administration strategy—or a combination of the two. This means, for instance, that one administrator can be responsible for the entire tree, several administrators responsible for branches of the tree, or one administrator responsible for the entire tree plus several administrators responsible for individual branches. This is accomplished with the help of three types of NDS administrators:

▸ *Centralized administrator*—A user (Admin, by default) that has been granted unrestricted (all) rights to manage the entire NDS tree.

▸ *Distributed administrator*—A user that has been granted the appropriate NDS rights needed to manage one or more branches of the NDS tree.

▸ *Exclusive container administrator*—A user that has been granted *exclusive* rights to manage one or more branches of the NDS tree. In such cases, other network administrators, including the Admin user, are blocked from managing these branches.

### Centralized Administration

In a *centralized administration* strategy, one or more users are granted unrestricted rights to manage the entire NDS tree. This is the NetWare 5.1 default. As we discussed earlier, the *Admin* User object is automatically created during initial NDS installation. By default, Admin receives Supervisor and Inheritable [SI] object rights to the [Root]. Consequently, Admin initially inherits all access rights to the entire NDS tree. (Because Admin is a regular User object, these rights can be modified or blocked at a later time, if desired.)

(**Note:** You may want to consider renaming the Admin User object to make it more difficult for intruders to locate it.)

Centralized administration is appropriate for small trees or large networks controlled by a central MIS department. The following tasks are appropriate for central administration:

▸ Renaming the Directory tree

▸ Creating the top layers of the NDS tree

▶ Partition management and time synchronization

▶ Assigning container administrators

**TIP**

**The Admin user has few special properties beyond [S1] rights to the [Root]. This user can be deleted, replaced, or generally abused. This is unlike the special Supervisor account from previous versions of NetWare, which was a "Super User" and couldn't be deleted. The moral of the story is, don't get delusions of grandeur if you log in as Admin. Remember, anyone can be Admin as long as he or she has Supervisor [S] rights to the [Root].**

### Distributed Administration

In a *distributed administration* strategy, one or more users are granted the rights needed to manage one or more branches of the NDS tree. In many situations, distributed administrators (also referred to as *container administrators*) can often respond to users' needs more quickly because network management responsibilities are not restricted to a single person.

The following administrative tasks can be distributed:

▶ Creating and managing user accounts, including managing passwords, assigning file system trustees, and creating workgroup managers

▶ Backing up and restoring data

▶ Creating and configuring print services

▶ Installing additional servers

In many cases, particularly in large networks, you may find that the optimal administrative strategy is to combine a central Admin user with multiple distributed administrators. In NDS, three common methods for creating distributed administrators include *explicit rights* (if only one person manages a container), use of an *organizational role* (if multiple users share container administration responsibilities), and *security equivalence* (not recommended, because the host object can accidentally be deleted).

### Exclusive Container Administrators

An *exclusive container administrator* is a special type of distributed administrator who is granted *exclusive* NDS rights to one or more branches of the NDS tree. In such cases, other network administrators, including the Admin user, are blocked from managing these branches.

This is accomplished in two steps:

**1.** A container administrator is granted [SBCDRI] object rights and [SCRWAI] property rights to a container.

**2.** The container administrator then applies an Inherited Rights Filter (IRF) to the container, effectively locking out all other network administrators.

Note: Using an IRF, the exclusive container administrator can choose to block all rights, all but the Browse [B] object right, or all but the Browse [B] object right and the Read [R] property right.

Figure 5.21 earlier showed two exclusive container administrators (SirKay in CHARITY.TOKYO and BThomas in PR.TOKYO) who have essentially locked out a higher-level network administrator (SHolmes). In each case, this was accomplished by placing an IRF of [B] on both of their containers.

When creating exclusive container administrators, keep several issues in mind. First, for fault tolerance purposes, make sure that always at least two trustees are assigned, such as an Organizational Role object (with multiple occupants) plus a user with explicit rights—or two User objects with explicit rights. This helps ensure that you don't lose administrative control of a portion of your NDS tree. Also, assign all object [SBCDRI] and property [SCRWAI] rights instead of just Supervisor and Inheritable [SI] rights. Finally, ensure that each container has an administrator that can regrant rights to Admin for NDS partitioning purposes.

► · · · · · · · · · · · · · · · · · · · · · · · · · · · · · · · · · · ◄

## REAL WORLD

The NDS Supervisor object right can be blocked by an IRF in the NDS tree. It cannot be blocked, however, by an IRF in the file system. If you attempt to block the Supervisor [S] right with an IRF, NetWare Administrator first requires you to make an explicit Supervisor [S] trustee assignment to someone else (assuming, of course, that one does not already exist). This is so that access to that portion of the tree is not permanently blocked.

### Other NDS Administrators

Furthermore, you can augment the centralized and distributed administration models by defining four other types of managers in NetWare 5.1:

► *Password Manager* — A password manager is a user (or organization role with individual user accounts as occupants) that has been granted the rights needed to perform the following tasks at the container level: reset user passwords, set password restrictions, track intruders, and set password expiration dates. To perform password manager responsibilities, a user (or organizational role) must be assigned [RWI] property rights to the Password Management property of the affected container(s).

► *Print Server Operator* — A print server operator is a user (or organization role with individual user accounts as occupants) that handles a subset of container administrator responsibilities, including loading and shutting down the print server, managing the print server, and maintaining print server configurations. To designate a user (or organizational role) as a print server operator, simply add the User or Organizational Role object to the Print Server Operator property of the respective Print Server object.

► *Print Queue Operator* — A print queue operator is a user (or organization role with individual user accounts as occupants) that assists the print server operator or container administrator in managing print jobs in a queue-based printing environment.

Print queue operators can delete print jobs, change the order of print jobs, and change the status of the print queue. To designate a user (or organizational role) as a print queue operator, simply add the User or Organizational Role object to the Print Queue Operator property of the respective Print Queue object.

▶ *Print Job Operator* — A print job operator is a user (or organization role with individual user accounts as occupants) that helps the container administrator manage print job flow in an NDPS printing environment. A print job operator can view, delete, modify, copy, or move print jobs as well as change the priority order of print jobs. To designate a user (or organizational role) as a print job operator, simply add the User or Organizational Role object to the NDPS Job Configurations property of the respective NDPS Printer.

Table 5.2 summarizes the actions and requirements of central and distributed administrators. For now, suffice it to say — you don't have to do it alone. No matter what networking challenges arise, a distributed administrator is always around to help you out.

TABLE 5.2

*Summary of Distributed Administrators*

| ROLE | ACCOUNT INFORMATION | FUNCTIONS |
|------|---------------------|-----------|
| Admin | Default Admin User object. Requires [SI] object rights to [Root] (by default). | Name the Directory tree; install the first server; create the top levels of the NDS tree; handle partition management and synchronization; assign distributed administrators; issue initial auditor password(s); and upgrade servers, clients, and applications. |

*Continued*

TABLE 5.2

*Summary of Distributed
Administrators (continued)*

| ROLE | ACCOUNT INFORMATION | FUNCTIONS |
|------|---------------------|-----------|
| Distributed Administrator | Exclusive container administrator or Organizational Role. Requires [BCDRSI] object rights to appropriate container. | Install supplemental servers; perform data backup and restoration; create and configure print services; write and maintain login scripts; monitor file server performance; track errors; monitor disk space usage, assign file system security; and upgrade respective servers, clients, and applications. |
| Password Manager | Organizational Role. Requires [RWI] property rights to the Password Management property of the container to be managed. | Reset user passwords to enable user to login when they forget their passwords, set password restrictions, track intruders, and set password expiration date. |
| Print Server Operator (Queue-based) | Print Server Operator object or Organizational Role. Must be added to Print Server Operator property of the respective Print Server object. | Load and shut down the print server, manage and maintain print server configurations. |
| Print Queue Operator (Queue-based) | Print Queue Operator object or Organizational Role. Must be added to the Print Queue Operator property of the respective print queue. | Delete print jobs, change the order of print jobs, change queue status. |
| Print Job Operator (NDPS) | Print Job Operator object or Organizational Role. Must be added to the NDPS Job Configurations property of the respective NDPS Printer. | View, delete, modify, copy, or move print jobs. Change the priority order of user print jobs. |

## NDS Security Management

Once you have established a secure foundation of NDS access rights, you should shift your management focus toward distributed resource access and troubleshooting. Following are three sections dedicated to advanced NDS security management:

- NDS Security Guidelines

- Managing NDS Resource Access

- Troubleshooting NDS Security

### NDS Security Guidelines

The goal of network security is to keep your network services and resources secure, while giving your network users the access they require. For example, most users typically have no need to create and delete NDS objects, or to modify most property values. With this in mind, check out the following guidelines for implementing NDS security:

- *Start with default assignments* — The purpose of default assignments is to give users access to the resources they need, without giving them access to resources or information they don't. When creating network access, you can start with default assignments and then make additional assignments to network or container administrators.

- *Don't forget that assigning the Supervisor object right implies granting the Supervisor property right to All Properties* — In some cases, you may want to grant container administrators all object rights except the Supervisor right and then assign specific property rights using the Selected Properties option.

- *Exercise caution when granting the Supervisor object right to a Server object* — Remember that granting a user the Supervisor object right to a Server object gives that user Supervisor file system rights to all volumes associated with the server. This is the one instance where NDS object rights are inherited into the file system. One way to avoid this problem is to grant container administrators all object rights except the Supervisor object right and then ensure that they do not have the Supervisor or Write property right to either All Properties or the ACL property of the Server object.

▶ *Avoid assigning rights using the All Properties option* — Although this may seem like the simplest way to assign rights, it's actually very dangerous. Using this option, it's very easy to inadvertently give users or perhaps even container administrators access to resources or information they do not need. It's very important, for example, to avoid accidentally granting users access to the Object Trustees (ACL) property of various objects. For example, if you assign an object Read and Write rights using the All Properties option, you are inadvertently given the trustee Write privileges to the object's ACL property.

▶ *Assign property rights using the Selected Properties option* — This option is much safer than the All Properties option, in that it allows you to be more selective in the rights that are granted.

▶ *Avoid assigning the Write property right to the Object Trustees (ACL) property of any object* — If a user has this right, he or she can grant anyone (including himself or herself) all rights, including the Supervisor right. This is another reason for exercising caution when grant rights via the All Properties option.

▶ *Exercise caution when filtering Supervisor rights with an IRF* — You should never have only one user with Supervisor rights to a container. If that user is inadvertently (or deliberately) deleted, you then lose control of that portion of the tree.

### Managing NDS Resource Access

Network resources are used, managed, and secured through NDS. Table 5.3 outlines the rights needed to create and manage access to various types of NDS objects.

**T A B L E   5.3**

*Summary of NDS Resource
Access Rights*

| NDS RESOURCE | ADMINISTRATIVE ACTION | NECESSARY RIGHTS |
| --- | --- | --- |
| Alias | Grant the user access rights to the aliased object. | Authority to grant NDS rights to the object in another container |

**TABLE 5.3**

*Summary of NDS Resource
Access Rights (continued)*

| NDS RESOURCE | ADMINISTRATIVE ACTION | NECESSARY RIGHTS |
|---|---|---|
| Application | *Step 1:* Grant the user the appropriate file system rights to the application associated with the Application object. | To perform Step 1, Supervisor [S] or Access Control [A] file system rights to the directory or file. |
| | *Step 2:* Associate the user with Application object. | To perform Step 2, Write [W] property right to Object Trustees (ACL) property of the Application and User objects. |
| Directory Map | *Step 1:* Grant the user the appropriate file system rights to the directory referred to by the Directory Map object. | To perform Step 1, Supervisor [S] or Access Control [A] file system rights to the directory or file. |
| | *Step 2:* Grant the user the Read [R] property right to the Path property of the Directory Map object. | To perform Step 2, Write [W] property right to Object Trustees (ACL) property of the Directory Map object. |
| Group | Add the user to the Group Membership list of the Group object. | Write [W] property right to the Member and Object Trustees (ACL) properties of the of the Group object. |
| Organizational Role | Add the user to the Occupant list of the Organizational Role object. | Write [W] property right to the Occupant and Object Trustees (ACL) properties of the Organizational Role object. |
| NDPS Printer | Add the user to the User Role list of the NDPS Printer object. | Write [W] property right to the Users and Object Trustees (ACL) properties of the NDPS Printer object. |
| Profile | *Step 1:* Add the Profile object to the User object's Profile property. | To perform both Steps 1 and 2, Write [W] property right to the Object Trustees (ACL) property of the Profile object. |
| | *Step 2:* Grant the user the Read [R] property right to the Login Script property of the Profile object. | |

*Continued*

TABLE 5.3

Summary of NDS Resource
Access Rights (continued)

| NDS RESOURCE | ADMINISTRATIVE ACTION | NECESSARY RIGHTS |
|---|---|---|
| Volume/directory | Grant the user the appropriate file system rights to the directory or file you want to target in the Volume object | Supervisor [S] or Access Control [A] file system right to the directory or file you want to target in the Volume object. |

### Troubleshooting NDS Security

NDS security is complex. Most NDS security problems occur at either end of the access rights spectrum: users either have too many rights or too few. Here are some troubleshooting hints:

▶ *Users who have unauthorized access* — If a user ends up with more access rights than you intended, you should determine the user's effective rights to the target resource (with NetWare Administrator), and identify the source of the access rights in question (by checking all the trustee types mentioned previously).

▶ *Users who can't access an authorized resource* — If a user is denied access to an authorized resource, consider the following troubleshooting questions: Has the user been made a member of any groups or occupant of any organizational roles? Has the user been made security equivalent to any other objects? Has the security of the user's home container changed recently? What explicit trustee assignments does this user have? And finally, are there any new IRFs assigned to the target object or parent containers?

That completes our *advanced* lesson in NDS security and administration. Now you should feel ready to secure the NDS tree from the top down and inside out. In the next two layers, we dive deeper into NetWare 5.1 resource access management with lessons in file system security and file/directory attributes.

Let's go to work.

## LAB EXERCISE 5.2: NDS ADMINISTRATION AT ACME

In this exercise, you use NetWare Administrator to create an exclusive container administrator for the FIN organizational unit. The basic technique for creating exclusive container administrators is to explicitly grant to one or more User objects all object and property rights to a container; next, modify the IRF of the container to block all rights from network administrators (and other objects) in parent containers. In this exercise, you assign the rights required to be an exclusive container administrator to an Organizational Role object as well as the Admin User object.

The following hardware is required for this exercise:

▶ A NetWare 5.1 server called WHITE-SRV1.WHITE.CRIME.TOKYO.ACME (which can be installed using the directions found in Appendix D).

▶ A workstation running either the NetWare 5.1 Novell Client for Windows 95/98 or NetWare 5.1 Novell Client for Windows NT/2000 (which can be installed using the directions found in Exercise 3.1).

Carefully perform the following tasks at your client workstation:

**1.** Log into the network as Admin, if you haven't already done so.

**2.** Execute NetWare Administrator.

**3.** In the WHITE Organizational Unit object, create a User object called RHood.

**4.** In the WHITE Organizational Unit object, create an Organizational Unit object called FIN.

**5.** In the FIN Organizational Unit object, create a User object called LJohn.

**6.** Attempt to remove all object and property rights from the IRF of the FIN Organizational Unit object.

  **a.** Right-click the FIN container.

**b.** Select Trustees of This Object from the pop-up menu that appears.

**c.** When the Trustees of FIN dialog box appears, click Inherited Rights Filter.

**d.** Follow these steps when the Inherited Rights Filter dialog box appears:

- In the Object Rights section, attempt to unmark all five object right check boxes (that is Supervisor, Browse, Create, Delete, and Rename), beginning with the Supervisor check box.

- When you attempt to unmark the Supervisor check box, an error message appears, indicating that you cannot filter the Supervisor object right because no user has explicitly been granted the Supervisor object right for this object. Click OK to acknowledge the message.

- When the Inherited Rights Filter dialog box reappears, click Cancel.

- When the Trustees of FIN dialog box reappears, click Cancel to return to the NetWare Administrator browser screen.

**7.** In the FIN Organizational Unit object, create an Organization Role object called FIN-Admin.

**a.** To create the FIN-Admin Organizational Role Unit, use *one* of the following methods:

- Click the FIN Organizational Unit and then press Insert, *or*

- Click the FIN Organizational Unit and then select Object ⇨ Create, *or*

- Right-click the FIN Organizational Unit and then choose Create from the pop-up menu that appears.

**b.** Follow these steps when the New Object dialog box appears:

- Click Organizational Role.

- Click OK.

**c.** When the Create Organizational Role dialog box appears, follow these steps:

- In the Organizational Role Name field, enter the following:

  FIN-Admin

- Mark the Define Additional Properties check box.

- Click Create.

**8.** Add the LJohn User object as an occupant of the FIN-Admin Organizational Role object.

**a.** Follow these steps when the Organizational Role: FIN-Admin dialog box appears:

- The Identification page is displayed, by default.

- Click the button to the right of the Occupant field.

**b.** When the Occupant dialog box appears, click Add.

**c.** When the Select Object dialog box appears, double-click the LJohn User object in the left pane to select it.

**d.** Follow these steps when the Occupant dialog box reappears:

- Notice that the LJohn.FIN.WHITE.CRIME.TOKYO.ACME object is listed.

- Click OK.

**e.** When the Organizational Role: FIN-Admin dialog box reappears, click OK to save your changes.

**f.** Follow these steps when the NetWare Administrator browser screen reappears:

- Double-click the FIN Organizational Unit object, if necessary, to expand it and display its contents.

- Notice that the FIN-Admin Organizational Role object you just created appears in the tree, as does the LJohn User object you created earlier in the exercise.

9. Make the FIN Organizational Unit object a trustee of itself and grant it the Browse [B] object right. This enables User objects in this container to view this container and its contents. (**Note:** This step is required because later in this exercise, we remove all object and property rights from the FIN Organizational Unit IRF — thereby blocking the Browse [B] right users in this container would normally inherit from above via the [Public] Trustee.)

   a. To assign the FIN Organizational Unit as a trustee of itself, use *one* of the following methods:

      • Click the FIN Organizational Unit object and then select Object ⇨ Trustees of This Object, *or*

      • Right-click the FIN Organizational Unit object and then choose Trustees of This Object from the pop-up menu that appears.

   b. Follow these steps when the Trustees of FIN dialog box appears:

      • In the Trustees list box, click FIN.WHITE.CRIME.TOKYO.ACME.

      • In the Object Rights section, you notice that all six object rights check boxes have gray check marks. This indicates that this trustee has not been granted these rights. Mark the Browse check box. When you do, notice that black check boxes appear in both the Browse and Inheritable check boxes. Also notice that the gray check marks disappear from the remaining four object right check boxes.

      • In the Property Rights section, notice that the All Properties radio button is marked, by default; and notice that all six check boxes contain gray check marks, meaning that these rights have not been granted to this trustee. Do not make any modifications.

      • Click OK to save your changes. (**Note:** Before clicking OK, you could have assigned an additional trustee for this object, if desired, by clicking the Add button. In our case, however, we want to explore another alternative method of assigning trustee rights in Step 10a.)

10. Make the FIN-Admin Organizational Role object a trustee of the FIN Organizational Unit object and grant it all object rights [SBCDRI] and all property rights [SCRWAI].

**a.** Drag the FIN-Admin Organizational Role object onto the FIN Organizational Unit object.

**b.** Follow these steps when the Trustees of FIN dialog box appears:

- In the Trustees list box, notice that FIN-Admin.FIN.WHITE. CRIME.TOKYO.ACME is highlighted.

- In the Object Rights section, mark the four of six object right check boxes that are not marked (that is, Supervisor, Create, Delete, and Rename).

- In the Property Rights section, notice that the All Properties radio button is marked, by default. Mark the three of six property right check boxes that are not marked (that is, Supervisor, Write, and Add Self).

- Click OK to save your changes.

**11.** Examine the effective rights of the LJohn User object to ensure he has all object and property rights to the FIN container.

**a.** Follow these steps when the NetWare Administrator browser screen reappears:

- Right-click the FIN container.

- Select Trustees of This Object from the pop-up menu that appears.

**b.** When the Trustees of FIN dialog box appears, click Effective Rights.

**c.** When the Effective Rights dialog box appears, click the Browse button to the right of the Object Name field.

**d.** When the Select Object dialog box appears, navigate the tree until the LJohn User object appears in the left pane and then double-click it to select it.

**e.** Follow these steps when the Effective Rights dialog box reappears:

- In the Object Name field, verify that LJohn.FIN.WHITE.CRIME.TOKYO.ACME is listed.

- In the Object Rights section, verify that all five object rights are displayed in black (that is, that none are grayed out).

- In the Property Rights section, verify that the All Properties radio button is marked and that all five property rights are displayed in black (that is, that none are grayed out).

- Click Close.

12. Attempt to remove all object and property rights from the IRF of the FIN Organizational Unit object.

   **a.** When the Trustees of FIN dialog box reappears, click Inherited Rights Filter.

   **b.** Follow these steps when the Inherited Rights Filter dialog box appears:

   - In the Object Rights section, attempt to unmark all five object right check boxes (that is Supervisor, Browse, Create, Delete, and Rename), beginning with the Supervisor check box.

   - When you attempt to unmark the Supervisor check box, an error message appears, indicating that you cannot filter the Supervisor object right because no user has explicitly been granted the Supervisor object right for this object. Click OK to acknowledge the message. (**Note:** Granting an Organizational Role the Supervisor object right does not satisfy this requirement.)

   - When the Inherited Rights Filter dialog box reappears, click Cancel.

13. Make the Admin User object a trustee of the FIN Organizational Unit object and grant it all object rights [SBCDRI] and all property rights [SCRWAI].

   **a.** When the Trustees of FIN dialog box appears, click Add Trustee.

   **b.** When the Select Object dialog box appears, double-click the Admin User object in the left pane to select it.

   **c.** Follow these steps when the Trustees of FIN dialog box appears:

   - In the Trustees list box, notice that Admin.WHITE.CRIME. TOKYO.ACME is highlighted.

- In the Object Rights section, mark the four of six object right check boxes that are not marked (that is, Supervisor, Create, Delete, and Rename).

- In the Property Rights section, notice that the All Properties radio button is marked, by default. Mark the three of six property right check boxes that are not marked (that is, Supervisor, Write, and Add Self).

- Click OK to save your changes.

14. Modify the IRF of the FIN Organizational Unit object so that all object and property rights are blocked. (This blocks inherited rights of objects in parent containers.)

   a. Follow these steps when the NetWare Administrator browser screen reappears:

   - Right-click the FIN container.

   - Select Trustees of This Object from the pop-up menu that appears.

   b. When the Trustees of FIN dialog box appears, click Inherited Rights Filter.

   c. Follow these steps when the Inherited Rights Filter dialog box appears:

   - In the Object Rights section, unmark all five object right check boxes (that is Supervisor, Browse, Create, Delete, and Rename).

   - In the Property rights section, verify that the All Properties radio button is marked and unmark all five property right check boxes (that is Supervisor, Compare, Read, Write, and Add Self).

   - Click OK to return to the Trustees of FIN dialog box.

   - Click OK to save your changes and return to the NetWare Administrator browser screen.

15. Examine the effective rights of the Admin User object to ensure that it still has all object and property rights for the FIN container.

**16.** Examine the effective rights of the LJohn User object to ensure that he still has all object and property rights for the FIN container.

**17.** Examine the effective rights of the RHood User object to ensure that he no longer has any object and property rights for the FIN container.

**18.** Exit NetWare Administrator.

**19.** Log into the network as RHood.

   **a.** Execute NetWare Administrator.

   **b.** Browse the WHITE container. Notice you cannot "see" the FIN Organizational Unit object in the tree because the Browse [B] right that RHood would normally have from the [Public] trustee is being blocked by the FIN Organizational Unit object's IRF.

   **c.** Exit NetWare Administrator.

**20.** Log into the network as LJohn. (**Hint:** In the Novell Login window, your current context is probably set to the WHITE Organizational Unit. Therefore, you can enter either LJohn.FIN or .LJohn.FIN.WHITE.CRIME. TOKYO.ACME in the Username field. If you decide to enter his full distinguished name, don't forget to include the preceding period.)

   **a.** Execute NetWare Administrator.

   **b.** Browse the WHITE container. Notice that you can "see" the FIN container.

   **c.** Modify the IRF of the FIN Organizational Unit to allow all inherited object and property rights to pass through, rather than being blocked. (In other word, reverse the IRF changes you made earlier in this exercise.)

   **d.** Exit NetWare Administrator.

**21.** Log into the network as Admin.

# Layer Four — File System Access Rights

NetWare 5.1 security exists on two functional planes:

- ▶ Above the server

- ▶ Within the server

To understand the two functional planes of NetWare 5.1 security, use the server as a midpoint (see Figure 5.27). NDS security occurs above the server, and in this plane, the server is at the bottom of the tree. It is treated as any other leaf object, just like users, printers, and groups. NDS security applied above the server ends when it gets to a leaf object. There's no transition into the file system (with one exception we discuss later).

FIGURE 5.27

*The two functional planes of NetWare 5.1 security*

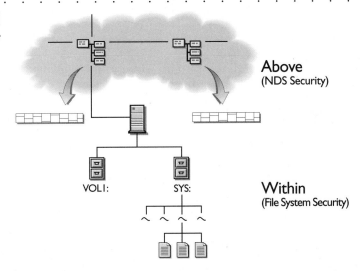

File system security, on the other hand, occurs within the server. In this case, the server is the top of the file system tree. The server contains the volumes that contain the directories that house the files. A user can't access a directory or file unless the proper rights have been assigned. Again, file system security ends once it gets up to the server. There's no transition into the NDS security structure.

Understanding the server's point of view helps you understand NDS and file system security.

The good news is NDS and file system security have a great deal in common: trustee assignments, inheritance, and security equivalence. Furthermore, the file system uses IRFs and the file system calculates effective rights in much the same way. However, a few minor differences exist between NDS and file system security:

▶ NDS has 12 access rights broken into two groups — object and property. The file system uses eight access rights.

▶ Rights do not flow from NDS into the file system except in one special instance. If a trustee is granted the Supervisor [S] object right to a Server object, the trustee also receives the Supervisor file system right to the root of all volumes associated with the server.

▶ In NDS, the Supervisor object and property rights can be blocked by an IRF. The Supervisor file system right, on the other hand, cannot be blocked by an IRF.

Because NDS and file system security are separate, administration can be divided among distributed *container* and *file system* administrators. For example, one network administrator could be given the responsibility of managing the central NDS tree and creating distributed workgroup managers for support. Another administrator could be put in charge of managing specific server volumes and their corresponding file systems.

Let's start our discussion of file system security within the server by describing the eight access rights that operate there.

## Understanding File System Access Rights

The NetWare 5.1 file system supports eight different access rights for securing directories and files:

▶ *Supervisor (S)* — Grants all privileges to a directory, its subdirectories, and files. This right cannot be blocked by an IRF (unlike NDS security).

▸ *Read (R)* — Grants the privilege to open files in a directory and read their contents or run applications.

▸ *Write (W)* — Grants the privilege to open and change the contents of files and directories.

▸ *Create (C)* — Grants the privilege to create new subdirectories and files.

▸ *Erase (E)* — Grants the privilege to delete a directory, its subdirectories, and files.

▸ *Modify (M)* — Grants the privilege to change the name or attributes of a directory or file.

▸ *File Scan (F)* — Grants the privilege to see files and directories.

▸ *Access Control (A)* — Grants the privilege to add or delete trustee assignments and IRFs involving all file system rights except Supervisor [S]. It also enables a user to modify a directory's disk space restrictions.

### REAL WORLD

The Supervisor access right is just as dangerous in the file system as it is in NDS. The tricky part is that it can leak its way into the file system without you knowing it. Any user with the Write [W] property right to a server's ACL implicitly receives Supervisor file system rights to the root of all volumes on the server. And to make this even worse, the user does not appear on any file or directory trustee list. There's a variety of ways to get the Write [W] property right to a server's ACL, including Supervisor object rights, Supervisor All Properties rights, and security equivalence. You may consider blocking these rights with a Server object IRF.

Understanding the eight file system access rights is only the beginning. To effectively configure and manage file system security, you must understand what each of them does. Table 5.4 summarizes the file system rights requirements for common network tasks.

| TABLE 5.4 | TASK | RIGHTS REQUIRED |
|-----------|------|-----------------|
| Rights Requirements for Common File System Tasks | Open and read a file | Read |
| | See a filename | File Scan |
| | Search a directory for files | File Scan |
| | Open and write to an existing file | Write, Create, Erase, and (sometimes) Modify |
| | Execute an .EXE file | Read and File Scan |
| | Create and write to a file | Create |
| | Copy files from a directory | Read and File Scan |
| | Copy files to a directory | Write, Create, and File Scan |
| | Make a new directory | Create |
| | Delete a file | Erase |
| | Salvage deleted files | Read and File Scan for the file and Create for the directory |
| | Change directory or file attributes | Modify |
| | Rename a file or directory | Modify |
| | Change the IRF | Access Control |
| | Change trustee assignments | Access Control |
| | Modify a directory's disk space restrictions | Access Control |

*So, where do you begin?* As with NDS, file system security starts with the defaults. NetWare 5.1 provides a sophisticated set of default file system access rights. These rights should become the foundation of your application and data security strategies. They aren't, however, as comprehensive as NDS defaults. You need to assign security whenever you create new application and data directories. Let's take a quick look at the NetWare 5.1 defaults:

▶ *User* — A user home directory can be created when the User object is created. By default, the user gets all file system rights except Supervisor to their home directory, namely [RWCEMFA]. The directory name matches the User object name unless otherwise specified. Its location is also configurable.

▸ *Supervisor* — Any user granted the Supervisor [S] object right to a Server object receives the Supervisor [S] file system right to the root of all volumes on that server.

▸ *Creator* — Whoever creates a File Server object (such as Admin) automatically receives the Supervisor [S] file system right to all volumes on the server.

▸ *Container* — A server's parent container is granted Read and File Scan [RF] rights to SYS:PUBLIC. This way, all users and objects in the server's home container can access NetWare 5.1 public utilities.

As you expand on the default file system security structure, consider planning your trustee assignments from the top down. This means starting with containers and working your way down to groups, and ultimately, to specific users. Here's the best top-down priority order for file system security:

▸ [Public]

▸ Containers (including [Root])

▸ Groups and Organizational Roles

▸ Users, and finally

▸ Security Equivalence (for temporary purposes only)

In addition, ensure that you only grant the rights that trustees need to access directories, files, and applications. Also, be sure to plan for inheritance and use IRFs accordingly (remember that the file system Supervisor [S] right cannot be blocked by an IRF). Finally, avoid granting excessive rights near the top of a file system structure.

This completes our discussion of file system access rights. Now that you know what to do, let's learn how to do it.

## Step One: Assigning Trustee Rights

File system security supports the same three-step trustee model as NDS security. However, in this case you are managing the assignment of eight different rights to directories and files:

▶ *Step One: Assigning Trustee Rights* — First, grant file system access rights using trustee assignments, inheritance, and security equivalence.

▶ *Step Two: Blocking Inherited Rights* — Next, you can block inherited rights by granting a trustee a new trustee assignment lower in the file system (which affects only the trustee), or by using one or more Inherited Rights Filters (which affects everyone).

▶ *Step Three: Calculating Effective Rights* — Finally, a trustee's effective rights are calculated as the combination of trustee assignments, inheritance (minus any rights blocked by an Inherited Rights Filter or a trustee assignment lower in the file system), and security equivalence.

In file system security, a *trustee* is any NDS object that has been placed in Access Control List (ACL) of a directory or file. Any trustee with the Access Control [A] or Supervisor [S] file system right to a directory or file can manipulate the ACL, and thus grant file system rights.

The file system supports the same trustee types as NDS, such as the following:

▶ *User*

▶ *Group*

▶ *Organizational Role*

▶ *Container*

▶ *[Root]*

▶ *[Public]*

Once you identify *who* the file system trustee is, you need to determine *which* rights you're going to give him/her and *where* the rights are assigned. This is shown in Figure 5.28. In the figure, MMarion is granted all rights except [SAM] to the SYS:SHARED directory. These rights are then inherited for all subdirectories underneath.

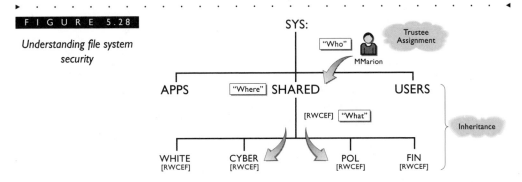

FIGURE 5.28

*Understanding file system security*

File system trustee rights can be assigned using the NetWare Administrator or ConsoleOne graphical utilities. Similar to NDS security, file system trustee assignments can be made from one of two perspectives:

- ▶ *Rights to Files and Directories* — This is from Maid Marion's point of view.

- ▶ *Trustees of this Directory* — This is from SYS:SHARED's point of view.

It really doesn't matter which option you choose. You can either assign rights from the user's point of view or the directory's point of view. In the first example, we assign security from Maid Marion's point of view. In ConsoleOne, double-click Maid Marion and her Properties window appears. Choose the Rights to Files and Directories tab from the top of the screen and then click Show. When the Select Object dialog box appears, navigate to and select the WHITE-SRV1_SYS volume and Figure 5.29 appears.

Assigning file system access
rights in ConsoleOne

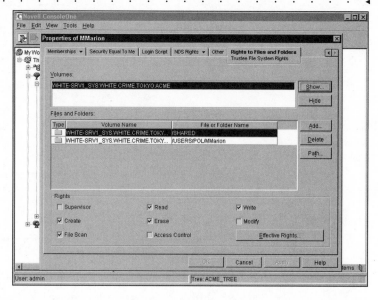

Figure 5.29 shows the security window from Maid Marion's point of view. As you can see, she has been granted [RWCEF] access rights to SYS:SHARED. In addition, she's also a trustee of SYS:\USERS\POL\MMARION — by default. You can create trustee assignments by using the Add button.

The second option enables you to assign access rights from SYS:SHARED's point of view. In this case, you would double-click WHITE-SRV1_SYS from the Browse window of NetWare Administrator. All of its directories should appear. Then, highlight SHARED and click the right mouse button. A pop-up menu appears — choose Details. Once the SYS:SHARED Details window appears, choose Trustees of this Directory from the right-hand list (see Figure 5.30).

In this screen, NetWare Administrator gives you the choice of adding trustees or setting the IRF (Inherited Rights Filter). Notice that MMarion has been added with the [RWCEF] access rights. You can create other trustee assignments for SYS:SHARED using the Add Trustee button. Also, notice the IRF allows all rights to flow through — this is the default.

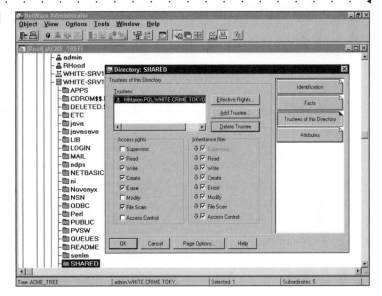

FIGURE 5.30

*Assigning file system access rights in NetWare Administrator*

There you have it. As you can see, it doesn't matter how we assign access rights. Both methods get the same result — Maid Marion (who) is granted [RWCEF] trustee rights (what) to SYS:SHARED (where).

**REAL WORLD**

In addition to NetWare Administrator and ConsoleOne, you can use FILER and RIGHTS (command-line utility) to assign file system access rights.

Like NDS security, file system rights flow down the directory structure — from volumes to directories to files. Unlike NDS security, file system inheritance is not dependent on the Inheritable (*I*) right. Instead, rights flow freely once they have been granted unless blocked by a new trustee assignment lower in the file system or by an IRF.

## Step Two: Blocking Inherited Rights

Both NDS and file system security provide two methods for blocking unwanted inherited rights:

▶ Granting a new trustee assignment

▶ Blocking rights with an Inherited Rights Filter (IRF)

If you want to block inherited file system rights for a specific user, grant him or her new trustee rights lower in the file system structure. File system rights that are inherited by an object are overwritten when the same object is granted a new trustee assignment lower in the file system — unless, of course, the assignment above includes the Supervisor [S] file system right. Remember, in the file system, the Supervisor right cannot be blocked by a new trustee assignment lower in the tree. (In other words, your only choice would be to remove the Supervisor [S] right from where it was originally assigned.)

On the other hand, if you want to block the inheritance of all users, then you can modify the IRF of a directory or file. Remember these three important points about how a *file system* IRF works:

▶ It's an inclusive filter, which means the rights that are in the filter are the ones that are allowed to pass through.

▶ An IRF can only block rights that have been inherited from object trustee assignments higher in the tree. (That's why it's called an Inherited Rights Filter.) It does not apply to trustee assignments themselves. In other words, if your User object is assigned rights to an object via a trustee assignment, that assignment would be unaffected by the object's IRF.

▶ An IRF applies to everyone in the tree except Admin or anyone else with the Supervisor file system right.

**TIP**

**Remember that an object's IRF can block the NDS Supervisor object or Supervisor property right, but a directory's IRF or file's IRF cannot block the file system Supervisor right. Also, you should know how to block rights in the file system — depending on whether or not the [S] right is one of the rights that needs to be blocked.**

## Step Three: Calculating Effective Rights

As we learned earlier, effective rights are the bottom line. This is the culmination of our three-step process. In Step One, we assign the rights. In Step Two, we filter the rights. In Step Three, we calculate exactly what the rights are.

Like NDS security, file system effective rights are the combination of the following:

▸ Explicit trustee assignments made to an object

▸ Inheritance minus rights blocked by an IRF (or a new trustee assignment lower in the file system)

▸ Rights granted to the [Root]

▸ Rights granted to the special [Public] trustee

▸ Security equivalence to parent containers, groups, organizational roles, and so on.

As we learned earlier, calculating effective rights for NDS can be mind-boggling and fun. The file system is no different. Let's use Maid Marion as an example. Suppose we're concerned about users making changes to our political database. To protect it, we assign an [RF] filter to SYS:SHARED\POL. This blocks MMarion's inherited rights of [RWCEF]. Therefore, her effective rights should be Read and File Scan [RF]. But as you can see in Figure 5.31, her effective rights in SYS:SHARED\POL are, in fact, [RWF]. How did this happen? She must be getting the [W] right from somewhere else. Ah, I remember. She's a member of the POL-Group and they've been granted Write privileges to SYS:SHARED\POL. Therefore, her effective rights become inherited rights minus the IRF plus group trustee assignments.

NetWare Administrator provides an excellent tool for viewing effective rights — check out Figure 5.31. All you have to do is identify the user (MMarion) and the directory (SYS:SHARED\POL) — NetWare Administrator does all the rest.

▶ · · · · · · · · · · · · · · · · · · · · · · · · ◀

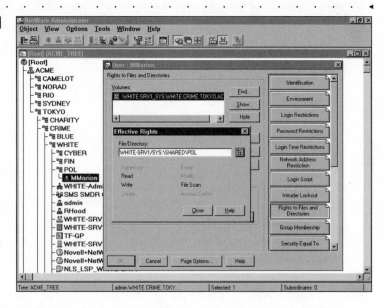

There you have it. The simple three-step file system security model. That was a fun review. It's fortunate for us that NetWare 5.1 basically uses the same model for both NDS and file system security. Even though these two layers apply to dramatically different network elements, they approach security in a similar way. Hopefully, now you have a firm handle on access rights, default assignments, trustees, inheritance, the IRF, and effective rights.

Now let's explore the final layer of NetWare 5.1 security — File/Directory Attributes.

**For some great hands-on experience with NetWare 5.1 file system access rights, check out Lab Exercise 5.4 at the end of the chapter.**

TIP

## LAB EXERCISE 5.3: CALCULATING FILE SYSTEM EFFECTIVE RIGHTS

Here you are, effective rights—Part 2. In this exercise, we're going to explore the wonderful world of file system effective rights. Now that you've helped "administrate" Sherlock Holmes and Wyatt Earp, it's time to "liberate" the rest of the crime-fighting team, namely Robin Hood, Maid Marion, Dr. Watson, Little John, and Friar Tuck.

Ah, a network administrator's job is never done.

### Case #1

FrTuck has been made a trustee of the SYS:SHARED directory and granted Read, Write, Create, and File Scan rights. The IRF for the SYS:SHARED directory contains all rights; the IRF for the SYS:SHARED\CYBER directory contains Supervisor, Read, and File Scan; and the IRF for the CYBER.DOC file contains Read, Write, Create, and File Scan. Calculate FrTuck's effective rights in the SYS:SHARED directory, the SYS:SHARED\CYBER directory, and the CYBER.DOC file, using the worksheet in Figure 5.32.

### Case #2

DrWatson was granted the Read, Write, Create, and File Scan rights to the SYS:SHARED directory. The CRIME Group, of which he is a member, was granted Read, Write, Create, Erase, Modify, and File Scan rights to the SYS:CRIME directory. The CRIME Group was also granted Read and File Scan rights to the CRIME.DB file. The IRF for the SYS:SHARED directory is all rights; the IRF for the SYS:SHARED\CRIME directory is Supervisor and Access Control; and the IRF for the CRIME.DB file is Supervisor, Read, Write, Create, and File Scan. Calculate DrWatson's effective rights in the SYS:SHARED directory, the SYS:SHARED\CRIME directory, and the CRIME.DB file, using the worksheet in Figure 5.33.

▶ · · · · · · · · · · · · · · · · · · · · · · · · · · · · · · ◀

FIGURE 5.32

*Calculating file system
effective rights — Case #1*

| SYS: SHARED | S | R | W | C | E | M | F | A |
|---|---|---|---|---|---|---|---|---|
| Inherited Rights Filter | | | | | | | | |
| Inherited Rights — User | | | | | | | | |
| Inherited Rights — Group | | | | | | | | |
| Trustee Assignment — User | | | | | | | | |
| Trustee Assignment — Group | | | | | | | | |
| Effective Rights | | | | | | | | |

| SYS: SHARED\CYBER | S | R | W | C | E | M | F | A |
|---|---|---|---|---|---|---|---|---|
| Inherited Rights Filter | | | | | | | | |
| Inherited Rights — User | | | | | | | | |
| Inherited Rights — Group | | | | | | | | |
| Trustee Assignment — User | | | | | | | | |
| Trustee Assignment — Group | | | | | | | | |
| Effective Rights | | | | | | | | |

| CYBER.DOC | S | R | W | C | E | M | F | A |
|---|---|---|---|---|---|---|---|---|
| Inherited Rights Filter | | | | | | | | |
| Inherited Rights — User | | | | | | | | |
| Inherited Rights — Group | | | | | | | | |
| Trustee Assignment — User | | | | | | | | |
| Trustee Assignment — Group | | | | | | | | |
| Effective Rights | | | | | | | | |

## Case #3

MMarion was granted the Modify and Access Control rights to the SYS:SHARED\POL directory. In addition, the POL Group, of which she is a member, was granted the Read, Write, Create, Erase, and File Scan rights to both the SYS:SHARED and SYS:SHARED\POL directories. The IRF for the SYS:SHARED directory contains all rights; the IRF for the SYS:SHARED\POL directory contains the Supervisor right; and the IRF for the CRIME.RPT file contains all rights. Calculate MMarion's effective rights to the SYS:SHARED directory, the SYS:SHARED\POL directory, and the CRIME.RPT file, using the worksheet in Figure 5.34.

**F I G U R E   5.33**

*Calculating file system effective rights — Case #2*

| SYS: SHARED | S | R | W | C | E | M | F | A |
|---|---|---|---|---|---|---|---|---|
| Inherited Rights Filter | | | | | | | | |
| Inherited Rights — User | | | | | | | | |
| Inherited Rights — Group | | | | | | | | |
| Trustee Assignment — User | | | | | | | | |
| Trustee Assignment — Group | | | | | | | | |
| Effective Rights | | | | | | | | |

| SYS: SHARED\CRIME | S | R | W | C | E | M | F | A |
|---|---|---|---|---|---|---|---|---|
| Inherited Rights Filter | | | | | | | | |
| Inherited Rights — User | | | | | | | | |
| Inherited Rights — Group | | | | | | | | |
| Trustee Assignment — User | | | | | | | | |
| Trustee Assignment — Group | | | | | | | | |
| Effective Rights | | | | | | | | |

| CRIME.DB | S | R | W | C | E | M | F | A |
|---|---|---|---|---|---|---|---|---|
| Inherited Rights Filter | | | | | | | | |
| Inherited Rights — User | | | | | | | | |
| Inherited Rights — Group | | | | | | | | |
| Trustee Assignment — User | | | | | | | | |
| Trustee Assignment — Group | | | | | | | | |
| Effective Rights | | | | | | | | |

## Case #4

SHolmes was granted all rights to the SYS:SHARED directory. The CRIME Group, of which he is a member, was granted Read, Write, Create, and File Scan rights to the SYS:SHARED\CRIME directory. The CRIME Group was also granted Read and File Scan rights to the CRIME.DB file. The IRF for the SYS:SHARED directory contains all rights; the IRF for the SYS:SHARED\CRIME directory contains the Supervisor right; and the IRF for the CRIME.DB file contains Supervisor, Read, and File Scan rights. Calculate SHolmes' effective rights to the SYS:SHARED directory, the SYS:SHARED\CRIME directory, and the CRIME.DB file, using the worksheet in Figure 5.35.

FIGURE 5.34

*Calculating file system effective rights — Case #3*

| SYS: SHARED | S | R | W | C | E | M | F | A |
|---|---|---|---|---|---|---|---|---|
| Inherited Rights Filter | | | | | | | | |
| Inherited Rights — User | | | | | | | | |
| Inherited Rights — Group | | | | | | | | |
| Trustee Assignment — User | | | | | | | | |
| Trustee Assignment — Group | | | | | | | | |
| Effective Rights | | | | | | | | |

| SYS: SHARED\POL | S | R | W | C | E | M | F | A |
|---|---|---|---|---|---|---|---|---|
| Inherited Rights Filter | | | | | | | | |
| Inherited Rights — User | | | | | | | | |
| Inherited Rights — Group | | | | | | | | |
| Trustee Assignment — User | | | | | | | | |
| Trustee Assignment — Group | | | | | | | | |
| Effective Rights | | | | | | | | |

| CRIME.RPT | S | R | W | C | E | M | F | A |
|---|---|---|---|---|---|---|---|---|
| Inherited Rights Filter | | | | | | | | |
| Inherited Rights — User | | | | | | | | |
| Inherited Rights — Group | | | | | | | | |
| Trustee Assignment — User | | | | | | | | |
| Trustee Assignment — Group | | | | | | | | |
| Effective Rights | | | | | | | | |

The answers to all of these case studies are in Appendix C.

FIGURE 5.35

*Calculating file system effective rights — Case #4*

| SYS: SHARED | S | R | W | C | E | M | F | A |
|---|---|---|---|---|---|---|---|---|
| Inherited Rights Filter | | | | | | | | |
| Inherited Rights — User | | | | | | | | |
| Inherited Rights — Group | | | | | | | | |
| Trustee Assignment — User | | | | | | | | |
| Trustee Assignment — Group | | | | | | | | |
| Effective Rights | | | | | | | | |

| SYS: SHARED\CRIME | S | R | W | C | E | M | F | A |
|---|---|---|---|---|---|---|---|---|
| Inherited Rights Filter | | | | | | | | |
| Inherited Rights — User | | | | | | | | |
| Inherited Rights — Group | | | | | | | | |
| Trustee Assignment — User | | | | | | | | |
| Trustee Assignment — Group | | | | | | | | |
| Effective Rights | | | | | | | | |

| CYBER.DB | S | R | W | C | E | M | F | A |
|---|---|---|---|---|---|---|---|---|
| Inherited Rights Filter | | | | | | | | |
| Inherited Rights — User | | | | | | | | |
| Inherited Rights — Group | | | | | | | | |
| Trustee Assignment — User | | | | | | | | |
| Trustee Assignment — Group | | | | | | | | |
| Effective Rights | | | | | | | | |

# Layer Five — Directory/File Attributes

Welcome to the final layer. I bet you never thought you'd get here. Directory and file attributes provide the final layer of NetWare 5.1 security. These attributes are rarely used, but provide a powerful tool for specific security solutions. If all else fails, you can always turn to attribute security to save the day.

Attributes are special assignments or properties that are assigned to individual directories or files. Attribute security overrides all previous trustee assignments and effective rights. Attributes can be used to prevent deleting a file, copying a file, viewing a file, and so on. Attributes also control whether files can be shared, mark files for backup purposes, or protect them from data corruption using the Transactional Tracking System (TTS). Directory and file attributes can be set using the NetWare Administrator, ConsoleOne, FLAG, or FILER utilities. They can also be viewed using the NDIR utility. Some NetWare 5.1 attributes are unavailable from DOS utilities.

Attributes enable you to manage what users can do with files once they have access to them. Attributes are global security elements that affect all users, regardless of their rights, and they override all previous levels of security. Let's say, for example, Maid Marion has all rights except [SAM] to the SYS:APPS\WP directory — [RWCEF]. You can still restrict her from deleting a specific file by assigning it the Read-Only attribute. Therefore, the true effective rights for Maid Marion in this directory are the combination of her effective file system rights and file attributes.

NetWare 5.1 supports two types of attributes: directory and file. Directory attributes apply to directories only, whereas file attributes can be assigned to files. In both of these cases, attributes fall into one of three categories:

- Security attributes

- Feature attributes

- Disk management attributes

Security attributes affect users' security access — what they can do with files. Feature attributes, on the other hand, affect how the system interacts with files. That is, whether the files can be archived, purged, or transactionally tracked.

Finally, disk management attributes apply to file compression, data migration, and block suballocation.

Let's take a closer look at NetWare 5.1 attribute security, starting with security attributes.

## Security Attributes

Security attributes protect information at the file and directory level by controlling two kinds of file access — file sharing and file alteration. File access security controls not so much who can access the files, but what kind of access they have. Once users have been given the proper trustee assignments to a given directory, they're in the door. Security attributes tell users what they can do with the files once they're there.

Here's a list of NetWare 5.1's security attributes and a brief description. An asterisk (*) indicates an attribute that applies to both directories and files.

▶ *All\** — Specifies the A, Ci, Di, H, Ic, P, Ri, Ro, Sh, Sy, and T attributes as a group. Primarily used to assign directories and files these special attributes.

▶ *Copy Inhibit (Ci)* — Only valid for Macintosh files. Prevents users from copying the file. Even if users have been granted the Read and File Scan [RF] rights, they still can't copy this specific file. Macintosh users can, however, remove the Copy Inhibit attribute if they have been granted the Modify [M] access right.

▶ *Delete Inhibit (Di)\** — Prevents a file from being deleted or copied over.

▶ *Execute Only (X)* — This is an extremely sensitive attribute and provides a very high level of NetWare 5.1 security. Once set, it cannot be cleared. The only way to remove the Execute Only attribute is to delete the file. The Execute Only attribute can be assigned to .EXE and .COM files. Files that have this attribute assigned cannot be copied or copied over (that is, backed up) — just executed or deleted. Note that some applications don't work properly if flagged with the Execute Only attribute — so test them carefully before granting access to your users.

▸ *Hidden (H)\** — Valid on both DOS and OS/2 machines. Hidden is reserved for special files or directories that should not be seen, used, deleted, or copied over. Prevents a filename from being displayed with the DOS DIR command, however, the NDIR command displays the directory if the user has File Scan [F] access rights.

▸ *Normal (N)\** — No directory or file attributes have been set. This is the default. Normal files are typically flagged non-sharable, Read/Write automatically.

▸ *Read-Only (Ro)* — No one can write to the file. When Read Only is set or cleared, NetWare 5.1 also sets or clears the Delete Inhibit and Rename Inhibit attributes. Consequently, a user can't write to, erase, or rename a file when Read Only is set. A user with the Modify or Supervisor access right can remove the Delete Inhibit and Rename Inhibit attributes without removing Ro. In this case, the file can be deleted or renamed, but not written to.

▸ *Read/Write (Rw)* — Enables users to change the contents of the file. This attribute is automatically assigned using the Normal (N) switch.

▸ *Rename Inhibit (Ri)\** — Prevents a user from renaming the file or directory.

▸ *Sharable (Sh)* — Allows the file to be accessed by more than one user at a time. This attribute is usually used in combination with Read-Only for application files. The default "Normal" setting is non-sharable.

▸ *System (Sy)\** — Applies to DOS and OS/2 workstations. The NetWare 5.1 OS assigns this attribute to system-owned files and directories. System files are hidden and cannot be deleted, renamed, or copied. Prevents a filename from being displayed with the DOS DIR command; however, the NetWare 5.1 NDIR command displays the file if the user has File Scan access rights.

That does it for security attributes. Now let's take a closer look at feature attributes.

## Feature Attributes

Feature attributes provide access to special NetWare 5.1 functions or features. These features include backup, purging, and transactional tracking. As a matter of fact, only three feature attributes exist in NetWare 5.1, and one of them applies to both directories and files (P). Here's how they work:

- ▶ *Archive Needed (A)* — A status flag set by NetWare 5.1 which indicates that the file has been changed since the last time it was backed up. NetWare 5.1 sets this attribute when a file is created or modified and clears it during SBACKUP full and incremental sessions.

- ▶ *Purge (P)* * — Tells NetWare 5.1 to purge the file immediately when it is deleted. The file then cannot be salvaged with the FILER utility. Purge at the directory level clears all files and directories from the salvage table once they're deleted. This attribute is best used on sensitive data.

- ▶ *Transactional (T)* — Indicates that the file is protected by NetWare 5.1's internal Transaction Tracking System (TTS), which prevents data corruption by ensuring that either all changes are made, or no changes are made when a file is being modified. The Transactional attribute should be assigned to TTS-tracked databases and accounting files.

That does it for NetWare 5.1 feature attributes. Now let's take a quick look at disk management.

## Disk Management Attributes

The remaining seven file and directory attributes apply to NetWare 5.1 disk management — file compression, data migration, and block suballocation. File compression enables more data to be stored on a volume by compressing files that are not being used. Once you enable this disk management feature, volume capacity increases up to 63 percent. Data migration is the transfer of inactive data from a NetWare 5.1 volume to an external optical disk storage device — such as a jukebox. This process is transparent to the user because files appear to be stored on the volume. Data migration is made possible through NetWare 5.1's internal High-Capacity Storage System (HCSS) — as seen in the previous chapter.

Finally, block suballocation increases disk storage efficiency by segmenting disk allocation blocks. Suballocation is turned on by default when you install NetWare 5.1. You can turn it off using one of the following seven attributes. Here's a quick look at NetWare 5.1's disk management attributes:

▶ *Can't Compress (Cc)* — A status flag set by NetWare 5.1. Indicates that the file can't be compressed because of insignificant space savings. To avoid the overhead of uncompressing files that do not compress well, the system calculates the compressed size of a file before actually compressing it. If no disk space is saved by compression, or if the size difference does not meet the value specified by the "Minimum Percentage Compression Gain" parameter, the file is not compressed. This attribute is shown on attribute lists, but cannot be set by the user or network administrators.

▶ *Compressed (Co)* — A status flag set by NetWare 5.1. Indicates that the file has been compressed by the system. Once again, this attribute is shown on attribute lists but cannot be set by the user or network administrators.

▶ *Don't Compress (Dc)\** — Prevents a file from being compressed regardless of what the volume or directory is set to. It is a way of managing file compression.

▶ *Don't Migrate (Dm)\** — Marks a file or directory so that it is never migrated to a secondary storage device backup system regardless of what the volume or directory is set to. This is the only way you can directly manage data migration. Otherwise, all files are automatically migrated once they exceed the timeout threshold (assuming, of course, that the Migration feature is turned on — which is the default).

▶ *Don't Suballocate (Ds)* — Prevents an individual file from being suballocated even if suballocation is enabled on the volume. This is typically used for files that are huge or appended to frequently, such as databases. This attribute is your only tool for managing suballocation once it's been activated.

▸ *Immediate Compress (Ic)\** — Marks a file or directory for immediate
compression as soon as the OS can. NetWare 5.1 compresses the file as soon
as it can without waiting for a specific event to initiate compression — such as
a time delay. As a network administrator, you can use Immediate Compress
to turn on compression and Don't Compress to turn it off. Both attributes
operate at the file and directory level.

▸ *Migrated (M)* — A status flag set by NetWare 5.1. Indicates that the file has
been migrated. This attribute is shown on an attribute list, but can't be set
by the user or network administrators.

You can set directory and file attributes with ConsoleOne, NetWare Administrator,
FILER, or FLAG. Refer to Figure 5.36 for an illustration of the ConsoleOne attribute
configuration screen.

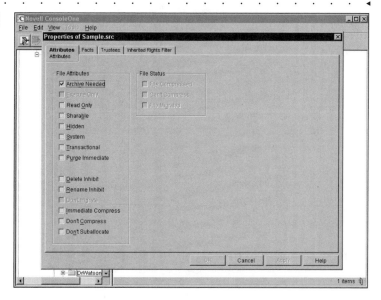

*Configuring attribute
security in ConsoleOne*

These file and directory attributes, when used in combination, can create effective security tools to control who has access to do what with specialized NetWare
5.1 files. The default attribute combination for all files is Normal — nonsharable

Read/Write. In some special instances, however, you can justify customizing these attributes. The following are examples:

▸ Standalone applications that are not to be shared should be flagged nonsharable Read-Only.

▸ Data files that are shared but not written to simultaneously should be flagged nonsharable Read/Write.

▸ Data files that are part of larger multi-user applications can be flagged Sharable Read/Write only if the application supports internal record locking.

▸ Application files that are accessed by simultaneous users should be flagged Sharable Read-Only.

▸ Large important database files should always be flagged with the Transactional (T) attribute, but be sure the application supports TTS.

▸ Sensitive archive files should be flagged with the attribute Hidden. These include records that are only accessed once a month.

▸ All System files owned by NetWare 5.1 should be flagged System. This is an attribute assigned by NetWare 5.1, not you.

▸ Sensitive application files that cost a significant amount of money should be flagged Execute Only by the network administrator. However, be careful, because not all applications will run when flagged "X."

**For some great hands-on experience with NetWare 5.1 directory/file attributes, check out Lab Exercise 5.4 later in this chapter.**

**TIP**

Congratulations! You have completed your lessons in all five of NetWare 5.1's security layers.

In Layer One, we learned how to log into the NDS tree with authentication. Then login restrictions took over. Layer Two was dominated by six different types of restrictions — login, password, network address, time, account balance, and Intruder Detection/Lockout. Once users pass through the first two barriers, their ability to access leaf and container objects is determined by a sophisticated NDS security structure — Layer Three. At the heart of NDS security is a simple three-step process: trustee assignments, IRF, and effective rights.

But what about security within the server? NDS security wasn't enough. In Layer Four, we learned how to configure file system security to grant file and directory access rights with the help of trustee assignments and inheritance. We learned how the eight different access rights can be used to protect NetWare 5.1 files and directories. But sometimes this isn't enough. That's where attributes came in. The final barrier enabled us to override previous security with three different attribute types — security, feature, and disk management.

As a network administrator, it is your responsibility to manage the NetWare 5.1 network. But most importantly, you must protect it. Hopefully now you've gained a new appreciation for the value of an impenetrable network armor. We've filled your brain with sophisticated security strategies and given you a utility belt full of advanced protection tools — like NetWare Administrator, ConsoleOne, and effective rights worksheets.

*So, where do you go from here?* So far, you can manage NDS, connect to the network, map drives, and secure the network. I'd say you're becoming a full-fledged NetWare 5.1 Superhero! But what about the big picture? Now I think you're ready to journey into the three realms of NetWare 5.1 workstation management with ZENworks.

**LAB EXERCISE 5.4: FILE SYSTEM SECURITY AT ACME**

In this exercise, we are going to explore the exciting world of NetWare 5.1 file system security. Now that you have made FIN-Admin Organizational Role an exclusive container administrator for the FIN container, you need to set up some initial file system rights for the FIN Organizational Unit object and the FIN-Admin Organizational Role object.

The following hardware is required for this exercise:

▸ A NetWare 5.1 server called WHITE-SRV1.WHITE.CRIME.TOKYO.ACME (which can be installed using the directions found in Appendix D).

▸ A workstation running either the NetWare 5.1 Novell Client for Windows 95/98 or NetWare 5.1 Novell Client for Windows NT/2000 (which can be installed using the directions found in Exercise 3.1).

In this exercise, you grant the grant the FIN-Admin Organizational Role object all file system rights to the WHITE-SRV1_SYS-Alias:SHARED\FIN subdirectory and then modify its IRF to block inherited rights from above. You also grant the FIN Organizational object Unit all file system rights except [SAM] to the WHITE-SRV1_SYS-Alias:SHARED\FIN subdirectory and CRIME Organizational Unit object all rights except [SAM] to the WHITE-SRV1_SYS-Alias:SHARED subdirectory.

Perform the following tasks at your client workstation.

**I.** Log into the tree as Admin, if you haven't already done so.

**2.** Execute ConsoleOne.

**3.** Create the WHITE-SRV1_SYS-Alias object.

    **a.** To create the WHITE-SRV1_SYS-Alias object, use one of the following methods:

        • Navigate to and click the FIN Organizational Unit object and press Insert, *or*

        • Navigate to and click the FIN Organizational Unit object and select File ⇨ New ⇨ Object, *or*

- Navigate to and right-click the FIN Organizational Unit object and select New ⇨ Object from the pop-up menu that appears.

**b.** When the New Object dialog box appears follow these steps:

- Click Alias.

- Click OK.

**c.** When the New Alias dialog box appears follow these steps:

- In the Name field, enter the following:

  `WHITE-SRV1_SYS-Admin`

- Click the Browse button to the right of the Object field.

- When the Select Object dialog box appears, navigate the tree until the WHITE-SRV1_SYS object appears in the left pane and then double-click it to select it.

**d.** Follow these steps when the New Alias dialog box reappears:

- In the Object field, Notice that WHITE-SRV1_SYS.WHITE. CRIME.TOKYO.ACME is listed.

- Click OK.

**4.** Assign the FIN-Admin Organizational Role all file system rights for the WHITE-SRV1_SYS-Alias:SHARED\FIN directory.

**a.** Navigate to and right-click the WHITE-SRV1_SYS-Alias:SHARED\FIN folder.

**b.** Select Properties from the pop-up menu that appears.

**c.** When the Properties of FIN dialog box appears, click the Trustees page tab.

**d.** When the Trustees page appears, click Add Trustee.

**e.** When the Select Object dialog box appears, navigate the tree until the FIN-Admin Organizational Role object appears in the large pane and then double-click it to select it.

**f.** Follow these steps when the Trustees page reappears:

- In the Trustees list box, verify that FIN-Admin.FIN.WHITE. CRIME.TOKYO.ACME is highlighted.

- In the Access Rights section, mark the six file system rights that are not marked (that is, Supervisor, Write, Create, Erase, Modify, and Access Control).

- Click Apply to save your changes.

**5.** Assign the FIN container the [RWCEF] rights for the WHITE-SRV1_SYS-Alias:SHARED\FIN subdirectory.

  **a.** Follow the basic procedures in Steps 4a through 4f to assign the FIN container the [RWCEF] file system rights to the WHITE-SRV1_SYS-Alias:SHARED\FIN directory.

  **b.** Click OK to save your changes.

**6.** Assign the CRIME container the [RWCEF] rights for the WHITE-SRV1_SYS-Alias:SHARED subdirectory.

  **a.** Follow the basic procedures in Steps 4a through 4f to assign the CRIME container the [RWCEF] file system rights to the WHITE-SRV1_SYS-Alias:SHARED directory.

  **b.** Click OK to save your changes.

**7.** Check LJohn's effective rights for the WHITE-SRV1_SYS-Alias: SHARED\FIN directory to verify that he has all file system rights.

  **a.** Right-click the WHITE-SRV1_SYS-Alias:SHARED\FIN folder.

  **b.** Select Properties from the pop-up menu that appears.

  **c.** When the Properties of FIN dialog box appears, click the Trustees page tab.

  **d.** When the Trustees page appears, click Effective Rights.

  **e.** When the Effective Rights dialog box appears, click the Browse button to the right of the Trustee field.

**f.** When the Select Object dialog box appears, navigate the tree until the LJohn User object appears in the large pane and then double-click it to select it.

**g.** Follow these steps when the Effective Rights dialog box reappears:

- Verify that LJohn has all eight file system rights.
- Click Close.

**8.** Modify the IRF of the WHITE-SRV1_SYS-Alias:SHARED\FIN directory.

**a.** When the Trustees dialog box reappears, click the Inherited Rights Filter page tab.

**b.** Follow these steps when the Inherited Rights Filter page appears:

- Unmark all check boxes, except for Supervisor (because the Supervisor right cannot be blocked by an IRF in the file system).
- Click Apply to apply your changes.

**9.** Examine the effective rights of the Admin User objects to verify that it has all file system rights to the WHITE-SRV1_SYS-Alias:SHARED\FIN subdirectory.

**10.** Examine the effective rights of the LJohn User object to make sure he has all file system rights to the WHITE-SRV1_SYS-Alias:SHARED\FIN subdirectory.

**11.** Examine the effective rights of the RHood User object to make sure he has no file system rights to the WHITE-SRV1_SYS-Alias:SHARED\FIN subdirectory.

**12.** Exit ConsoleOne.

**13.** Log into the network as RHood.

**a.** Execute ConsoleOne.

**b.** Browse the WHITE-SRV1_SYS-Alias:SHARED subdirectory. Notice you cannot "see" the FIN subdirectory.

**c.** Exit ConsoleOne.

**14.** Log into the network as LJohn.

    **a.** Execute ConsoleOne.

    **b.** Browse the WHITE-SRV1_SYS-Alias:SHARED subdirectory. Notice you can see the FIN subdirectory.

    **c.** Exit ConsoleOne.

**15.** Log into the network as Admin.

## LAB EXERCISE 5.5: FIVE-LAYER SECURITY MODEL

Circle the 15 security-related terms hidden in this word search puzzle using the hints provided. No punctuation characters (such as blank spaces, hyphens, brackets, and so on) should be included. Numbers should always be spelled out.

```
T  T  S  G  R  A  C  E  L  O  G  I  N  S  T  R
P  R  O  P  E  R  T  Y  R  I  G  H  T  S  L  T
A  U  T  H  E  N  T  I  C  A  T  I  O  N  P  H
C  S  B  A  R  G  O  J  T  J  P  O  V  G  I  N
L  T  T  L  K  K  M  M  M  I  U  O  X  K  I  T
C  E  V  M  I  T  V  E  R  T  O  W  V  S  W  Z
M  E  F  F  E  C  T  I  V  E  R  I  G  H  T  S
D  R  O  B  J  E  C  T  R  I  G  H  T  S  W  Z
U  I  O  R  L  D  V  I  C  G  Y  X  S  I  Y  L
Q  G  R  E  N  A  M  E  I  S  Z  V  K  T  K  F
Y  H  D  F  M  D  N  N  H  O  D  J  D  I  H  Q
G  T  E  C  N  A  T  I  R  E  H  N  I  E  G  T
J  S  S  G  X  Q  W  B  X  L  C  N  I  C  F  N
```

**Hints**

1. Property of an object that lists trustees of the object.
2. Making sure you are who you say you are.
3. Object right that is only valid for containers.
4. Object right that allows you to remove an object from the NDS tree.
5. The rights that an object can actually exercise for an object, directory, or file.
6. The number of times a user can log in with an expired password.
7. Object used for assigning rights to multiple users.
8. Flowing down of money or trustee rights.
9. Controls the rights that can be inherited from a parent container or directory.
10. Privileges required to view or modify a container or leaf object.
11. Privileges required to view or modify the values associated with an NDS object.

12. Special trustee which is somewhat similar to the EVERYONE Group found in earlier versions of NetWare.
13. Object right that allows you to change an object's name.
14. Privileges granted to an object that determine its access to another object, directory, or file.
15. System Fault Tolerance feature that protects database applications from corruption by backing out incomplete transactions.

See Appendix C for answers.

**LAB EXERCISE 5.6: NETWARE 5.1 SECURITY**

**Across**

2. Required for changing file attributes
7. Required for deleting a directory or file
8. Required for looking at file contents
9. Required for changing a file system IRF
10. Required for viewing objects in the NDS tree
12. Restricts access to directories and files
13. Automatically granted with the Read property right
14. Charges users for access to network resources

**Down**

1. What is the 'O' for?
3. NDS rights flow down the tree
4. Can be blocked by an NDS IRF
5. Handy for creating multiple users
6. File system rights to consider restricting
11. Required for changing file contents
12. Is initially granted access to entire tree
    See Appendix C for answers.

# CHAPTER 6

# NetWare 5.1 Workstation Management

**U**nlike its name implies, ZENworks has nothing to do with ancient meditation and wisdom. In actuality, it's a clever acronym for "Zero Effort Networks." While it's impossible to achieve "zero effort" networking, ZENworks greatly improves the manageability of user access to the information superhighway.

ZENworks is an integrated set of applications that reduces the cost and complexity of managing Windows-based network workstations through NDS. ZENworks provides policy-enabled workstation management, desktop management, and application control.

ZENworks 2.0 is available in two forms: the *ZENworks 2.0 Starter Pack* (on the *Novell Client CD-ROM* included with NetWare 5.1) and the *ZENworks 2.0 full package* (purchased separately). The ZENworks 2.0 Starter Pack includes the Application Launcher and Desktop Management components. The full ZENworks 2.0 package includes the functionality found in the Starter Pack, as well as hardware and software inventory management, remote control, inventory and distribution reporting, and HelpDesk policies.

ZENworks extends the NDS schema to include several new objects. These objects enable you to configure and control workstations from within the NDS tree, and include the following:

▶ Application and Application Folder objects

▶ User and User Group objects

▶ Workstation and Workstation Group objects

▶ Policy packages

**REAL WORLD**

To take full advantage of the NDS integration features of ZENworks, you must use the 32-bit version of NetWare Administrator. By default, NetWare Administrator 32 is copied to the SYS:PUBLIC\WIN32 directory during ZENworks installation.

In this chapter, we explore each of these objects and learn how they enhance workstation, desktop, and application management for NetWare 5.1 administrators. Let's begin our new "ZEN" training with a comprehensive lesson in ZENworks construction — also known as installation.

# ZENworks Installation

As I mentioned earlier, NetWare 5.1 ships with a *ZENworks 2.0 Starter Pack* CD-ROM. The ZENworks Starter Pack consists of an Application Launcher and the Workstation Manager. In this section, we explore the detailed steps of ZENworks server installation.

Before we tackle the step-by-step instructions of ZENworks construction, let's take a closer look at ZENworks design guidelines and installation requirements.

## ZENworks Design Guidelines

A full ZENworks implementation is a sophisticated and complex project. In general, it consists of the following five phases:

▸ *Phase 1: Planning* — First, you should determine how many workstations will be added to your NDS tree. Second, you should plan the distribution of policy objects and redesign the NDS tree as needed.

▸ *Phase 2: Installation* — Third, you should install ZENworks on all servers and workstations that require it. Also, be sure to update your existing NetWare 5.1 Client with full ZENworks functionality. Finally, consider creating a Workstation Import Policy.

▸ *Phase 3: Initial NDS Registration* — Once ZENworks is installed, the new and improved workstations must send NDS registration information to the Workstation Registration property of select NDS containers. Don't worry, this is accomplished automatically when users log in.

▶ *Phase 4: Import Workstations* — Next, you must import all your new ZENworks workstations into the NDS tree using the 32-bit version of NetWare Administrator.

▶ *Phase 5: Final NDS Registration* — Finally, your NDS-enhanced workstations automatically register themselves with their own logical NDS objects the next time users log in.

To use ZENworks efficiently, you must focus on four sets of NDS objects: Application, User, Workstation, and policy packages. Let's take a closer look.

### ZENworks Design for Application Objects

ZENworks includes an application management feature called *Application Launcher*. This integrated tool relies on two ZENworks-enhanced NDS objects: Application and Application Folder. Application objects store configuration and launching information for network applications, and can be further organized into functional Application Folder objects.

Using Application Launcher, you can quickly and easily distribute applications to users' workstations and manage those applications as objects in the NDS tree.

During ZENworks design, you must determine where to place Application and Application Folder objects in the NDS tree. Follow these ZENworks design guidelines:

▶ *Application objects* — place Application objects close to the users who will be accessing them.

▶ *Application Folder objects* — place Application Folders in centralized locations for easy management. Users never access these objects, so you don't have to worry about distributed NDS traffic.

### ZENworks Design for User and Group Objects

The best way to connect User and Application objects is to use groups. Group objects include a number of User members, who will inherit any application associations given to the group.

Follow these ZENworks design guidelines for Group objects:

▶ Place Group objects in the same containers as associated Application objects.

▶ Limit the number of group members to 1,500.

▶ Keep users in the group within the same partition so external references and associated network traffic are minimized. Never span group membership across a WAN.

### ZENworks Design for Workstation Objects

Once ZENworks has been installed on the network, you can create a Workstation object corresponding to each network workstation by *registering* the workstation and then *importing* it into the NDS tree. After a Workstation object has been created for a workstation, you can configure, control, and troubleshoot the workstation remotely (without having to leave your desk).

ZENworks also allows you to assign Workstation objects as members of a Workstation Group object. This way, you can apply workstation management rules to multiple clients using a single NDS object.

### ZENworks Design for Policy Package Objects

ZENworks includes various Policy Package objects that can be used for workstation configuration and management. The number of Policy Package objects you create depends on the platforms present on your network and the complexity of your management needs.

ZENworks supports three Policy Package object types in a variety of platform-specific configurations: Container, User (Win31, Win95-98, and WinNT), and Workstation (Win31, Win95-98, and WinNT). See Figure 6.1 for an illustration of the ZENworks policies included in the Win95-98 Workstation Policy Package object.

Follow these ZENworks design guidelines for Policy Package objects:

▶ Create Container Policy Packages at the highest level in the NDS tree (within a given site or location).

▶ Create User and Workstation Policy Packages close to the objects and users/workstations that will access them (preferably in the same container).

▶ If you create a single-purpose container for Workstation objects, place Workstation Policy Packages in this container.

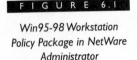

F I G U R E   6.1

*Win95-98 Workstation Policy Package in NetWare Administrator*

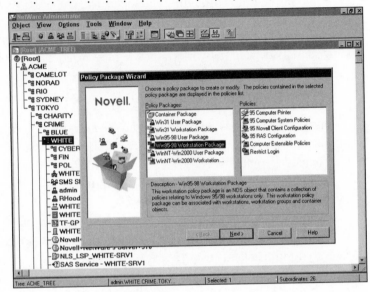

That completes our lesson in ZENworks design. Now, let's take these guidelines to the next level — installation.

## ZENworks Installation Requirements

To install ZENworks, you must ensure that your server and workstations meet the minimum requirements discussed here. In addition, you must have appropriate NDS and file system rights. Remember, ZENworks is a fully network-integrated client connectivity solution.

### ZENworks Server Requirements

ZENworks relies on a high level of synergy between the NetWare 5.1 server and the Novell Client. Let's begin with the server. The following is a checklist of minimum hardware and software requirements for ZENworks server installation:

- ▶ A Novell NetWare 4.11 (or later) server with Support Pack 6 (Recommended: NetWare 5.1)

- ▶ NDS-integration (bindery emulation not supported) with Version 6.*x* or higher (Recommended: Version 8)

▸ 128MB of server RAM for NetWare 5.*x* servers, or 64MB of server RAM for NetWare 4.*x* servers (at least 7MB free)

▸ 175MB of available server disk space on the SYS:volume if you copy the client installation software to the server; 40MB of available disk space on the SYS:VOLUME if you don't copy the client installation software to the server

▸ The NetWare server must also have the 32-bit version of NetWare Administrator (NWADMN32.EXE) installed in the SYS:PUBLIC\WIN32 subdirectory

**ConsoleOne does not currently support ZENworks.**

TIP

### ZENworks Client Requirements

Next, you must ensure that the Novell Clients meet ZENwork's minimum installation requirements. Here's a quick checklist:

▸ Windows 95/98 and Windows NT/2000 clients can use all the ZENworks features.

▸ Windows 3.1 and DOS clients use a subset of the ZENworks features.

▸ Workstations must support the latest Novell Client software with the Management component installed: Version 3.1 or better for Windows 95/98, or Version 4.6 or better for Windows NT/2000.

▸ A network connection via NDS. Bindery connections do not support ZENworks.

▸ A Pentium/250Mhz processor or better. (Recommended: Pentium III/500Mhz.)

▸ 16MB of workstation RAM. (Recommended: 64MB.)

▸ 5MB of available hard disk space.

**TIP**

**Windows 3.1 cannot use all the ZENworks features because the Registry (found only in Windows 95/98 and Windows NT/2000) is needed to store some of the advanced configuration information created by ZENworks.**

### ZENworks Rights Requirements

To install ZENworks, you must have a minimum set of NDS and file system rights. In addition, users need special file system rights to access Application Launcher-delivered applications. The following are the minimum set of rights. How secure do you feel?

▶ *NDS rights* — To install ZENworks, you must have Supervisor object rights to the [Root] of the NDS tree. This right allows you to extend the NDS schema and accommodate new ZENworks objects. In addition, users need Read and Compare property rights to All Properties for any Container, Group, or User object associated with an Application Launcher application. Fortunately, these NDS rights are assigned automatically when you associate a user with an Application object.

▶ *File system rights* — To use the ZENworks application-management features, users need certain file system rights to the directory in which Application Launcher is installed and the directories containing Application Launcher applications. Fortunately, ZENworks automatically assigns users Read and File Scan file system rights to the default Application Launcher directory (SYS:PUBLIC). The second rights assignment occurs when users are associated with Application Launcher-delivered Application objects. And here's the cool part — these rights are revoked when the user is disassociated from the Application object.

That's all there is to it . . . no sweat. Now that your NetWare server and clients are ready, it's time for ZENworks server installation.

## ZENworks Server Installation

Before you begin ZENworks server installation, you must establish Admin rights on the NetWare server where you will be installing the ZENworks 2.0

Starter Pack. Also, make sure this server is locally accessible (that is, not over a WAN). Finally, make sure to terminate all programs running from the SYS:PUBLIC directory on the target server.

Following are the seven steps of ZENworks server installation:

▶ *Step 1*: Getting Started

▶ *Step 2*: ZENworks Installation Type

▶ *Step 3*: Choose ZENworks Components

▶ *Step 4*: Choose ZENworks Parts

▶ *Step 5*: Choose ZENworks Servers

▶ *Step 6*: Workstation Registration Rights

▶ *Step 7*: The End

That's all there is to it. Now let's install ZENworks on one of ACME's SYDNEY servers.

### Step 1: Getting Started

You must install ZENworks separately on each ZEN-based server. To start off, you must log on to the server as an Administrator with Supervisor object rights to the [Root] of the NDS tree. Next, close all applications on your administrative workstation and insert the *NetWare 5.1 Novell Client Software* CD-ROM into the appropriate drive.

The *NetWare 5.1 Novell Client Software* CD-ROM is designed with an auto-run feature that automatically launches the first screen when you insert the CD-ROM. Otherwise, you can run WINSETUP.EXE from the root directory of the CD.

The first ZENworks server installation screen (shown in Figure 6.2) allows you to select from the following number of installation options:

▶ ZENworks — Installs the ZENworks Starter Pack 2.0 desktop tool on selected servers, but you must be currently logged onto each.

▶ *Windows 95/98 Client* — Installs the NetWare 5.1 Novell Client for Windows 95/98.

▶ *Windows NT/2000 Client* — Installs the NetWare 5.1 Novell Client for Windows NT/2000.

▶ *Windows 3.x Client* — Installs the NetWare 5.1 Novell Client for Windows 3.x.

▶ *Documentation* — Launches a Web browser to view client documentation in HTML format (at `http://www.Novell.com/documentation`).

▶ *Browse CD-ROM* — Enables you to view the contents of the *NetWare 5.1 Novell Client Software* CD-ROM.

When you click ZENworks, an Installation Wizard guides you through the process of installing the ZENworks desktop tool on one or more NetWare servers. Follow the onscreen prompts to read the introductory information and accept the license agreement.

▶ · · · · · · · · · · · · · · · · · · · · · · · · · ◀

**FIGURE 6.2**

*The opening ZENworks server installation screen*

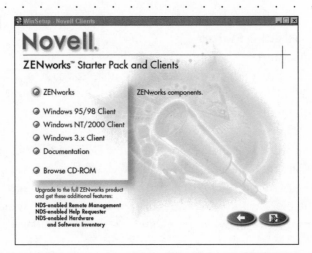

> **REAL WORLD**
>
> The installation instructions are based on the ZENworks Version 2.0 Starter
> Pack. Subsequent versions may behave slightly differently. Stay on your toes!

### Step 2: ZENworks Installation Type

Once you've activated the ZENworks server Installation Wizard, you are at the
"ZENworks Setup Type" screen shown in Figure 6.3. At this point, you must
choose among the following three types of ZENworks installation:

FIGURE 6.3

*The ZENworks Setup Type
installation screen*

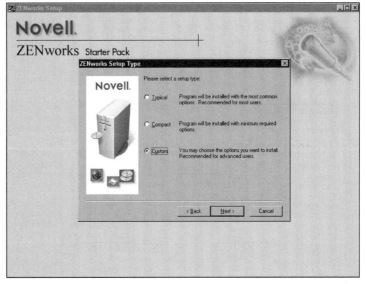

- ▶ *Typical* — A Typical installation copies all the server-based components of
  ZENworks to the server on which you're logged. This includes application
  management, workstation maintenance, desktop management, and the
  NetWare Administrator 32. However, copies of the Novell Client software
  for Windows are *not* copied to the network.

▶ *Compact* — A Compact installation copies only the minimum program options. This is a subset of the typical installation type. Choose this option only if your server is short on disk space.

▶ *Custom* — The Custom installation type enables you to choose the options you want to install, including the Novell Client software for Windows. In addition, this advanced Wizard enables you to specify multiple target servers.

In this section, we're going to explore the Custom installation type. Why not? We're network administrators, we can handle it. Make the appropriate choice and click Next to continue.

**Step 3: Choose ZENworks Components**

If you choose the Custom option, the Installation Wizard responds with a list of ZENworks components. As seen in Figure 6.4, the first two components correspond to the two main features described in this chapter. The final two options are administrative.

▶ · · · · · · · · · · · · · · · · · · · · · · · · · · ◀

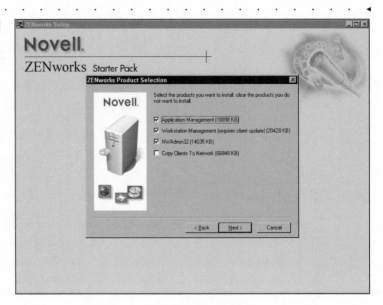

**FIGURE 6.4**

*The ZENworks Product Selection installation screen*

Here's the list of products:

▸ *Application Management* — This is the Application Launcher piece. Choosing this component enables you to distribute network-based applications to users' workstations and manage the applications as objects in the NDS tree.

▸ *Workstation Management* — This represents the first and largest feature offered by the ZENworks 2.0 Starter Pack. Workstation Management encompasses all the network administration tasks associated with daily user productivity, including policies and NDS registration.

▸ *NWAdmin32* — Choosing this component copies a ZENworks-enhanced version of NetWare Administrator to the target server(s). This is a good idea.

▸ *Copy Clients to Network* — This option copies the Novell Client Installation Wizard to each target server. This enables you to execute the ZENworks Client installation from a central network repository. It saves you time shuffling CD-ROMs all around the network.

If you want a fully functional ZENworks server, choose all the components and click Next to continue.

### Step 4: Choose ZENworks Parts

Once you've selected the ZENworks installation components, you must further refine your focus to include Parts. ZENworks installation Parts are logical network entities that enable you to implement the components you just selected. As seen in Figure 6.5, ZENworks installation Parts include Files, Schema Extensions, Application Objects, and Workstation Registry Entities.

Select all the ZENworks installation Parts check boxes and click Next to continue.

▶ · · · · · · · · · · · · · · · · · · · · · · ◀

The ZENworks Part
Selection installation screen

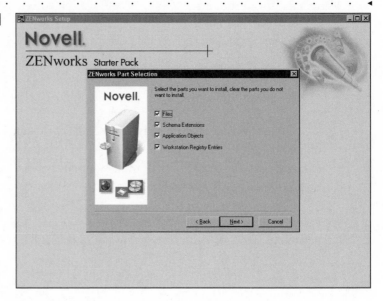

### Step 5: Choose the ZENworks Servers

On the next screen, verify that the correct tree is marked and then click Next. The Wizard automatically lists all servers to which you've been authenticated. By default, your initial login server is selected. Check it out in Figure 6.6.

To install ZENworks on multiple servers, you must be authenticated to each server, have rights to NDS, and be mapped to each SYS:volume *before* launching the ZENworks installation program. As you can see in Figure 6.6, only one server is selected. To install ZENworks on multiple servers on the list, click the Select All button. Doing so makes all configurations made during the remainder of the installation process apply to all servers selected.

Once you've selected the ZENworks target servers, click Next to continue. At this point, you must confirm the language you selected in Step 1 and acknowledge the ZENworks summary information. At this point, the Installation Wizard begins copying files to your target ZENworks servers.

### Step 6: Workstation Registration Rights

After the files have been copied to the server, a Workstation Registration Rights screen appears, allowing you to define an NDS rights scope for workstation registration. Before ZENworks can create Workstation objects in NDS, users of those workstations must be granted appropriate rights. Check out the workstation registration rights assignment screen in Figure 6.7.

FIGURE 6.6

The ZENworks List of Tree/Servers installation screen

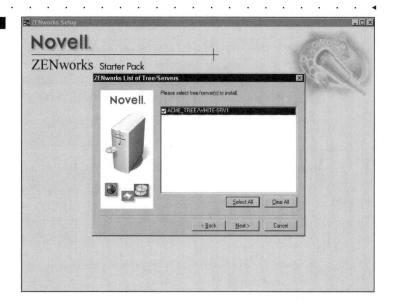

FIGURE 6.6

The ZENworks List of Tree/Servers installation screen

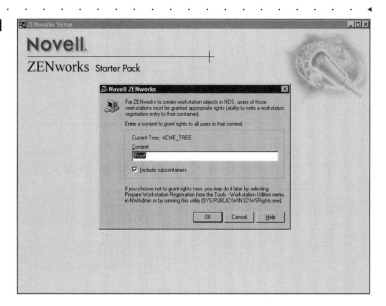

FIGURE 6.7

The ZENworks workstation registration rights assignment screen

Granting rights at the [Root] level facilitates registration throughout the tree. If you restrict the workstation registration context, you limit your own ability to manage workstations outside that context. Input [Root] in the Context field and mark the Include Subcontainers check box. Click OK to continue.

**TIP**

**If you currently choose not to grant workstation registration rights, you may do it later by selecting Prepare Workstation Registration from the Tools menu of NetWare Administrator. You can also accomplish the same task by running the WSRIGHTS.EXE program in SYS:PUBLIC\WIN32.**

### Step 7: The End

By default, the README file and Setup Log should be opened in the Windows WordPad utility. If you do not want to view these files, simply remove the checkmarks from the Launch Readme File and Launch Setup Log File boxes before you click Finish.

Congratulations—you're finished! You've successfully constructed your own ZENworks system. In this section, we activated the ZENworks server(s) with the help of an administrative workstation, *ZENworks 2.0 Starter Pack* CD-ROM, and seven simple steps.

Now that ZENworks is installed, you can take full advantage of its three powerful features:

▶ Workstation Management

▶ Desktop Management

▶ Application Management

Now, let's take a comprehensive tour through each of these three features and learn what it takes to master the ZENworks 2.0 Starter Pack.

LAB EXERCISE 6.1: INSTALLING ZENWORKS IN THE

Welcome back to ACME!

Now it's time to bring some "Zen" into ACME's network. As you learned in this section, ZENworks relies on synergy between the NetWare server and the Novell Client. In this exercise, we install the ZENworks 2.0 Starter Pack on the WHITE-SRV1 server.

The following hardware is required for this exercise:

▶ A NetWare 5.1 server called WHITE-SRV1.WHITE.CRIME.TOKYO.ACME (which can be installed using the directions found in Appendix D). You also need to make sure that this server meets the minimum hardware requirements for installing ZENworks.

▶ A workstation running either the NetWare 5.1 Novell Client for Windows 95/98 or NetWare 5.1 Novell Client for Windows NT/2000 (which can be installed using the directions found in Lab Exercise 3.1).

The *NetWare 5.1 Novell Client Software* CD-ROM is required for this exercise. (It contains the Novell ZENworks 2.0 Starter Pack.)

To perform this exercise, you need the following NDS rights (which is why you log on to the tree as Admin):

▶ Supervisor object rights to the NetWare 5.1 server (WHITE-SRV1) where you will install ZENworks.

▶ Supervisor object rights to the NDS container (WHITE.CRIME.TOKYO.ACME) where you will install ZENworks.

▶ Rights to modify the schema of the NDS tree (ACME_TREE) into which you are installing ZENworks.

As we learned in this section, the ZENworks server installation consists of seven simple steps. Follow the bouncing ball:

**1.** Getting Started

**a.** Log on to your tree as Admin, if you have not already done so.

    **b.** Exit any other applications that are running.

    **c.** Insert the *NetWare 5.1 Novell Client Software* CD-ROM in your workstation's CD-ROM drive. The WINSETUP.EXE file launches automatically.

    **d.** When the "WinSetup — Novell Clients" screen appears, click ZENworks to install ZENworks on the server.

    **e.** Follow these steps when the "Welcome to ZENworks!" window appears:

       • Read the information onscreen. Note that it strongly recommends that all programs using files in SYS:PUBLIC and its subdirectories be terminated prior to running this Setup program. It also strongly recommends that you exit all Windows programs before running this Setup program. (You should have done the latter in Step 1b.)

       • Click Next.

    **f.** When the Software License Agreement window appears, read the agreement and then click Yes to accept its terms.

**2.** ZENworks Installation Type

    **a.** When the ZENworks Setup Type window appears, click Custom to perform a custom installation and then click Next.

**TIP**

**You must select the Custom installation method to be able to specify which ZENworks components you want to install. For example, the Typical and Compact methods do not allow you to copy the Novell client software for Windows 95/98, Windows NT/2000, and DOS/WIN clients to the server.**

**3.** Choose ZENworks Components

    **a.** When the ZENworks Product Selection window appears, ensure that the first three check boxes are marked and then click Next.

**4.** Choose ZENworks Parts

   **a.** When the ZENworks Part Selection window appears, verify that all check boxes are marked and then click Next.

**5.** Choose ZENworks Servers

   **a.** When the ZENworks List of Trees window appears, confirm that only the ACME_TREE check box is marked and then click Next.

   **b.** When the ZENworks List of Tree/Servers window appears, confirm that only the ACME_TREE/WHITE-SRV1 check box is marked and then click Next.

   **c.** When the ZENworks Language Selection window appears, ensure that the language you want to use for installation is checked and then click Next.

   **d.** When the Start Copying Files window appears, review the summary of components to be installed in the Current Settings list box. If everything is correct, click Next.

   **e.** Wait while the ZENworks files are copied to the server. (This may take awhile.)

**6.** Workstation Registration Rights

   **a.** ZENworks Workstation Auto-Registration requires that users have the rights to write a registration request to their container in order to register their workstations with NDS and to keep the workstations synchronized with NDS. Because object rights flow down through the NDS tree unless modified or blocked lower in the tree, assigning the rights at the [Root] level facilitates workstation registration throughout the tree. Follow these steps when the Novell ZENworks window appears:

     • Read the information onscreen.

     • Verify that the following context is listed in the Context field:

       `[Root]`

     • Confirm that the Include Subcontainers check box is marked.

     • Click OK.

**b.** Follow these steps when the Novell ZENworks Workstation Auto-Registration Rights Utility window appears:

- Read the information onscreen indicating that the Novell ZENworks Workstation Auto-Registration rights were successfully set up.

- Click OK to acknowledge the message.

**7.** The End

**a.** Follow these steps when the Setup Complete window appears:

- Ensure that the Launch Read Me File check box is marked.

- Confirm that the Launch Setup Log File check box is marked.

- Click Finish.

**b.** When the "Readme.txt — Notepad" window appears, read the ZENworks Release Notes and then select File ⇨ Exit to exit the Notepad utility.

**c.** When the "Setuplog.txt — Notepad" window appears, read the information in the Setup Log and then select File ⇨ Exit to exit the Notepad utility.

**d.** When the ZENworks window appears, click the Exit icon located in the lower-right corner of the screen.

**8.** Using the NetWare Administrator utility, follow these steps to view the NDS objects that were created by the ZENworks installation process:

**a.** Execute NetWare Administrator.

**b.** Navigate to the WHITE container and view the objects that ZENworks has added to your NDS tree.

**c.** Exit the NetWare Administrator utility.

**TIP**

If you launch NetWare Administrator using a shortcut that you created on a Windows 95/98 or Windows NT/2000 desktop prior to installing ZENworks, you may find that the shortcut does not point to the correct version of NetWare Administrator (because there are different versions in different directories). If this happens, ZENworks objects will not appear within the Create menu. To solve this problem, either use Start ⇨ Run or re-create the NetWare Administrator shortcut and have it point to the NetWare Administrator version in **SYS:PUBLIC\WIN32**.

▶ · · · · · · · · · · · · · · · · · · · · · · · · · · · · ◀

# Workstation Management Using ZENworks

There's a lot more to a Novell client workstation than meets the eye. It's a complex collection of user tools and connectivity hardware that makes Workstation Management an incredible challenge. Furthermore, workstations and users provide an even greater challenge — *diversity*.

ZENworks Workstation Management enables you to control network diversity and user productivity by integrating workstations with NDS. Look for the following when you implement ZENworks Workstation Management:

- ▶ *ZENworks policies* — ZENworks 2.0 Starter Pack includes various *policy packages,* which are NDS objects you create to help you maintain Workstation objects in the NDS tree. Each package is a collection of *policies* that enable you to set up parameters for managing workstations, users, groups, or containers. For example, the policies found in the Workstation Package help you set up controls that apply to Windows workstations on your network — including printers, systems, Remote Access Server (RAS), and login restrictions.

- ▶ *NDS registration* — Workstations must be registered with NDS before they can be imported into the tree and managed as other NDS objects. Once ZENworks is installed on the network, you can create a Workstation object corresponding to each network workstation by *registering* the workstation, and then *importing* it into the NDS tree. As a network administrator, you can use one of three methods for invoking the Workstation Registration Agent: Application Launcher, ZENworks Scheduler, or a customized login script. After a Workstation object has been created for a workstation, you can configure, control, and troubleshoot the workstation remotely.

In summary, ZENworks Workstation Manager is your best tool for controlling network diversity at the Novell Client. Let's start this lesson with a detailed look at the Workstation Manager.

## Using the ZENworks Workstation Manager

ZENworks Workstation Manager is a collection of workstation-resident modules and integrated NetWare Administrator snap-in files. Together, these tools enable you to limit the time you spend troubleshooting desktop configurations, printer driver delivery, diverse user settings, and any other problems requiring that you visit a user's workstation to resolve.

**TIP**     **The ZENworks installation includes the automatic installation of Workstation Manager on the server. Workstations receive Workstation Manager components during a Typical Novell Client installation.**

The greatest advantage of Workstation Manager is the configuration of Microsoft's policies through NetWare Administrator 32. This enables you to do the following:

- ▶ Configure policies and apply them to workstations through a Policy Package object in NDS.

- ▶ Push policies to multiple workstations by associating Policy Package objects with User or Workstation objects.

- ▶ Modify configurations for multiple workstations by reconfiguring policy details in the Policy Package object.

- ▶ Avoid copying policies between servers, thus increasing network bandwidth requirements.

The ZENworks Workstation Manager is made up of two components: workstation-resident modules and NetWare Administrator snap-in files. The *workstation-resident modules* work together to log in to NDS as the Workstation object, maintain two connections to NDS, launch the Workstation Registration agent, read policy information from the NDS, and execute workstation tasks. The *NetWare Administration snap-in files* are .DLL files that enable you to create, view, and configure the various Workstation Management objects though NetWare Administrator.

Refer to Table 6.1 for a list of the most useful Workstation Manager features.

| T A B L E  6.1 | FEATURE | CAPABILITY |
|---|---|---|
| ZENworks Workstation Manager Features | Scheduled Updates | Schedule software updates to occur at workstations at a specific time, such as when the workstation is not in use. (**Note:** Users don't need to be logged in for the update to occur.) |
| | Novell Client Configuration | Configure Novell Client properties for multiple workstations from a single screen. |
| | Workstation Profile Management | Create and manage mandatory user profiles and desktop options. You can also establish user interface standards (such as display, keyboard, and mouse attributes) and lock them with NDS security access rights. |
| | NDS Storage for Policies | Create policies in NetWare Administrator and manage user desktops from a central utility. This approach reduces policy management workload and improves fault tolerance by centralizing changes in NDS and replicating them throughout the network. |
| | Dynamic Printer Configuration | Associate a print queue and its corresponding printer driver with specific workstations and users. |

Now that the Workstation Manager is in place, let's learn how we can use it to create and manage ZENworks Policies.

## ZENworks Policies

ZENworks includes various *Policy Package* objects that can be used for workstation configuration and management. Each policy package (except for the Container Policy Package) contains a collection of *policies* that are grouped together according to the type of workstation platform being managed. Each policy, in turn, contains parameters that can be enabled, disabled, or modified as needed.

ZENworks provides seven Policy Package objects from which to choose, in three different categories: Container, Workstation, and User. Table 6.2 lists the types of Policy Package objects you can create, and the NDS objects with which each can be associated.

| TABLE 6.2 | POLICY PACKAGE OBJECT | ASSOCIATION |
| --- | --- | --- |
| *ZENworks Policy Packages and Associations* | Container Package | Containers only |
| | Windows 3.1 User Package Windows 95 User Package Windows NT User Package | User objects, User Group objects, and containers |
| | Windows 3.1 Workstation Package Windows 95 Workstation Package Windows NT Workstation Package | Workstation objects, Workstation Group objects, and containers |

Except for the Container Policy Package, all objects are organized according to the workstation's OS platform. Once you configure a policy package, you can associate it with other NDS objects—such as Users and Workstations. This way, distributed users can experience changes in their desktop configurations, printer availability, and application privileges immediately—if the workstation has been upgraded to the Novell Client. Refer to Figure 6.8 for a list of the ZENworks policy packages you can manage in the NetWare 5.1 Policy Package Wizard of NetWare Administrator.

FIGURE 6.8

*ZENworks Policy Package
Wizard in NetWare
Administrator*

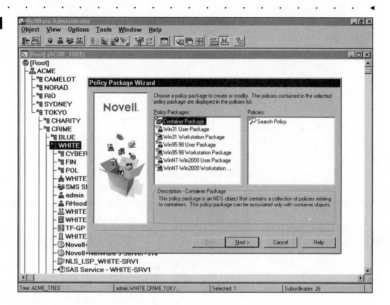

Furthermore, when you associate Packages with a Container object, the policies you enable in the Package apply to all Workstation and User objects in the container. This is an easy way of implementing sweeping changes throughout the network. Let's learn more about ZENworks policies by exploring each of these three Package categories.

### Container Policy Package

The Container Policy Package is simple. It contains only one ZENworks policy — Search. The Search policy helps you determine which policies are in effect for an object (such as a User) in a given container. You can also use it to increase network security by identifying NDS objects that shouldn't have policies in effect, but do.

## REAL WORLD

Even though ZENworks policies are NDS objects, they do not appear in the NDS tree browser of NetWare Administrator. Instead, you must access Policy objects through their parent Package. Policy configurations allow you to customize numerous policies within a Package.

Policy package associations flow down the NDS tree much like NDS inheritance. When you view the associated policy packages for a given object, the search begins with the object and moves up the tree in the following default order:

**1.** Object

**2.** Groups of which the object is a member

**3.** Parent containers leading to the [Root]

While Workstation Manager is walking the tree, only policy packages that are associated with the User (or groups of which he or she is a member) are applied.

You can modify the Search policy for a container to change the default search order described previously. You can also reduce unnecessary network traffic by limiting searches to one or more specific containers and/or NDS partitions. Figure 6.9 shows the Container Policy Package Configuration screen in NetWare Administrator.

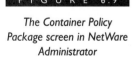

FIGURE 6.9

*The Container Policy Package screen in NetWare Administrator*

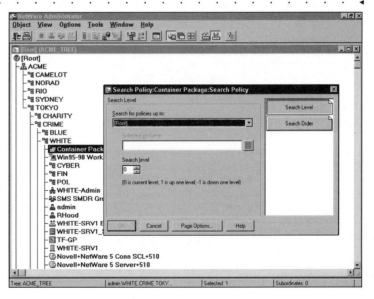

The Search Policy in Figure 6.9 includes two configurable properties:

▸ *Search Level* — The Search Level setting enables you to set a policy limiting where NetWare searches for associated policy packages in the NDS tree. This setting includes four options: [Root] (by default), Object Container (where the imported Workstation object exists), Partition (limited to the Partition root where the imported Workstation object exists), and Selected Container (enables you to browse and choose a starting point).

▸ *Search Order* — The Search Order setting enables you to set rules on how the system searches for associated policy packages in the NDS tree. As we learned earlier, the default search order is as follows: Object, Group, and Container.

**TIP**

**If a User is associated with multiple policy packages of the same type, only the first policy found is used. Also, the Workstation object must be imported into the same NDS partition as the Search policy in order for Workstation Manager to limit the Search Level.**

### Workstation Policy Packages

ZENworks includes three Workstation Policy Package objects. Each policy package is platform-specific and applies to a particular type of workstation (such as Windows 95/98, Windows NT, or Windows 3.*x*). The policies in each Workstation Policy Package apply to workstations only — regardless of the user who logs on to the network.

You can create Workstation Policy Packages before registering Workstation objects in the NDS tree. After you have configured the policies in a particular Workstation Policy Package, you can associate it with one or more container, Workstation Group, or Workstation objects.

Check out Figure 6.10 for an illustration of the policies available in the WIN95-98 Workstation Policy Package. For a more detailed description of these Workstation policies, check out Table 6.3.

FIGURE 6.10

The WIN95-98 Workstation Policy Package screen in NetWare Administrator

| TABLE 6.3 | WORKSTATION POLICY PACKAGE | POLICY | DESCRIPTION |
|---|---|---|---|
| ZENworks Policies in Workstation Policy Packages | WIN95-98 Workstation Policy Package | 95 Computer Printer | Assigns printers and printer drivers to Windows 95/98 workstations. Using this policy, the Printer object appears in the workstation Control Panel and the printer driver is automatically installed on the workstation. |
| | | 95 Computer System Policies | Used to define applications that are automatically delivered to Windows 95 desktops, regardless of the user who authenticates to the network. |

*Continued*

| TABLE 6.3 | WORKSTATION POLICY PACKAGE | POLICY | DESCRIPTION |
|---|---|---|---|
| ZENworks Policies in Workstation Policy Packages (continued) | WIN95-98 Workstation Policy Package | 95 Novell Client Configuration | Used to set Client configuration parameters for Novell Client protocols and services. Novell Client settings include client, login, and default CAPTURE parameters. Protocol settings include IPX 32-bit protocols and NetWare/IP configurations. Service settings include Host Resources Management Information Base (MIB), Simple Network-Management Protocol (SNMP), IP Gateway, and Target Service Agent (TSA) configurations. |
| | | 95 RAS Configuration | Used to configure dial-up network settings for Windows 95/98 workstations. |
| | | Computer Extensible Policies | Allows you to control any application function that is configured in the Windows 95/98 Registry by extending policy-editing capabilities into NDS. This is configured at the workstation level. |

| TABLE 6.3 | WORKSTATION POLICY PACKAGE | POLICY | DESCRIPTION |
|---|---|---|---|
| ZENworks Policies in Workstation Policy Packages (continued) | WIN95-98 Workstation Policy Package (continued) | Restrict Login | Used to set rules regarding login times and occurrences for workstations associated with the policy package containing this policy. |
| | WinNT Workstation Policy Package | Computer Extensible Policies | Allows you to control any application function that is configured in the Windows NT Registry by extending policy-editing capabilities into NDS. This is configured at the workstation level. |
| | | NT Computer Printer | Identical to the 95 Computer Printer Policy, except that this policy assigns printers and print drivers to Windows NT workstations. |
| | | NT Computer System Policies | Used to define applications that are automatically delivered to Windows NT desktops, regardless of the user who authenticates to the network. |
| | | NT Novell Client Configuration | Same as WIN95 Workstation Policy Package. |

*Continued*

| TABLE 6.3<br>ZENworks Policies in<br>Workstation Policy Packages<br>(continued) | WORKSTATION<br>POLICY PACKAGE | POLICY | DESCRIPTION |
|---|---|---|---|
| | WIN95-98 Workstation<br>Policy Package<br>(continued) | Restrict Login | Same as WIN95<br>Workstation Policy<br>Package |
| | WIN 3x Policy<br>Workstation Package | 3x Computer<br>System | Used to specify<br>network files to<br>be downloaded<br>to one or more<br>workstations. The<br>types of files you can<br>manage using this<br>policy include ASCII<br>text (such as .BAT,<br>.INI, or .CFG) or<br>binary files (such as<br>.EXE, .COM, or<br>.DLL). The Windows<br>3.x platform<br>supports a limited<br>number of policies<br>because it does not<br>contain a Registry<br>like the one in<br>Windows 95/98 and<br>Windows NT/2000. |

**TIP**

**The Windows 3.x Policy Packages contain fewer policies than the Windows 95-98 and Windows NT Packages. Because Windows 3.x doesn't support the Registry, policies that require access to the Windows 95/98 and Windows NT/2000 Registry are unavailable to Windows 3.x workstations.**

### User Policy Packages

ZENworks includes three User Policy Packages. Each policy package is platform-specific and applies to a particular type of workstation (such as Windows 95/98, Windows NT/2000, or Windows 3.x). The policies in each User Policy Package only apply to a user who is associated with the package and who logs onto the network using a Windows workstation that matches the platform specified by the package.

After you set up policies for a particular User Policy Package, you can associate the package with one or more of the following objects: container, group, and user. Check out Figure 6.11 for an illustration of the policies found in the WIN95-98 User Package. For a more detailed description of these policies, refer to Table 6.4.

FIGURE 6.11

The WIN95-98 User Package screen in NetWare Administrator

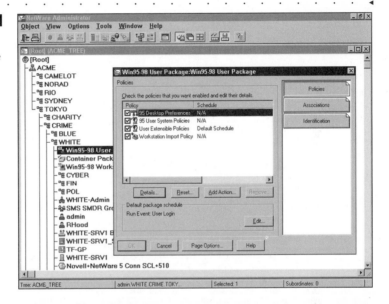

TABLE 6.4

ZENworks Policies in User Policy Packages

| USER POLICY PACKAGES | POLICY | DESCRIPTION |
| --- | --- | --- |
| WIN95-98 User Policy Package | 95 Desktop Preferences | Used to set up a default desktop configuration through the workstation Control Panel for users who access this policy from a Windows 95/98 workstation. |
| | 95 User System Policies | Used to define restrictions to desktop applications for Windows 95/98 users associated with the policy package containing this policy. |

*Continued*

| TABLE 6.4 | USER POLICY PACKAGES | POLICY | DESCRIPTION |
|---|---|---|---|
| *ZENworks Policies in User Policy Packages (continued)* | WIN95-98 User Policy Package *(continued)* | User Extensible Policies | Allows you to control any application function that is configured in the Windows 95/98 registry by extending policy-editing capabilities into NDS. This is configured at the user level. |
| | | Workstation Import Policy | Used to set rules about how workstations are named and where Workstation objects should appear in the NDS tree once they are imported. |
| | WinNT User Policy Package | Dynamic Local User | Used to manage user access to Windows NT workstations using NDS. |
| | | NT Desktop Preferences | Used to set up a default desktop configuration through the workstation Control Panel for users who access this policy from a Windows NT workstation. |
| | | NT User Printer | Assigns printers and printer drivers to Windows NT workstation users who are associated with the policy package containing this policy. |
| | | NT User System Policies | Used to define restrictions relating to desktop applications for Windows NT users who are associated with the policy package containing this policy. |
| | | Workstation Import Policy | Same as WIN95 User Policy Package. |

| | USER POLICY PACKAGES | POLICY | DESCRIPTION |
|---|---|---|---|
| **TABLE 6.4** *ZENworks Policies in User Policy Packages (continued)* | WIN 3*x* User Policy Package | Workstation Import | Same as WIN95 User Policy Package. |

That completes our journey through the seven different ZENworks policy packages. Now, let's complete our discussion of ZENworks policies by learning a thing or two about policy management.

## ZENworks Policy Management

ZENworks policies are very powerful Workstation Management tools. If used incorrectly, however, they can reduce the effectiveness and productivity of your network.

In this section, we explore a variety of policy management guidelines that apply to policy planning, policy troubleshooting, and policy management.

### Policy Planning Guidelines

You need to consider a plethora of criteria when creating ZENworks policies and policy packages. Follow these planning and configuration guidelines to build, associate, and distribute ZENworks policies intelligently:

> ▶ *Consider platform when creating policy packages* — Consider the following criteria when creating policy packages: the size of the network, the platforms in use, and the need for multiple policy packages of the same type and the same container. Sometimes it's necessary to create multiple policy packages of the same type in a single container because users have different needs. Keep in mind that ZENworks policies can be used to manage common NetWare tasks. These task include restricting Windows desktop applications (such as Network Neighborhood), establishing user interface standards (such as wallpaper and mouse settings), configuring Novell Client properties, and enabling Windows NT/2000 users to create a dynamic local user at login to bypass Windows security.

▸ *Place policy packages high (containers) and low (leaf objects)* — Create Container Policy Packages at the highest level possible in the tree without exceeding a container representing a location or site. Place User and Workstation Policy Packages in the lowest container that contains Workstation and User objects. Although not generally recommended, you can create a single-purpose container for Workstation objects. If so, place the Workstation Policy Packages in that container.

▸ *Create Admin policy packages* — Because Container and Group Policy Packages affect Admin users as well as everyone else, you must create "super-user" policy packages for Admin objects that override Container and Group packages. These Admin packages should enable all configuration settings and be associated with Admin User objects directly.

▸ *Policy configuration* — Some policies can actually affect the structure of the NDS tree or impact network performance and bandwidth. Creating too many policies reduces network access speed, limits the scalability of the NDS tree, creates a need for future partitioning, or clutters user search capabilities. When configuring policies, make sure that each NDS partition still has fewer than 3,500 objects after Workstation objects are added to the tree. Also, be sure to place Workstation objects in the same container as their associated users. Finally, try to avoid single-purpose containers whenever possible.

### Policy Troubleshooting

ZENworks policies and policy packages can become complex very quickly. Following are three guidelines for troubleshooting policy-related problems:

▸ *Verify Workstation objects and associations* — If you are having problems with ZENworks Workstation Management, you may want to verify that the problematic workstation is linked with a valid Workstation object. Do this by viewing the Workstation object value in the following Windows Registry key:

```
HKEY_LOCAL_MACHINE\SOFTWARE\Novell\Workstation_Manager\
Identification
```

In addition, make sure that the Workstation and/or User are associated with the correct type of policy package. You can verify policy associations by viewing the Details of the Policy Package in NetWare Administrator and choosing Associations.

▸ *Expedite the synchronization of enabled policies* — Users must restart their workstations for new policies to take effect immediately. Otherwise, the Workstation Manager policy synchronization rate is set to 30 minutes, by default. You can expedite the synchronization refresh rate using the Workstation Manager component in the Network Control panel or the Scheduler in the Windows System Tray. Before you set a new default synchronization refresh rate, you should identify the existing rate within the Properties menu of Novell Workstation Manager.

▸ *Make sure the active tree is a "Trusted Tree"* — The ZENworks Workstation Manager relies on the concept of *Trusted Trees*. A ZENworks Search policy only works if the active tree is defined as a Trusted Tree in the Novell Client's NetWare Connections properties. To view the active Trusted Tree on a Windows NT/2000 workstation, select Properties from the Novell Workstation Manager tab and verify that "Enable Workstation Manager" is checked. To view the active Trusted Tree on a Windows 95/98 workstation, browse the Windows Registry with REGEDIT and verify that the tree name in the following Identification key is correct: HKEY_LOCAL_MACHINE\ SOFTWARE\Novell\Workstation Manager\Identification.

**REAL WORLD**

You can define a specific Trusted Tree for each workstation during Novell Client installation (using the Custom Install option). Otherwise, the Novell Client automatically defines your authentication tree as the Trusted Tree. Also, the Novell Client does not report an error if a Trusted Tree is not defined on the workstation. It simply won't search the NDS tree for policy packages.

### Policy Management

As you establish policy packages in NDS and enable workstation policies, you must understand how ZENworks policies are managed, associated, and disabled. Following are some fundamental policy management guidelines:

▶ *Associate policy packages with objects, groups, and containers (in order)* — Policy packages can be associated with individual NDS objects, groups, or containers. Policy package associations, such as NDS access rights, flow down the tree. As such, explicit object associations take precedence over Group associations, which in turn take precedence over container associations. When a single policy in a Package associated with an object is not enabled, the next enabled policy of its type up the tree is applied. However, three "cumulative" policy types *combine* to create a single set of workstation settings: User/Computer System Policies, User/Computer Extensible Policies, and Scheduled Actions.

▶ *Disable individual policies instead of policy packages* — you can disable individual policies in specific policy packages. This has two administrative advantages: 1) users can log in faster because NDS doesn't apply disabled policies and 2) problems with a specific policy can be isolated without affecting the entire policy package. To disable a specific policy, you must change the policy settings in NetWare Administrator, restart the workstation, and authenticate to the target user's home container. The following policy packages allow you to disable a policy and still use the last setting recorded in the workstation's registry: User Extensible, Computer Extensible, User System, and Computer System.

▶ *Understand system policy states* — ZENworks includes three possible system policy states that affect how policies are applied to workstation settings: Disabled (policy settings don't apply at all), Ignore (the workstation reverts to the last entry recorded in the Windows registry), and Enabled (policy settings are applied).

That completes our discussion of ZENworks policies. Policies are powerful allies if configured and distributed correctly. Now, let's continue our Workstation Management studies with a lesson in NDS workstation registration.

▶ · · · · · · · · · · · · · · · · · · · · · · ◀

**REAL WORLD**

When an explicit Workstation association and a User Policy Package affect an individual leaf object, the User package takes precedence.

## NDS Workstation Registration

NetWare 5.1 workstations must be registered with NDS before they can be imported into the tree and managed as NDS objects. ZENworks includes a Workstation Registration Agent that automatically or manually registers workstations according to several predefined configurations. During NDS registration, the Workstation Registration Agent creates a workstation entry in the Workstation Registration property of the user's parent container. This entry contains a variety of statistics related to the workstation, including registration time, network address, last server, and last user information.

Once a workstation appears in the Workstation Registration property, it can then be imported into the tree. However, you must first configure a Workstation Import Policy by performing the following tasks:

▶ Create a User Policy Package for each workstation platform on your network.

▶ Configure the Workstation Import policy to create Workstation objects in the desired container and with the desired naming features.

▶ · · · · · · · · · · · · · · · · · · · · · · · · · · · ◀

**REAL WORLD**

The Workstation Name and MAC Address are the default naming attributes for Workstation NDS object names. You can also use the workstation's IP and IPX network address to identify it in NDS. These naming attributes are configured in the workstation's home container's Workstation Import policy.

In short, ZENworks NDS workstation registration is accomplished in two steps:

▸ *Step 1*: Register Workstations with NDS

▸ *Step 2*: Import Workstations into the NDS tree

Ready, set, "registrate."

### Step 1: Register Workstations with NDS

Before you can import a workstation into the NDS tree, it must appear on the Registration List stored in the Workstation Registration property of the User's parent container. Furthermore, this container must be *prepared* before workstations can be registered and imported into it.

NDS container preparation involves assigning registration rights to each worstation's user (specifically, the Write NDS right to the WM: Registered Workstations property of the target container). This can be accomplished automatically or manually. Automatic container preparation occurs using the WSRIGHTS.EXE utility during ZENworks installation. Manual container preparation is available from the Prepare Workstation Registration utility in the Tools menu of NetWare Administrator (see Figure 6.12).

▸ · · · · · · · · · · · · · · · · · · · · · · · · · · · · · ◂

F I G U R E   6 . 1 2

*The Prepare Workstation Registration utility in NetWare Administrator*

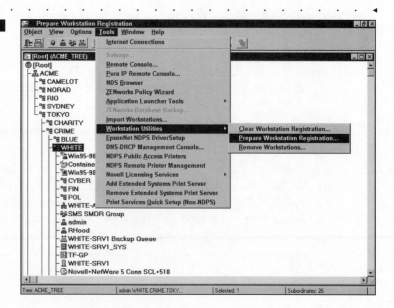

**REAL WORLD**

If workstation registration rights are not granted to the [Root] during ZENworks installation, you need to assign each user the Write NDS right to the WM: Registered Workstations property of each container that will house associated workstation objects. In addition, if you create a container after ZENworks installation, then it must be prepared manually using the Tools menu of NetWare Administrator. However, on a Windows NT/2000 workstation, you must manually prepare each container even before ZENworks installation.

Once the target container is prepared, it's time to automatically activate the Workstation Registration Agent. ZENworks provides three options for registering NDS workstations:

▶ *ZENworks Scheduler* — To use this method, three conditions must be met. First, all ZENworks components must be installed. Second, all workstations must be running either Windows 95/98 or Windows NT/2000. Third, the Novell Client for NetWare 5.1 must be installed on all workstations. The Scheduler relies on the Desktop Management component of ZENworks to run properly, and uses the WSREG32.DLL file to run the Workstation Registration Agent. This process is automatically activated the first time the user logs onto the network after all three conditions have been met. The Scheduler icon appears in the Windows system tray.

▶ *Application Launcher* — If the Desktop Management component of ZEN works is not installed, you can use the Application Launcher to run the Workstation registration Agent. To do so, use NetWare Administrator to locate the Application object corresponding to the executable file needed in the server's parent container — namely WSREG32.EXE (for Windows 95/98 and Windows NT/2000 workstations) or WSREG16.EXE (for Windows 3.*x* and DOS workstations). Next, associate each Application object with one or more container, group, or user objects and set the application to a Forced Run. Finally, when users log in, the Workstation Registration Agent runs (as configured in the Application Launcher), and the workstations are registered using the appropriate Workstation Import Policy.

▶ *Login Script* — If both the Desktop Management component and the Application Launcher are not installed, you can use a login script to automatically activate the Workstation Registration Agent. This is accomplished by executing the appropriate Agent program within a Container or Profile login script — that is, WSREG32.EXE or WSREG16.EXE. (**Hint**: Use the "#" command to run these programs. In addition, you may want to use the "% PLATFORM" identifier variable to specify Windows NT/2000 [WNT], Windows 95/98 [W95], and/or Windows 3.*x* (WIN) workstation platforms.)

Once your workstations are registered with NDS, you should use one of the following two methods to verify that they have been properly configured. First, check the appropriate log file in the root directory on each workstation's local hard drive — namely WSREG32.LOG (Windows 95/98 or Window NT/2000) or WSREG16.LOG (Windows 3.*x*). These log files record information about the success or failure of the NDS Registration process.

Alternately, you can use NetWare Administrator to verify registration by viewing the Registered Workstations property page for the parent container of each workstation. Refer to Figure 6.13 for an illustration of the Workstation Registration page in NetWare Administrator.

FIGURE 6.13

The Workstation
Registration page in
NetWare Administrator

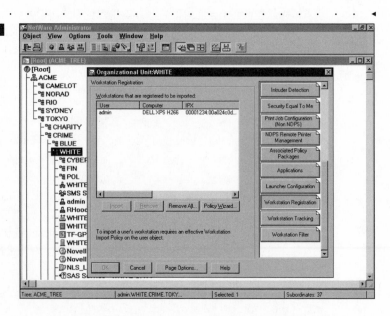

Now, your target workstations should appear in the container's Workstation Registration page. If they don't, make sure that the Workstation Manager component of the Novell Client is installed on each workstation, and verify that none of the workstations are registered in another NDS tree. Finally, check registration security and make sure that each user has Supervisor or Write NDS rights to the WM: Registered Workstation property of each target container.

Once your workstations have appeared in the Workstation Registration page, they can be imported into the NDS tree. That's Step 2.

### Step 2: Import Workstations into the NDS Tree

A Workstation object is not created for a registered workstation until the workstation is imported into the NDS tree. Even after you import workstations, you must periodically re-import them to keep the network addresses updated. This ensures that NIC replacement, reassigned network addresses, or changes in a workstation's location do not affect your ability to access the Workstation object.

Before you can import NetWare 5.1 workstations into the NDS tree, you must decide where to place them — in each user's home container or a central WORK-STATIONS container. Placing Workstation objects in the same container as their associated users enables you to keep the NDS design flexible and efficient. However it causes user containers to grow rapidly and requires that you closely monitor NDS growth.

On the other hand, you can place all Workstation objects in a single-purpose WORKSTATIONS container. This strategy allows you to make a single trustee assignment for decentralized workstation management and limits container growth to a single partition. On the downside, it reduces access speed to workstation resources, increases synchronization traffic across partitions, and creates inflexibility at the bottom of the NDS tree design.

Follow these four steps to import a workstation from the Workstation Registration page into the NDS tree:

▸ *Step 1: Create a User Policy Package* — Start by opening NetWare Administrator and browsing to the Workstation's home container. Highlight the container and click Object and Create to build a new User Policy Package. Match the platform of the Package to the workstations you want to import — such as WIN95 or WinNT. Click Create to continue.

▶ *Step 2: Configure the Workstation Import Policy* — First, you need to enable
the Workstation Import Policy of your new User Policy Package and click
the Details button. Second, configure the host location for the Workstation
object by clicking the Workstation Location button. Then, configure a
naming convention for the Workstation objects by accessing the Workstation Naming button. By default, the Computer Name and workstation's
network MAC address are the naming attributes. You can also choose to
use the workstation's IP or IPX network address to identify it. Refer to
Figure 6.14 for more information. Finally, you should associate the new
User Policy Package with the workstation's home container and click OK
to continue.

▶ · · · · · · · · · · · · · · · · · · · · · · · · · · · · · · · ◀

**FIGURE 6.14**

*Configuring the Workstation
Import Policy*

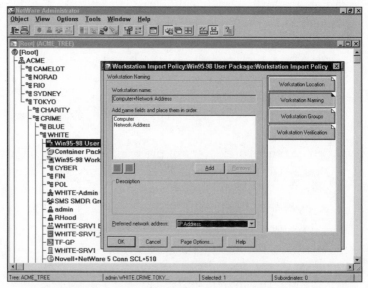

▶ *Step 3: Import the Workstations* — With the home container still highlighted
in NetWare Administrator, select the Import Workstations command
from the Tools menu. Check it out in Figure 6.15. Next, specify the full
Distinguished Name of the home container in the Import From tab and
click OK to begin the import process.

FIGURE 6.15

*The Import Workstations
option in NetWare
Administrator*

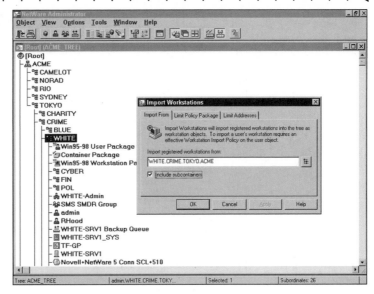

▶ *Step 4: The End* — Once you've activated the Import Workstations utility,
NDS begins building Workstation objects. At the end of this process, a
verification screen appears and lists the total number of workstation entries
created. You can further verify the import procedure by reviewing the
Success Log. Finally, you should ensure that the Workstation objects were
placed in the right container by collapsing and expanding the NetWare
Administrator browser. In Figure 6.16, our Workstations found their way
into the correct ACME container.

**REAL WORLD**

You can also configure the Import Workstations utility to update Workstation
objects automatically. Simply associate the application with Application Launcher or
the ZENworks Scheduler. This way, you can ensure that the latest workstation
address information finds its way to the central NDS database.

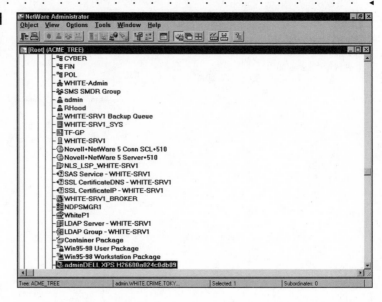

That does it . . . mission accomplished. Your ZENworks clients are now part of the global NDS tree. This level of synergy provides you with centralized access to critical workstation maintenance and desktop management tasks. Let's take a closer look.

## LAB EXERCISE 6.2: ZENWORKS POLICIES AND NDS

To fully tap the Zen of our ACME workstations, you must integrate them with the NDS tree. In effect, workstations must be registered with NDS before they can be imported into the tree and fully managed. The actual process of registering ZENworks clients involves NDS and NetWare 5.1 policies. Here's a quick preview:

▸ *Stage 1:* Prepare the WHITE Container for Registration

▸ *Stage 2:* Create a Workstation Import Policy

▸ *Stage 3:* Register the Workstation(s)

▸ *Stage 4:* Import the Registered Workstation(s)

You need the following hardware for this exercise:

▸ A NetWare 5.1 server called WHITE-SRV1.WHITE.CRIME.TOKYO.ACME (which can be installed using the directions found in Appendix D). The ZENworks Starter Pack must be installed (see Lab Exercise 6.1).

▸ A workstation running either the NetWare 5.1 Novell Client for Windows 95/98 or NetWare 5.1 Novell Client for Windows NT/2000 (which can be installed using the directions found in Lab Exercise 3.1).

Let's help our friends in Tokyo with some Crime Fighting workstation registration. Check it out!

### Stage 1: Prepare the WHITE Container for Registration

Before ZENworks can create Workstation objects in the NDS tree, we need to grant users the rights to write a workstation registration entry to their container. In this first step, we grant the User objects located in the WHITE container the rights to write a workstation registration entry to the WHITE container.

Perform the following tasks on your first workstation:

**1.** Log on to the tree as the Admin User, if you haven't already done so.

**2.** Launch the NetWare Administrator utility. (**Note:** To use ZENworks, you must use NWADMN32 in WHITE-SRV1_SYS:PUBLIC\WIN32\ NWADMN32, which is the version you should have been using in previous lab exercises.)

**3.** At this point, you must prepare the container for registration, if you haven't already done so. This involves granting users the rights they need to write a workstation registration entry to the container. In our case, we did this during the ZENworks server installation process by granting these rights at the [Root] level (which gives you more flexibility). Because we have not done anything to modify these rights since that time, you're finished with this step.

### Stage 2: Create a Workstation Import Policy

Before you can import a workstation into the NDS tree, you must create a Workstation Import Policy and associate it with the WHITE container. Perform the following steps on Workstation #1:

**1.** Create a WIN95-98 or WinNT-2000 User Policy package:

**a.** In NetWare Administrator, right-click the WHITE container, and then click Create.

**b.** When the New Object dialog box appears, navigate to and double-click Policy Package to select it.

**c.** When the first Policy Package Wizard dialog box appears, follow these steps:

• Click the User Policy Package that matches your workstation platform. For instance, if you're a Windows 95 or Windows 98 user, click Win95-98 User Package. If you're a Windows NT or Windows 2000 user, click WinNT-Win2000 User Package.

• Click Next.

**d.** When the second Policy Package Wizard dialog box appears, follow these steps:

- In the Name field, verify that the default name listed matches the type of workstation platform you are using. For instance, if you are using Windows 95 or Windows 98, it should list "Win95-98 User Package."

- In the Create In field, verify that it lists WHITE.CRIME.TOKYO.ACME.

- Click Next.

**e.** When the third Policy Package Wizard dialog box appears, follow these steps:

- Mark the Workstation Import Policy check box.

- Click Details.

**2.** Configure the Workstation Import policy.

**a.** When the Workstation Import Policy dialog box appears, follow these steps:

- You'll notice that the Workstation Location page is displayed by default.

- Verify that the "Allow Importing of Workstations" check box is marked.

- Open the pull-down menu in the Create Workstation Objects In field, and choose Selected Container.

- Ensure that the Path field contains the following path:

  `WHITE.CRIME.TOKYO.ACME`

- Click the Workstation Naming tab.

**b.** When the Workstation Naming page appears, click Add to add another attribute to the workstation naming convention.

**c.** When the Add Name Field dialog box appears, double-click User.

**d.** When the Workstation Naming page reappears, note that User now appears in the "Add Name Fields and Place Them in Order" list box.

**e.** Next, reorder the names in the "Add Name Fields and Place Them in Order" list box:

- In the "Add Name Fields and Place Them in Order" list box, click User.

- Ensure that the following is listed in the Preferred Network Address field:

  IPX Address

- Click the up-arrow twice to move User above Computer. (Workstation objects in your container will now be listed by username, followed by computer name and IPX address.)

- Click the Workstation Verification page tab.

**f.** Follow these steps when the Workstation Verification page appears:

- In the "Time Interval to Verify Workstation Creation After Registration" field, change the existing value as follows (since we're in a hurry):

  1

- Click OK to close the Workstation Import Policy dialog box.

**3.** Associate the User Package with your container.

**a.** When the Policy Package Wizard dialog box reappears, click Next.

**b.** When the next Policy Package Wizard dialog box appears, follow these steps:

- In the Associations list box, verify that WHITE.CRIME.TOKYO.ACME is listed.

- Click Next.

**c.** Follow these steps when the next Policy Package Wizard dialog box appears:

- Review the selections that are listed to ensure that they are correct.

- Click Finish.

**d.** Exit NetWare Administrator.

**Stage 3: Register the Workstation(s)**

Once the users and containers are prepared, we can begin the registration process. Register a ZENworks workstation with one of the following three methods:

▶ Use the ZENworks Scheduler to automatically perform workstation registration for workstations that have the NetWare 5.1 Client installed. This occurs the first time a user logs in from such a workstation after the users and containers have been prepared.

▶ Run WSREG32.EXE manually or from a login script for Windows 95/98 and Windows NT/2000 workstations (or WSREG16.EXE for Windows 3.1*x* workstations).

▶ Run the WSREG Application object using the Application Launcher (Application Launcher).

In this exercise, we will use the first of the three methods listed above. Perform the following steps to register a ZENworks workstation and to verify the registration:

**1.** Log on to the network as Admin.

**2.** Verify workstation registration through the log file. Perform the following steps on your workstation:

**a.** Launch the Window Explorer utility by right-clicking Start in the Windows taskbar, and then clicking Explore.

**b.** Follow these steps when the main Windows Explorer window appears:

- In the left pane, click the C: drive.

- In the right pane, find the WSREG32.LOG file, and then double-click it to view it.

- When the Open With dialog box appears, scroll down and click Notepad to associate the Notepad utility with this file, and then click OK.

- View the contents of the log file. (You'll notice that it says that the workstation has been successfully registered for importation.)

**TIP**

**If the log file is empty, close it, wait a few minutes, and then open it again. If a registration error is listed, exit the Windows Explorer utility, and then check both the Novell Login window and the Control Panel Network folder (Novell NetWare Properties page) to verify that the information in the following fields is correct: Tree (ACME_TREE), Server (WHITE-SRV1), and Context (WHITE.CRIME.TOKYO.ACME). Then repeat Steps 1 and 2 of this procedure. If you still experience a registration error, you can try rebooting the workstation, and then repeating Steps 1 and 2. With any luck, your workstation will be registered at this point.**

**c.** Click File ⇨ Exit to close the WSREG32.LOG log file.

**d.** Click File ⇨ Close to Exit the Windows Explorer utility.

**3.** Verify workstation registration in NDS. Perform the following tasks on your workstation:

**a.** Execute NetWare Administrator.

**b.** Right-click the WHITE container.

**c.** Click Details in the pop-up menu that appears.

**d.** The Identification page appears by default. Use the scroll bar to locate the Workstation Registration tab, and then click it.

**e.** Do as follows when the Workstation Registration page appears:

- View the information that is shown for the registered workstation. (Use the horizontal scroll bar to show the fields that are out of view.)

- Click Cancel.

### Stage 4: Import the Registered Workstation(s)

Now that the Workstation Import policy exists and the users and containers are prepared, we can get on with the real work — importing the workstations in the WHITE container.

A registered workstation does not become an NDS object until it is imported into the NDS tree. You need to perform the following when you import registered workstations into the tree:

▸ Update each existing Workstation object with the network address of the workstation to which it corresponds.

▸ Create a Workstation object for each registered workstation that does not already have one.

You can use several methods to import registered workstations into the NDS tree. You can schedule workstation importation to occur automatically using the Novell Workstation Manager Scheduler feature or the Application Launcher. You can also import workstations manually using the Import Workstations option in the NetWare Administrator Tools menu.

In this final step, we import workstations manually using the Import Workstations utility in the NetWare Administrator Tools menu.

**1.** Import registered workstations.

**a.** Follow these steps in NetWare Administrator:

- Click the WHITE container to select it.

- Select Tools ⇨ Import Workstations.

**b.** When the Import Workstations dialog box appears, the Import From page should be displayed by default.

- Ensure that the following container is listed in the "Import Registered Workstations From" field:

  WHITE.CRIME.TOKYO.ACME

- Mark the Include Subcontainers check box.

- Click OK.

**c.** When the Import Workstations dialog box appears, note the number of workstations created (which is probably one), and then click Close.

**If workstation importation does not occur, wait a few minutes, and then try Step 1b again.**

TIP

**2.** Follow these steps to view your Workstation object in NetWare Administrator:

**a.** Double-click the WHITE container to collapse it.

**b.** Double-click the WHITE container again to expand it.

**c.** Scroll down and find the new Workstation object(s). Note that the naming convention used is Username+Computer Name+IPX address.

**d.** Exit NetWare Administrator.

# Desktop Management Using ZENworks

In addition to workstation management, ZENworks offers numerous benefits to the user. First, you can customize the user desktop by enabling two specific ZENworks policies: the User System Policy (in the User Policy Package) and the Computer System Policy (in the Workstation Policy Package). These policies allow you to hide sensitive applications and customize the Windows properties of a specific workstation. Second, you can create user profiles that standardize and control the following desktop settings: Wallpaper, Screen Saver, and Sounds.

This desktop management functionality is employed via two different features:

▶ Customizing Desktop Applications

▶ Standardizing User Profiles

You can use ZENworks to configure the desktop environment by defining user-specific and workstation-specific policies. These policies work together to customize desktop applications and the Windows user interface.

## Customizing Desktop Applications

You can customize a Windows 95/98 or Windows NT/2000 desktop by enabling the following policies in User and Workstation Policy Packages:

▶ 95-98 or NT User System Policies

▶ 95-98 or NT Computer System Policies. Check them out.

### 95-98 or NT User System Policies

The 95-98 or NT User System Policies allow you to control the desktop for specific applications from users. Accomplish this using the User System users. You should first hide Policies Page button in NetWare Administrator (see Figure 6.17).

Hiding applications (such as Network Neighborhood, Run, and Find) can help reduce network access problems, increase network security, and improve server performance.

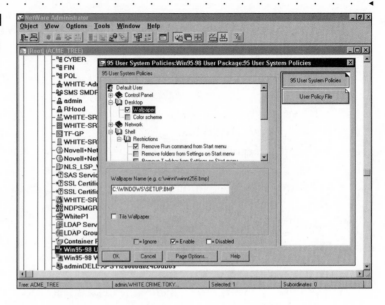

FIGURE 6.17

*Hiding desktop applications
with a User System Policy*

### 95-98 or NT Computer System Policies

The 95-98 or NT Computer System Policy (in a Workstation Policy Package) allows you to control the Windows desktop for specific workstations. For example, you can use a Computer System Policy (like the one illustrated in Figure 6.18) to launch a utility that Force-Runs a desktop application when the workstation connects to the network. Two such applications you should consider force-feeding to users are NAL.EXE and the Remote Control User Agent (as shown in Figure 6.18). (**Note:** the Remote Control feature is only available in the full ZENworks package, which can be purchased separately.)

Any changes that you make to either a User System Policy or a Computer System Policy affect only the users and workstations that are associated with the corresponding host policy package. Desktop applications that you've hidden from users through the User System Policy take effect as soon as the policy is enabled. Applications that are set to launch automatically on a workstation through the Computer System Policy won't launch until the next time the workstation is used to log on to the network.

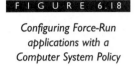

FIGURE 6.18

*Configuring Force-Run applications with a Computer System Policy*

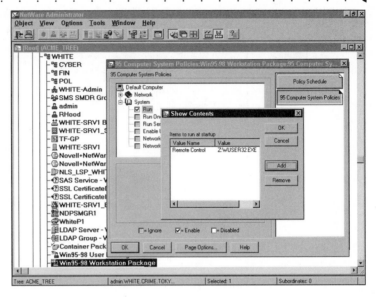

**TIP**

**Desktop applications that you've hidden from users through the User System Policy take effect as soon as the policy is enabled. However, applications that you set to launch automatically on a workstation through the Computer System Policy won't launch until the workstation logs back onto the network.**

## Standardizing User Profiles

Desktop settings such as Wallpaper, Screen Saver, and Sounds can be standardized and deployed to every user in the organization. In addition, these settings can be locked so users cannot modify them.

As you can see in Figure 6.19, the Desktop Preferences Policy allows you to lock most of the user-defined preferences set in the Windows Control Panel by creating a Mandatory user profile. Once a user is associated with the customized policy package, his or her desktop takes on a standard company-wide look and feel.

▶ · · · · · · · · · · · · · · · · · · · · · · · · · · · · · · · ◀

FIGURE 6.19

*Standardizing the user desktop with a Desktop Preferences Policy*

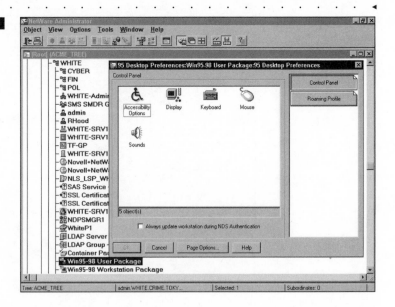

**TIP**

**If your users revolt against a standardized desktop, you can spoon-feed them a dose of individuality. The Desktop Preferences configuration in Figure 6.19 allows you to choose which settings are mandatory. I suggest you let your users choose their own Wallpaper as a start.**

That completes our second lesson in NetWare 5.1 workstation management — Workstation Management. In this lesson, we learned how to transform the user desktop by customizing applications and standardizing the workstation's look and feel. As a ZENworks network administrator, it's important to keep tight control over user desktop management.

Now let's complete our exhaustive journey through ZENworks by exploring the final feature — Application Management.

▶ · · · · · · · · · · · · · · · · · · · · · · · · · · · · · · · ◀

## Application Management Using ZENworks

Network productivity is a tenuous balance between user individuality and standardization. It's your responsibility to set up and continually maintain a productive software environment for each user. Doing so enables users to perform their tasks in synergy with other network users while maintaining some unique job specialization. You can accomplish this strategy by intelligently pushing application software to each client. Software, then, is not only shared by everyone on the network but also customized for each user's needs.

Installing shared network applications is easier, but the process has many drawbacks. For example, you must install an icon on each user's desktop, you may have to visit each geographically separated workstation, and you may assume more complex support responsibilities.

ZENworks solves all these problems with the *Application Launcher*. This special workstation management tool enables you to distribute network-based applications to users' workstations and to manage the applications as objects in the NDS tree. Users then access the applications assigned to them using the Application Launcher Window or Application Explorer.

In addition, Application Launcher implements solutions such as fault tolerance and load balancing to guarantee that users always have access to the applications they need. Furthermore, if the user deletes application .DLL files from his or her hard disk, Application Launcher automatically detects the missing files and restores them when the user attempts to launch the application.

So, what can Application Launcher do for you? Here's a list:

▶ Application Launcher provides multilevel folders to hierarchically order Application objects in the NDS tree.

▶ Application Launcher automatically grants file rights to users so that they can access the applications assigned to them.

▶ Application Launcher automatically grants NT Supervisor rights to the Admin user so that Admin can handle advanced Registry settings in Windows NT/2000. Accomplish this by using the Windows NT/2000 Service Control Manager, which enables network administrators to make changes to secure NT/2000 servers/workstations.

▶ Application Launcher provides an application-suspension configuration to enable you to schedule a time when application access will terminate.

▸ Application Launcher provides the snAppShot utility—which can be used to capture a workstation's configuration before and after an application is installed. The purpose of snAppShot is to assist in creating Application objects by comparing the pre- and post-installation configuration of the test workstation.

The ZENworks Application Launcher feature enables you to distribute application software to network workstations without having to physically visit each workstation. Once the applications are distributed, they can be installed, launched, and even repaired by Application Launcher.

## Application Launcher Architecture

Using Application Launcher, you can install applications on each user's workstation individually, or as shared applications on the network. When you install applications on each user's workstation individually, you must also upgrade and support the application individually for each user.

While installing shared network applications is easier, it still has a number of disadvantages. For example, you must install an application icon on each user's desktop, you may need to make additional visits to each workstation to perform upgrades or other changes, you may need to provide additional support to users who try to launch an application without having the proper drive mappings, and you must re-create network application icons that users have deleted.

Application Launcher consists of four separate programs, broken into two functional categories:

▸ *Administrator components*—Application Launcher Snap-In extends NetWare Administrator for Application object management, and snAppShot enables you to capture workstation configurations and generate an Application Object Template (AOT).

▸ *User components*—the Application Launcher Window displays Application Launcher-delivered applications on the user desktop, and the Application Explorer offers more sophisticated access to Application Launcher-delivered applications.

Let's learn more about how these four ZENworks pieces fit together to complete the Application Management puzzle.

### Administrator Components of Application Launcher

Application Launcher includes two powerful application management utilities for network administrators:

- Application Launcher Snap-In for NetWare Administrator

- snAppShot

*Application Launcher Snap-In* is a Windows-based .DLL file that extends the application management capabilities of NetWare Administrator and enables you to distribute applications to users. This snap-in enables you to create, configure, and view Application objects in the NetWare Administrator browser. It also enables you to manage applications by modifying the properties of an Application object, as well as through the Applications property page of a container, User Group, or User object. In addition, the Application Launcher snap-in also adds the following items to the NetWare Administrator Tools menu: Export Application Object, Show All Inherited Applications, Migrate Application Objects, Check Schema Extensions, Search and Replace, Sync Distribution GUIDS, Generate New GUIDS, and AOT/AIX File Tools.

*snAppShot* works in conjunction with the enhanced version of NetWare Administrator to automate the process of creating Application objects. First, snAppShot captures the current configuration of your workstation and prompts you to install the target application on your own machine. Second, snAppShot captures a delta configuration to discover the changes made by your application's installation process. Third, snAppShot generates an Application Object Template (AOT) that identifies the changes between the two captures.

Network administrators can use snAppShot AOT files to create Application objects in NetWare Administrator. Then, when the Application objects are distributed to workstations, the new application dependencies are also distributed— including Registry settings, .INI file entries, text files, .DLLs, and application programs. In addition, you can also use an Application Object Text Template (AXT) to create Application objects. An AXT differs from an AOT in that the AXT is an editable text file, rather than a binary file. Although you can use a text editor to make changes to an AXT file, AOT files are often preferable because they can be processed more quickly. Also, AXT files are subject to inaccuracies if you don't follow the proper format when editing the file.

Application Launcher provides the following benefits to network administrators:

▶ *Single-point of application administration* — Application Launcher enables you to create Application objects in the NDS tree and manage the following properties: drive mapping or Universal Naming Convention (UNC) path to the executable file, printer port CAPTURE commands required to print from this application, registry and INI entries necessary to run the application, program files necessary to run the application, and drive mappings or search drives necessary to run the application or access its data. Once you create Application objects, you can associate them with Organization, Organizational Unit, User or Workstation Groups, or individual User and Workstation objects. Then, when users log on to the tree, they are granted location-independent access to applications as a result of these associations.

▶ *Centralized application maintenance and control* — Application Launcher enables you to control exactly what users see and do at their workstations. An additional advantage is that if a user accidentally deletes one or more program files associated with an Application Launcher-delivered application, he or she can right-click the application and select Verify. The appropriate application files and configuration settings are then restored. This level of control enables you to easily deliver new and updated applications to users, thus reducing the cost of workstation administration and the overall cost of network management.

▶ *Push-and-pull software distribution to workstations* — Application Launcher gives you the option of pulling or pushing software to network workstations. *Pull distribution* places application icons on the user's desktop and runs remote installation programs when the user requests them. *Push Distribution* does the same thing — only automatically.

**REAL WORLD**

When a user clicks an Application icon in ZENworks, one of the following actions occurs: the associated application is installed on the local workstation and all relevant changes are made to the Windows registry, the executable file launches as defined in the "Path to executable file" field of the Application NDS object, or the application installs *and* launches automatically.

**User Components of Application Launcher**

Application Launcher includes two powerful application delivery tools for users:

▶ Application Launcher Window

▶ Application Explorer

The *Application Launcher Window* is an automated desktop that displays icons corresponding to applications that have been delivered via Application Launcher and set up for the user (see Figure 6.20). This window runs on Windows 3.1*x*, Windows 95/98, or Windows NT/2000 workstations. The Application Launcher Window is executed as SYS:\PUBLIC\NAL.EXE, which in turn activates NALW31. EXE (Windows 3.*x*) or NALWIN32.EXE (Windows 95/98 or Window NT). Once the appropriate application is launched, the NAL.EXE program automatically terminates. This allows you to add a single command to a login script without being concerned about the client platform. In addition, NAL.EXE updates appropriate files on the local workstation (in WINDOWS\SYSTEM) prior to activating the Application Launcher Window.

F I G U R E   6 . 2 0

*The ZENworks Application
Launcher Window*

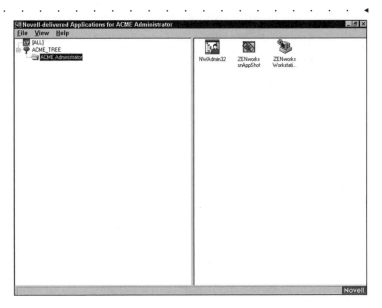

The *Application Explorer* is an alternative to the Application Launcher Window that can only be run on Windows 95/98 and Windows NT 4.0 workstations. The Application Explorer can deliver distributed applications to a variety of locations — including the Application Explorer Window, Windows Explorer, Start Menu, System Tray, and/or the Windows Desktop. Keep in mind that shortcuts on the desktop delivered through Application Explorer use a red arrow instead of the standard black one.

Application Launcher provides the following benefits to users:

▶ *Location-independent access to applications* — Provides users with access to network applications on distributed servers, as well as automated drive mappings and local configurations.

▶ *Application fault tolerance* — Replicates primary applications to backup servers and automatically restores local configurations if they are deleted. This level of fault tolerance is transparent to users.

▶ *Application load balancing* — Stores applications on multiple servers where they can be distributed to users intelligently and efficiently. Application Launcher sends you an alternate copy of an application when the primary server is overworked.

▶ *Roaming profile support* — Detects your current setup and pushes the components you need to the desktop.

▶ *Rights assignments via applications* — The ZENworks 2.0 Starter Pack includes the ability to assign file system rights to an NDS application object, and therefore pass those rights to the user during application association.

## Distributing Applications Using Application Launcher

Once Application Launcher is installed, you can distribute applications to users by following these steps. First, capture workstation configurations with snAppShot. Second, create an Application object from the AOT template. Third, associate the Application object with Organization, Organizational Unit, User Group, and/or

User objects. Fourth, launch applications using NAL.EXE or NALEXPLD.EXE from Container, Profile, and/or User login scripts. Users can then launch applications using either the Application Launcher Window or Application Explorer. Let's explore these steps in more detail.

### Step 1: Capture Workstation Configurations with snAppShot

Application Launcher includes a separate administrator utility, called snAppShot, that can be used to create an Application Object Template (AOT) file. A template file can be used to create customized Application objects with standard settings, icons, and drive mappings. Follow these steps to capture workstation configurations with snAppShot and create a network-wide AOT:

▸ *Run snAppShot* — From a *clean* Windows workstation (a workstation that *only* has freshly installed versions of Windows and the Novell Client running), execute SNAPSHOT.EXE from the SYS:PUBLIC\SNAPSHOT directory. Use the input fields on the Information dialog box to identify a name and description for the Application object. A period (.), equal sign (=), or plus sign (+) are not allowed. Next, use the input fields on the Configuration Information dialog box to specify details about how the workstation will be configured, including directory paths, drive mappings, and text-based configuration files. Refer to Figure 6.21 for more snAppShot configuration details.

F I G U R E   6.21

*Naming your applications in the snAppShot Wizard*

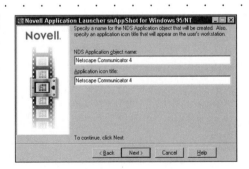

▶ *"Before" picture* — Next, snAppShot takes a "before" picture of your workstation's folders, files, Windows shortcuts, .INI files, system configurations, and Registry settings (for Windows 95/98 and Windows NT/2000). This is used to identify the delta changes once the application is installed. When this process is complete, the Wizard returns a snAppShot Process Summary (see Figure 6.22).

▶ *Install the application* — Next, you must click the Run Application Install button to install the Application Launcher-delivered application. snAppShot monitors the application installation process and indicates when it's complete by displaying the "Wait for Setup to finish" screen. Once the application is properly installed, snAppShot takes an "after" picture and generates the AOT file.

F I G U R E   6.22

*SnAppShot process
summary screen*

### Step 2: Create Application Objects from the AOT Template

The newly created AOT file contains all the application-specific settings and program files that your network workstations need to run the application. To create an Application object from an AOT or AXT file, highlight the home container in NetWare Administrator and select Object ➪ Create. Then, from the Object list, double-click Application. Finally, click "Create an Application Object with an .AOT/.AXT file" option to embed AOT data into NDS (see Figure 6.23).

NetWare Administrator supplies the source and target paths based on information it extracts from the AOT file. Verify that these paths are correct and click Finish to complete the Application Object Creation Wizard.

▶ • • • • • • • • • • • • • • • • • • • • • • • • • • ◀

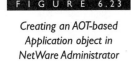

FIGURE 6.23

*Creating an AOT-based
Application object in
NetWare Administrator*

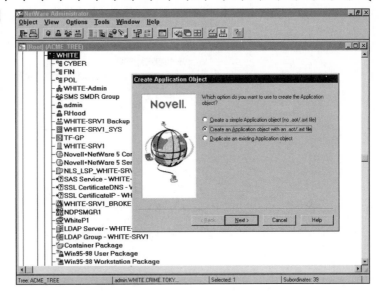

## Step 3: Associate the Application Object

Once you've created an Application object, use its Associations property page to link it with target users or groups. An Application object must be associated with a container, User Group, or User object in order for it to be delivered to workstations. If you associate an Application object with a container, existing or new users created below the container receive the application. For a more restrictive distribution, you should associate the Application object with a User Group or User object.

To define an Application object's associations, simply double-click the object in NetWare Administrator and choose the Associations page (see Figure 6.24). Click the Add button and enter an object's complete name. In addition, you must define the application's program source on the "Path to Executable File" page. This path can be either stated as a drive mapping or UNC path. Finally, NDS doesn't automatically assign file system rights when you associate Application objects with User, User Group, or container objects. This is not usually a problem, as the default Read and File Scan rights that users typically have to SYS:PUBLIC are sufficient (because Application Launcher resides in that directory). However, some applications store user-specific information on the server and additional rights may be needed.

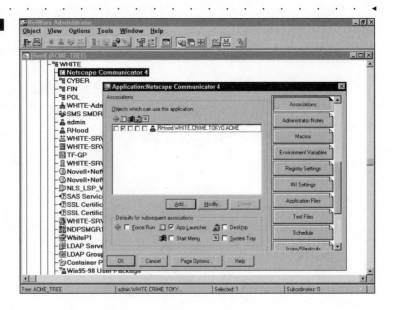

*The Application object
Associations page in
NetWare Administrator*

### Step 4: Launch Applications with NAL.EXE

Finally, you need to make the Application Launcher Window available to users by placing NAL.EXE (Application Launcher) or NALEXPLD.EXE (Application Explorer) in each workstation's Startup folder or in a login script.

To add NAL.EXE or NALEXPLD.EXE to a login script, access the Details window of a User, Organization, or Organizational Unit object and click Login Script. Next, add the appropriate command to the bottom of the login script:

```
@\\servername\SYS\PUBLIC\NAL.EXE
```

or

```
@\\servername\SYS\PUBLIC\NALEXPLD.EXE
```

In these examples, the @ symbol executes the Application Launcher program concurrently with the processing of the login script. You can also use the pound sign (#) to suspend login script processing while the program is executed. Finally, when the user logs in, Application Launcher executes automatically. The user can then access any of the available applications by double-clicking the appropriate icon in the Application Launcher Window or Application Explorer.

## Managing Applications Using Application Launcher

Application Launcher and NetWare Administrator enable you to perform the following application management tasks:

▸ *Set up an application's identification* — Application Launcher does not use separate icons to designate Windows 3.1, Windows 95/98, or Windows NT/2000 applications. Instead, you can use the Identification property page in NetWare Administrator to specify a preferred operating system. In addition, you can use the Identification property page to supply an executable path, designate the application for installation only, specify that Application Launcher run the application only once, or create custom icons.

▸ *Set up an application's environment* — You can use the Environment property page in NetWare Administrator to specify how the application should run. First, you can define command-line parameters for the application and identify a working directory. You can specify whether the application should run minimized or maximized. You can enable error logging for installation programs and use a Wrapper Executable (which launches the appropriate executable, based on the workstation's platform). In addition, you can configure Application Launcher to clean up drive mappings and print captures after the application has terminated. Finally, the Environment property page allows you to enable 16-bit Windows-On-Windows (WOW) support. This feature enables you to protect your 32-bit applications from a "crash" in 16-bit space.

▸ *Filter applications* — You can use the System Requirements property page in NetWare Administrator to filter applications against a broad range of criteria. *Operating System* only offers application icons that match the local operating system. (**Note:** You must select at least one Windows platform, or the Application object will be hidden from *all* Windows users.) *MB of RAM* disallows applications if the local machine doesn't have enough RAM installed. This field is only valid for Windows 95/98 and Windows NT/2000 machines. *Processor* disallows applications if the local machine doesn't have a fast enough processor. The choices are 386, 486, and Pentium. And *Free Disk Space* demands a minimum amount of free disk space on three different drives: Windows drive, TEMP drive, and D: drive.

▶ *Set up distribution schedules* — You can use the Schedule property page in NetWare Administrator to control when users get Application Launcher-delivered applications. For example, you may want to distribute a large service pack to all users next week. You may also want to stagger the delivery times.

▶ *Set up load balancing and fault tolerance* — The Fault Tolerance page in NetWare Administrator enables you to configure Application objects for load balancing and fault tolerance. *Load balancing* enables you to store applications on multiple servers and then intelligently distribute them according to load. When you load-balance your applications, be sure to note that Application Launcher does not distribute applications according to server CPU usage. Instead, it uses a random number to decide who gets which application. Also, be sure to enable load balancing on the same sides of a WAN link, and to give users the security rights they need to access applications on multiple servers. *Fault tolerance* enables you to set up primary and alternate sources for application delivery. This protects you in case the primary server goes down, or the network link is lost.

That completes our comprehensive journey through NetWare 5.1 workstation management via ZENworks. In this chapter, we learned how to install the powerful ZENworks desktop management tool and take full advantage of its three primary features:

▶ Workstation Management

▶ Desktop Management

▶ Application Management

This client environment is one of the most important aspects of your network because it's where your users interface with NetWare. Good luck.

## LAB EXERCISE 6.3: DISTRIBUTING ACME APPLICATIONS

As an ACME network administrator, you must market the worldwide network to your users. This involves helping them use their workstations productively and with a general peace of mind.

Application Launcher enables you to distribute network-based applications to user workstations and manage them as objects in the NDS tree. This feature enables you to maintain network standardization while pushing individuality to each user.

In this exercise, we explore Application Launcher from the network administrator's point of view. This way, we can maintain enterprise standardization while helping each time-traveling hero unlock his or her own individuality. Here's a quick preview:

- ▶ *Stage 1* — Create and associate an Application Object

- ▶ *Stage 2* — Add Application Launcher and Application Explorer to a Container Login Script

- ▶ *Stage 3* — Launch an Application from the Application Launcher Window and Application Explorer

You need the following hardware for this exercise:

- ▶ A NetWare 5.1 server called WHITE-SRV1.WHITE.CRIME.TOKYO.ACME (which can be installed using the directions found in Appendix D). The ZENworks Starter Pack must be installed (see Lab Exercise 6.1).

- ▶ A workstation running either the NetWare 5.1 Novell Client for Windows 95/98 or NetWare 5.1 Novell Client for Windows NT/2000 (which can be installed using the directions found in Lab Exercise 3.1).

### Stage 1: Create and Associate an Application Object

First, let's begin by creating a simple NDS Application object with NetWare Administrator. Then, we associate the object with the Crime Fighting heroes in the WHITE organizational unit.

Here's how to do it:

1. Log on to the network as Admin, if you haven't already done so.

2. Create an Application Object.

    a. Launch NetWare Administrator.

    b. When the NetWare Administrator browser screen appears, right-click the WHITE container.

    c. Click Create in the pop-up menu that appears.

    d. When the New Object dialog box appears, double-click Application.

    e. Follow these steps when the first Create Application Object dialog box appears:

    • Ensure that the "Create a Simple Application Object (No .aot/.axt File)" radio button is marked.

    • Click Next.

    f. Follow these steps when the second Create Application Object dialog box appears:

    • In the Object Name field, enter the following:

      `Calculator`

    • In the Path to Executable field, enter the following:

      `C:\WINDOWS\CALC.EXE`

    • Click Finish.

**Stage 2: Add Application Launcher to a Container Login Script**

Once you've created the simple Calculator Application object, you can automatically distribute it throughout the WHITE organizational unit using an NDS Container login script.

**1.** Add the Application Launcher window and Application Explorer to the WHITE Container login script.

   **a.** When the NetWare Administrator browser screen reappears, right-click the WHITE container.

   **b.** Click Details in the pop-up menu that appears.

   **c.** When the Organizational Unit: WHITE dialog box appears, click the Login Script tab.

   **d.** When the Login Script page appears, enter the following lines in the Login Script list box:

```
@WHITE-SRV1\SYS:PUBLIC\NAL.EXE

@WHITE-SRV1\SYS:PUBLIC\NALEXPLD.EXE
```

**2.** Make Application Launcher icons available in the Start Menu, on the Desktop, and in the System Tray.

   **a.** Scroll down and click the Applications page tab.

   **b.** When the Applications page appears, click the Add button under "Associated with Users" list box.

   **c.** When the Select Object dialog box appears, navigate to the Calculator Application object, and then double-click it in the left pane.

   **d.** When the Applications page reappears, follow these steps in the "Associated with Users" list box:

- Ensure that the Calculator.WHITE.CRIME.TOKYO.ACME object is listed.

- Leave the Force Run check box unmarked.

- Verify that the App Launcher check box is marked.

- Mark the Start Menu, Desktop, and System Tray check boxes.

- Click OK.

   **e.** Exit NetWare Administrator.

### Stage 3: Launch an Application from the Application Launcher Window and Application Explorer

Well done! Now it's time to use the NetWare 5.1 Application Launcher Window and Application Explorer to access the new Calculator application. Follow these steps and go!

**1.** Log on to the tree as Admin.

**2.** After a brief wait, the Application Launcher should execute automatically. (**Hint:** If it doesn't, try rebooting the workstation and logging onto the network as Admin.)

**3.** Launch the Calculator application from the Application Launcher.

   **a.** When the "Novell-Delivered Applications for ACME Administrator" dialog box appears, double-click the Calculator icon in the right pane to launch it.

   **b.** When the Calculator window appears, click Close (X) to close the Calculator application.

   **c.** When the "Novell-Delivered Applications for ACME Administrator" dialog box reappears, click Close (X) to close the window.

**4.** Launch the Calculator application from the System Tray.

   **a.** You'll notice a Calculator icon in the System Tray. (The System Tray is located at the right end of the Windows taskbar.) Click the Calculator icon to launch it.

   **b.** When the Calculator window appears, click Close (X) to close the Calculator window.

**5.** Launch the Calculator from the Windows Start Menu.

   **a.** Click Start ⇨ .WHITE.CRIME.TOKYO.ACME ⇨ Calculator.

   **b.** When the Calculator window appears, click Close (X) to close the Calculator window.

**6.** Launch the Calculator from Desktop.

   **a.** Double-click the Calculator icon on your Windows Desktop.

   **b.** When the Calculator window appears, click Close (X) to close the Calculator window.

**7.** Launch the Calculator application from Application Explorer.

   **a.** Double-click the Application Explorer icon on your Windows Desktop.

   **b.** When the Application Explorer window appears, double-click the ACME_TREE icon.

   **c.** When the ACME_TREE (Novell Directory Services) window appears, double-click WHITE.CRIME.TOKYO.ACME.

   **d.** When the WHITE.CRIME.TOKYO.ACME (in tree ACME_TREE) window appears, double-click the Calculator icon to launch the Calculator program.

   **e.** When the Calculator window appears, click Close (X) to close the Calculator window.

   **f.** When the WHITE.CRIME.TOKYO.ACME (in tree ACME_TREE) window reappears, click File ➪ Exit Application Explorer.

   **g.** When the Application Explorer dialog box appears asking if you want to close the Application Explorer, click Yes.

**8.** Prevent the Application Launcher and Application Explorer utilities from executing automatically.

   **a.** Log on to the tree as Admin.

   **b.** Execute NetWare Administrator.

   **c.** When the NetWare Administrator browser screen appears, navigate to and right-click the WHITE container.

   **d.** Click Details in the pop-up menu that appears.

   **e.** When the Organizational Unit: WHITE property sheet appears, click the Login Script tab.

**f.** When the Login Script property page appears, delete the following lines in the Login Script list box:

```
@WHITE-SRV1\SYS:\PUBLIC\NAL.EXE

@WHITE-SRV1\SYS:\PUBLIC\NALEXPLD.EXE
```

**9.** Prevent the Calculator utility from appearing in the Application Launcher, Application Explorer, Windows Desktop, Start menu, and System Tray.

**a.** Scroll down and click the Applications tab.

**b.** When the Applications page appears, perform the following tasks in the "Associated with Users" list box:

- Click the Calculator.WHITE.CRIME.TOKYO.ACME.

- Click Delete.

- Click OK.

**c.** Exit the NetWare Administrator utility.

**d.** Log on to the network as Admin.

**e.** Verify that the Application Launcher is no longer executed automatically.

**f.** Verify that the Application Explorer and Calculator icons (that is, shortcuts) no longer appear on your Windows desktop.

**g.** Verify that the Calculator utility no longer appears in your Start menu or System Tray.

Hooray!

That completes our tour of ZENworks Application Management. In this Lab, we've struggled to find a balance between heroic individuality and network-wide ACME standardization. I think we achieved an excellent balance with Application Launcher.

Are you having fun yet?!

## LAB EXERCISE 6.4: ZENWORKS 2.0

Circle the 15 ZENworks-related terms hidden in this word search puzzle using the hints provided. No punctuation characters (such as blank spaces, hyphens, brackets, and so on) should be included. Numbers should always be spelled out.

```
P  U  B  L  I  C  S  Y  S  V  F  H  U  N  Q  S
O  S  M  W  L  Q  O  O  B  G  W  R  O  Y  A  R
L  C  D  I  S  A  B  L  E  D  T  I  L  W  X  N
I  H  W  V  D  S  N  A  P  P  S  H  O  T  K  D
C  E  U  S  E  R  P  R  O  F  I  L  E  S  K  N
Y  D  W  O  R  K  S  T  A  T  I  O  N  D  K  M
P  U  L  L  D  I  S  T  R  I  B  U  T  I  O  N
A  L  Y  E  P  H  G  L  X  Q  E  Z  C  B  R  O
C  E  I  Y  K  H  Q  H  Q  Q  E  D  V  B  M  N
K  R  E  U  F  L  H  H  T  W  R  Q  K  X  B  E
A  X  S  U  P  E  R  V  I  S  O  R  A  X  G  Y
G  O  R  B  J  H  D  E  Z  E  N  W  O  R  K  S
E  W  E  I  D  R  C  V  Y  A  G  O  C  N  E  D
R  J  A  P  P  L  I  C  A  T  I  O  N  R  J  P
```

**Hints**

1. Can be used to create an Application object in NetWare Administrator.
2. NDS object that stores configuration and launching information for network applications.
3. System policy state that allows you to isolate problematic policies without affecting the entire policy package.
4. System policy state that causes the Workstation to disable a given policy and revert to the last entry recorded in the Windows Registry.
5. .EXE file that enables you to distribute network-based applications to workstations and manage them as objects in the NDS tree.
6. Collection of policies that enables you to set up parameters for managing workstations, users, groups, or containers.
7. Default directory for Application Launcher installation.

· · · · ·

8. Application Launcher feature that places application icons on a user's desktop and runs remote installation programs when the user requests them.
9. ZENworks feature that enables you to run programs automatically from the Windows 95/98 and Windows NT/2000 System Tray.
10. Utility that can be used to capture a workstation's configuration before and after an application is installed.
11. To install ZENworks, you must have these object rights to the [Root] of the NDS tree. This allows you to extend the NDS Schema.
12. Can be created and configured using the Novell Workstation Manager component of ZENworks.
13. ZENworks extends the NDS schema to include this type of leaf object.
14. NetWare 5.1 utility that automatically prepares a container for NDS workstation registration during ZENworks installation.
15. Integrated set of applications that reduces the cost and complexity of managing Windows-based network workstations through NDS.

See Appendix C for answers.

LAB EXERCISE 6.5: NETWARE 5.1 WORKSTATION

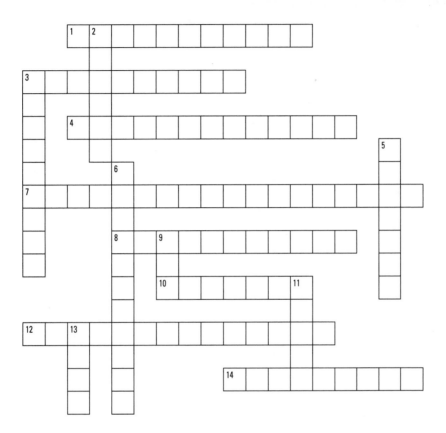

## Across

1. Desktop Preferences policy standardizes this
3. NetWare 5.1 utility not supported by ZENworks
4. Application Launcher benefit
7. NetWare Administrator Tools option
8. Used to install a subset of ZENworks 2.0
10. Most common ZENworks installation method
12. Another Application Launcher benefit
14. More Desktop Preferences standardization

**Down**

2. Installs ZENworks on multiple target servers
3. Policy package includes one policy: Search
5. Type of workstations managed using ZENworks
6. Authentication tree for ZENworks Workstation Manager
9. Application Object Text Template
11. Non-remote ZENworks installation method
13. Policy package takes precedence over this when a conflict exists
   See Appendix C for answers.

# CHAPTER 7

# NetWare 5.1 Printing

The last stop on our tour of NetWare 5.1 Administration is printing. I always like to save the best for last. Now that you've lived through all the administrative responsibilities of NetWare 5.1, I think that you're ready to explore Novell's latest printing wonder — Novell Distributed Print Services (NDPS).

NDPS represents a revolution in NetWare printing. It is the result of a joint development effort by Novell, Hewlett-Packard, and Xerox. NDPS is designed to replace the traditional queue-based printing system found in earlier versions of NetWare — although the two can peacefully coexist together.

Bottom line: easier setup, better management, and more flexibility. Novell certainly hasn't solved your printing problems entirely, but it has given you some great tools with NDPS. You no longer have to create, link, and manage Print Queue, Print Server, and Printer objects. NDPS combines these objects into one software entity called a *Printer Agent*. Although NDPS does not require print queues, you can continue to use queue-based printers on your network because NDPS offers full backward compatibility.

Benefits of NDPS include the following:

▸ Improved overall network performance

▸ Reduced network printing problems

▸ Reduced administration costs and management time

In this chapter, we're going to learn about NDPS architecture and practice installing NDPS printing objects. But first, let's spend a few moments exploring the underlying features offered by NDPS.

## The Essence of NDPS

We already know what a great job NetWare 5.1 does with its file services, but printing is just as important to users. Initially, all users need access to file storage and shared print services to get the most out of NetWare. Let's begin by taking a close look at the theoretical realm of NDPS:

▶ NDPS Features

▶ NDPS versus Queue-Based Printing

## NDPS Features

NDPS is designed to handle the increasing complexity of today's large networks — specifically, to help network administrators manage printing devices in any type of network environment, ranging in size from small workgroups to enterprise-wide systems. In addition, NDPS is designed with Novell Directory Services (NDS) in mind. In other words, it's fully network-centric. This design enables administrators to create, configure, and automatically install and initialize printer drivers without having to physically leave their desks.

To this end, NDPS offers a myriad of business solutions and features. Here's a quick list:

▶ Plug and Print

▶ Automatic printer driver download and installation

▶ Greater printer control

▶ Bi-directional feedback

▶ NDS integration

▶ Configurable event notification

▶ Multiple printer configurations

▶ Network traffic reduction

▶ Print job scheduling

▶ Backward compatibility

> ▸ Remote Printer Management (RPM)

> ▸ Internet Printing Protocol (IPP)

Let's take a closer look.

### Plug and Print

Once you set up NDPS, you can plug a printer into the network and have it become immediately available to all users. This is accomplished using automatic hardware detection. (**Note:** Plug-and-Print capabilities require an NDPS-aware printer. That is, a printer with the Printer Agent functionality embedded in its hardware.)

### Automatic Printer Driver Download and Installation

NDPS enables you to designate common printer drivers to be automatically downloaded and installed on each workstation (see Figure 7.1). Keep in mind that NDPS ships with English-only printing drivers. Therefore, you'll have to manually add non-English drivers, as needed.

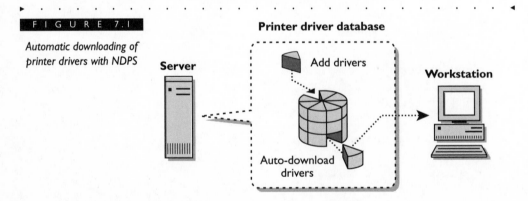

**FIGURE 7.1**

*Automatic downloading of printer drivers with NDPS*

Printer driver database

Server

Add drivers

Workstation

Auto-download drivers

### Greater Printer Control

NDPS allows clients and printers to exchange real time information about printers and print jobs. This interchange enables users and network administrators to access all sorts of information about printers—such as availability status, configuration properties, and features. As you can see in Figure 7.2, all of these printer control features are available from a single NetWare Administrator Printer Control page.

FIGURE 7.2

*Greater printer control offered by NetWare 5.1 NDPS*

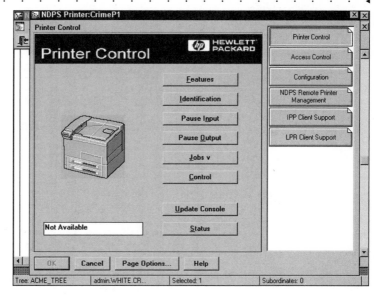

### Bi-directional Feedback

NDPS enables clients and printers to exchange real-time information about printers and print jobs, as illustrated in Figure 7.3. For example, network administrators and users can obtain information about printers, including printer properties and features (such as color or duplexing support) and printer availability or status (such as toner low, paper out, lid open, or off-line). They can also obtain information about print jobs, such as print job properties and status, the number of job copies being printed, job hold and scheduling information, and job completion notification.

### NDS Integration

NDPS offers increased security and easier management via Novell Directory Services (see Figure 7.4). In the NDS tree, printers can be conveniently grouped by department, location, workgroup, and so on. Bottom line: network administrators can administer all printing devices from a single location using NetWare Administrator.

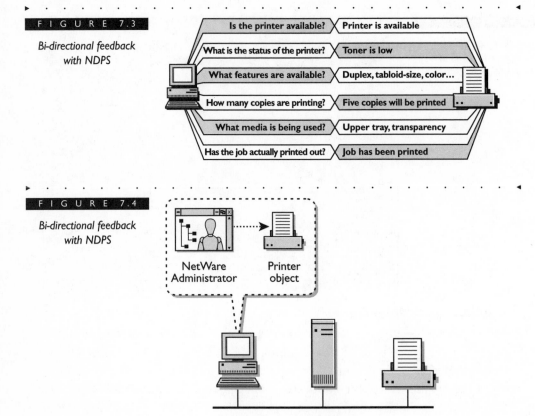

FIGURE 7.3

Bi-directional feedback
with NDPS

| Is the printer available? | Printer is available |
| What is the status of the printer? | Toner is low |
| What features are available? | Duplex, tabloid-size, color... |
| How many copies are printing? | Five copies will be printed |
| What media is being used? | Upper tray, transparency |
| Has the job actually printed out? | Job has been printed |

FIGURE 7.4

Bi-directional feedback
with NDPS

NetWare Administrator          Printer object

NDPS technology allows you to configure the
printer as a Directory object and access it
through NetWare Administrator

### Configurable Event Notification

NDPS enables you to specify which users, operators, and administrators receive which types of notification (see Figure 7.5).

### Multiple Printer Configurations

NDS enables you to set up a printer with multiple configurations. For example, you might allow all users in a department to print to a color printer using only the black-and-white capabilities, but allow two or three individuals to use the color capabilities. This increases network printing efficiency and productivity.

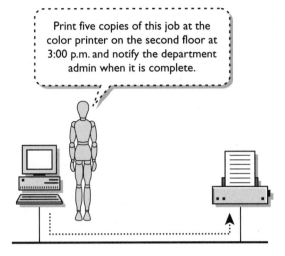

FIGURE 7.5

*Configurable event notification with NDPS*

### Network Traffic Reduction

In an IP-Only configuration, NDPS can operate independently from the IPX-based Service Advertising Protocol (SAP) and communicate directly with printers. This decreases unnecessary network traffic and increases network bandwidth.

### Print Job Scheduling

NDPS offers much more flexibility in the area of configuring print job scheduling options. For example, you can schedule a job based on the time of day, type of medium, or job size.

### Backward Compatibility

NDPS is fully compatible with all types of printers, whether or not they have been configured to take advantage of the advanced features that NDPS offers. For example, NDPS can be configured to work with NPRINTER and queue-based technology in conjunction with NetWare 4.11. Also, the backward compatibility and cross-platform support offered by NDPS ensures that all of your current Queue Management Services (QMS) printers will work just as they always have, even if you do not convert them to NDPS. Finally, backward compatibility enables NDPS clients to access legacy queue-based printers and enables non-NDPS clients to print through a queue to NDPS printers. Check out Figure 7.6.

FIGURE 7.6

*Backward compatibility with NDPS*

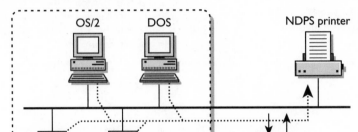

### Remote Printer Management (RPM)

NDPS allows network administrators to remotely install printers to workstations without user intervention.

### Internet Printing Protocol (IPP)

NDPS allows non-NetWare clients to access NetWare printers through TCP/IP and IPP (the open standard protocol for Internet printing).

As you can see, NDPS offers an exhaustive list of features and benefits. Probably one of the most critical features is backward compatibility. Along these lines, let's take a closer look at how NDPS differs from legacy queue-based printing systems.

## NDPS versus Queue-Based Printing

The architecture of Novell legacy queue-based print services is based on the creation and linking of three components: printers, print queues, and print servers. As you can see in Figure 7.7, this creates a circle of administrative responsibility for you and the NetWare operating system.

FIGURE 7.7

*Understanding queue-based
printing architecture*

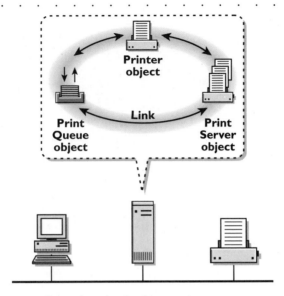

Queue-based technology requires you to
create Print Queue, Printer, and Print
Server objects, and link them together.

Setting up queue-based printing is often a complex task. To print, user data follows a wondrous journey from the workstation to the network printer. First, there is *capturing*. This process redirects the print job from a local workstation to the server hard drive containing the specified print queue. Next, the print job waits in the *print queue* until the print server is ready to handle the print job. Finally, the *print server* sends the print job to the correct printer.

NDPS combines printer, print queue, and print server functions into a single entity called a *Printer Agent*. The need to create print queues has been eliminated because users send print jobs directly to network printers. As you can see in Figure 7.8, the queue-based redirection complexity has been eliminated, with Printer Agents transparently managing the entire printing journey.

▶ · · · · · · · · · · · · · · · · · · · · · · · ◀

FIGURE 7.8

Understanding NDPS
printing architecture

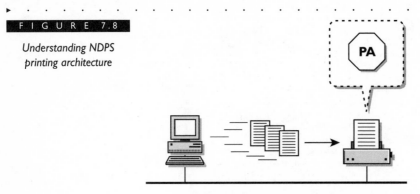

NDPS allows users to print directly to
network printers using a single
component: the Printer Agent.

Now, let's take a quick look at some of the most obvious differences between
queue-based printing and NDPS. (Follow along in Table 7.1.)

▶ *Setup* — In queue-based printing systems, network administrators must
create and link Print Queue, Printer, and Print Server objects. With NDPS,
network administrators create Printer Agents, instead.

▶ *User Printing* — In queue-based printing systems, the client must
capture the printer port on the workstation and redirect the data to
a server-based queue file. The file (that is, a print job) then waits in
line until the print server sends it to the correct printer. With NDPS,
a user simply submits a print job directly to a printer and the appropriate Printer Agent takes care of the rest. Also, printer drivers can
automatically be installed on user workstations.

▶ *Communications* — In queue-based printing systems, printing
communications are unidirectional. Feedback consists of pop-up
windows reporting a nonconfigurable set of events. With NDPS,
communications are bi-directional. Network administrators can
configure event notification utilizing the following methods: e-mail
(GroupWise), pop-up windows, or event logs. Third parties can also
develop other mechanisms, such as the use of beepers and faxes.

As a matter of fact, reported events are limited only by the printer's capability. This provides a framework for more intelligent printers in the future.

▶ *Snap-ins* — Queue-based printing systems don't support add-ons or extensions from third-party companies. With NDPS, you can customize the capabilities of your printing system. In addition, Novell and other third-party manufacturers offer snap-in interfaces for enhanced printing.

▶ *Plug and Print* — Queue-based printing systems don't support automatic hardware detection or Plug-and-Print technology, meaning that you must create and configure Printer objects manually. With NDPS, Plug-and-Print options are available for installing public access printers. In addition, NDPS enables you to select common printer drivers and have them automatically downloaded and installed on each workstation. (**Note:** Plug-and-Print capabilities require an NDPS-aware printer. That is, a printer with the Printer Agent functionality embedded in its hardware.)

**T A B L E   7.1**

*NDPS versus Queue-Based Printing*

| FEATURE | QUEUE-BASED PRINTING | NDPS |
|---|---|---|
| Setup | Queues, printers, and print servers | Printer Agents |
| User printing | Capture redirection | Directly to printers |
| Communications | Unidirectional | Bi-directional |
| Snap-ins | None | Supported |
| Plug and Print | None | Supported |

So, that's the essence of printing. As you can see, NDPS offers a simplified journey from the user workstation to the printer down the hall. Now, let's continue our exploration of NDPS by taking a close look at its detailed architecture.

# NDPS Printing Architecture

As we just learned, NDPS offers important improvements over the Novell legacy queue-based printing architecture. First of all, the functions of printer, print queue, and print server have been combined into a single logical entity called a Printer Agent. This architecture ensures the scalability of NetWare 5.1 printing and enables you to print in any type of network environment. The NDPS scalability architecture also enables you to print to a variety of devices — ranging from simple dot-matrix printers to laser printers and large-scale production devices.

Figure 7.9 illustrates the major components of the NDPS architecture:

- *NDPS Printer Agent* — This is the heart of NetWare 5.1 NDPS printing. A Printer Agent combines the functions previously performed by a printer, print queue, print server, and spooler into one intelligent, simplified entity.

- *NDPS Manager* — The NDPS Manager is a logical entity used to create and manage Printer Agents. It is represented as an object in the NDS tree. The NDPS Manager object stores information used by NDPSM.NLM.

- *NDPS Gateway* — NDPS gateways enable you to support printing environments that include non-NDPS-aware printers and print systems that require jobs to be placed in queues. NDPS currently supports two types of gateways: the Novell Gateway and third-party gateways. The Novell Gateway is implemented through a Print Device Subsystem (PDS) and a Port Handler (PH).

- *NDPS Broker* — When NDPS is installed, the installation utility ensures that a Broker object is loaded on your network. An NDPS Broker provides three network support services not previously available in NetWare. Although these services are transparent, you should be aware of them in case a Broker decides to take a vacation. The three NDPS support services are Service Registry Services (SRS), Event Notification Services (ENS), and Resource Management Services (RMS).

Now, let's take a closer look at each of these four NDPS components and learn how they can be combined to create a powerful NDPS printing system.

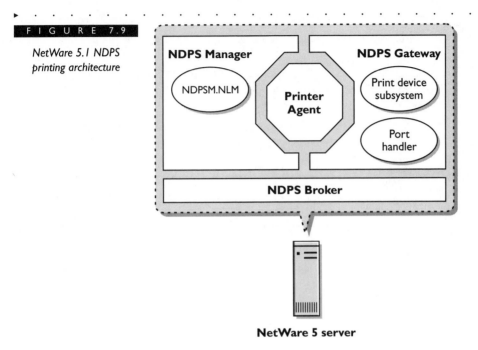

*NetWare 5.1 NDPS printing architecture*

## NDPS Printer Agent

A Printer Agent combines the functions previously performed by queue-based print queues, printers, and print servers into one intelligent, integrated entity. A printer has a one-to-one relationship with a Printer Agent. This means that a Printer Agent cannot represent more than one printer, nor can a printer be represented by more than one Printer Agent. A Printer Agent can represent either a Public Access printer or a Controlled Access printer (both of which are discussed later in this chapter).

A Printer Agent can exist as software (running on a NetWare 5.1 server) or firmware (embedded within a network-attached printer). In either case, a Printer Agent provides the following NDPS services (see Figure 7.10):

▶ It manages print job processing and many operations performed by the physical printer.

▶ It answers queries from network clients concerning print jobs, documents, or printer attributes.

▸ It generates event notification for job completion, printing problems, errors, or changes in the status of a print job, document, or printer.

▸ It ensures the scalability of the printing environment, allowing you to print in LANs, WANs, and/or enterprise systems.

▸ It enables you to print to a wide range of physical printing devices.

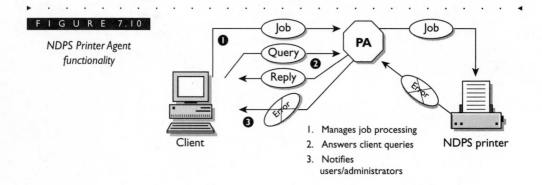

FIGURE 7.10

NDPS Printer Agent functionality

Client

1. Manages job processing
2. Answers client queries
3. Notifies users/administrators

NDPS printer

## NDPS Manager

An NDPS Manager object is used to create and manage Printer Agents. You must create an NDPS Manager object before creating server-based Printer Agents. The good news is that a single NDPS Manager object can control an unlimited number of Printer Agents (assuming, of course, that there is enough memory). A good rule of thumb is to create an NDPS Manager object for each server that hosts NDPS printers. Only one NDPS Manager is allowed per server.

The NDPS Manager software runs on a NetWare 5.1 server as NDPSM.NLM. This NLM carries out instructions provided by the NDPS Manager object. As you can see in Figure 7.11, NDPSM.NLM can be loaded in one of two ways:

▸ *Manually*—You can manually load NDPSM.NLM at the server console by typing

```
LOAD NDPSM.NLM <NDPS Manager distinguished name>
```

For example,

```
LOAD NDPSM.NLM .NDPSMGR1.WHITE.CRIME.TOKYO.ACME
```

▶ *Automatically* — The NDPS Manager can also be loaded automatically by placing the LOAD command in the server's AUTOEXEC.NCF file. This is the preferred method. Naturally, you'll need to reboot the server for this change to take effect. If you don't want to reboot the server, you can simply execute the command manually, as well.

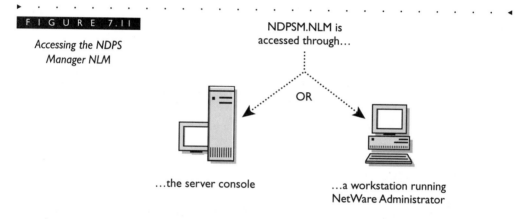

**FIGURE 7.11**

*Accessing the NDPS Manager NLM*

NDPSM.NLM is accessed through...

OR

...the server console

...a workstation running NetWare Administrator

**REAL WORLD**

If an NDPS Manager is not running when you create the first Printer Agent, NetWare prompts you to load it by displaying an error message.

While you can perform some configuration and management tasks directly through the NDPS Manager console interface, NetWare Administrator is a much better tool for performing these tasks. Refer to Figure 7.12 for a quick look at configuring an NDPS Manager object using NetWare Administrator.

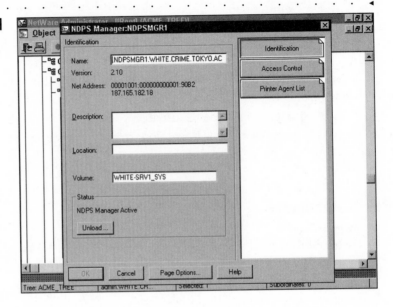

*Configuring an NDPS Manager in NetWare Administrator*

## NDPS Gateways

NDPS gateways are a collection of software that run on the NDPS Broker server and ensure backward compatibility for non-NDPS-aware printers (that is, printers that are not equipped with embedded NDPS Printer Agents). You must select and configure an NDPS gateway whenever you create a Printer Agent.

One benefit of NDPS gateways is that they enable you to support printing environments using printers that are not NDPS-aware. Using an NDPS gateway, an NDPS client can do the following:

▶ Send print jobs to printers that are not NDPS-aware (that is, printers that are not equipped with embedded NDPS controllers)

▶ Send print jobs to non-NDPS printing systems (such as UNIX, Macintosh, queue-based, and/or mainframe systems)

▶ Access print systems that require jobs to be placed in queues

▶ Query printer attributes, including Status

▶ Manage the printer

In short, an NDPS gateway acts as a software bridge that directly links Printer Agents to NDPS printers (see Figure 7.13). This is accomplished by translating NDPS instructions into device-specific commands. NDPS currently supports a number of generic and manufacturer-specific gateways:

▶ *Novell Gateway* — This is a generic gateway that provides NDPS support for devices without an embedded Printer Agent and printers that don't have their own manufacturer-specific gateway.

▶ *Manufacturer-specific Gateways* — The following manufacturer-specific gateways ship with NetWare 5.1 and provide access to non-NDPS-aware printers: Cannon, EPSON, Hewlett-Packard, IBM, Lexmark, OKIDATA, Ricoh, Kyocera, Tektronix, and Xerox.

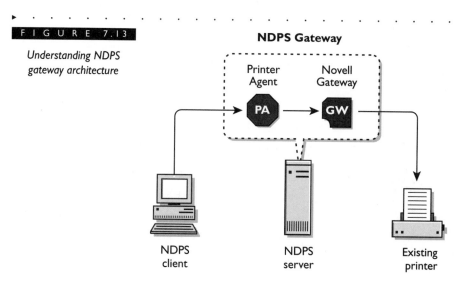

**FIGURE 7.13**

*Understanding NDPS gateway architecture*

**NDPS Gateway**

Printer Agent — Novell Gateway

PA → GW

NDPS client

NDPS server

Existing printer

**TIP**

**The Novell Gateway is generally used for printers that are attached to the server itself via a parallel cable. The manufacturer-specific gateways are usually used for printers that have some form of network interface and that are attached directly to the network.**

## NDPS Broker

An NDPS Broker is a special management component that provides three important services to the NetWare 5.1 printing architecture (explained later in this section). The Broker is composed of two complementary parts: an NDS leaf object (NDPS Broker) and a server-based NLM (BROKER.NLM).

The good news is you don't have to worry about creating your own NDPS Broker. When NDPS is installed for the first time in an NDS tree, the setup tool ensures that an NDPS Broker object is automatically created in the same container as the server upon which NDPS is being installed. If you install NDPS on subsequent servers, the Customize button presented at the end of the NetWare installation process enables you to install an additional Broker (if necessary). An additional Broker is only created automatically if you install NDPS on a server that is more than three hops away from the nearest existing Broker.

Furthermore, you don't have to worry about activating an NDPS Broker that has been installed because it's automatically loaded when NDPS is initialized. To do its job, an NDPS Broker must log into the NDS tree and authenticate itself to the server.

So, what is an NDPS Broker's job? Good question. An NDPS Broker provides three network support services:

▸ *Service Registry Services (SRS)* — An NDPS Broker allows Public Access printers (discussed later in this session) to advertise themselves to the network. This is important because it enables network administrators and users to find printers that are not represented by an NDPS Printer object. This service maintains information about device type, device name, device address, and other device-specific data such as the printer manufacturer and model number.

▸ *Event Notification Services (ENS)* — An NDPS Broker enables printers to send users and operators customized notifications about printer events and print job status. ENS supports several delivery methods, including pop-up windows, log files, and e-mail.

▸ *Resource Management Services (RMS)* — An NDPS Broker provides a central repository for printing resources. It enables you to install NDPS drivers, definition files, banners, and fonts in a central location, and then it enables you to automatically download them to clients, printers, or anyone else who needs them.

This completes our lesson on NDPS architecture. Now, let's take a moment to explore the two different NDPS printer types: Public Access and Controlled Access.

## NDPS Printer Types

With NetWare 5.1, network printers can be connected to the network in a variety of different ways:

- *Network printers* — These are attached directly to the network cable.

- *Remote printers* — These are attached to a workstation (or remote file server) using special software provided by NDPS.

- *Local printers* — These are attached directly to a server running NDPS.

Regardless of the way you connect your printer to the network, it must be defined as one of two types: *Public Access* or *Controlled Access*. A Public Access printer is available without restriction to everyone on the network. A Controlled Access printer, on the other hand, has an associated NDS object and provides a tighter degree of administrative control and security. Let's take a closer look.

### Public Access Printers

A Public Access printer is simply *public*. In other words, *anyone* on the network can use it without any restrictions. The following are important points to remember about a Public Access printer:

- It has no corresponding NDS object.

- It provides Plug-and-Print capabilities.

- It has limited security.

- It limits job event notification.

- It allows little administrative configuration.

A Public Access printer is created using the Printer Agent List tab of the NDPS Manager object. Because a Public Access printer is not represented in the NDS tree as an NDS object, it cannot be viewed using the Directory tree browser in Net-Ware Administrator. It can, however, be managed using the Tools menu of NetWare Administrator or the NDPS Manager object that the Printer Agent is associated with.

**For a complete comparison of Public Access and Controlled Access printers, refer to Table 7.2.**

TIP

### Controlled Access Printers

Controlled Access printers, on the other hand, are represented as objects in the NDS tree. Because of this, you can use NetWare Administrator to change printer values, restrict access, or set up event notification. Controlled Access printers provide the following advantages over Public Access printers: They offer a full range of network security options, they offer a full range of event and status notification options, and they can be customized with a full range of printer configurations.

There are several ways to create a Controlled Access printer:

1. *Create a New Printer Agent* — This creates an NDPS Printer object automatically.

2. *Existing NDPS Printer Object in NDS* — This upgrades an existing NDPS Printer object.

3. *Public Access Printer* — This converts an existing Public Access printer.

See Table 7.2 for a summary of the most important differences between Public Access and Controlled Access printers.

### REAL WORLD

When you create a Controlled Access printer, NDS rights are automatically granted to all users in the printer's context (that is, the parent container of the NDPS Printer object). Other users will need to be specifically assigned NDS rights to access the printer.

**TABLE 7.2**

*Comparing Controlled
Access and Public Access
Printers in NDPS*

| FEATURE | CONTROLLED ACCESS PRINTERS | PUBLIC ACCESS PRINTERS |
|---|---|---|
| NDS object | Yes | No |
| Security | High | Low |
| Configuration | Full range | Limited |
| NetWare Administrator support | As an NDS object | Via the Tools menu or the NDPS Manager object the Printer Agent is associated with |
| Event notification | Full range | Limited |
| Plug and Print | Yes | Yes |
| Automatic client installation | Yes | Yes |
| Printer accessibility | User objects in the parent container of the NDPS Printer object | All network users |

In this chapter, we've been unraveling the mysteries of NetWare 5.1's printing revolution — NDPS. So far, you've uncovered the fundamental features of NDPS and discovered how its architecture works. Now it's time to leave the realm of NDPS theory and take *action*! Let's start at the beginning . . . NDPS construction.

## LAB EXERCISE 7.1: UNDERSTANDING NDPS

Match the following terms with their descriptions.

**a.** NDPS Broker

**b.** NDPS Manager

**c.** Printer Agent

**d.** Printer driver

**e.** Printer gateway

**f.** Public Access printer

**g.** Controlled Access printer

**Item  Definition**

____  Logical entity used to create and manage Printer Agents

____  Converts print job into printer-specific format

____  Provides the following support services: event notification, resource management, and service registration

____  Has no corresponding NDS object

____  Combines the functionality previously performed by Print Queue, Printer, and Print Server objects

____  Can be configured with a full range of printer configuration and security options

____  Provides a bridge between NDPS clients and legacy printers

See Appendix C for Answers.

▶ . . . . . . . . . . . . . . . . . . . . . . . . . . ◀

# NDPS Printing Setup

Welcome to NDPS printing setup. Now that you understand the fundamental architecture of NetWare 5.1 printing, it's time to explore NDPS construction. This involves installation and configuration of the following three NDPS elements:

▶ *NDPS Broker* — Runs on a NetWare 5.1 server and provides three important support services

▶ *NDPS Manager* — Creates and manages Printer Agents

▶ *NDPS Printer Agent* — Combines the functions previously performed by a printer, print queue, print server, and spooler into one intelligent, simplified entity

Believe it or not, NDPS printing setup is as simple as 1-2-3-4. First, you must install NDPS Services on your NetWare 5.1 file server. This authenticates the NDPS Broker and activates NetWare 5.1 printing. Once an NDPS Broker is in place, you must create an NDPS Manager. The NDPS Manager provides a platform for Printer Agents that will reside on the server. This is all accomplished using NDPSM.NLM.

Once an NDPS Manager is in place, it's time to begin creating NDPS printers — using Printer Agents. NDPS supports both Public Access and Controlled Access printers. It's up to you, as a NetWare 5.1 network administrator, to determine when you need the advanced services and security provided by Controlled Access printers. Otherwise, Public Access provides *elementary* functionality.

Finally, there is Step 4 — workstation configuration. Before you can use your new NDPS printing system, you must install printers and activate NDPS services on each distributed workstation. Fortunately, NetWare 5.1 supports both automatic and manual installation options.

Here's a quick preview of the NetWare 5.1 NDPS printing setup process:

▶ *Step 1:* Install NDPS on the server.

▶ *Step 2:* Create and Load an NDPS Manager.

▶ *Step 3:* Create NDPS Printer Agents.

▶ *Step 4:* Install NDPS printers and activate NDPS services on the workstations.

There you have it — four simple steps. Of course, all this techno-wizardry requires a little bit of planning. Just like any network administration task, NDPS Printing Setup has minimum requirements that must be met. To support NDPS, your NetWare 5.1 servers and workstations must exceed the following minimum requirements:

▶ *NDPS server* — Your NDPS server must first meet the minimum hardware and software requirements for NetWare 5.1. In addition, it must have 140MB of available disk space on the SYS: volume and at least 4MB of RAM above the NetWare 5.1 requirements for NDPS. Finally, the server must have CD-ROM capability to read the NDPS installation media.

▶ *NDPS workstations* — The NDPS workstation must support Windows 95/98, Windows NT/2000, or Windows 3.1 and be running the latest NetWare 5.1 Novell Client. In addition, the workstation must support Windows 95/98 or Windows NT/2000, if access to the NDPS administrative utilities is desired from this workstation.

**REAL WORLD**

To install NDPS, you must have the NDS Supervisor right to the first NDPS NetWare 5.1 Server object and the [Root] of the NDS tree. For all other servers, you must have all rights except Supervisor for the container of the server on which you are installing NDPS.

Now, let's build a NetWare 5.1 NDPS printing system, starting with Step 1: Install NDPS on the Server.

## Step 1: Install NDPS on the Server

Before you can use NDPS, you must determine which setup strategy you want to use. You can either upgrade your current queue-based printing resources to NDPS or create a completely new NDPS printing system from the ground up.

If you want to upgrade your existing printing environment with all its current printing objects and users intact, you'll need to use the Novell Upgrade Wizard. On the other hand, it's safer and cleaner to create a new NDPS printing system from the ground up. Regardless of the strategy you use, NDPS will not disable your current printing setup. The good news is your users can continue to print just as they always have, until you decide to disable queue-based printing. This can be done gradually, or all at once.

NDPS can be installed on a NetWare 5.1 server in one of two ways:

▸ You can install NDPS during initial NetWare 5.1 server installation.

▸ You can add NDPS to an existing NetWare 5.1 server by choosing Novell ⇨ Install from the Java-based NetWare 5.1 GUI console.

The first time NDPS is installed in a Directory tree, an NDPS Broker object is created automatically in the container where the Server object resides. Subsequent NDPS servers don't require a new Broker if they are three hops or less from an existing Broker.

## Step 2: Create and Load an NDPS Manager

After an NDPS Broker is in place, you must create an NDPS Manager. The NDPS Manager is used to control server-based Printer Agents, similar to the way PSERVER was used to manage printing resources on queue-based servers.

The good news is that a single NDPS Manager can control an unlimited number of Printer Agents (assuming, of course, that there is enough memory). The best rule of thumb is to create an NDPS Manager object for each server that will host NDPS printers. Also, be sure that each server-based local printer sits on the same server as its host NDPS Manager.

To create an NDPS Manager in NetWare Administrator, perform the following tasks:

**1.** In NetWare Administrator, browse to the container where you want the NDPS Manager object to reside and then click the container to select it.

**2.** Select Object ⇨ Create.

**3.** When the New Object dialog box appears, select NDPS Manager and click OK.

**4.** When the Create NDPS Manager Object dialog box appears, fill in the following fields (as shown in Figure 7.14):

- In the NDPS Manager Name field, enter the NDPS Manager name.

- In the Resident Server field, indicate the server where you want this NDPS Manager to reside. (This can be any server in the current NDS tree on which you have installed NDPS. The server should not have an NDPS Manager already running.)

- In the Database Volume field, identify the volume to be used for print spooling.

- Click Create to create the NDPS Manager object.

**5.** Once you've created the NDPS Manager object, you'll need to activate it. To do so, type the following command at the server console:

```
LOAD NDPSM.NLM <NDPS Manager distinguished name>
```

For example,

```
LOAD NDPSM.NLM .NDPSMGR1.LABS.NORAD.ACME
```

Also, insert this command in the server's AUTOEXEC.NCF file so that it will be activated automatically whenever the server is rebooted.

FIGURE 7.14

*Creating an NDPS Manager
in NetWare Administrator*

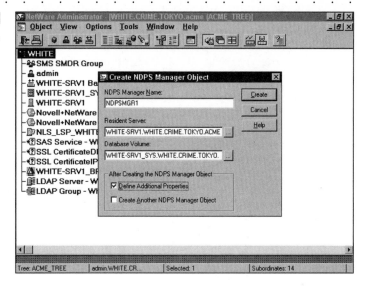

**REAL WORLD**

You must activate the NDPS Manager before its Printer Agents can be created. If you forget this final task, NetWare 5.1 automatically prompts you to load the NDPS Manager manually.

## Step 3: Create NDPS Printer Agents

Each Printer Agent has a one-to-one relationship with a printer. In this section, we're going to focus on the NetWare Administrator setup tool, and learn how to create Public Access and Controlled Access printers with it. So, without any further ado, let's create some printers.

### Creating Public Access Printers

To create a Public Access printer, perform the following tasks:

**1.** In NetWare Administrator, browse the NDS tree and locate the NDPS Manager you created previously in the "Step 2: Create and Load an NDPS

Manager" section. Access the NDPS Manager Identification page by double-clicking the NDS object. Click the Printer Agent List page tab.

**2.** When the Printer Agent List page appears, click New.

**3.** When the Create Printer Agent dialog box appears, perform the following tasks:

- In the Printer Agent (PA) Name field, enter the name of the new Public Access printer.

- In the NDPS Manager Name field, verify that the correct NDPS Manager is listed.

- In the Gateway Types field, select the appropriate gateway (that is, Cannon, EPSON, Hewlett-Packard, IBM, Lexmark, OKIDATA, Ricoh, Kyocera, Tektronix, or Xerox). Click OK.

**4.** The remaining screens vary, depending on the gateway you chose and the type of printer. After configuring the gateway, select a printer driver for each client operating system. Click Continue to save your changes and then click OK to acknowledge the list of printer drivers to be installed. Finally, click Cancel to return to the main NetWare Administrator screen.

Remember, Public Access printers don't appear as objects in the NDS tree. They are simply NDPS resources available to *all* network users. If you want better security and/or enhanced services, consider creating a Controlled Access printer.

### Creating Controlled Access Printers

To create a Controlled Access printer, perform the following tasks:

**1.** In NetWare Administrator, browse to the container where you want to create the Controlled Access printer and then right-click the container. When the pop-up menu appears, select Create. When the New Object dialog box appears, double-click NDPS Printer to select it.

**2.** When the Create NDPS Printer dialog box appears, fill in the following fields (as shown in Figure 7.15):

- In the NDPS Printer Name field, type a unique name for the Controlled Access printer.

- In the Printer Agent Source section, choose a method for creating the Controlled Access printer.

- In the "After Creating the NDPS Printer Object" section, mark the Define Additional Properties check box. Click Create.

▶ • • • • • • • • • • • • • • • • • • • • • • • • • • • ◀

F I G U R E   7.15

*Creating a Controlled Access printer in NetWare Administrator*

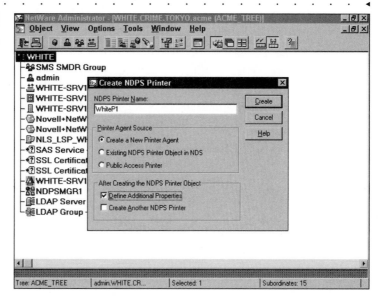

3. If you chose the "Create a New Printer Agent" option previously in the "Step 2: Create and Load an NDPS Manager" section, the Create Printer Agent dialog box appears:

- In the Printer Agent (PA) Name field, the name you selected earlier should be listed.

- In the NDPS Manager Name field, browse to and select the NDPS Manager object that you want to use to control this printer.

- In the Gateway Types field, select the appropriate gateway (that is, Cannon, EPSON, Hewlett-Packard, IBM, Lexmark, OKIDATA, Ricoh, Kyocera, Tektronix, or Xerox). Click OK.

**4.** The remaining screens vary, depending on the gateway you chose and the type of printer. After configuring the gateway, select a printer driver for each client operating system. Click Continue to save your changes and then OK to acknowledge the list of printer drivers to be installed. Finally, click Cancel to return to the main NetWare Administrator screen.

**5.** If you chose the "Existing NDPS Printer Object in NDS" or "Public Access Printer" option previously in the "Step 2: Create and Load an NDPS Manager" section, indicate which existing NDPS Printer object or Public Access printer to use and then click OK. When the Printer Control dialog box appears, use the Access Control page tab, if necessary, to add additional users, groups, or containers as authorized users.

This completes the core steps of NDPS Printing Setup. Let's review. First, we activated server-based NDPS printing with the creation of an NDPS Broker. This was accomplished automatically, by default, using the NetWare 5.1 server installation procedure. Second, we created an NDPS Manager object to support multiple Printer Agents on a particular server. Third, we created Public Access and Controlled Access printers using NetWare Administrator.

Congratulations, you are printing . . . sort of. Actually, the server is printing, but the users aren't! To open up NDPS printing to your users (and make it truly productive), you'll need to install printing services on each workstation. Let's take a look.

## Step 4: Install NDPS Printers and Activate NDPS Services on the Workstations

For users to take full advantage of NDPS, each workstation must have the latest NetWare 5.1 Novell Client installed, including the NDPS client component. Workstation access to NDPS printers is accomplished using a printer driver database.

NDPS allows you to choose which drivers you want to automatically download to Windows 3.1, Windows 95/98, and Windows 2000/NT workstations. When you create an NDPS printer, you can configure it for automatic installation on each workstation within a specific container. Or you can install NDPS manually on specific workstations. In summary, NDPS supports two workstation installation options:

▸ Automatically configure NDPS to download printer drivers and configure printing on workstations

▸ Manually configure each workstation using the Novell Printer Manager

### Automatic NDPS Printer Installation on the Workstation

While NDPS allows users to download and install printers on workstations manually, it also enables you (as a NetWare 5.1 network administrator) to designate certain printers to be downloaded and installed automatically. Check out Figure 7.16.

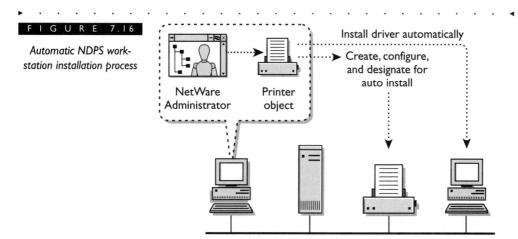

**F I G U R E   7.16**

*Automatic NDPS work-station installation process*

NetWare Administrator    Printer object

Install driver automatically

Create, configure, and designate for auto install

From NetWare Administrator, an administrator can create and configure Printer objects and designate printers to be automatically installed on user workstations.

Designate a printer to be installed automatically by using the Remote Printer Management (RPM) feature in NetWare Administrator. Once you have designated a printer for automatic installation, it magically appears on the workstation's installed printers list next time the user logs in. To enable automatic printer driver installation within a particular container, perform the following tasks:

**I.** In NetWare Administrator, browse to the target container and highlight it.

**2.** Select Object ⇨ Details.

**3.** When the Organizational Unit Identification page appears, click the NDPS Remote Printer Management page tab (as shown in Figure 7.17). Next, mark the "Show the Results Window on Workstations" check box and click the Add button under the "Printers to Install to Workstations" field.

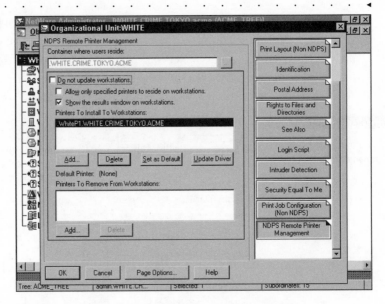

FIGURE 7.17

*Automatic NDPS workstation installation screen in NetWare Administrator*

**4.** When the Available Printers Options dialog box appears, browse to and click the desired Controlled Access or Public Access printer and then click OK.

**5.** When the NDPS Remote Printer Management page reappears, perform the following tasks:

- Click the printer you just added to the list.

- (Optional) If this printer is the default printer for the users in this container, click Set as Default.

- Click Update Driver. A notice appears informing you that the driver for this printer will download to workstations the next time users in this container log in. Click OK to acknowledge the message. Click OK to save your changes.

## Manual NDPS Printer Installation on the Workstation

If you want to live dangerously, you can choose to *manually* install NDPS printers on each user workstation. This is accomplished using the Novell Printer Manager tool. Novell Printer Manager enables users to manage NDPS printing tasks from their workstations. When you install the client software, a list of installed printers appears in the Novell Printer Manager main window. Following is a list of tasks that you can accomplish using the Novell Printer Manager:

▶ Add printers

▶ View a list of print jobs; change job order; submit jobs with a hold; and pause, resume, and delete jobs

▶ Maintain and update the printer list

▶ Receive real-time status information for print jobs and event notification for jobs and printers

Here's how the Novell Printer Manager works:

**I.** Click Start ➪ Run.

**2.** When the Run dialog box appears, browse to or enter the following and click OK:

```
\\server_name\SYS\PUBLIC\WIN32\NWPMW32
```

**3.** When the Novell Printer Manager screen appears, select Printer ➪ New. When the Novell Printers dialog box appears, click Add.

**4.** When a list of available printers appears, select the printer you want to install and click Install. When the Novell Printers — Install dialog appears, modify the printer name that appears and select a predefined configuration, if desired, and then click OK. The printer driver is then installed on the workstation. Wait until the Novell Printers dialog box reappears, showing the new printer in the Installed Printers list. If a license agreement screen appears, read the agreement, and then click Accept to accept the terms and conditions.

**5.** Click Close to return to the main Novell Printer Manager screen. Select Printer ⇨ Close to exit the Novell Printer Manager utility.

Congratulations, you are printing! You've passed the final ACME test by building an NDPS printing system.

This final chapter started with the Essence of Printing. Then, we learned all the steps involved in NDPS Printing Setup. There are only four steps, and they're not very hard. First, you install the NDPS Broker, then create an NDPS Manager, and finally, configure Printer Agents and Printers. Then, to top it all off, you must activate the NDPS workstation.

*NOW WHAT!?!*

This concludes our tour of Novell's newest operating system — NetWare 5.1. It is a powerful tool for saving the world. In this book, we've focused on the six main features required for Novell Course 560, "NetWare 5.1 Administration":

▸ Novell Directory Services (Chapter 2)

▸ NetWare 5.1 Connectivity (Chapter 3)

▸ NetWare 5.1 File System (Chapter 4)

▸ NetWare 5.1 Security (Chapter 5)

▸ NetWare 5.1 Workstation Management (Chapter 6)

▸ NetWare 5.1 NDPS Printing (Chapter 7)

Oh, my goodness! Would you look at the time — where has it all gone? I've just been rambling away here . . . sorry, if you missed your train, plane, or supercar. I guess I'm done. There's not much more that can be said about NetWare 5.1. Are you interested in Golf? Aliens? Neurogenetic Recombination? We could talk about that for a while. Nah, I better save those topics for another book.

It's been quite a wild ride, and you should be proud of yourself for surviving it in one piece — or so it seems. Do you still want to be a CNA? A NetWare 5.1 Superhero? Great. Because the world needs a few good CNAs, and you're a great place to start.

You are the final piece in our globe-trotting puzzle. You will save the world with NetWare 5.1. Your mission — should you choose to accept it — is to pass the NetWare 5.1 Administration exam. You will need courage, security, ConsoleOne, and this book. If you succeed, you will save the world and become a CNA!

All in a day's work . . .

Well, that does it! The End . . . Finito . . . Kaput. Everything you wanted to know about NetWare 5.1, but were afraid to ask. I hope you've had as much fun reading this book as I've had writing it. It's been a long and winding road — a life changer. Thanks for spending the last 500 pages with me, and I bid you a fond farewell in the only way I know how:

*"See ya' later, alligator!"*
*"After a while, crocodile!"*
*"Hasta la vista, baby!"*
*"Live long and prosper!"*
*"So long and thanks for all the fish!"*
*"May the force be with you . . ."*

GOOD LUCK, AND BY THE WAY....
THANKS FOR SAVING THE WORLD!!

BEST WISHES,

*David James Yorke IV*

## LAB EXERCISE 7.2: SETTING UP NDPS PRINTING IN THE CRIME FIGHTING DIVISION OF ACME

Welcome back to ACME! In this final ACME exercise, we will build an NDPS printing system for the Crime Fighting division of ACME. Specifically, we will create three NDPS printing components on the WHITE-SRV1 server in the WHITE.CRIME.TOKYO.ACME Organizational Unit.

First, we will activate server-based NDPS printing with the creation of an NDPS Broker. If you accepted the defaults for "optional components" during the NetWare 5.1 installation process (see Appendix D), this occurred automatically. Second, we will create an NDPS Manager to support multiple Printer Agents. And third, we will create a Public Access Printer and then convert it to a Controlled Access printer using NetWare Administrator.

Here's a quick preview:

▶ *Step 1:* Verify NDPS Broker activation.

▶ *Step 2:* Create and Load an NDPS Manager.

▶ *Step 3:* Create a Public Access printer.

▶ *Step 4:* Configure a container for automatic printer driver download.

▶ *Step 5:* Test a Public Access printer configuration on your workstation.

▶ *Step 6:* Configure a container to remove a printer driver.

▶ *Step 7:* Convert a Public Access printer to a Controlled Access printer.

▶ *Step 8:* Manually configure the Admin workstation to use a Controlled Access printer.

▶ *Step 9:* Test a Controlled Access printer configuration on the Admin workstation.

In order to accomplish this ACME exercise, you need the following network hardware:

▸ A NetWare 5.1 server called WHITE-SRV1.WHITE.CRIME.TOKYO.ACME (which can be installed using the directions found in Appendix D) with the NDPS component installed.

▸ A workstation running either the NetWare 5.1 Novell Client for Windows 95/98 or NetWare 5.1 Novell Client for Windows NT/2000 (which can be installed using the directions found in Lab Exercise 3.1), with the NDPS component installed.

▸ A printer physically attached to your server (rather than your workstation). Also, you'll need to determine the following information for your printer: printer type, gateway type, and printer driver.

Let's get started.

**1.** Verify NDPS Broker activation.

   **a.** Make sure your printer is powered on. If it is not, perform the following tasks:

      • Do a normal shutdown/poweroff of your NetWare 5.1 server.

      • Ensure that the printer has paper.

      • Turn the printer on and verify that it's online.

      • Power on your server. Wait until the NetWare 5.1 operating system is finished loading on your server.

   **b.** You'll need to verify that an NDPS Broker was created and activated when you originally built the WHITE-SRV1 server (see Appendix D). On your WHITE-SRV1 server console, press Alt+Esc until the NDPS Broker screen appears.

**c.** On the NDPS Broker screen, verify that the following three services are enabled:

- Service Registry Service (SRS)
- Event Notification Service (ENS)
- Resource Management Service (RMS)

**d.** If the NDPS Broker is not running, use Alt+Esc to find the server console prompt. Once there, type the following and press Enter:

```
LOAD BROKER.NLM
```

**2.** Create and Load an NDPS Manager.

**a.** On your workstation, log into the tree as Admin, if you haven't already done so.

**b.** Launch NetWare Administrator.

**c.** Right-click the WHITE container and then choose Create from the pop-up menu that appears.

**d.** When the New Object dialog box appears, scroll down and select NDPS Manager, and then click OK.

**TIP**

**If NDPS Manager is not listed as an option, it probably means that the NDPS client function is not installed on your workstation. If so, you'll need to do a Custom reinstall of the NetWare 5.1 Novell Client (see Lab Exercise 3.1).**

**e.** When the Create NDPS Manager Object dialog box appears, perform these tasks:

- In the NDPS Manager Name field, enter the following:

```
NDPSMGR1
```

- Click the Browse button to the right of the Resident Server field.

**f.** When the Select Object dialog box appears, follow these tasks:

- Select WHITE-SRV1 in the left pane.

- Click OK.

**g.** When the Create NDPS Manager Object dialog box reappears, follow these tasks:

- Verify that WHITE-SRV1.WHITE.CRIME.TOKYO.ACME is listed in the Resident Server field.

- Click the Browse button to the right of the Database Volume field.

**h.** When the Select Volume dialog box appears, perform these tasks:

- Verify that WHITE-SRV1_SYS.WHITE.CRIME.TOKYO.ACME is selected in the Volumes field.

- Click OK.

**i.** When the Create NDPS Manager Object dialog box reappears, perform these tasks:

- Verify that WHITE-SRV1_SYS.WHITE.CRIME.TOKYO.ACME is listed in the Database Volume field.

- Click Create to create the NDPS Manager object.

**j.** When the main NetWare Administrator browser screen reappears, you'll notice that the NDPS Manager object you just created (that is, NDPSMGR1) now appears in the tree. Next, you need to activate it at the server. You'll also want to add the LOAD statement to the server's AUTOEXEC.NCF file so that the LOAD statement automatically loads each time the server boots. Here's how it works:

- At the server console, press Alt+Esc until you get to a console prompt.

- At the console prompt, type the following and press Enter:

```
EDIT AUTOEXEC.NCF
```

- Insert the following command at the bottom of the file:

```
LOAD NDPSM.NLM .NDPSMGR1.WHITE.CRIME.TOKYO.ACME
```

- Press Esc to save the file.

- Verify that Yes is selected and then press Enter when asked if you want to save SYS:SYSTEM\AUTOEXEC.NCF.

- Next, a screen appears. This screen gives you the opportunity to edit another file. Press Esc to exit this screen.

- Verify that Yes is selected and then press Enter when asked whether to exit the EDIT utility.

k. Next, you'll need to load the NDPS Manager manually on the server (so that you don't have to reboot the server to execute the command you just added to the AUTOEXEC.NCF file). To do so, type the following at the server console prompt and press Enter:

```
LOAD NDPSM.NLM .NDPSMGR1.WHITE.CRIME.TOKYO.ACME
```

A blank Printer Agent List screen then appears on the server console.

3. Create a Public Access printer.

a. Return to your workstation. In NetWare Administrator, double-click the NDPSMGR1 object you just created.

b. The Identification page for the NDPS Manager object appears, by default. After it appears, perform these tasks:

- Verify that the Version field has a version number in it.

- Confirm that the Net Address field lists the network address for your server.

- Verify that the Status section indicates that the NDPS Manager is active.

- Click the Printer Agent List tab.

c. When the Printer Agent List page appears, click New.

**d.** When the Create Printer Agent dialog box appears, perform these tasks:

- In the Printer Agent (PA) Name field, enter the following:

  WhitePA1

- Verify that the NDPS Manager object you created earlier (that is, NDPSMGR1.WHITE.CRIME.TOKYO.ACME) is listed in the NDPS Manager Name field.

- Normally, you would select the appropriate gateway in the Gateway Type field. (For more details, refer to the documentation that comes with NetWare 5.1.) For the purposes of this exercise, however, select the Novell Gateway, instead.

- Click OK.

**e.** When the Configure Novell PDS for Printer Agent "WhitePA1" dialog box appears, perform these tasks:

- In the Printer Type list box, select the appropriate printer driver for your printer.

- In the Port Handler Type field, verify that Novell Port Handler is selected.

- Click OK.

**f.** When the first Configure Port Handler for Printer Agent "WhitePA1" dialog box appears, perform these tasks:

- In the Connection Type section, mark the Local (Physical Connection to Server) radio button.

- In the Port Type section, verify that the LPT1 radio box is marked (assuming, of course, that your printer is attached to the LPT1: port on your server).

- Click Next.

**g.** When the second Configure Port Handler for Printer Agent "WhitePA1" dialog box appears, perform these tasks:

- In the Controller Type field, verify that Auto Select is selected.

- In the Interrupts section, verify that the None (Polled Mode) radio button is marked.

- Click Finish.

**h.** Wait for the Printer Agent to load.

**i.** When the Select Printer Drivers dialog box appears. perform these tasks:

- Verify that the tab corresponding to your workstation platform is selected.

- Confirm that the appropriate printer driver for your printer is selected.

- Click Continue.

**j.** When the Information — NDPS v2.00 dialog box appears, perform these tasks:

- Review the list of printer drivers to be installed.

- Click OK.

**k.** When the Printer Agent List page reappears, perform these tasks:

- Verify that the status of the WhitePA1 Printer Agent is "Idle."

- Click Cancel to return to the main NetWare Administrator browser screen.

**4.** Configure a container for automatic printer driver download.

**a.** In NetWare Administrator, right-click the WHITE container and then choose Details from the pop-up menu that appears.

**b.** When the Identification page for the WHITE Organizational Unit object appears, select the NDPS Remote Printer Management tab. (You may have to use the scrollbar to find it.)

**c.** When the NDPS Remote Printer Management page appears, perform these tasks:

- Mark the "Show the Results Window on Workstations" check box.

- Click the Add button below the "Printers to Install to Workstations" field.

**d.** When the Available Printers Options dialog box appears, perform these tasks:

- In the Available Printers field, select the WhitePA1 printer.

- Click OK.

**e.** When the NDPS Remote Printer Management page reappears, perform these tasks:

- In the "Printers to Install to Workstations" field, click WhitePA1 to select it.

- (Optional) If this printer is the default printer for the users in this container, click Set as Default.

- Click Update Driver.

**f.** A notice appears informing you that the driver for this printer will be copied to workstations the next time users log in.

- Click OK to acknowledge the message.

- Click OK to save your changes.

**g.** Exit the NetWare Administrator utility.

**h.** Restart your workstation.

**5.** Test a Public Access printer configuration on your workstation.

    **a.** Log back into the tree as Admin:

- Log into the tree as the Admin user.

- Wait while NDPS modifies your printer setup. (This may take awhile.) Eventually, the NDPS Remote Printer Management dialog box displays a variety of messages, including one message advising you that Printer WhitePA1 is installed. Wait until the process is complete and then click Close to acknowledge the message.

- If a printer driver license agreement appears, read the license agreement, and then click Accept to agree to its terms and conditions.

- You'll notice that a printer icon corresponding to the printer driver appears in the Printer folder of your Windows workstation.

    **b.** Launch NetWare Administrator.

    **c.** Click Object ➪ Print Setup.

    **d.** When the Print Setup dialog box appears, perform these tasks:

- In the Printer section, open the pull-down box in the Name field and select WhitePA1.

- Click OK.

    **e.** On the main NetWare Administrator browser screen, click the Printer icon in the toolbar.

    **f.** When the Print dialog box appears, perform these tasks:

- Verify that WhitePA1 is listed in the Printer field.

- Confirm that the "Print in Two Columns" check box is marked.

- Select the print quality of your choice from the Print Quality drop-down list.

- Click OK.

**g.** A printout of your NDS tree should appear on your printer. If this happens, congratulations — you are now the proud owner of a new Public Access Printer.

**6.** Configure a container to automatically remove a printer driver.

**a.** In NetWare Administrator, right-click the WHITE container and then choose Details from the pop-up menu that appears.

**b.** When the Identification page for the WHITE Organizational Unit object appears, select the NDPS Remote Printer Management page tab. (You may have to use the scrollbar to find it.)

**c.** When the NDPS Remote Printer Management page appears, perform these tasks:

- Verify that the "Show the Results Window on Workstations" check box is marked.

- Click the Add button under the "Printers to Remove from Workstations" field.

**d.** When the Available Printers Options dialog box appears, perform these tasks:

- In the Available Printers field, click WhitePA1.

- Click OK.

**e.** When the NDPS Remote Printer Management page reappears, perform these tasks:

- You'll notice that WhitePA1 has disappeared from the "Printers to Install to Workstations" field and has appeared in the "Printers to Remove from Workstations" field.

- Click OK to save your changes.

**f.** Exit the NetWare Administrator utility.

**g.** Restart your workstation.

**h.** Log back into the tree as Admin:

- Log into the tree as the Admin user.

- Wait while NDPS modifies your printer setup. (This may take awhile.) Eventually, the NDPS Remote Printer Management dialog box displays a series of messages. One of the messages advises you that Printer WhitePA1 has been removed. Wait until the process is complete and then click Close to acknowledge the message.

**i.** Verify that the printer is no longer installed on the workstation.

- Click Start ⇨ Settings ⇨ Printers.

- The WhitePA1 icon should no longer appear in the Printers window.

- Click File ⇨ Close to close the window.

**j.** Delete the printer driver icon from the workstation.

- From the Printer folder, click the printer driver icon corresponding to WhitePA1 to select the corresponding printer. (**Hint:** The icon name will list the printer driver name, rather than WhitePA1.)

- Press Delete to delete the icon.

- Click Yes when asked if you are sure you want to delete the icon.

**7.** Convert a Public Access printer to a Controlled Access printer.

**a.** In NetWare Administrator, right-click the WHITE container and select Create from the pop-up menu that appears.

**b.** When the New Object dialog box appears, perform these tasks:

- Click NDPS Printer.

- Click OK.

**c.** When the Create NDPS Printer dialog box appears, perform these tasks:

- In the NDPS Printer Name field, type **WhiteP1**.

- In the Printer Agent Source section, click the Public Access Printer radio button.

- In the After Creating the NDPS Print Object section, mark the Define Additional Properties check box.

- Click Create.

**d.** A Warning—NDPS v2.00 dialog box appears, advising you that converting a Public Access Printer to an NDPS Printer object will require every client installation of this printer to be reinstalled. Click OK to acknowledge the warning.

**e.** When the Select Printer Agent dialog box appears, verify that WhitePA1 is selected, and then click OK.

**f.** Wait while NDPS creates the NDPS Printer object. When the Printer Control page for the WhiteP1 NDPS Printer object appears, click the Access Control tab.

**g.** When the Access Control page appears, perform these tasks:

- By default, Admin is assigned as a Manager, Operator, and User (because you created this printer while logged on as Admin). Also, you'll notice that the printer's home container (WHITE.CRIME. TOKYO.ACME) is designated as a User. This means that everyone in the WHITE container can use the new printer. Let's restrict access to the Admin user.

- In the Role field, click Users.

- In the Current Users field, click WHITE.CRIME.TOKYO.ACME.

- Click Delete.

**h.** When the Delete Member dialog box appears, asking if you want to delete this user, click OK to confirm.

**i.** In case something goes wrong with the new Controlled Access printer, you may want to notify the WhiteP1 Manager with a pop-up notification message. To activate this NetWare 5.1 feature

- Click Managers in the Role field.
- Click Admin.WHITE.CRIME.TOKYO.ACME in the Current Managers field.
- Click Notification.

**j.** When the Notification dialog box appears, perform these tasks:

- If your printer driver allows you (some may not), set up pop-up notification parameters.
- Click OK.

**k.** When the Access Control Page reappears, click OK to save your changes.

**l.** Exit NetWare Administrator.

**8.** Manually configure the Admin workstation to use a Controlled Access printer.

**a.** Click Start ➪ Run.

**b.** When the Run dialog box appears, browse to or enter the following and click OK:

`\\server_name\SYS\PUBLIC\WIN32\NWPMW32`

**c.** When the Novell Printer Manager screen appears, select Printer ➪ New.

**d.** When the Novell Printers dialog box appears, click Add.

**e.** When a list of available printers appears, perform these tasks:

- Select WhiteP1.
- Click Install.

**f.** When the Novell Printers—Install dialog appears, modify the printer name that appears and select a predefined configuration, if desired, and then click OK.

**g.** Wait while the printer driver is installed on the workstation. Do not touch the keyboard!

**h.** If a license agreement screen appears, read the agreement, and then click Accept to accept the terms and conditions.

**i.** Wait until the Novell Printers dialog box reappears, showing the new printer in the Installed Printers list. (**Note:** Do *not* respond to any interim dialog boxes, even if you think you should! Doing so will produce undesirable results. Interestingly, you'll find that interim dialog boxes disappear from the screen without any response from you, if you ignore them.)

**j.** Click Close to return to the main Novell Printer Manager screen.

**k.** Select Printer ⇨ Close to exit the Novell Printer Manager utility.

**l.** Restart your workstation.

**9.** Test a Controlled Access printer configuration on the Admin workstation.

**a.** Use NetWare Administrator (or the application of your choice) to test the White P1 printer configuration. (If you want to use NetWare Administrator, refer to Step 5 above.)

## LAB EXERCISE 7.3: THE MYSTERY OF NDPS

Circle the 15 NDPS-related terms hidden in this word search puzzle using the hints provided. No punctuation characters (such as blank spaces, hyphens, and so on) should be included. Numbers should always be spelled out.

```
N  E  T  W  O  R  K  P  R  I  N  T  E  R  K  B  V
D  D  R  E  M  O  T  E  P  R  I  N  T  E  R  V  O
S  A  P  R  I  N  T  E  R  C  O  N  T  R  O  L  P
I  I  M  S  F  I  Y  J  B  K  F  O  W  N  C  L  A
N  E  G  W  B  E  P  L  L  K  M  F  G  F  T  K  Q
T  X  V  W  M  R  E  R  J  B  J  R  P  Y  E  N  O
E  V  E  N  T  N  O  T  I  F  I  C  A  T  I  O  N
G  W  P  T  Q  T  V  K  E  N  S  X  H  I  K  R  H
R  X  M  S  R  B  V  O  E  D  T  T  T  R  V  R  H
A  T  F  P  E  R  J  N  J  R  J  Q  P  U  B  J  X
T  N  G  N  I  R  U  T  P  A  C  X  U  C  D  O  V
I  G  P  K  N  O  V  E  L  L  G  A  T  E  W  A  Y
O  T  N  E  G  A  R  E  T  N  I  R  P  S  U  B  Z
N  Q  R  E  V  I  R  D  R  E  T  N  I  R  P  E  M
```

### Hints

1. Legacy process for redirecting print jobs from a local workstation port to a network printer.
2. An NDPS feature that can utilize e-mail (GroupWise), pop-up windows, or event logs.
3. Provides SRS, ENS, and RMS support services.
4. NDPS feature that enables network administrators to administer all printing devices from a single location using NetWare Administrator.
5. A printer that is attached directly to the LAN cabling.
6. Provides a generic software bridge between NDPS and legacy local and remote printers, including those using NPRINTER or queue-based technology.

7. Legacy printing object required in earlier versions of NetWare.

8. Printing component that combines the functions previously performed by a printer, print queue, print server, and spooler into one intelligent, simplified entity.

9. NetWare Administrator screen that displays real-time information about NDPS printers and print jobs.

10. Can be downloaded automatically to workstations after NDPS is installed.

11. Legacy printing utility that most closely resembles the services provided by an NDPS Manager.

12. Attached to a workstation or remote file server using special software provided by NDPS.

13. Acronym for a NetWare Administrator feature that enables you to configure printers for remote installation.

14. IPX-based protocol that can be turned off by NDPS in an IP-Only network to decrease unnecessary network traffic and increase network bandwidth.

15. An NDPS feature which is "High" for Controlled Access Printers and "Low" for Public Access Printers.

See Appendix C for answers.

## LAB EXERCISE 7.4: NETWARE 5.1 PRINTING

### Across

2. Software bridge for printers
6. Printer advertising service
8. Relies on automatic hardware detection
10. More secure than Public Access
12. Less secure than Controlled Access
15. Legacy printing object that controls print queues

**Down**

1. NDPS Broker software
3. Central repository for printing resources
4. Customized Broker notification service
5. Open standard printing protocol
7. Manages Printer Agents
9. Is attached directly to an NDPS server
11. Houses embedded Printer Agent
13. Focus of this chapter
14. NDPS RAM requirement (MB)

See Appendix C for answers.

# NetWare 5.1 Certification:
# A World of Knowledge

In a world where people, businesses, organizations, governments, and nations are being connected and sharing information at a dizzying rate, Novell's primary goal is to be the infrastructure that connects people and services together all over the world.

To help fulfill this goal, Novell Education is providing quality education programs and products to help create a strong support base of trained networking professionals. By itself, the Novell Education department isn't nearly large enough to provide high-quality training to the vast number of people who will require training. Therefore, Novell Education has developed training partnerships throughout the world that provide authorized training. In addition, Novell Education has created certification programs to help ensure that the standard for networking skills is maintained at a high level.

Today, Novell has more than 1,500 authorized education partners worldwide, including colleges, universities, professional training centers, e-Learning companies, and so on.

This appendix describes Novell Education and the CNA program. It also provides some practical tips, such as alternatives to formal classes, finding out how to take the test, and where to go from here. Specifically, we're going to learn how Novell Education and NetWare 5.1 helps you build your own on-ramp to the global Web — also known as a whole new "World of Knowledge."

## Novell Certification

Every year, Novell certifies thousands of professionals around the world to manage and support its information technology (IT) products. Whether you are a network administrator, systems integrator, or other networking professional, you'll undoubtedly find that Novell offers one or more network certifications to meet your needs. If you want to learn more about the various types of certifications available, you should check out the information at `http://www.novell.com/education/certinfo/`.

## NetWare 5.1 CNA Certification

If you are new to the Novell certification process, you may find that the NetWare 5.1 CNA certification is the right one for you. This certification track consists of *one* course and *one* exam. Table A.1 lists the latest course and associated exam number that were valid as of the writing of this study guide.

| T A B L E   A.1 | COURSE NUMBER | COURSE TITLE | EXAM NUMBER |
|---|---|---|---|
| *NetWare 5.1 CNA Exam Requirements* | Course 560 | NetWare 5.1 Administration | Exam 50-653 |

## NetWare 5.1 CNE Certification

If you're looking for a more comprehensive certification, you may find that the NetWare 5.1 CNE certification is the right one for you. This certification track consists of *six* courses and *six* required exams. (You'll notice that one of the required courses, Course 560, is also a requirement for the CNA certification.) Five of the courses are preselected for you. You'll also be asked to select one of four electives. Table A.2 lists the latest courses and exam numbers that were valid as of the writing of this book.

| T A B L E   A.2 | COURSE NUMBER | COURSE TITLE | EXAM NUMBER |
|---|---|---|---|
| *NetWare 5.1 CNE Exam Requirements* | Course 560 | NetWare 5.1 Administration v2.0 | Exam 50-653 |
| | Course 565 | Networking Technologies v1.0 | Exam 50-632 |
| | Course 570 | NetWare 5.1 Advanced Administration v2.0 | Exam 50-654 |
| | Course 575 | NDS Design and Implementation, v2.0 | Exam 50-659 |
| | Course 580 | Service and Support v2.0 | Exam 50-635 |
| | **Electives: Select *one* of the following:** | | |
| | Course 350 | GroupWise 5.5 System Administration | Exam 50-633 |

*Continued*

· · · · ·

| TABLE A.2 | COURSE NUMBER | COURSE TITLE | EXAM NUMBER |
|---|---|---|---|
| *NetWare 5.1 CNE Exam Requirements (continued)* | Course 555 | Integrating NetWare & Windows NT | Exam 50-644 |
| | Course 606 | TCP/IP for Networking Professionals | Exam 50-649 |
| | Course 730 | Management Using ManageWise 2.6 | Exam 50-641 |
| | Course 770 | Internet Security Management with Border Manager Enterprise Edition 3.5 v1.02 | Exam 50-650 |
| | Course 780 | Desktop Management with ZENworks | Exam 50-656 |
| | Course 990 | Oracle Database Operator for NetWare | Exam 50-436 |

While you are working toward your certification, it's important that you always have access to an up-to-date version of the *certification track* relating to the certification you are interested in. If you plan to obtain a NetWare 5.1 CNA certification, check out the CNA Certification Track at `http://www.novell.com/education/certinfo/cna/`. If you are interested in the NetWare 5.1 CNE certification, check out the various CNE Certification Tracks at `http://www.novell.com/education/certinfo/cne/`.

## Continuing Education Requirements

Like other networking technology, Novell products are constantly being updated and enhanced. Because of this, you will eventually find that the Novell product related to your certification has become obsolete. When this happens, you will typically have approximately 12 to 18 months to recertify by taking an exam on the new product. If you fail to do so, your existing certification may be invalidated.

# Exam Preparation

You can obtain most Novell certifications by simply signing a Novell Education Certification Agreement and passing the required exams. Neither the CNA or CNE certifications require you to attend formal training classes.

## Preparation Methods

There are many ways to prepare for an exam, including formal Novell-authorized classroom training, CNA/CNE Study Guides from Novell Press, Clarke Notes books from Novell Press, Novell Student Kits, online training from CyberStateU.com (an official Novell Online Training Provider), computer-based training, videos, and practice exams. No matter which method(s) you choose, it is critical that you gain a thorough understanding of the technical concepts, as well as a firm grasp of the hands-on material.

## Study Hints

As you prepare for the CNA and CNE exams, be sure that you tailor your study habits toward the testing objectives. The exam questions are based on the testing objectives listed and cross-referenced in Appendix B of this book. Also, be sure that you know the course material *well*. You'll find that some exam questions rely on *memorization* of facts, while others require you to actually *apply* the knowledge that you've acquired.

Here are a few more study hints that should help you prepare for the CNA and CNE exams:

▶ Remember that exam questions may be presented in a variety of different formats, including single-answer multiple choice, multiple-answer multiple choice, true/false, fill-in-the-blank, and drag-and-drop. You may also get a number of simulation (performance-based) questions and exhibit-related questions. In simulation situations, you may be asked to perform a number of sequential tasks. Unfortunately, you may find that the simulator is not programmed to allow your favorite method of performing a certain task — so it's always wise to be familiar with alternative methods. Be prepared!

> ► After you've read this entire study guide, go back and take a second look at the Real World and Tip icon references. If you don't have a high degree of confidence, read the book again and spend additional time practicing the hands-on lab exercises.

> ► Interestingly, you may occasionally find exam questions that do not appear to be in the official Novell course material. This is unfortunate, but cannot be avoided. If this occurs, your best bet is to use your overall knowledge of the subject to architect the correct answer(s).

## The Exam

Okay. You've finished the course, you've studied this book, you've spent hours in the lab or on your own network practicing hands-on tasks. Now, you're ready to show your stuff and prove that you have the baseline of knowledge required to take on network administrator duties in the real world. You're ready to take the exam and become a CNA (or alternately, take your first step toward becoming a CNE).

### Registering for the Exam

In the United States and Canada, Novell exams are administered by one of two professional testing organizations: Prometric or Virtual University Enterprises (VUE). If you take a Novell-authorized course, your instructor will probably be able to give you information about where to take the exam locally. Otherwise, to find a location that administers this exam, simply call one of the following numbers:

> ► Novell Education, at 1-800-233-EDUC (toll-free in Canada and the United States) or 1-801-861-3382.

> ► Prometric, at 1-800-RED-TEST or 1-800-RED-EXAM (both toll-free in Canada and the United States), or 1-952-820-5706.

> ► Virtual University Enterprises (VUE), at 1-800-TEST-CNE (toll-free in Canada and the United States) or 1-952-995-8970.

Outside of the United States and Canada, contact your local Novell office, a local Prometric office, or a VUE office.

When you call the testing organization, you'll be asked to provide the following information: your testing ID (which is your Social Security Number if you are in the United States), name, organization, address, telephone number, exam title, exam number, and method of payment (credit card is recommended).

The standard fee for the exam at the time of this writing is $100. When you register for the exam, write down the name of the testing center, the address, phone number, driving directions to the testing center, the exam date and time, as well as the final date and time you can call to reschedule or cancel the exam without penalty. Also, confirm that the exam number you have requested is the correct one. You should also confirm the exam format (form or adaptive), the time limit, and the total number of questions.

## What Is the Exam Like?

The NetWare 5.1 Administration exam, like all Novell exams, is computer based. In other words, you take the exam by answering questions on the computer. However, unlike more traditional exams, the NetWare 5.1 Administrator exam is also performance based. This means that instead of just asking you to regurgitate facts, the exam also requires you to apply your knowledge to solve problems. For example, the exam may include scenarios describing network problems or tasks (such as adding a user with specific properties). In those cases, you'll need to use simulations of NetWare utilities to complete the tasks or solve the problems.

The exam is closed book and is graded on a pass/fail basis. You will not be allowed to take any notes into or out of the exam room, although the testing center should provide you with two pieces of paper and a pencil (or the equivalent) for temporary notes.

### Form Exams

The exam format, number of questions, and time limit varies, depending on when you take the exam. Novell changes these parameters from time to time. If you take the exam early in a product's life cycle, you'll probably be given a *form* exam. Form exams offer a fixed number of questions (and simulations) in a specific time period—such as 67 questions (including simulations) in 90 minutes.

### Adaptive Exams

Adaptive exams, on the other hand, offer questions of varying difficulty based on your last answer. In other words, the exam begins with a fairly easy question. If you answer it correctly, the next question is slightly more difficult. If you answer that one correctly, the next question is even more difficult. If you answer a question incorrectly, on the other hand, the next question is slightly easier. If you miss that one, too, the next will be easier yet, until you get one right (or reach the maximum number of questions allowed).

Adaptive exams allow less time than form exams, because they include fewer questions—typically 15-25 questions in 30, 45, or 60 minutes. The number of questions you'll be asked varies, depending on your level of knowledge. If you answer all the questions correctly, you'll be presented with the minimum number of questions. If you answer any questions incorrectly, you'll be asked one or more additional questions—up to the maximum allowed.

## Hints for Taking the Exam

Once you've completed your in-depth studies, it's time to take the test. Here are some hints you may find helpful while taking a Novell certification exam:

▶ Show up early and bring two appropriate forms of ID (one must have a picture and one must have a signature). Leave everything else in your car trunk or at home. (You will not be allowed to bring study materials into the exam room.)

▶ When you sit down at the computer, take a deep breath and try to relax. Try not to hyperventilate. (It will only make you dizzy.) The good news is that you'll probably find that taking exams usually tends to get a bit less nerve wracking after you've taken several of them.

▶ If this is your first certification exam, you may want to take the (sample) orientation exam before you take the real one, to get a general feel for how the exam process works. (On the sample exam, don't worry about getting the answers right—just concentrate on understanding the exam process itself.)

▶ Before you begin the actual exam, reconfirm the time limit, total number of questions, and whether questions must be answered sequentially, or if you can skip around and go back to previous questions. Also, make sure that the information on the opening screen is correct (such as your name, your testing ID, the exam title, and the exam number). If any of the information is incorrect — do not begin the exam! (Instead, discuss the matter with the exam administrator.)

▶ Keep track of the time. Don't be concerned, however, if a particularly complex question takes five minutes, because you will probably be able to answer other questions in 30 seconds or less. Don't panic if most of the early questions seem to be long and complex. If so, the later questions will hopefully be shorter and simpler.

▶ You'll be given something to write on during the exam (such as a pencil and paper, dry erase board and marker, laminated paper and grease pencil, and so on). Although you will not be able to leave the building with it, you may find that it comes in quite handy during the exam. As soon as you begin the exam, you may want to take a moment and write down those things you have memorized that you don't want to forget. Also, during the exam, you may want to write down anything important you see in an exam question that you think might help you later on.

▶ Read each question *carefully*. Don't glance at key words in a question and assume that you understand the question. (This is a very common mistake.) For example, some questions may ask you to indicate which statements are *not* correct.

▶ Remember that exam questions may be presented in a variety of different formats, including single-answer multiple choice, multiple-answer multiple choice, true/false, fill-in-the-blank, and drag-and-drop. You may also get a number of simulation (performance-based) questions and exhibit-related questions. In simulation situations, you may be asked to perform several sequential tasks.

▶ In most form exams, you're not allowed to skip ahead or go back—so be sure of your answer before you move on. If you simply do not know the correct answer, start by eliminating the answers that appear to be the most unlikely. Then, review each remaining answer to see if you can find anything subtle that would make it incorrect. Do not simply pick the answer that leaps out as the obvious correct answer—because it may be a trick!

▶ In questions that require multiple answers, be sure that you select the correct number of choices.

▶ In any situation where multiple screens are involved (such as simulations and those that include exhibits), use Alt+Tab to toggle between the screens and/or tile the windows to see more information onscreen at one time.

▶ Be careful about typographical errors.

▶ Don't waste mouse clicks on simulator questions. Plan ahead.

▶ These exams were developed by Novell Education. Therefore, it's generally best to give the answer found in the courseware, rather than, for example, relying on information found in some obscure Technical Information Document (TID) you found on the Web.

▶ When you finish the exam, be sure that you obtain the exam results printout from the exam administrator. It will list information such as the passing exam score required, your score, whether you passed, and any topics that you missed questions on. It will not, however, tell you which questions you missed.

If you fail the exam, take heart. You can take it again. In fact, you can take it again as many times as it takes to pass the exam (or until your checkbook runs dry, whichever comes first). Be aware that there may be a mandatory waiting period imposed, however, between each exam attempt. (Check with the testing center that you registered with for further details.) Because of the way the exam is designed, questions are drawn from a large database. Therefore, you may not get the same exam questions twice, no matter how often you take the exam.

## Checking Your Certification Status

To receive your official certification status, you must sign a Novell Education Certification Agreement and complete any exam requirements. The certification agreement contains the usual legal jargon you might expect with such certification. Among other things, the certification agreement grants you permission to use the trademarked name "CNA" on your resume or other advertising, as long as you use the name in connection with providing network administration services on a NetWare 5.1 network. It also reminds you that if the network administration services you offer don't live up to Novell's high standards of quality, Novell can require you to meet those standards within "a commercially reasonable time."

If you'd like to check your new or existing certification status, you can do so at http://www.novell.com/education/community/. At this site, you can do the following:

▸ Update your personal information, such as name, address, phone, fax, e-mail address, and so on

▸ View a list of certifications that you have already been awarded

▸ Verify the exams that you have already completed

This site requires a username and password, so you'll need to contact Novell CNA (or CNE) Administration if you don't know your username and password.

## For More Information

And, of course, you can always get more information about Novell products and services by surfing over to any of the Web sites described in Table A.3. Keep in mind that Novell changes its Web sites frequently. Therefore, URLs may change over time. If this happens, simply browse to the Novell home page and perform a search for the topic you're interested in. Remember, we're here for you, and *we care!*

T A B L E  A.3

*For More Information*

| TYPE OF INFORMATION | WEB SITE URL |
|---|---|
| Novell Education | `http://www.novell.com/education/` |
| Novell Education Contact Information (Phone Numbers) | `http://www.novell.com/education/about/contacts.html` |
| Novell Education Feedback (E-mail Addresses) | `http://www.novell.com/education/about/feedback.html` |
| Novell Certification Information | `http://www.novell.com/education/certinfo/` |
| Certification Headline News | `http://www.novell.com/education/certinfo/certnews.html` |
| Novell CNA Program Information | `http://www.novell.com/education/cna/` |
| Novell CNE Program Information | `http://www.novell.com/education/cne/` |
| Novell Certification Brochure | `http://www.novell.com/education/certinfo/certbroc.pdf` |
| Novell Certification Explorer | `http://www.novell.com/education/certinfo/explorer.html` |
| Continuing Certification Requirements | `http://www.novell.com/education/certinfo/cneccr.html` |
| Novell Training Options | `http://www.novell.com/education/training/index.html` |
| Novell Authorized Training Locator | `http://www.novell.com/education/locator/` |
| Novell Press | `http://www.novell.com/books` |
| IDG Books | `http://www.idgbooks.com/` |
| CyberStateU.com (an official Novell Online Training Provider) | `http://www.cyberstateu.com` |
| Novell Education Certification Agreement | `http://www.novell.com/education/certinfo/certagrm.html` |
| Novell Testing Information | `http://www.novell.com/education/testinfo/` |
| CNENET (for current CNEs; requires username and PIN) | `http://cnenet.novell.com/` |

**TABLE A.3**

*For More Information*
*(continued)*

| TYPE OF INFORMATION | WEB SITE URL |
| --- | --- |
| Novell Education Personal Status Information (for current CNAs and CNEs; requires username and PIN) | http://www.novell.com/education/community/ |
| Novell, Inc. | http://www.novell.com/ |
| NetWare 5.1 Home Page | http://www.novell.com/products/netware/ |
| Novell Online Documentation | http://www.novell.com/documentation/ |
| Novell Technical Support | http://support.novell.com/ |

# Cross-Reference to Novell Course Objectives

**N**ovell's *CNA Study Guide for NetWare 5.1* enables you to learn the Novell-authorized course objectives (see the page-number cross-references) in conjunction with Novell-authorized courseware. This appendix clarifies that relationship by pointing you in the right direction.

Have fun and good luck!

# Section 1: Introduction to NetWare and NDS

1. Identify what a network is and list its components: **2–27, 81–88.**

2. Identify the features of NetWare: **2–27.**

3. List the responsibilities of a Network Administrator: **4.**

4. Install the Novell Client software and perform the login procedure: **88–95.**

5. List the resources and services you administer: **2–27.**

6. Identify the features of Novell Directory Services: **37–42.**

7. Browse the NDS tree: **43–57, 128–138, 142–157.**

8. Identify how the NDS tree affects resource access: **58–72, 148–151.**

# Section 2: Using a Workstation

1. Describe how a workstation communicates with the network: **82–88.**

2. Identify workstation hardware and its functions: **84–88.**

3. Identify workstation software and its functions: **84–88.**

**4.** Identify the components of a workstation dataflow model: **86–88.**

**5.** List the configuration options for the Novell Client and Windows: **88–95.**

**6.** Identify network resources: **81–88, 148–151.**

**7.** Identify browser configurations: **96–100, 136–138.**

# Section 3: Setting Up and Managing Network Access for Users

**1.** Identify the function of the User object: **54, 139.**

**2.** Create and modify NDS objects using ConsoleOne: **144–147, 158–171.**

**3.** Create and modify User accounts using NetWare Administrator: **140–144, 158–171.**

**4.** Identify the types of network security provided by NetWare: **256–257.**

**5.** Determine and establish login security: **257–274.**

# Section 4: Managing the File System

**1.** Identify the basic components of the network file system: **178–179.**

**2.** Identify guidelines for planning and creating custom volumes in the network file system: **180–183, 190–192.**

**3.** List the system-created directories and identify their contents and functions: **183–186.**

# Section 5: Managing File System Security

# Section 6: Creating and Managing Login Scripts

**4.** Create and execute login scripts: **120–127.**

**5.** Edit login scripts using the LOGIN utility: **92–95.**

# Section 7: Managing NDS Security

**I.** Define NDS security: **275.**

**2.** Identify how NDS security differs from file system security: **325–326.**

**3.** Control access to NDS objects: **281–301.**

**4.** Determine rights granted to NDS objects: **275–281.**

**5.** Block inherited rights: **281–301.**

**6.** Determine effective rights: **293–301.**

**7.** Troubleshoot NDS security problems: **316.**

# Section 8: Securing the NDS Tree

**I.** List and explain NDS default rights: **302–306.**

**2.** List and explain guidelines for implementing NDS security: **312–314.**

**3.** Compare centralized and distributed administration: **307–310.**

**4.** Determine administrative roles and rights assignments: **310–312.**

# Section 9: Implementing Novell Distributed Print Services

**1.** Describe the purpose and function of NDPS: **440–446**.

**2.** Describe the differences between queue-based printing and NDPS: **446–449**.

**3.** Explain the four NDPS components and their functions: **450–460**.

**4.** Explain the difference between Controlled Access printers and Public Access printers: **457–459**.

**5.** Configure the network for NDPS: **461–468, 474–487**.

**6.** Configure workstations to print to NDPS printers: **468–473, 474–487**.

# Section 10: Using ZENworks to Manage Workstations

**1.** Identify ZENworks design guidelines: **361–364**.

**2.** Install the ZENworks 2.0 Starter Pack: **364–379**.

**3.** Define the Workstation Manager component of ZENworks: **380–382**.

**4.** Determine workstation management needs: **380, 393–397**.

**5.** Configure the Search Policy in a Container Policy Package: **383–397, 405–412**.

**6.** Register workstations in NDS: **397–401, 405–412**.

**7.** Important Workstation objects into NDS: **401–404, 405–412**.

**8.** Explain how policies are applied in NDS: **393–397**.

**9.** Identify policy package problems and solutions: **393–397**.

# Section 11: Using ZENworks to Manage Applications

**1.** Identify how Application Launcher leverages NDS: **416–422**.

**2.** Create Application object templates for applications: **422–424**.

**3.** Configure Application objects for distribution: **424–428**.

**4.** Distribute applications using Application Launcher and Application Explorer: **424–428**.

# Section 12: Managing Resources in a Multicontainer Environment

**1.** Identify how NDS structure affects network administration: **35–57**.

**2.** Identify NDS planning guidelines: **58–59**.

**3.** Provide users with access to resources: **59–74**.

**4.** Configure shortcuts to access and to manage resources: **148–151**.

**5.** Identify guidelines for setting up resources in a multicontainer environment: **148–151, 313–317**.

**6.** Identify the actions and rights needed to grant access to NDS resources: **314–316.**

**7.** Create login scripts that identify resources in other contexts: **107–127.**

# Solutions to Puzzles and Exercises

# Chapter 1: Introduction to NetWare 5.1

## Lab Exercise 1.1: OneNet!

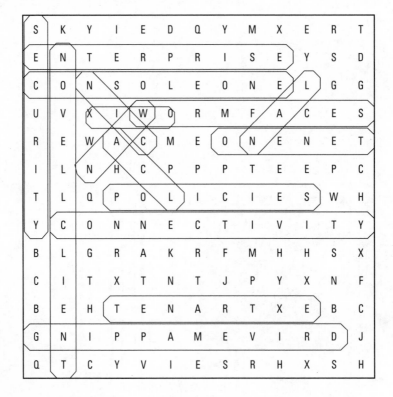

1. ACL
2. ACME
3. Connectivity
4. ConsoleOne
5. Drive Mapping

6. Enterprise
7. Extranet
8. LAN
9. NIC
10. Novell Client
11. OneNet
12. Policies
13. Security
14. WAN
15. Wormfaces

## Lab Exercise 1.2: Introduction to NetWare 5.1

Across:
1. NDPS
6. NETWORKING
7. INTRANET
9. GATEWAY
10. CNA
11. ZENWORKS
15. AUTHENTICATION

Down:
2. DIRECTORYMAP
3. INTERNET
4. CONTAINER
5. FILESYSTEM
8. NEDS
12. CONTEXT
13. CE
14. VOLUME

# Chapter 2: Novell Directory Services

## Lab Exercise 2.1: Getting to Know NDS (Matching)

### Part I

  1. L
  2. C
  3. L
  4. L
  5. C
  6. L
  7. L
  8. L
  9. L
 10. C

### Part II

  1. Container (Organizational Unit)
  2. Leaf
  3. Leaf
  4. Leaf
  5. Container (Organization)
  6. Leaf
  7. Container (Country or Organizational Unit)
  8. Leaf
  9. Organizational Unit
 10. Leaf

## Lab Exercise 2.2: Understanding NDS Naming

1. .BMasterson.BLUE.CRIME.TOKYO.ACME
2. .CN=RHood.OU=WHITE.OU=CRIME.OU=TOKYO.O=ACME
3. CRIME.TOKYO.ACME
4. CN=BLUE-SRV1.OU=BLUE.OU=CRIME.OU=TOKYO.O=ACME (because the default current context is the [Root])
5. SHolmes
6. LJohn.WHITE.CRIME
7. CN=SirKay.OU=CHARITY.
8. Admin...
9. CN=BThomas.OU=PR..
10. CN=BLUE-SRV1_SYS.OU=BLUE.OU=CRIME.OU=TOKYO.O=ACME....
11. .BLUE.CRIME.TOKYO.ACME (because it's the context of the server)
    LOGIN .DHolliday.BLUE.CRIME.TOKYO.ACME
    LOGIN DHolliday (because NetWare 5.1 searches the server's context by default)
12. CX CHARITY..
13. LOGIN .CN=SHolmes.OU=CRIME.OU=TOKYO.O=ACME
    LOGIN .SHolmes.CRIME.TOKYO.ACME
    LOGIN SHolmes.
    LOGIN CN=SHolmes.
    LOGIN SHolmes.CRIME..
    LOGIN CN=SHolmes.OU=CRIME..
    LOGIN SHolmes.CRIME.TOKYO...
    LOGIN CN=SHolmes.OU=CRIME.OU=TOKYO...
    LOGIN SHolmes.CRIME.TOKYO.ACME....
    LOGIN CN=SHolmes.OU=CRIME.OU=TOKYO.O=ACME....
14. CX /R

## Lab Exercise 2.3: Plant a Tree in a Cloud

```
O  R  G  A  N  I  Z  A  T  I  O  N  Q  O  E  R  X  V  I  O
R  B  I  N  D  E  R  Y  R  T  N  U  O  C  U  R  R  E  N  T
G  L  J  C  H  V  I  K  W  V  J  N  U  G  X  X  N  X  E  W
A  J  Q  E  T  D  O  I  R  E  P  G  N  I  L  I  A  R  T  S
N  G  W  H  C  L  I  C  P  W  B  K  O  S  G  Y  T  Y  W  Q
I  H  X  Y  S  T  G  U  H  J  T  Y  Y  O  B  S  P  M  A  L
Z  X  L  I  G  Q  I  Y  Q  O  D  A  L  K  Y  E  E  H  R  N
A  B  Y  D  P  I  Z  V  G  G  V  N  T  G  F  M  B  D  E  P
T  X  G  N  A  T  U  R  A  L  G  R  O  U  P  G  E  W  S  R
I  G  R  C  C  I  W  K  O  Q  O  N  L  X  P  Y  U  Y  E  E
O  R  G  A  N  I  Z  A  T  I  O  N  A  L  R  O  L  E  R  L
N  T  Y  P  E  L  E  S  S  N  A  M  E  G  M  Q  I  V  V  C
A  R  C  J  O  J  R  V  M  M  T  H  X  T  O  C  B  V  E  C
L  E  A  D  I  N  G  P  E  R  I  O  D  N  E  W  L  M  R  I
U  G  Z  G  B  I  C  C  M  P  Y  O  X  U  Z  X  V  L  D  P
N  U  Q  N  J  U  E  R  D  Y  N  L  Q  F  Q  P  X  M  P  L
I  H  Z  R  W  J  T  M  N  Q  N  O  F  Y  V  G  Q  L  G  N
T  K  S  C  J  D  F  D  G  X  T  R  W  E  S  B  I  J  U  Z
```

1. Bindery
2. Country
3. Current
4. CX
5. Leading Period
6. Login
7. Natural Group
8. NetWare Server
9. Object
10. Organization
11. Organizational Role
12. Organizational Unit
13. Trailing Period
14. Typeful Name
15. Typeless Name

## Lab Exercise 2.4: Novell Directory Services

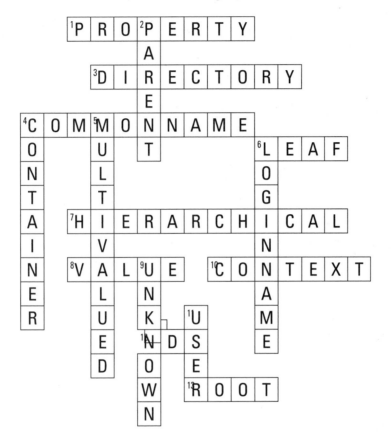

· · · · · · · · · · · · · · · · · · · · · · · · · · · ◄

# Chapter 3: NetWare 5.1 Connectivity

## Lab Exercise 3.2: Configuring ACME'S Login Scripts

```
*  This TF-GP Profile login script was designed by Cathryn Ettelson on August 1, 2000.

*  Map network and search drives.

MAP INS S1:=WHITE-SRV1_SYS:PUBLIC
```

```
REM  MAP S16:= WHITE-SRV1_SYS:APPS\WHITE\TF-GP

REM MAP S:= WHITE-SRV1_SYS:SHARED\WHITE\TF-GP

REM MAP ROOT U:= WHITE-SRV1_SYS:USERS\WHITE\TF-GP\%HOME_DIRECTORY

*  Display greeting.

WRITE "Good %GREETING_TIME, %FULL_NAME"

WRITE "Today is %DAY_OF_WEEK, %MONTH_NAME, %DAY, %YEAR."

WRITE "You are logging into the network from Station %STATION."

*  Display important news.

REM DISPLAY WHITE-SRV1_SYS:SHARED\WHITE\TF-GP\MESSAGE.TXT

*  Display Wednesday Staff Meeting advisory.

IF DAY_OF_WEEK="Wednesday" THEN BEGIN

   WRITE "Staff meeting today is at 9:00 a.m."

WRITE "in Conference Room 3-D"

   FIRE PHASERS 2

   PAUSE
END

*  Run Dr. Watson's login script for task force managers.

REM IF MEMBER OF "TF-GPMGR" THEN INCLUDE .DrWatson.WHITE.CRIME.TOKYO.ACME
```

(**Note:** In an actual login script, each command should appear on its own line. In the example above, however, some commands are split across multiple lines because of margin limitations in this book.)

## Lab Exercise 3.4: Building ACME's NDS Tree

### Part III: Special Cases

1. Each site needs a revolving administrator. Consider creating an Organizational Role object under each location OU. Use the following naming standard:

    ```
    NORAD-Admin in OU=NORAD.O=ACME

    RIO-Admin in OU=RIO.O=ACME
    ```

```
CAM-Admin in OU=CAMELOT.O=ACME

SYD-Admin in OU=SYDNEY.O=ACME

TOK-Admin in OU=TOKYO.O=ACME
```

Then, assign the divisional administrator as the first occupant in each location: AEinstein, GWashington, KingArthur, Gandhi, and SHolmes, respectively.

2. Next, create a common Profile login script object for all the administrators to share. It should be called ADMIN-Profile and placed in the O=ACME container. Remember, shared objects are placed higher in the tree. Finally, associate each Organizational Role with the shared login script by referencing the Profile object within each Organizational Role's Login Script property.

3. If the Human Rights (HR) tracking program is constantly changing, consider creating a Directory Map object. Then, all the HR login scripts can point to the Directory map object rather than the physical application directory. In this case, create a Directory Map object called HR-App and place it in the .OU=HR.OU=SYDNEY.O=ACME container. Then, place the following directory in the Directory Map object's Path property:

```
HR-SRV1_SYS:APPS\HRT
```

4. In addition, each of the HR administrators needs access to the Human Rights tracking application in HR-SRV1_SYS:APPS\HRT. Security could be a problem. Create a Group leaf object called HR-Group and place it in the .OU=HR.OU= SYDNEY.O=ACME container. Then, create a Group Membership list containing each of the HR administrators — Gandhi, ASchweitzer, MTeresa, FNightingale, and Buddha.

5. The people in the Auditing department need easy access to the Financial resources. There's a simple solution, and it allows the auditors to access these resources from within their home OU=AUDIT container. Simply create an Alias object for .OU=FIN.OU=OPS.OU=CAMELOT.O=ACME and place it in the OU=AUDIT container. The Alias will point to the original objects from within the auditor's home context.

6. In addition, the auditors and financial accountants need access to the ever-changing financial database program. In this case, create a Directory Map object called FIN-App and place it in the .OU=AUDIT.OU=ADMIN.OU=RIO.O=ACME and .OU=FIN.OU=OPS.OU=CAMELOT.O=ACME containers. Then, place the following directory in the Directory Map object's Path property:

```
CAM-FIN-SRV1_SYS:APPS\FIN
```

7. The same holds true for the auditing application, except this time only the auditors need access to the Directory Map object. In this case, create a Directory Map object called AUD-App and place it in the .OU=AUDIT.OU=ADMIN.OU=RIO.O=ACME container. Then, place the following directory in the Directory Map object's Path property:

```
AUDIT-SRV1_SYS:APPS\AUDIT
```

8. To accommodate traveling users, consider creating corresponding Alias objects for them at the very top of the ACME tree. This way, they can log in from anywhere with a simple name context. For example, MCurie's alias becomes .MCurie.ACME. That's a big improvement over MCurie.NUC.R&D.LABS.NORAD.ACME. To accomplish this, create three user Alias objects (MCurie, AEinstein, and DHoliday) and place them in the O=ACME container.

9. Everyone in the Crime Fighting division needs access to a common login script. Simply create a Profile login script called CRIME-profile and place it in the .OU=CRIME.OU=TOKYO.O=ACME container. Don't forget to add CRIME-profile to each user's Login Script property.

10. To empower Leonardo's scientists, you'll need to create an Organizational Role called R&D-Admin. Place it in the OU=R&D.OU=LABS.OU=NORAD.O=ACME container and give the Organizational Role administrative rights over all R&D resources. Then, you can rotate the scientists through the organizational role, starting with LDaVinci. Make him the first occupant.

## Lab Exercise 3.5: Connecting to the NetWare 5.1 Network

```
B  U  L  K  L  O  A  D  C  E  L  P  T  M
R  W  O  H  U  C  E  K  L  Q  Y  I  T  M
E  O  G  T  P  I  B  G  R  P  C  N  K  A
A  O  I  F  D  I  S  P  L  A  Y  F  K  P
K  J  N  Z  Z  E  B  K  P  V  M  N  N  D
S  V  S  U  W  D  M  X  Q  L  N  E  E  I
T  H  C  F  I  R  E  P  H  A  S  E  R  S
A  G  R  E  E  T  I  N  G  T  I  M  E  P
T  U  I  S  T  E  N  T  B  Q  X  C  H  L
I  F  P  Q  X  T  C  Y  E  I  M  R  Q  A
O  Z  T  M  A  P  L  O  I  F  D  V  O  Y
N  O  D  E  F  A  U  L  T  M  N  B  A  F
K  P  H  D  U  U  D  I  M  M  G  U  Y  S
Q  J  J  O  J  S  E  W  V  X  S  P  S  R
N  B  A  F  B  E  N  Q  H  C  Q  Q  M  L
```

1. BREAK
2. BULKLOAD
3. FDISPLAY
4. FIRE PHASERS
5. GREETING_TIME
6. INCLUDE
7. LOGIN SCRIPT
8. MAP
9. MAP DISPLAY

10. NO_DEFAULT
11. PAUSE
12. REMARK
13. STATION
14. TEN
15. WRITE

## Lab Exercise 3.6: Let Me In!

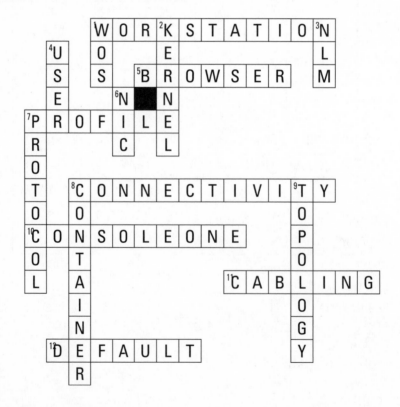

# Chapter 4: NetWare 5.1 File System

### Lab Exercise 4.3: Mapping Drives with MAP

1. MAP /?
2. MAP
3. MAP U:=SYS:USERS\WHITE\%HOME_DIRECTORY
4. MAP G:=SYS:\SHARED\POL
5. MAP J:=F:
6. MAP S:=.WHITE.SRV1_SYS.WHITE.CRIME.TOKYO.ACME:SHARED
7. MAP INS S1:=SYS:\PUBLIC
8. MAP INS S2:=SYS:\PUBLIC\IBM_PC\MSDOS\V6.22
9. MAP S3:=APPS\SS30
10. MAP ROOT S4:=SYS:\APPS\DB50
11. At the DOS prompt, a false root has no space after the volume name, but it does have a space followed by a backslash after the name of the directory it points to.
    In the Results window, a false root has no space after the volume name, but it does have a space followed by a backslash after the name of the directory it points to.
12. MAP S5:=W:=SYS:\APPS\WP70
13. The Z: drive letter would now be pointing to the root of the volume instead of SYS:PUBLIC — which means that the corresponding search drive (such as S1:) would also be pointing to the wrong location. To fix the problem, you could type CD \PUBLIC at the DOS prompt to modify the path that the drive letter points to.
14. MAP DEL J:
15. MAP REM S3:
    The search drives with higher search drive numbers would be renumbered accordingly.
    The network drive associated with the search drive would be deleted.
16. MAP C S4:
    The search drive would be deleted.
    The network drive associated with the search drive would be moved to the top portion of the map list.

## Lab Exercise 4.5: File Cabinet of Life

```
Y  D  I  R  E  C  T  O  R  Y  J  M  O  U  P
P  U  R  G  E  E  J  F  P  X  B  L  K  K  J
O  O  D  A  T  A  M  I  G  R  A  T  I  O  N
C  T  T  B  K  T  D  N  G  O  E  C  P  Q  N
N  E  T  W  O  R  K  D  R  I  V  E  H  K  M
S  S  E  A  R  C  H  D  R  I  V  E  M  G  O
U  X  K  W  R  U  N  D  I  R  H  S  I  M  J
F  I  L  E  C  O  M  P  R  E  S  S  I  O  N
I  I  A  J  B  T  K  M  C  S  E  T  I  G  L
L  T  L  U  F  E  H  T  F  U  G  O  F  Y  Q
E  G  H  E  U  J  R  P  B  D  A  F  V  D  Q
R  M  N  V  S  Q  J  R  G  A  V  U  Z  T  O
F  U  N  U  W  C  R  F  A  W  L  D  R  M  Z
L  H  I  W  Z  F  A  Z  T  R  A  C  Q  F  Q
Y  H  W  C  I  J  E  N  Q  P  S  T  K  U  T
```

1. CREATE
2. DATA MIGRATION
3. DIRECTORY
4. FILE COMPRESSION
5. FILE SCAN
6. FILER
7. NCOPY
8. NDIR

9. NETWORK DRIVE
10. PURGE
11. READ
12. SALVAGE
13. SEARCH DRIVE
14. SET
15. USER

## Lab Exercise 4.6: NetWare 5.1 File System

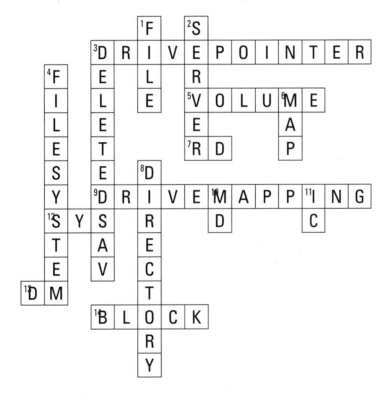

▶ · · · · · · · · · · · · · · · · · · · · · · · · · · · · · · · · · ◀

# Chapter 5: NetWare 5.1 Security

## Lab Exercise 5.1: Calculating NDS Effective Rights

### Case #1

In this case, we are helping Sherlock Holmes gain administrative rights to the Crime Fighting division of ACME. Refer to Figure C5.1 for the completed effective rights calculation worksheet.

▶ · · · · · · · · · · · · · · · · · · · · · · · · · · · · · · · · · ◀

**FIGURE C.I**

*Calculating NDS effective rights — Case #1*

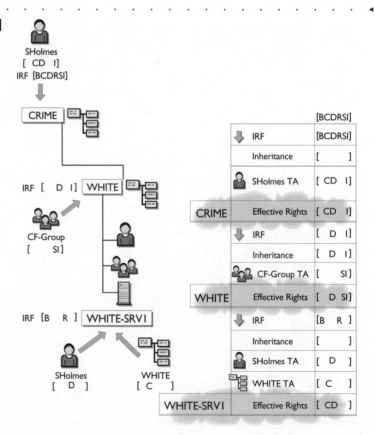

As you can see from the figure, Sherlock Holmes is granted [ CD I] rights to the .OU=CRIME Organizational Unit. Because he has no rights from any other source and explicit trustee assignments override the Inherited Rights Filter (IRF) for this container, his effective rights for the CRIME Organizational Unit are the same — [ CD I].

These rights then flow down to the .OU=WHITE Organizational Unit as inherited rights, where they are partially blocked by an IRF of [ D I] — leaving inherited rights of [ D I]. Sherlock Holmes also gets the [ SI] rights to the WHITE Organizational Unit as a member of the CF-Group object. If you add his individually inherited rights of [ D I] to the group-inherited [ SI] rights, you'll find that his effective rights for the WHITE container are [ D SI]. (**Note:** The fact that he has the [ SI] object rights means that he implicitly has all object rights and all property rights for this object. However, the Supervisor right stands alone when it comes to the IRF . . . as you're about to see in the next section).

Finally, Sherlock's effective rights of [ D SI] in the WHITE container flow down and become inherited rights at the WHITE-SRV1 server, where they are totally blocked by the IRF of [B R ]. (Even though he implicitly had all rights to the WHITE container, implied rights do not flow down — only explicit rights. Also, remember, that the [ S ] right *can* be blocked by an IRF in the NDS tree.) Sherlock Holmes does, however, receive an explicit trustee assignment of [ D ] to the WHITE-SRV1 server as an individual. Also, his home container, the WHITE Organizational Unit, receives a trustee assignment of [ C ] — meaning that his effective rights for the WHITE-SRV1 server are [ CD ].

### Case #2

After careful consideration, you decide that the previous rights are inadequate for Sherlock and his administrative needs. So, let's try it one more time. But, in this case, we're going to use the CF-Role Organizational Role instead of the CF-Group. This gives us more administrative flexibility and narrows the scope of rights assignments. Refer to Figure C5.2 for the completed effective rights calculation worksheet.

In Case #2, Sherlock Holmes receives an explicit trustee assignment of [B R ] to the CRIME Organizational Unit. Because he has no rights from other sources, and an explicit assignment overrides the IRF, his effective rights in the CRIME Organizational Unit are [B R ].

▶ · · · · · · · · · · · · · · · · · · · · · · · · · · · · · · · ◀

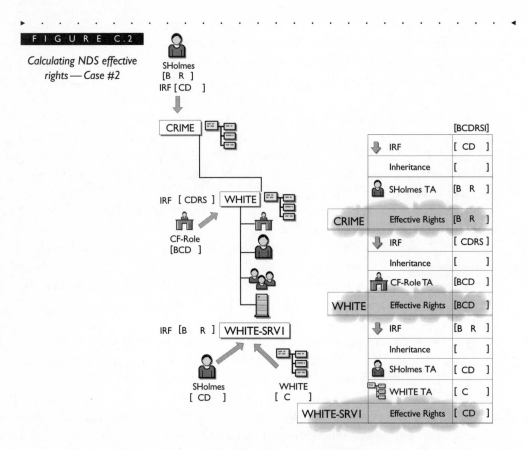

FIGURE C.2

*Calculating NDS effective rights — Case #2*

These rights would usually flow down and become inherited rights at the WHITE Organizational Unit. However, NetWare 5 requires the Inherited [I] right in order for rights to flow down the tree. Because Sherlock Holmes doesn't have the Inherited [I] right at CRIME, he won't inherit the [B  R  ] rights in the WHITE subcontainer. Interesting, huh? Therefore, his effective rights in WHITE are the same as his explicit rights from the CF-Role Organizational Role object — that is, [BCD  ].

Similarly, Sherlock's effective rights to the WHITE-SRV1 Server object are simply a combination of the individual rights he gains as SHolmes and the ancestral rights he gains from his home container (OU=WHITE). In this case, the IRF is meaningless because there are no inherited rights due to the lack of the [I] right in the parent container.

Bottom line — Sherlock Holmes' effective rights to the WHITE-SRV1 object are [ CD  ]. Viola!!

### Case #3

In this final case, let's bounce over to the .BLUE.CRIME.TOKYO.ACME container and help out Wyatt Earp — their administrator. Refer to Figure C5.3 for the completed effective rights calculation worksheet.

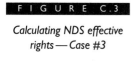

FIGURE C.3

*Calculating NDS effective rights — Case #3*

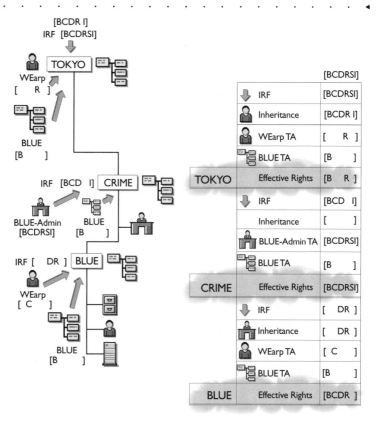

In Case #3, Wyatt Earp inherits [BCDR I] rights to the TOKYO Organizational Unit through a trustee assignment to his User object somewhere higher in the tree. These rights are then filtered by the Tokyo Organizational Unit's IRF of [BCDRSI] — which allows all five rights to flow through. He doesn't get to keep these rights, however, because his User object receives a new trustee assignment to the Tokyo Organizational Unit at this level — and such an assignment blocks inheritance from his User object from higher in the tree. Wyatt Earp does, however, receive the [B    ] trustee right for the TOKYO Organizational Unit from the Blue Organizational Unit, which is his home container, and the [ R ] right from his User object. This means that his inherited rights for the TOKYO container are [B    ] plus [ R ] or [B R ].

None of these rights flows down to the CRIME subcontainer because there's no Inherited [I] right in the TOKYO parent. It doesn't matter, though, because Wyatt Earp receives an explicit trustee assignment of all rights to CRIME through his BLUE-Admin Organizational Role object. This overshadows his [B    ] rights from BLUE and gives him effective rights for the CRIME Organizational Unit of [BCDRSI].

Finally, these rights flow down and become inherited rights at the BLUE Organizational Unit and are partially blocked by an IRF of [ DR ] — leaving inherited rights of [ DR ]. (Remember, the [    S] right *can* be blocked by an IRF in the NDS tree.) Wyatt Earp also receives the [ C  ] right to the BLUE Organizational Unit from his User object and the [B    ] right from the BLUE Organizational Unit, which is his home container. This means that his effective rights to the BLUE Organizational Unit are the [ DR ] rights, which he received through inheritance; plus the [ C  ] right, which he received from his User object; plus the [B    ] right, which he received from the BLUE Organizational Unit — or [BCDR ].

## Lab Exercise 5.3: Calculating File System Effective Rights

### Case #1

See Figure C5.4 for the answer to this case.

FIGURE C.4

*Calculating file system effective rights — Case #1*

| SYS: SHARED | S | R | W | C | E | M | F | A |
|---|---|---|---|---|---|---|---|---|
| Inherited Rights Filter | S | R | W | C | E | M | F | A |
| Inherited Rights — User | | | | | | | | |
| Inherited Rights — Group | | | | | | | | |
| Trustee Assignment — User | | R | W | C | | | F | |
| Trustee Assignment — Group | | | | | | | | |
| Effective Rights | | R | W | C | | | F | |

| SYS: SHARED\CYBER | S | R | W | C | E | M | F | A |
|---|---|---|---|---|---|---|---|---|
| Inherited Rights Filter | S | R | | | | | F | |
| Inherited Rights — User | | R | | | | | F | |
| Inherited Rights — Group | | | | | | | | |
| Trustee Assignment — User | | | | | | | | |
| Trustee Assignment — Group | | | | | | | | |
| Effective Rights | | R | | | | | F | |

| CYBER.DOC | S | R | W | C | E | M | F | A |
|---|---|---|---|---|---|---|---|---|
| Inherited Rights Filter | | R | W | C | | | F | |
| Inherited Rights — User | | R | | | | | F | |
| Inherited Rights — Group | | | | | | | | |
| Trustee Assignment — User | | | | | | | | |
| Trustee Assignment — Group | | | | | | | | |
| Effective Rights | | R | | | | | F | |

## Case #2

See Figure C5.5 for the answer to this case.

▶ · · · · · · · · · · · · · · · · · · · · · · · ◀

**FIGURE C.5**

*Calculating file system effective rights — Case #2*

| SYS: SHARED | S | R | W | C | E | M | F | A |
|---|---|---|---|---|---|---|---|---|
| Inherited Rights Filter | S | R | W | C | E | M | F | A |
| Inherited Rights — User | | | | | | | | |
| Inherited Rights — Group | | | | | | | | |
| Trustee Assignment — User | | R | W | C | | | F | |
| Trustee Assignment — Group | | | | | | | | |
| Effective Rights | | R | W | C | | | F | |

| SYS: SHARED\CRIME | S | R | W | C | E | M | F | A |
|---|---|---|---|---|---|---|---|---|
| Inherited Rights Filter | S | | | | | | | A |
| Inherited Rights — User | | | | | | | | |
| Inherited Rights — Group | | | | | | | | |
| Trustee Assignment — User | | | | | | | | |
| Trustee Assignment — Group | | R | W | C | E | M | F | |
| Effective Rights | | R | W | C | E | M | F | |

| CRIME.DB | S | R | W | C | E | M | F | A |
|---|---|---|---|---|---|---|---|---|
| Inherited Rights Filter | S | R | W | C | | | F | |
| Inherited Rights — User | | | | | | | | |
| Inherited Rights — Group | | | | | | | | |
| Trustee Assignment — User | | | | | | | | |
| Trustee Assignment — Group | | R | | | | | F | |
| Effective Rights | | R | | | | | F | |

## Case #3

See Figure C5.6 for the answer to this case.

FIGURE C.6

*Calculating file system effective rights — Case #3*

| SYS: SHARED | S | R | W | C | E | M | F | A |
|---|---|---|---|---|---|---|---|---|
| Inherited Rights Filter | S | R | W | C | E | M | F | A |
| Inherited Rights — User | | | | | | | | |
| Inherited Rights — Group | | | | | | | | |
| Trustee Assignment — User | | | | | | | | |
| Trustee Assignment — Group | | R | W | C | E | | F | |
| Effective Rights | | R | W | C | E | | F | |

| SYS: SHARED\POL | S | R | W | C | E | M | F | A |
|---|---|---|---|---|---|---|---|---|
| Inherited Rights Filter | S | | | | | | | |
| Inherited Rights — User | | | | | | | | |
| Inherited Rights — Group | | | | | | | | |
| Trustee Assignment — User | | | | | | M | | A |
| Trustee Assignment — Group | | R | W | C | E | | F | |
| Effective Rights | | R | W | C | E | M | F | A |

| CRIME.RPT | S | R | W | C | E | M | F | A |
|---|---|---|---|---|---|---|---|---|
| Inherited Rights Filter | S | R | W | C | E | M | F | A |
| Inherited Rights — User | | | | | | M | | A |
| Inherited Rights — Group | | R | W | C | E | | F | |
| Trustee Assignment — User | | | | | | | | |
| Trustee Assignment — Group | | | | | | | | |
| Effective Rights | | R | W | C | E | M | F | A |

## Case #4

See Figure C5.7 for the answer to this case.

▶ · · · · · · · · · · · · · · · · · · · · · · · · · · · · · · · ◀

**FIGURE C.7**

*Calculating file system effective rights — Case #4*

| SYS: SHARED | S | R | W | C | E | M | F | A |
|---|---|---|---|---|---|---|---|---|
| Inherited Rights Filter | S | R | W | C | E | M | F | A |
| Inherited Rights — User | | | | | | | | |
| Inherited Rights — Group | | | | | | | | |
| Trustee Assignment — User | S | R | W | C | E | M | F | A |
| Trustee Assignment — Group | | | | | | | | |
| Effective Rights | S | R | W | C | E | M | F | A |

| SYS: SHARED\CRIME | S | R | W | C | E | M | F | A |
|---|---|---|---|---|---|---|---|---|
| Inherited Rights Filter | S | | | | | | | |
| Inherited Rights — User | S | | | | | | | |
| Inherited Rights — Group | | | | | | | | |
| Trustee Assignment — User | | | | | | | | |
| Trustee Assignment — Group | | R | W | C | | | F | |
| Effective Rights | S | R | W | C | (E) | (M) | F | (A) |

| CYBER.DB | S | R | W | C | E | M | F | A |
|---|---|---|---|---|---|---|---|---|
| Inherited Rights Filter | S | R | | | | | F | |
| Inherited Rights — User | S | | | | | | | |
| Inherited Rights — Group | | | | | | | | |
| Trustee Assignment — User | | | | | | | | |
| Trustee Assignment — Group | | R | | | | | F | |
| Effective Rights | S | R | (W) | (C) | (E) | (M) | F | (A) |

## Lab Exercise 5.5: Five-Layer Security Model

| T | T | S | G | R | A | C | E | L | O | G | I | N | S | T | R |
|---|---|---|---|---|---|---|---|---|---|---|---|---|---|---|---|
| P | R | O | P | E | R | T | Y | R | I | G | H | T | S | L | T |
| A | U | T | H | E | N | T | I | C | A | T | I | O | N | P | H |
| C | S | B | A | R | G | O | J | T | J | P | O | V | G | I | N |
| L | T | T | L | K | K | M | M | M | I | U | O | X | K | I | T |
| C | E | V | M | I | T | V | E | R | T | O | W | V | S | W | Z |
| M | E | F | F | E | C | T | I | V | E | R | I | G | H | T | S |
| D | R | O | B | J | E | C | T | R | I | G | H | T | S | W | Z |
| U | I | O | R | L | D | V | I | C | G | Y | X | S | I | Y | L |
| Q | G | R | E | N | A | M | E | I | S | Z | V | K | T | K | F |
| Y | H | D | F | M | D | N | N | H | O | D | J | D | I | H | Q |
| G | T | E | C | N | S | T | I | R | E | H | N | I | E | G | T |
| J | S | S | G | X | Q | W | B | X | L | C | N | I | C | F | N |

1. ACL
2. Authentication
3. Create
4. Delete
5. Effective Rights
6. Grace Logins
7. Group
8. Inheritance
9. IRF
10. Object Rights
11. Property Rights
12. [Public] (**Note:** Don't enter the brackets ([]).)
13. Rename
14. Trustee Rights
15. TTS

## Lab Exercise 5.6: NetWare 5.1 Security

```
        W
   ²M O D ³I  F Y        ⁴S              ⁵T
        R    N              U              E
        M    H    ⁶S        P              M
        F   ⁷E R A S E      E              P
        A    R    M    ⁸R E A D            L
        C    I         V              A
        E    T         I              A
        S   ⁹A C C E S S C O N T R O L
             B         O              E
             L        ¹⁰B R O ¹¹W S E
             E              R
                  ¹²A T T R I B U T E S
                    D         T
                  ¹³C O M P A R E
                    I
        ¹⁴A C C O U N T I N G
```

# Chapter 6: NetWare 5.1 Workstation Management

## Lab Exercise 6.4: ZENworks 2.0

```
P  U  B  L  I  C  S  Y  S  V  F  H  U  N  Q  S
O  S  M  W  L  Q  O  O  B  G  W  R  O  Y  A  R
L  C  D  I  S  A  B  L  E  D  T  I  L  W  X  N
I  H  W  V  D  S  N  A  P  P  S  H  O  T  K  D
C  E  U  S  E  R  P  R  O  F  I  L  E  S  K  N
Y  D  W  O  R  K  S  T  A  T  I  O  N  D  K  M
P  U  L  L  D  I  S  T  R  I  B  U  T  I  O  N
A  L  Y  E  P  H  G  L  X  Q  E  Z  C  B  R  O
C  E  I  Y  K  H  Q  H  Q  Q  E  D  V  B  M  N
K  R  E  U  F  L  H  H  T  W  R  Q  K  X  B  E
A  X  S  U  P  E  R  V  I  S  O  R  A  X  G  Y
G  O  R  B  J  H  D  E  Z  E  N  W  O  R  K  S
E  W  E  I  D  R  C  V  Y  A  G  O  C  N  E  D
R  J  A  P  P  L  I  C  A  T  I  O  N  R  J  P
```

1. AOT
2. Application
3. Disabled
4. Ignore
5. NAL
6. Policy Package
7. PUBLIC
8. Pull Distribution
9. Scheduler
10. snAppShot

11. Supervisor
12. User Profiles
13. Workstation
14. WSRIGHTS
15. ZENworks

## Lab Exercise 6.5: NetWare 5.1 Workstation Management

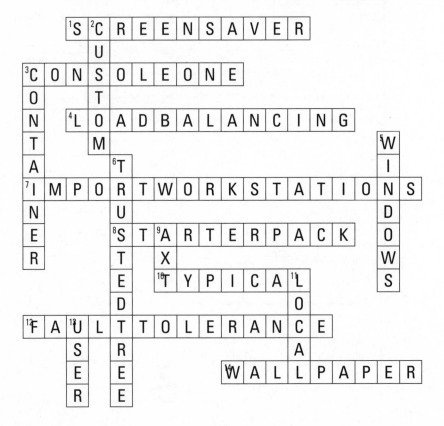

# Chapter 7: NetWare 5.1 Printing

## Lab Exercise 7.1: Understanding NDPS

1. b (NDPS Manager)
2. d (Printer driver)
3. a (NDPS Broker)
4. f (Public Access printer)
5. c (Printer Agent)
6. g (Controlled Access printer)
7. e (Printer gateway)

## Lab Exercise 7.3: The Mystery of NDPS

```
N  E  T  W  O  R  K  P  R  I  N  T  E  R  K  B  V
D  D  R  E  M  O  T  E  P  R  I  N  T  E  R  V  O
S  A  P  R  I  N  T  E  R  C  O  N  T  R  O  L  P
I  I  M  S  F  I  Y  J  B  K  F  O  W  N  C  L  A
N  E  G  W  B  E  P  L  L  K  M  F  G  F  T  K  Q
T  X  V  W  M  R  E  R  J  B  J  R  P  Y  E  N  O
E  V  E  N  T  N  O  T  I  F  I  C  A  T  I  O  N
G  W  P  T  Q  T  V  K  E  N  S  X  H  I  K  R  H
R  X  M  D  T  B  V  O  E  D  T  T  T  R  V  R  H
A  T  F  P  E  R  J  N  J  R  J  Q  P  U  B  J  X
T  N  G  N  I  R  U  T  P  A  C  X  U  V  D  O  V
I  G  P  K  N  O  V  E  L  L  G  A  T  E  W  A  Y
O  T  N  E  G  A  R  E  T  N  I  R  P  S  U  B  Z
N  Q  R  E  V  E  R  D  R  E  T  N  I  R  P  E  M
```

1. Capturing
2. Event Notification
3. NDPS Broker

4. NDS Integration
5. Network Printer
6. Novell Gateway
7. Print Queue
8. Printer Agent
9. Printer Control
10. Printer Driver
11. PSERVER
12. Remote Printer
13. RPM
14. SAP
15. Security

## Lab Exercise 7.4: NetWare 5.1 Printing

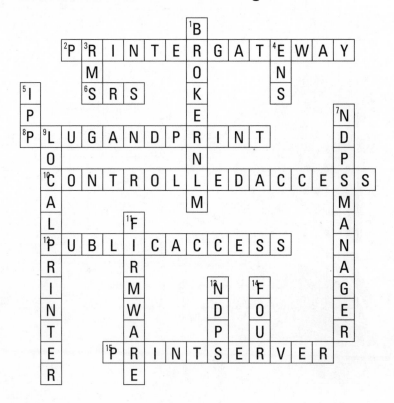

# NetWare 5.1 Installation

**N**etWare 5.1 can be installed using a variety of installation, upgrade, and migration methods. Only the Basic installation method is covered in this appendix. With this method, NetWare 5.1 can be installed from scratch. In other words, it assumes that the target computer does not contain any programs or data that must be retained.

Unlike earlier versions of NetWare, you no longer have to decide whether to perform a Simple or Custom installation before you begin. Instead, you simply install the NetWare 5.1 operating system and then choose whether or not to customize any parameters at the end of the process.

**When performing the lab exercises in this book, it is imperative that you use a nonproduction (that is, a practice) server in an isolated tree. You should use nonproduction workstation(s), as well.**

**TIP**

The NetWare 5.1 installation program provides the following features:

▶ *The Novell Installation Wizard* — This program uses a Java-based GUI during the later stages of the server installation process. (The earlier stages of the process still use a text-mode interface.)

▶ *Automatic hardware detection and selection of drivers* — The installation program attempts to auto-detect platform support modules, Peripheral-Component Interconnect (PCI) Hot Plug Support modules, storage adapters, storage devices (such as hard disks, CD-ROMs, and tape units), and local area network (LAN) adapters.

▶ *Batch support* — This feature enables you to install one server and then use the same profile to install other servers.

▶ *Multiple protocol support* — This feature enables you to choose IPX-Only, Pure IP, or both.

▶ *Version checking* — This feature ensures that only the latest files are copied to the server.

Before you can install NetWare 5.1, you must ensure that your server satisfies a minimum set of hardware, software, and protocol requirements. Keep in mind that these are just *minimum* requirements — the *recommended* values are considerably higher (as shown in parentheses).

Here's the minimum and recommended hardware requirements for a NetWare 5.1 server:

▸ A server-class PC with a Pentium II or higher processor

▸ A VGA or higher-resolution display adapter (SVGA with VESA support recommended)

▸ 128MB of RAM (256MB for standard NetWare products plus WebSphere Application Server for NetWare, with 512MB recommended; 512MB all products, including Oracle8)

▸ 50MB DOS partition with 35MB of available space (256MB recommended for core dump)

▸ 1.3GB free disk space for the SYS: volume (for NetWare 5.1 products plus WebSphere Application Server for NetWare)

▸ One or more network boards

▸ The appropriate network cabling (Ethernet, Token Ring, FDDI, ARCnet, baseband, and so on) and related components (hubs, uninterruptible power supplies, and so on)

▸ A CD-ROM drive that can read ISO 9660-formatted CD-ROM disks (if NetWare 5.1 is being installed from a CD-ROM). (**Note:** Bootable CD-ROM drives must meet the El Torito specification.)

▸ (Optional, but recommended) PS/2 or serial mouse

The NetWare 5.1 Basic server installation process consists of multiple steps in four stages. Following is a brief preview of these four stages:

▸ *Stage 1*: Getting Started

▸ *Stage* 2: Text-based Input Screens

▸ *Stage* 3: GUI Input Screens

▸ *Stage* 4: Customization

It all starts in Stage 1, where you perform pre-installation tasks and run INSTALL.BAT. Then, in Stage 2, you get to attack the text-mode portion of the installation process, including choosing the type of installation, selecting regional settings, modifying selected drivers, creating the NetWare partition and SYS: volume, and mounting the SYS: volume.

Once you've built the foundation of the NetWare 5.1 server, it's time to plug in the key functional components. Next, in Stage 3, you build on the text-based platform with some GUI-mode tasks, including naming the server, selecting networking protocols, choosing the server time zone, installing NDS, and installing NLS. Finally, in Stage 4, you finish the installation by selecting additional products and services, and customizing server parameters.

**In this Appendix, we'll use the local CD-ROM method for all installation options, because it's the most common.**

**TIP**

▸ · · · · · · · · · · · · · · · · · · · · · · · · · · · · · ◀

# Stage 1: Getting Started

In the first installation stage, we'll prepare the server for installation and execute the main installation program — called INSTALL.BAT.

## Step 1: Complete Pre-Installation Tasks

There are a number of tasks you'll need to perform before you can install your NetWare 5.1 server, such as the following:

▸ Determine if your computer room meets recommended power and operating environment requirements.

▸ Verify that your server meets the minimum NetWare 5.1 hardware requirements and that all hardware is compatible. (See the minimum hardware requirements, listed earlier in this appendix.) Be sure that you install and configure any necessary hardware (such as network interface cards, hubs, cabling, uninterruptible power supplies, and so on).

▸ Confirm that you have all the appropriate DOS, NetWare 5.1, and application software and/or documentation that you need.

▸ Be sure that you have performed all of the planning required for the installation and have any required information handy. (Obviously, the best time to make installation-related decisions is *before* you begin the actual installation.) For example, a few of the numerous decisions you'll want to make before you start are whether to use the CD-ROM or network installation method, which protocol(s) to use (that is, IPX and/or IP), whether to install the server in a new or existing tree, how big to make the DOS partition, and so on.

▸ Back up your existing system. Create at least two full server backups on tape or on other storage media. Remember that all data on the server will be destroyed during pre-installation.

▸ Boot the server using the DOS version supplied by your computer manufacturer. NetWare requires DOS 3.3 or higher. (**Note:** Do *not* use the version of DOS that comes with Windows 95/98 or Windows NT/2000.)

▸ Create a boot diskette. To format a diskette and make it bootable, insert the diskette in the floppy drive (or drive A:) and type the following:

```
FORMAT A: /S
```

After the disk is formatted, you'll need to use the DOS COPY command to copy two important utilities to the diskette: FDISK.EXE and FORMAT.COM. You may also want to include copies of your AUTOEXEC.BAT and CONFIG.SYS files, DOS CD-ROM drivers (plus MSCDEX.EXE), and utilities such as EDIT.COM (to edit ASCII files), XCOPY.EXE (to copy files), and MEM.EXE (to display information about available RAM).

▶ Create the DOS partition. The DOS partition is required because NetWare 5.1 does not have its own cold-boot loader. This means that to start the server, you must load the NetWare 5.1 operating system via SERVER.EXE from a DOS prompt. When determining the appropriate size for your DOS partition, make sure that it is large enough to support disk drivers, LAN drivers, namespace modules, the SERVER.EXE boot file, and repair utilities. Once you've determined the appropriate DOS partition size, use the DOS FDISK utility to delete existing partitions and to create a new, active DOS partition of 50MB or more — leaving the rest of the hard disk space unpartitioned. (**Note:** When determining how large a DOS partition to create, don't forget to make sure that you end up with at least 35MB of available disk space after you've loaded any non-network-related files.)

▶ Format the DOS partition. Use the DOS FORMAT utility contained on the boot diskette that you made to format the new partition and make it bootable. In other words, type the following at the DOS prompt:

```
FORMAT C: /S
```

(Be sure to copy all DOS CD-ROM drivers from your computer *before* you run FDISK or FORMAT. Doing so afterward won't help because you will have wiped out the files.)

▶ Install the CD-ROM drive as a DOS device, following the instructions provided by the drive manufacturer.

▶ Use the DOS DATE and TIME commands to verify the computer's date and time and then modify them, if necessary.

## Step 2: Run INSTALL.BAT

At the server console, insert the *NetWare 5.1 Operating System* CD into the CD-ROM drive, switch to the drive letter assigned to the drive, and then type the following:

```
INSTALL
```

**Note:** If you have a bootable CD-ROM drive that meets the El Torito specification, the installation program automatically boots when the CD-ROM is inserted in the CD-ROM drive.

## Stage 2: Text-based Input Screens

In the second stage, we'll build the foundation of the server using a text-based interface. This early server foundation consists of regional configurations, disk drivers, LAN drivers, one or more NetWare 5.1 partitions, and the SYS: volume.

### Step 3: Choose the Type of Installation

As the installation program begins to load, a colorful NetWare title screen will eventually appear. (It may take awhile.) Wait for a few minutes until the next screen appears. If you have an International version of the program, a NetWare Installation screen eventually appears, giving you the opportunity to select the language to be used during the installation process. Next, the "NetWare 5.1 Software License" screen appears. Press F10 to accept the terms of the License Agreement.

When the "Welcome to the NetWare Server Installation" screen appears, indicate the type of installation you are interested in (New Server or Upgrade) and the startup directory (that is, the destination for the NetWare 5.1 server boot files). You'll notice that the defaults are Upgrade (installation type) and C:\NWSERVER (startup directory). (**Note:** For the purposes of the lab exercises in this book, you need to create a new server. Therefore, make sure that Upgrade is highlighted and then press Enter to toggle it to New Server. Also, verify that C:\NWSERVER is listed in the Startup Directory field.)

### Step 4: Select Server Settings

The Server Settings screen appears next, listing the following default values:

- NDS Version: NDS 8

- CD-ROM Driver to Access Install: NetWare

▸ Server ID Number: (random number)

▸ Load Server at Reboot: Yes

▸ Server Set Parameters: Edit

Review the default settings and modify them, as necessary. You'll probably find that the defaults are fine.

## Step 5: Select Regional Settings

The Regional Settings screen appears next. Regional settings are used to customize server language and keyboard settings. If you are located in the United States, the default values are as follows:

▸ Country: 001 (USA)

▸ Code Page: 437 (United States English)

▸ Keyboard: United States

Review the default settings and modify them as necessary.

## Step 6: Modify Selected Drivers

During Step 6, the Installation Wizard attempts to automatically detect certain types of hardware and determine the appropriate drivers. Other drivers must be selected manually.

The first NetWare 5.1 driver screen lists mouse type and video mode parameters. Because the installation program does not attempt to auto-detect these parameters, you will need to select the appropriate settings manually.

▸ *Mouse type* — Although the installation program supports PS/2 and serial mouse types, a mouse is not required (although it is recommended). Optionally, you can use the keyboard's arrow keys to control pointer movement.

▶ *Video mode* — The installation program is optimized to use Super VGA resolution and to work with display hardware that is VESA 2 complaint. You should only choose Standard VGA if your video card does not support 256 colors.

Review the values listed on this screen and modify them as necessary.

The system then automatically copies a number of server boot files from the CD-ROM to the startup directory. These include files such as SERVER.EXE, disk drivers, LAN drivers, NWCONFIG.NLM, NWSNUT.NLM, VREPAIR.NLM, and other NetWare Loadable Modules (NLMs).

The second NetWare 5.1 driver screen lists the following types of auto-detected drivers:

▶ *Platform Support Module* — The performance of servers with multiple processors and other configurations can be optimized by loading a platform support module driver. (Platform support modules have a .PSM filename extension.)

▶ *Hot Plug Support Module* — Computers that provide support for PCI Hot Plug technology allow storage adapters and network boards to be inserted and removed while the computer is powered on. (Hot Plug modules have an .NLM extension.)

▶ *Storage adapters* — Storage adapters require a software driver called a *host adapter module* (HAM) to communicate with the computer (host). Because a single storage adapter can control more than one type of storage device, only one HAM may be required. Various types of storage adapters (such as Integrated-Drive Electronics [IDE] and Small Computer System Interface [SCSI]) may be auto-detected. If a particular storage adapter is not detected, choose the appropriate driver from the list or load it from a manufacturer-specific diskette.

Review the values listed on this screen and modify them as necessary.

The third NetWare 5.1 driver screen lists the following types of drivers:

- *Storage devices* — Storage devices require a software driver, called a *custom device module* (CDM), to communicate with the storage adapter that controls it. Each type of storage device requires a separate CDM. The Installation Wizard auto-detects many types of storage devices, such as SCSI/IDE drives, CD-ROM drives, and tape drives.

- *Network boards* — Network boards require a software driver called a *LAN driver* to communicate with the network. The installation program auto-detects many types of network boards. If a particular network board is not detected, choose the appropriate driver from the list provided or load it from a manufacturer-specific diskette.

- *NetWare Loadable Modules* — Some servers and network configurations require that you load a NetWare Loadable Module (NLM) before completing the server installation. For example, if you are installing the server in a Token Ring environment, you may need to load ROUTE.NLM. If so, add it to the NetWare Loadable Modules field.

Review the values listed on this screen and modify them as necessary.

## Step 7: Create the NetWare Partition and Mount the SYS: Volume

To complete the NetWare 5.1 server foundation, you'll need to create internal disk partitions and volumes. In Step 7, the "Volume SYS and Partition Properties" screen appears. This text-mode screen displays the default parameters for creating NetWare partitions and the SYS: volume. If a server contains only one hard disk, the Installation utility creates a single NetWare 5.1 partition consisting of all free disk space beyond the DOS partition.

If you plan to have additional volumes on this partition, you must decrease the size of the SYS: volume in order to leave room for the other volume(s). It's probably a good idea to create one or more additional volumes for your data in order to keep it separate from your NetWare operating system files. This also makes it easier to restrict access to specific directories or files. Also, don't forget that if you plan to use Novell Storage Services (NSS), you must leave additional unpartitioned space on each hard disk that will contain an NSS partition, rather than using all of the free space on each disk for a NetWare partition.

Although the basic NetWare operating system requires only about 350MB, it's important to make sure that the SYS: volume is large enough to handle any additional NetWare products and services, online documentation, and applications that may be installed. (**Note:** Novell recommends that the SYS: volume has at least 1.3GB for NetWare 5.1 and other networking products.)

**TIP**

**Don't forget that if you plan to use NSS, you will need to leave additional free space on the hard disk for the NSS partition, rather than using all of the free space for the NetWare volume. Also, you can create additional partitions and volumes after installation by loading NWCONFIG.NLM at the server console.**

## Stage 3: GUI Input Screens

In Stage 3, we will establish networking protocols, an NDS context, and licensing authentication. In this stage, we will leave the boring text-mode world and switch to a Java interface. Although a mouse is recommended, you can use keystrokes to navigate through the installation program.

### Step 8: Name the NetWare 5.1 Server

At this point, the Installation Wizard copies a number of files to the server hard drive (called the "preparatory file copy" process). A Java Virtual Machine (JVM) is then created on the server and the GUI portion of the Installation Wizard is loaded. This step may take awhile.

When the Server Properties dialog box appears, type the server name in the Server Name field. The name should consist of 2 to 47 characters (including letters, numbers, hyphens, and/or underscores — but no spaces). The first character cannot be a period. Don't forget that each server in your NDS tree must have a unique name.

**Note:** For the lab exercises in this book, you'll need to use the following server name:

WHITE-SRV1

You'll notice this screen also has an Advanced button that lets you modify your server's AUTOEXEC.BAT file, CONFIG.SYS file, and your Server ID Number (which we set to 1001 earlier in the installation process), as well as language information.

## Step 9: Configure the File System

If the Configure File System dialog box appears, review the information listed. If you modified the size of the SYS volume in an earlier step, you can create additional volumes at this point using available free space. To do so, click the Free Space icon and then click Create.

When the New Volume dialog box appears, type the name of the new volume in the Volume Name field and click OK. The new volume should then be listed on the Configure File System screen.

If the Mount Volumes dialog box appears, you will be asked whether you want all volumes mounted when the server reboots or if you want them mounted now. Verify that Yes is selected so that all volumes will be mounted immediately. Otherwise, they will all be mounted when the server reboots.

## Step 10: Select Networking Protocols

At this point, the Protocols dialog box should appear. It asks you to specify the network protocol(s) for each internal server Network Interface Card (NIC).

To configure the IP protocol, follow these simple steps:

**1.** In the Network Boards pane on the left, click the icon for your network board (if it's not already selected).

**2.** In the Protocols section on the right, mark the IP check box.

**3.** Enter the IP address in the IP Address field. (If your server is *not* connected to the Internet, use 187.165.182.18.)

**4.** Enter the subnet mask in the Subnet Mask field. (If your server is *not* connected to the Internet, use 255.255.0.0.)

**5.** (Optional) In the Protocols section, enter the router (gateway) address in the Router (Gateway) field.

**6.** To configure the IPX protocol, in the Protocols section on the right, mark the IPX check box.

You'll notice that there's also an Advanced button which enables you to configure a number of protocol-related parameters, such as IPX frame types, IPX Compatibility settings, and SNMP information.

**NOTE**

**Know that to configure the IP protocol, you must be familiar with and know the IP address, the subnet address, and the router (gateway) address. (**Note: **The Installation utility uses default frame types of Ethernet_802.2 [for Ethernet] and Ethernet_II [for TCP/IP]).**

## Step 11: Domain Name Service

When the Domain Name Service screen appears, you would normally fill in the information required. Leave all of these fields blank for now, however. When you click Next, a message will appear warning you that because you have not configured Domain Name Service, you will obtain limited functionality from products that require this service. Click OK to acknowledge the message.

## Step 12: Choose the Server Time Zone

In Step 12, the Time Zone dialog box appears. Choose the correct time zone for your server and make sure that the "Allow System to Adjust for Daylight Saving Time" check box is marked, if appropriate.

## Step 13: Install Novell Directory Services (NDS)

This is probably one of the most important steps in the installation process. At the beginning of Step 13, the NDS Install dialog box appears. If this is the first

NetWare server in your NDS tree, select New NDS Tree. (**Note:** For the lab exercises in this book, you'll need to select New NDS Tree. Be aware that the resources available in the new tree will *not* be available to users who are logged into a different tree.)

If this is a new tree (which it should be, because you are using a nonproduction server for the lab exercises in this book), follow these steps:

**1.** Enter the tree name in the Tree Name field. This is usually the [Root] name of your tree followed by the term TREE.

**Note:** For the lab exercises in this book, you'll need to use the following tree name:

```
ACME_TREE
```

**2. Warning:** Do *not* type the server location in the "Context for Server Object" field. Instead, you will need to build the context using the browse button to the right of the "Context for Server Object" field.

**Note:** For the lab exercises in this book, you'll need to build the following server context:

```
OU=WHITE.OU=CRIME.OU=TOKYO.O=ACME
```

To do so, follow these steps:

**a.** Create the ACME Organization. Click the browse button to the right of the "Context for Server Object" field. On the NDS Context Browser screen, click ACME_TREE and then click Add. When the New Container dialog box appears, enter ACME in the Container Name field, verify that the Organization radio button is selected in the Container type field, and then click OK.

**b.** Create the TOKYO Organizational Unit. When the NDS Context Browser screen reappears, verify that ACME is highlighted and then click Add. When the New Container dialog box appears, enter TOKYO in the Container Name field, verify that the Organizational Unit radio button in the Container type field is selected, and then click OK.

**c.** Create the CRIME Organizational Unit. When the NDS Context Browser screen reappears, verify that TOKYO is highlighted and then click Add. When the New Container dialog box appears, enter CRIME in the Container Name field, verify that the Organizational Unit radio button in the Container type field is selected, and then click OK.

**d.** Create the WHITE Organizational Unit. When the NDS Context Browser screen reappears, verify that CRIME is highlighted and then click Add. When the New Container dialog box appears, enter WHITE in the Container Name field, verify that the Organizational Unit radio button in the Container type field is selected, and then click OK. Finally, click OK to return to the NDS Install screen.

**3.** In the Administrator Information section, enter the leaf name of the Admin User object in the Admin Name field, if you want it to be something other than Admin. (**Note:** For the lab exercises in this book, you need to leave it as Admin.)

**4.** Enter the context for the Admin User object in the Admin Context field, if you want it to be different than the context of the Server object. (**Note:** For the lab exercises in this book, you need to leave the default context that is displayed.)

**5.** Enter the password for the Admin User object in the Password and Retype Password fields. Keep track of this information for future reference. If you lose any of the Admin configuration details, your life will get much more complicated.

**Note:** For the lab exercises in this book, you'll need to enter:

ACME

If you had instead chosen to install the server in an existing tree, you would have been asked to provide the tree name (if there's more than one), the Admin username, and the Admin password.

At this point, the Installation Wizard checks for duplicate tree names and installs NDS. When the NDS Summary screen appears, write down the following information and store it in a safe place for future reference:

- ▶ NDS Tree Name: ACME_TREE

- ▶ Server Context: OU=WHITE.OU=CRIME.OU=TOKYO.O=ACME

- ▶ Administrator Name:
  CN=Admin.OU=WHITE.OU=CRIME.OU=TOKYO.O=ACME

- ▶ Administrator Password You Entered on Previous Screen: ACME

**REAL WORLD**

Remember that the Admin User object is the one NDS User object created by default during the installation of the first NDS tree. A non-NDS (bindery) Supervisor User object is also created that can be used to log into the tree in Bindery Emulation mode (LOGIN /B). Because Supervisor is not an NDS object, it is not displayed in the NDS tree.

## Step 14: Install Novell Licensing Services (NLS)

Now it's time to license the NetWare 5.1 server. To do so, you would normally insert your NetWare license diskette in the floppy drive and select the appropriate license file. (Be sure to use a unique license diskette.) If using a license diskette, make sure you actually browse to and select the license file, instead of just listing the drive letter (a common mistake). When you click the file, you'll notice that the type of license appears in the Description section, such as "NetWare 5.1 Server, Plus Fifty User Connections."

**Note:** If you are using a "demo version" of the *NetWare 5.1 Operating System* CD (that is, one that does not have an associated license diskette), use the license file in the LICENSE/DEMO directory on the CD (if one exists). If not, mark the "Install without Licenses" check box, although you may experience problems with NDPS, which uses a couple of connections.

NetWare 5.1 itself is a *licensed application*. As such, the number of users connected to the network is restricted to the number of licenses provided by the NetWare license. When NetWare is installed, the following NetWare license objects are added to the NDS tree:

▶ *License Service Provider object* — The License Service Provider (LSP) object resides in the same container as the Server object and includes the server's name in its object name. For example, the License Service Provider for WHITE-SRV1 would be named "NLS_LSP_WHITE-SRV1". The LSP object provides trending information and tells the licensing service how far up the tree to search for licensing certificates.

▶ *License Container Objects* — NetWare 5.1 supports two different types of License container objects: a *User License* (that is, Connection License) container and a *Server License* container. These objects are added to the NDS tree when NetWare 5.1 is installed, and they appear as leaf objects in the container that includes the Server object. License container objects can contain multiple License Certificate objects. The name of a License container object is a compound name consisting of publisher, product, and version segments. For example, a User Connection License container might be named "Novell + NetWare 5.1 Conn SCL+500"; whereas a Server Connection License container might be named "Novell+NetWare 5.1 Server+500".

▶ *License Certificate Objects* — License Certificate objects are typically created in NDS when a NetWare 5.1 server is installed. All License Certificate objects are installed in a User (Connection) License container. By default, the user who installed the license (such as Admin) is the owner of this certificate, and, therefore, always has access to the network.

These objects contain information about the product (such as the Publisher, Product name, version, how many licenses the certificate allows, and whether additional licenses are available). Each license included in the certificate allows a *licensed connection* to be made. A licensed connection is initiated when a user requests a network connection by logging in. When a server receives the request, it checks to make sure a licensed unit is available in the license certificate stored in NDS. If a license unit is available, the server allows the client to complete the network connection.

**REAL WORLD**

In NetWare Administrator, locate a User (Connection) License container and then double-click it to view any License Certificates that it contains. Finally, double-click a License Certificate to view information about the license.

You can restrict the use of licenses by assigning License Certificates to the following objects: User, Group, Organization, and Organizational Unit. If you choose to do so, consider assigning License Certificates to objects that represent the greatest number of users rather than assigning them to individual users. For example, if you assign a container object to a license certificate, it allows all users in the container and subcontainers to use the licenses. Once you make assignments, only those objects that have been assigned to the License Certificates can use the licenses. Therefore, if you don't want to restrict the licenses in this way, don't make the assignments.

# Stage 4: Customization

In the fourth and final stage, you are given the choice to install additional products and services and/or customize numerous operating system parameters.

## Step 15: Install Additional Products and Services

Toward the end of the NetWare 5.1 Installation process, the Additional Products and Services dialog box appears, allowing you to select from the follow list:

▸ Install Standard NetWare Products

▸ Install Standard NetWare Products Plus WebSphere App Server

▸ Custom

If you click a radio button, you'll notice that a corresponding list of products to be installed will appear in the Description section. For instance, if you select Install Standard NetWare Products, you would install the following products and services: FTP Server, LDAP, Catalog Services, Storage Management Services, Secure Authentication Services, Novell Certificate Server, Novell Distributed Print Services, and Novell Internet Services. If you select the Custom option, indicate the products you wish to install. (**Note:** For the purposes of the lab exercises in this book, you need to use the Install Standard NetWare Products option.)

The screens that are displayed next are determined by which option you chose from the preceding list of options. If you selected Install Standard NetWare products, you will see the screens described in the next three paragraphs.

When the Novell Certificate Server 2.0 Objects screen appears, review the onscreen information. When the Organizational CA Warning dialog box appears, read the information and then click OK to acknowledge the warning. The Novell Certification Server 2.0 Objects screen then reappear briefly. Ignore it and wait until the next screen appears.

When the NetWare Enterprise Web Server Settings screen appears, make note of the onscreen information. You'll notice an optional setting that allows you to optimize WebBench performance, if desired. When the NetWare Web Manager Settings screen appears, make note of the onscreen information.

When the Summary screen appears, review the additional NetWare 5.1 products to be installed. When you are satisfied with the list of products, click Customize to be allowed to customize various installation parameters.

### Step 16: Customize the Server

You can enhance the *basic* NetWare 5.1 server with some additional configurations using the Product Customization dialog box. Categories of customizable options include the core operating system, file system, protocols, time synchronization, Novell Directory Services, and additional products and services. Browse the tree to find the first NetWare 5.1 component you want to modify, select the component, and then click Configure. When you have finished customizing your selections, click OK to return to the Summary screen.

### Step 17: Complete the Installation

On the Summary screen, click Finish to complete the installation process.

The Installation Wizard then performs the main file copy. (This step may take awhile.) When the final copy is complete, the Installation Complete window appears. Select View Log or View Readme, if desired. Then, remove the NetWare 5.1 License diskette from the floppy drive (if you actually used one) and click Yes to restart your computer.

Congratulations—you've done it! You have successfully traversed the four stages and 17 steps of NetWare 5.1 installation! Now it's time to use your new server to help *save the Net!*

# ACME Mission Briefing

In the social hierarchy of needs, the world is pretty out of whack. Almost two-thirds of our population doesn't have sufficient resources to satisfy the lowest basic needs—medicine, food, shelter, and peace—while a smaller percentage takes higher needs—like digital watches—for granted. Something needs to change.

As a matter of fact, the Alpha Centurions have discovered this and have decided to do something about it. As it turns out, they are great fans of Planet Earth and would hate to see us destroy it. The good news is they are a benevolent and intelligent race. They understand the Pyramid of Needs and recognize that everyone should be able to enjoy digital watches. They have discovered that the top 1 percent of the Earth's population is destroying the world at an alarming pace, while the other 99 percent is just trying to survive. In an effort to save the world, they have issued an ultimatum:

*Clean up your act or find another planet to exploit!*

They have given us until January 1, 2010, to clean up our act—or else! It's safe to say that the fate of the human race is in your hands. To help measure our progress, the Alpha Centurions have developed a World Health Index (WHI). The WHI is a balanced calculation of seven positive and seven negative factors that determine how good or bad we're treating the Earth. They've decided that 100 is a good number to shoot for. It represents a good balance between basic and higher needs. Once the world achieves a WHI of 100, almost everyone will be able to afford a digital watch. Here's a quick list of the 14 positive and negative WHI factors:

| WHI *Positive* | WHI *Negative* |
|---|---|
| Charity | Crime |
| Love | Pollution |
| Birth | Starvation |
| Education | Disease |
| Health | War |
| Laughter | Poverty |
| Sports | Corruption |

*Bottom line:* The Alpha Centurions have given us a little more than nine years to increase our WHI from its current level (–2) to 100. We have until January 1, 2010. If we don't clean up our act by then, they will mercifully eradicate all humans, and let the animals and plants live peacefully on Planet Earth.

**TIP**

**Throughout this book, we will use ACME as a global case study for key NetWare 5.1 network management tasks. You will build ACME's enterprise NDS tree, construct a multilayered security model, distribute ZENworks clients, and build a comprehensive NDPS printing system. Pay attention! ACME may just change your life ... and help you become a NetWare 5.1 CNA.**

ACME has been designed as "A Cure for Mother Earth." It is staffed by some of the greatest heroes from our unspoiled history. These are the founding mothers and fathers of Earth's Golden Age — before instant popcorn, talking cars, and daytime television. It's clear that somewhere along the human timeline, progress went amok. We need help from heroes before that time. To vortex back in history and grab the ACME management, we've used a prototype of the Oscillating Temporal Overthruster (OTO). We've hand chosen only the brightest and most resourceful characters and then meticulously trained each one of them for special tasks. They're a little disoriented, but more than happy to help.

These historical heroes have been placed in an innovative organizational structure. As you can see in Figure E.1, ACME is organized around these five main divisions:

▸ *Human Rights (Gandhi)* — Taking care of the world's basic needs, including medicine, food, shelter, and peace. These tasks are handled jointly by Albert Schweitzer, Mother Teresa, Florence Nightingale, and Buddha. This division's work has the most positive impact on the WHI.

▸ *Labs (Albert Einstein)* — Putting technology to good use. This division is the technical marvel of ACME. In addition to research and development (R&D) efforts, the Labs division is responsible for the WHI tracking center in NORAD. This division is staffed by the wizardry of Leonardo da Vinci, Sir Isaac Newton, Charles Darwin, Marie Curie, and Charles Babbage.

▸ *Operations (King Arthur)* — Saving the world can be a logistical nightmare. Fortunately, we have King Arthur and the Knights of the Round Table to help us out. In this division, ACME routes money from caring contributors (Charity) to those who need it most (Financial) — there's a little Robin Hood in there somewhere. Also, with the help of Merlin, we will distribute all the Human Rights and Labs material to the four corners of the globe.

> ▸ *Crime Fighting (Sherlock Holmes and Dr. Watson)* — Making the world a safer place. This division tackles the almost insurmountable task of eradicating world crime. It's a good thing we have the help of Sherlock Holmes and some of our greatest crime-fighting superheroes, including Robin Hood, Maid Marion, Wyatt Earp, and Wild Bill Hickok. These heroes deal with the single most negative factor in WHI calculations — crime. This is important work.

> ▸ *Admin (George Washington)* — Keeping the rest of ACME running smoothly. It's just like a well-oiled machine with the help of some of America's Founding Fathers and famous presidents — George Washington, Thomas Jefferson, Abraham Lincoln, Franklin Delano Roosevelt (FDR), and James Madison. Their main job is public relations under the command of one of our greatest orators, FDR. In addition to getting the word out, Admin tracks ACME activity (auditing) and keeps the facilities operating at their best.

Now it's your turn. You are the final piece in our globe-trotting puzzle. You are ACME's management information services (MIS) department. ACME has a daunting task ahead of it, so we don't have any time to mess around. I'd like to begin by thanking you for choosing to accept this mission. You'll find some NDS schematics included in the next few pages. They are for your eyes only. Once you have read the inputs, eat them! There's other good news — you don't have to save the world alone. The project team is here to help you. Remember, we're counting on you. Be careful not to let these facts fall into the wrong hands. Believe it or not, there are forces at work that don't share our love for the human race.

FIGURE E.1

*ACME organizational chart*

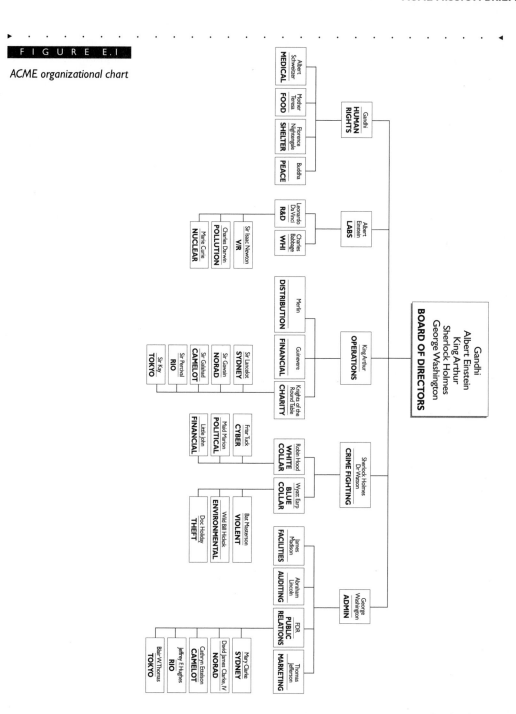

# ACME Chronicles

A day in the life . . .

What you're about to read is for your eyes only. This is extremely confidential information. The ACME *Chronicles* is an interactive newsletter that provides a detailed look at the life and times of ACME. This is an exceptional organization created for a singular purpose — to save the world. As you can see in Figure E.1, ACME is organized around five main divisions:

- ▶ Human Rights

- ▶ Labs

- ▶ Operations

- ▶ Crime Fighting

- ▶ Admin

Let's go inside and see what makes them tick.

## Human Rights — Gandhi in Sydney

This is the heart of ACME's purpose. Human Rights has the most profound positive effect on the WHI. Efforts here can save lives and increase our chances of surviving beyond 2010. The goal of Human Rights is to raise people from the bottom of the Pyramid of Needs. By satisfying their basic needs (medicine, food, shelter, and peace), we hope to give humans the strength to fight for higher needs (equality, justice, education, and digital watches). This makes the world a better place and dramatically improves the WHI.

All Human Rights materials developed here are distributed every day through ten different distribution centers around the world. The Sydney site is ACME's manufacturing facility for food, shelter, and medical aid. Check out Figure E.2. In addition, the peacekeepers use any means necessary to thwart global wars. Let's take a closer look at the four different departments of Human Rights.

- *Medical (Albert Schweitzer)* — This department is collecting basic medical materials, and training doctors and nurses for field work. Also, ACME is eagerly developing vaccines and working overtime to cure serious diseases. Finally, the medical staff is taking steps to clean up the sanitation of "dirty" countries. This is all accomplished with the help of Albert Schweitzer and his dedicated staff.

- *Food (Mother Teresa)* — With the help of her country-trained culinary heroes, Mother Teresa will determine how much opossum stew the whole world can eat. In addition, they are developing a series of genetically engineered organisms that will transform inedible materials into food stock. Finally, ACME's Food department has teamed up with R&D to create virtual reality (VR) programming that teaches people how to grow food of their own. After all, if you give a person a fish, they eat for a day; but if you teach them to fish, they eat for a lifetime (and get a guest spot on ESPN's "Outdoor World").

- *Shelter (Florence Nightingale)* — With all the new healthier and happier people in the world, our attention shifts to shelter. Fortunately, Florence Nightingale and her crack construction team have developed a cheap, recyclable, geodesic dome called a Permaculture. It has central heating, air conditioning, water, plumbing, and computer-controlled maid service. The most amazing thing about the dome is that it can be constructed from any native materials — that's cacti and sand in the desert, lily pads in the marsh, and snow in the Arctic. If all else fails, they're edible.

- *Peace (Buddha)* — One of the most overlooked basic needs is peace. All the other stuff doesn't mean a hill of beans if you're living in a war zone. Buddha's job is to somehow settle the 101 wars currently plaguing our earth. He relies on a combination of wisdom, diplomacy, military presence, and fortune cookies.

▶ · · · · · · · · · · · · · · · · · · · · · · · ◀

FIGURE E-2

The SYDNEY site at ACME

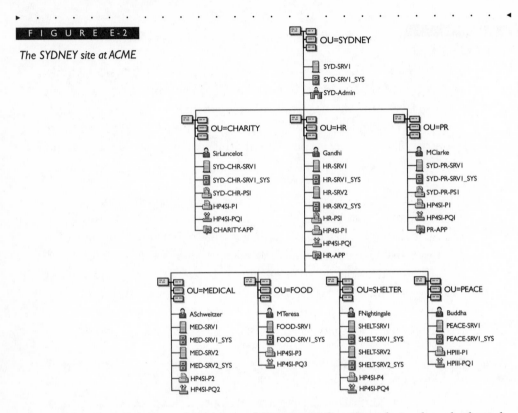

That completes our discussion of Human Rights. Now, let's take a look at the ACME Labs division.

## Labs — Albert Einstein in NORAD

Albert Einstein is one of the greatest minds in our history, but how far can he push technology? The U.S. Military has loaned us the NORAD facility in Colorado as a base for technical wizardry. In addition to Research & Development (R&D), this is the central point of a vast WHI data-collection network. Check out Figure E.3.

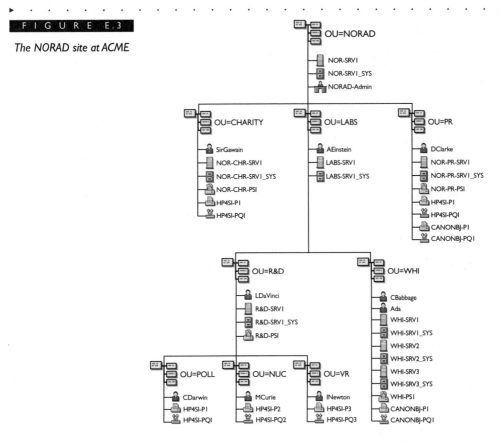

ACME's R&D efforts are controlled by Leonardo da Vinci and his dream team of scientists. They use technology and a little bit of magic to save the earth. Current projects include alternative power sources, VR programming, antipollutants, NDS, and a cure for bad-hair days. Let's take a closer look:

▶ *Pollution (Charles Darwin)*—This department is developing antipollutants and methods of transforming garbage into fuel. Also, this group is working to eradicate the world's largest scourge—ElectroPollution. Currently Leonardo da Vinci and Charles Darwin are working on airplanes powered by pencil erasure grit.

▸ *Nuclear (Marie Curie)* — Cybernetic soldiers (Nuclear Disarmament Squads or NDS) are being designed to infiltrate and neutralize nuclear weapons facilities. Finally, somebody's splitting atoms for good.

▸ *VR (Sir Isaac Newton)* — VR programming is being developed to convince the world that a cure is necessary. The VR devices will be sold as video games and will help ACME tap the minds of the world. This borders on mind control, but in a good way (if that's possible). There's nothing that brain power and a little bit of magic can't cure.

In addition to R&D, NORAD is the central point of a vast WHI data-collection network. This network is the pulse of ACME. Collection of world data and calculation of the WHI occur here every day. Currently, the WHI sits at –2. And, as we all know, it must climb to more than 100 by January 1, 2010. Charles Babbage and Ada diligently guard the computers and make daily adjustments to WHI calculations. Ada's sacrifice is particularly notable because she used to be the "Countess of Lovelace." But, fortunately for us, she has a soft spot in her heart for mathematics and Mr. Babbage.

Distributed world data-collection centers are scattered to all four corners of the earth. There are ten ACME WHI hubs — one in every divisional headquarters — and five more scattered to strategic points around the earth. From each of these sites, world data is sent to NORAD and calculated on a daily basis. The results are distributed to every major newspaper so that the world can chart ACME's progress. In addition to the ten WHI hubs are hundreds of collection clusters are distributed around each hub. Each cluster sends data directly to the closest hub (via dial-up lines) and eventually back to the central site at NORAD.

This completes our journey through ACME technology. Now, let's take a look at the Operations division.

## Operations — King Arthur in Camelot

King Arthur and his court will keep ACME financed through charity drives and financial spending. After all, "money makes the world go 'round." Never before has it been more true. In addition, the Operations division handles the arduous task of distributing ACME aid to all the people who need it. Check out Figure E.4. Here's how it works:

*The CAMELOT site at ACME*

OU=CAMELOT
- CAM-SRVI
- CAM-SRVI_SYS
- CAM-Admin

OU=CHARITY
- SirGalahad
- CAM-CHR-SRVI
- CAM-CHR-SRVI_SYS
- CAM-CHR-PSI
- HP5-PI
- HP5-PQI

OU=OPS
- KingArthur
- OPS-SRVI
- OPS-SRVI_SYS
- OPS-PSI
- CANONBJ-PI
- CANONBJ-PQI

OU=PR
- CEttelson
- CAM-PR-SRVI
- CAM-PR-SRVI_SYS
- CAM-PR-PSI
- HP4SI-PI
- HP4SI-PQI

OU=FIN
- Guinevere
- CAM-FIN-SRVI
- CAM-FIN-SRVI_SYS
- CAM-FIN-SRV2
- CAM-FIN-SRV2_SYS
- CAM-FIN-SRV3
- CAM-FIN-SRV3_SYS
- CAM-FIN-PSI
- CAM-FIN-PS2
- HP4SI-PI
- HP4SI-PQI
- HP4SI-P2
- HP4SI-PQ2

OU=DIST
- Merlin
- DIST-SRVI
- DIST-SRVI_SYS
- DIST-SRV2
- DIST-SRV2_SYS
- DIST-PSI
- HPIII-PI
- HPIII-PQI

- *Financial (Guinevere)* — This is the money-out department. Guinevere handles the distribution of charity contributions, including the purchase of human-rights material, bailing out bankrupt nations, and the funding of internal ACME activities. For a more detailed discussion of Financial operations, refer to the ACME Workflow section later in this chapter.

▸ *Distribution (Merlin)* — We're going to need all the magic we can get. This department handles the distribution of human rights materials, medical supplies, doctors, nurses, food, hardware, building supplies, and prefabricated geodesic domes. No guns! It also handles implementation of WHI devices from R&D, such as antipollutants, Nuclear Disarmament Squads (NDS), antihacking viruses, and VR programming. The latter is handled through satellite TV transmissions and video games. ACME distribution takes place through the same ten hubs as WHI. Think of it as data in (WHI), and aid out (Distribution).

▸ *Charity (Knights of the Round Table)* — This is the money-in department. The Knights collect charity from world organizations and distribute it to the Financial department for disbursement. Each of the five major Knights oversees one of five charity centers — in each of the divisional headquarters. Sir Lancelot is in Sydney, Sir Gawain is in NORAD, Sir Galahad handles Camelot, Sir Percival oversees Rio, and Sir Kay is in Tokyo. I haven't seen such dedication since the Medieval Ages.

Well, that's how ACME's Operations work. Now, let's take a look at Crime Fighting.

### Crime Fighting — Sherlock Holmes in Tokyo

Crime has one of the most negative effects on the WHI. Fortunately, we have history's greatest crime-fighting mind to help us out — Sherlock Holmes. With the help of Dr. Watson, he has identified two major categories of world crime (see Figure E.5):

▸ White Collar

▸ Blue Collar

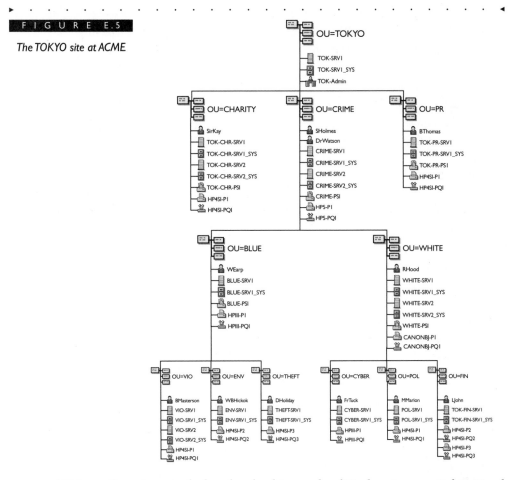

White-collar crimes include cyber-hacking and political espionage. Robin Hood and his Band of Superheroes direct white-collar crime-fighting efforts from Tokyo. Here are some of the different types of crimes with which they're concerned:

▶ *Cyber (Friar Tuck)* — With the help of the Cyberphilia underground, Friar Tuck attempts to thwart cyber-crime. Most cyber-crimes occur on the Net, so ACME must constantly monitor global communications. Tuck also has the help of an offshoot group of guardian angels known as the Cyber Angels.

▶ *Political (Maid Marion)* — She can charm her way through any politically tense situation. Political crimes are especially rampant in emerging nations, so Maid Marion enlists the help of the United Nations.

▶ *Financial (Little John)* — With some creative financing and the help of ex-IRS agents, Little John thwarts financial crimes throughout the world. These crimes especially hurt the middle class, so he has recruited some key Yuppies as undercover agents.

Blue-collar crimes are a little more obvious — such as violence and theft. This is familiar ground for Wyatt Earp and his band of western heroes. They're not glamorous, but they're effective. Here's a look at ACME Crime Fighting from the blue-collar point of view:

▶ *Violent (Bat Masterson)* — This cowboy is in his element. He thwarts violent crime by getting inside the criminal's mind — literally.

▶ *Environmental (Wild Bill Hickok)* — A great fan of the environment, Mr. Hickok uses his country charm to thwart environmental crimes such as excessive deforestation, toxic waste, whaling, oil spills, ElectroPollution, and forced extinction.

▶ *Theft (Doc Holliday)* — With his legendary sleight of hand, Doc Holliday stays one step ahead of the world's thieves.

So, that's what's happening on the crime-fighting front. Now, let's take a close look at the final ACME division — Admin.

## Admin — George Washington in Rio

Ever since the beginning of time, humans have quested for wisdom and knowledge. Now we'll need to put all of our enlightenment to good use — or else. A few centuries ago, the United States' Founding Fathers joined a growing group of men and women called Illuminoids. These people were dissatisfied with everyday life on Planet Earth and began to reach above, within, and everywhere else for a better way. The Illuminoids formed a variety of organizations dedicated to creating a

New World Order, including the Masons, the Trilateral Commission, the Council on Foreign Relations (CFR), and the Bilderberg Group.

Regardless of their ultimate motivation, the Illuminoids' hearts were in the right place — "Let's make the world a better place." The founder of the Trilateral Commission has always claimed it is just a group of concerned citizens interested in fostering greater understanding and cooperation among international allies. Whether or not it's true, it sounds like a great fit for ACME. Once again, we've used the Oscillating Temporal Overthruster (OTO) to grab some of the earliest Illuminoids and to solicit their help for ACME administration.

George Washington keeps the ACME ship afloat. Along with FDR, he keeps things running smoothly and makes sure the world hears about our plight. In addition, James Madison keeps the facilities running, while Abraham Lincoln makes sure ACME is held accountable for all its work. For years, the Trilateral Commission has been rumored to covertly run the world. Now they get a chance to overtly save it!

Now, let's take a look at the four departments that make up ACME's administration (see Figure E.6):

▸ *Public Relations (Franklin Delano Roosevelt)* — This department solicits help from the rest of the world by enlisting the help of heroes from our own age — the 1990s and the turn of the millennium. We're not going to be able to save the world alone. The PR department is responsible for communicating our plight to the four corners of the earth. Department members inform everyday citizens about the Alpha Centurion ultimatum, daily WHI quotes, and requests for charity. A local PR office is in each major location. For more details, see the organizational chart in Figure E.1, shown earlier in this appendix.

▸ *Auditing (Abraham Lincoln)* — This department makes sure that everyone stays in line. Financial trails for all charity moneys and complete records of all changes to the WHI are tracked by the Auditing department. Although it's part of the internal ACME organization, Auditing is an independent tracking company that generates bonded reports.

▸ *Facilities (James Madison)* — This department keeps everyone working, happy, and fed. The Facilities department also organizes field trips and ACME parties. Imagine the doozy they're going to have when we finally succeed!

▸ *Marketing (Thomas Jefferson)* — Educating the rest of the world and soliciting help is another Marketing department responsibility. In addition to advertising, this department develops materials for distributed PR offices. Its goal is to rally all nations around ACME and our cause in order to save the earth. They also bake really good apple pies and chocolate chip cookies.

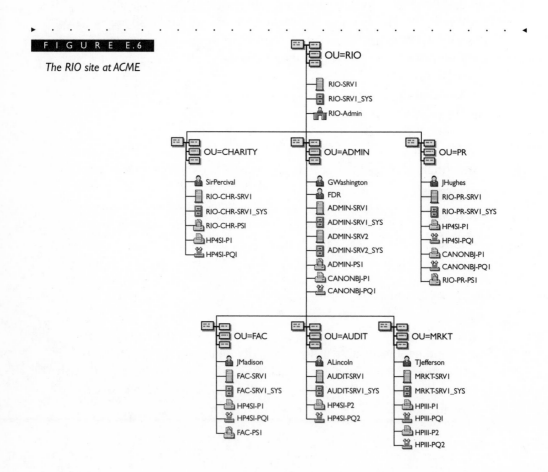

**F I G U R E  E.6**

*The RIO site at ACME*

Well, there you have it. That's everything there is to know about ACME. I hope these *Chronicles* have helped you and the project team to better understand what ACME is up against. This is no normal organization. If ACME goes out of business, the world is either lost or saved — it's up to you.

▶ · · · · · · · · · · · · · · · · · · · · · · · · · · · · · · · · · · ◀

## ACME Workflow

Although it may look complicated, the daily grind at ACME is really pretty simple. It's a combination of workflow and dataflow. *Workflow* describes the daily operations of ACME staff and their task-oriented responsibilities. *Dataflow* describes the daily or weekly movement of data from one location to another. Although the two are not always the same, they should be compatible. This is the goal of ACME synergy.

In this section, we're going to take a detailed look at how work and data flow through the ACME organization. This data has a dramatic impact on NDS design. After all, work and data flow over the WAN infrastructure. Refer to Figure E.7 as you follow along.

▶ · · · · · · · · · · · · · · · · · · · · · · · · · · · · · · · · · · ◀

**FIGURE E.7**

*ACME workflow diagram*

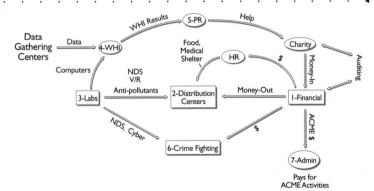

## Financial

Of course, money makes the world go 'round! The Financial department has two main responsibilities:

▸ Money-in

▸ Money-out

*Money-in* focuses on funding ACME activities and distributing charities to needy people. With *Money-out*, Guinevere pays for Human Rights materials, Admin work, and Crime Fighting tools. Next, she disburses charity money through distribution centers. Money-in comes from the various Charity activities. All financial activity is audited by the internal Auditing organization.

Technically, this is accomplished from a central database at the Financial headquarters in Camelot. No money changes hands. Quarterly budgets are developed in Camelot and distributed to local banks for Human Rights, Crime Fighting, Distribution, and Admin. Each of these distributed sites sends weekly updates to the central database with the help of local servers.

## Distribution Centers

The Distribution department is the hub of ACME achievements. Distribution centers disburse three kinds of aid:

▸ Human Rights materials (such as food, medicine, and shelter)

▸ Money from the Financial department

▸ Exciting inventions from Labs

Each of the ten distribution centers maintains its own distributed database. They move material to local warehouses for delivery to needy people. Weekly summary updates are sent to the central inventory management database in Camelot. The central database oversees the big picture of aid distribution.

If a center runs out of a particular resource, one of two things happens:

**1.** Camelot updates the center's budget, and it purchases the resource locally.

**2.** Camelot orders the movement of resources from another distribution center. This option makes sense for finite materials, such as special inventions from Labs or medical supplies.

## Labs and Their Inventions

This is where the brainiacs hang out. Scientists in the Labs division develop world-saving toys for the following:

- *Crime Fighting* — NDS and cyber-viruses

- *Distribution* — VR programming and antipollutants

The Labs division supports WHI and all its technical needs. New product updates are sent to Distribution and Crime Fighting for internal consumption. This is secure information.

## WHI Calculations

Labs is also where the WHI is calculated. Charles Babbage and Ada collect data from data-gathering centers (DGCs) throughout the world. The following DGCs are housed in divisional headquarters and distribution centers throughout the ACME WAN:

| | |
|---|---|
| NORAD | Seattle |
| Rio | Cairo |
| Camelot | New York |
| Sydney | Moscow |
| Tokyo | St. Andrews |

Ironically, the distribution centers send aid out and the DGCs pull data in — from the same ten locations. Daily WHI summary calculations are sent to NORAD each day so that the final WHI calculation can be made. Results are distributed to PR daily for inclusion in global periodicals — including the ACME *Chronicles* (an hourly interactive newsletter).

## Public Relations

This is the voice of ACME. In addition to distributing daily WHI reports, Public Relations (PR) educates the world and helps solicit money for Charity. PR pulls the daily WHI results from NORAD twice a day. They're also the online editors of the ACME *Chronicles*, which gives them some great financial leads for Charity.

Money-In Charity is ACME's open door. It is the funnel for ACME contributions. There is a charity center in each of the five divisional headquarters. This is how the top 1 percent helps the rest of us. Here's their motto:

*Spread the wealth, or the Alpha Centurions will eat you!*

All money collected by Charity is sent to the Financial department for disbursement. Two of the most important uses for this money are Crime Fighting and Admin. Note that the money doesn't actually change hands. It is deposited in local divisional banks, and daily updates are sent to the central financial database in Camelot.

## Crime Fighting

Remember, crime has one of the greatest negative effects on the WHI. The Crime Fighting department relies on the following sources:

▶ Labs' inventions (NDS and cyber-viruses)

▶ Money from the Financial department

▶ The guile of Robin Hood, Wyatt Earp, and their respective heroes

## ACME Administration

The ACME staff has to eat. Admin relies on money from Financial to keep things running smoothly. You can't fight bureaucracy. In addition, the Auditing department needs audit-level access to the central financial database in Camelot. They are responsible for tracking money-in from Charity and money-out from Financial.

That's all there is to it. No sweat. As you can see, ACME runs like a well-oiled machine. Someone sure put a lot of effort into designing its organizational structure — and it shows! We're in good hands with ACME.

Good luck; and by the way, thanks for saving the world!

# What's On the CD-ROM

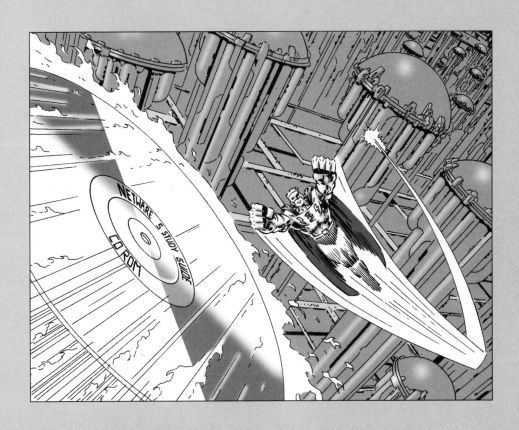

This appendix includes information and installation instructions for the contents of the two CD-ROMs included with this book. The CD-ROMs contain the following information:

### Disc 1

▸ NetWare 5.1 Operating System — 3-User Demo

### Disc 2

▸ Client Software (including ZENworks Starter Pack)

# NetWare 5.1 Operating System — 3-User Version

The *NetWare 5.1 Operating System* CD-ROM (Disc 1) that comes with this book contains a 3-user version of NetWare 5.1 with the NetWare 5.1 license embedded in the NetWare 5.1 code. No separate license disk is required to install this software. During installation, the license loads itself from the CD-ROM. Additionally, this software has no expiration date, so you can install it at any time.

## NetWare 5.1 Minimum Requirements

Here are the minimum requirements for server hardware in order to run NetWare 5.1:

▸ Server-class PC with a Pentium processor

▸ VGA display adapter

▸ 64MB of RAM

▸ 600MB available disk space (50MB for the boot partition, 550MB for the NetWare partition)

▸ Network board

▸ CD-ROM drive

▸ PS/2 or serial mouse recommended

## Installing NetWare 5.1

The following steps guide you through the installation of NetWare 5.1 on your system:

**1.** Create a 50MB DOS boot partition.

**2.** Install a CD-ROM drive and drivers according to your hardware vendor's instructions.

**3.** Insert the NetWare 5.1 Operating System CD-ROM (Disc 1) and type **INSTALL**.

**4.** Accept the License Agreement.

**5.** Choose the server language, if prompted.

**6.** Select New Server.

**7.** Confirm computer settings.

**8.** When prompted for the License Diskette, select the license located in the \LICENSE directory on the NetWare 5.1 Operating System CD-ROM. *Please note that there is no separate license diskette.*

**9.** Complete the installation by following the onscreen instructions.

# Client Software

Disk 2 of the CD-ROM set contains the Client Software from Novell, which includes the Zenworks Starter Pack.

## Installing Client Software

Follow these steps to install the Client Software:

**1.** On a computer running Windows, insert the Client Software CD-ROM (Disc 2) and run WINSETUP.EXE.

**2.** Select a language for the installation.

**3.** Select a platform for the installation.

**4.** Select the software to install.

**5.** Complete the installation by following the onscreen instructions.

# *I*ndex

*Continued*

**B**

## E

*Continued*

*Continued*

# Notes

# Notes

# Notes

# Notes

# Notes

_____

_____

_____

_____

_____

_____

_____

_____

_____

_____

_____

_____

_____

_____

_____

_____

_____

# Hungry Minds, Inc.
# End-User License Agreement

**READ THIS.** You should carefully read these terms and conditions before opening the software packet(s) included with this book ("Book"). This is a license agreement ("Agreement") between you and Hungry Minds, Inc. ("HMI"). By opening the accompanying software packet(s), you acknowledge that you have read and accept the following terms and conditions. If you do not agree and do not want to be bound by such terms and conditions, promptly return the Book and the unopened software packet(s) to the place you obtained them for a full refund.

1. **License Grant.** HMI grants to you (either an individual or entity) a nonexclusive license to use one copy of the enclosed software program(s) (collectively, the "Software") solely for your own personal or business purposes on a single computer (whether a standard computer or a workstation component of a multi-user network). The Software is in use on a computer when it is loaded into temporary memory (RAM) or installed into permanent memory (hard disk, CD-ROM, or other storage device). HMI reserves all rights not expressly granted herein.

2. **Ownership.** HMI is the owner of all right, title, and interest, including copyright, in and to the compilation of the Software recorded on the disk(s) or CD-ROM ("Software Media"). Copyright to the individual programs recorded on the Software Media is owned by the author or other authorized copyright owner of each program. Ownership of the Software and all proprietary rights relating thereto remain with HMI and its licensers.

3. **Restrictions On Use and Transfer.**

   **(a)** You may only (i) make one copy of the Software for backup or archival purposes, or (ii) transfer the Software to a single hard disk, provided that you keep the original for backup or archival purposes. You may not (i) rent or lease the Software, (ii) copy or reproduce the Software through a LAN or other network system or through any computer subscriber system or bulletin-board system, or (iii) modify, adapt, or create derivative works based on the Software.

   **(b)** You may not reverse engineer, decompile, or disassemble the Software. You may transfer the Software and user documentation on a permanent basis, provided that the transferee agrees to accept the terms and conditions of this Agreement and you retain no copies. If the Software is an update or has been updated, any transfer must include the most recent update and all prior versions.

4. **Restrictions on Use of Individual Programs.** You must follow the individual requirements and restrictions detailed for each individual program in Appendix F of this Book. These limitations are also contained in the individual license agreements recorded on the Software Media. Tnese limitations may include a requirement that after using the program for a specified period of time, the user must pay a registration fee or discontinue use. By opening the Software packet(s), you will be agreeing to abide by the licenses and restrictions for these individual programs that are detailed in Appendix F and on the Software Media. None of the material on this Software Media or listed in this Book may ever be redistributed, in original or modified form, for commercial purposes.

5. **Limited Warranty.**

   **(a)** HMI warrants that the Software and Software Media are free from defects in materials and workmanship under normal use for a period of sixty (60) days from the date of purchase of this Book. If HMI receives notification within the warranty period of defects in materials or workmanship, HMI will replace the defective Software Media.

**(b) HMI AND THE AUTHOR OF THE BOOK DISCLAIM ALL OTHER WARRANTIES, EXPRESS OR IMPLIED, INCLUDING WITHOUT LIMITATION IMPLIED WARRANTIES OF MERCHANTABILITY AND FITNESS FOR A PARTICULAR PURPOSE, WITH RESPECT TO THE SOFTWARE, THE PROGRAMS, THE SOURCE CODE CONTAINED THEREIN, AND/OR THE TECHNIQUES DESCRIBED IN THIS BOOK. HMI DOES NOT WARRANT THAT THE FUNCTIONS CONTAINED IN THE SOFTWARE WILL MEET YOUR REQUIREMENTS OR THAT THE OPERATION OF THE SOFTWARE WILL BE ERROR FREE.**

(c) This limited warranty gives you specific legal rights, and you may have other rights that vary from jurisdiction to jurisdiction.

6. **Remedies.**

   (a) HMI's entire liability and your exclusive remedy for defects in materials and workmanship shall be limited to replacement of the Software Media, which may be returned to HMI with a copy of your receipt at the following address: Software Media Fulfillment Department, Attn.: *Novell's CNA Study Guide for NetWare 5.1,* Hungry Minds, Inc., 10475 Crosspoint Blvd., Indianapolis, IN 46256, or call 1-800-762-2974. Please allow four to six weeks for delivery. This Limited Warranty is void if failure of the Software Media has resulted from accident, abuse, or misapplication. Any replacement Software Media will be warranted for the remainder of the original warranty period or thirty (30) days, whichever is longer.

   (b) In no event shall HMI or the author be liable for any damages whatsoever (including without limitation damages for loss of business profits, business interruption, loss of business information, or any other pecuniary loss) arising from the use of or inability to use the Book or the Software, even if HMI has been advised of the possibility of such damages.

   (c) Because some jurisdictions do not allow the exclusion or limitation of liability for consequential or incidental damages, the above limitation or exclusion may not apply to you.

7. **U.S. Government Restricted Rights.** Use, duplication, or disclosure of the Software for or on behalf of the United States of America, its agencies and/or instrumentalities (the "U.S. Government") is subject to restrictions as stated in paragraph (c)(1)(ii) of the Rights in Technical Data and Computer Software clause of DFARS 252.227-7013, or subparagraphs (c) (1) and (2) of the Commercial Computer Software - Restricted Rights clause at FAR 52.227-19, and in similar clauses in the NASA FAR supplement, as applicable.

8. **General.** This Agreement constitutes the entire understanding of the parties and revokes and supersedes all prior agreements, oral or written, between them and may not be modified or amended except in a writing signed by both parties hereto that specifically refers to this Agreement. This Agreement shall take precedence over any other documents that may be in conflict herewith. If any one or more provisions contained in this Agreement are held by any court or tribunal to be invalid, illegal, or otherwise unenforceable, each and every other provision shall remain in full force and effect.

# CD-ROM Installation Instructions

For complete contents and descriptions of the software included on the two CD-ROMs that accompany *Novell's CNA Study Guide for NetWare 5.1*, please see Appendix F, "What's On the CD-ROM." Detailed installation instructions and system requirements are also provided for all included programs.

To install the software on any of the two CD-ROMs included with this book with Windows 95, 98, or NT 4.0, follow these steps:

1. Place the desired CD-ROM disc in your CD-ROM drive.

2. Click the Start button and select Run.

3. Type the letter of your CD-ROM drive with a colon and backslash (for instance, **D:\**) and the directory name that contains the program you wish to run, followed by the name of the appropriate executable installation file. For example, to install the Visio Solution Pack for NDS (Disc 3), you would type the following:

   `D:\nds\setup.exe`

4. Click OK and follow the onscreen installation instructions.